Protecting Societal Interests in Corporate Takeovers

Huizi Ai

Protecting Societal Interests in Corporate Takeovers

A Comparative Analysis of the Regulatory Framework in the U.K., Germany and China

Springer

Huizi Ai
Law School
Beijing Normal University
Beijing, China

This work was supported by China Scholarship Council (CSC) grant number is 201707070042.

ISBN 978-981-19-7545-5 ISBN 978-981-19-7546-2 (eBook)
https://doi.org/10.1007/978-981-19-7546-2

This Springer imprint is published by the registered company Springer Nature Singapore Pte Ltd.
The registered company address is: 152 Beach Road, #21-01/04 Gateway East, Singapore 189721, Singapore

Acknowledgements

I started my Ph.D. research in Maastricht in September 2017 with the support of the China Scholarship Council. I really enjoyed the attractive journey in the past 4 years and there are many people to whom I owe my sincere gratitude.

First and foremost, I want to give my utmost gratitude to my two supervisors of the Ph.D. research, Prof. Niels Philipsen and Prof. Mieke Olaerts. I met Niels first in 2015 when I was a student at the China-EU School of Law (CESL) at China University of Political Science and Law (CUPL), and Niels was one member of the "flying faculty" of CESL and gave us the course "Competition Law". He provided us with a thorough and interesting introduction to the EU competition law. After class, whenever my classmates and I had questions, he was always glad and patient to discuss with us. Several months after I met Niels, I had a chance to go to Maastricht University to attend the elective course "Comparative Corporate Governance", which was given by Mieke. Mieke's course was very interesting and enlightening. It was also my first time to go abroad and I was really excited to find out how lovely the city of Maastricht is. Later, when I decided to pursue a doctorate abroad, Maastricht University became my first choice, and I was very lucky to have Niels and Mieke as my supervisors. During the past 4 years, they gave consistent support to me. This research would never be accomplished without their encouragement and guidance.

I also want to give my sincere gratitude to Prof. Michael Faure, for providing me with the opportunities to meet many thoughtful researchers through the Ius Commune Research School, and for giving me encouragement and suggestions on my research. I owe my gratitude to two professors from CUPL. Prof. Hongyao Wu was the first one to encourage me to pursue my doctorate abroad. He gave me a lot of guidance when I was confused about my career. My appreciation also goes to Dr. Jun Wang, the supervisor of my master's thesis in CESL. During the past 4 years, he gave me many suggestions on my research when I came back to China and visited him. Prof. Wu and Dr. Wang's devotion and dedication to work and their humble attitude towards students set me a good role model.

Last but certainly not least, my deepest gratitude goes to my family, especially my beloved mother and my husband. Thank you for all the love, care, respect and support you give me in my life.

Abbreviations

Regulations and Self-Regulatory Rules

Of the EU

Directive (EU) 2017/828	Directive (EU) 2017/828 of the European Parliament and of the Council of 17 May 2017 amending Directive 2007/36/EC as regards the encouragement of long-term shareholder engagement [2017] OJ L 132/1
Directive 2007/36/EC	Directive 2007/36/EC of the European Parliament and of the Council of 11 July 2007 on the exercise of certain rights of shareholders in listed companies [2007] OJ L 184/17
TFEU	Consolidated version of the Treaty on the Functioning of the European Union (TFEU) [2016] OJ C 202/1
The EC Merger Regulation	Council Regulation (EC) No 139/2004 of 20 January 2004 on the control of concentrations between undertakings [2004] OJ L 24/1
The EU FDI Screening Regulation	Regulation (EU) 2019/452 of the European Parliament and of the Council of 19 March 2019 establishing a framework for the screening of foreign direct investments into the Union [2019] OJ L 79 I/1
The EU Non-financial Reporting Directive	Directive 2014/95/EU of the European Parliament and of the Council of 22 October 2014 amending Directive 2013/34/EU as regards

	disclosure of non-financial and diversity information by certain large undertakings and groups Text with EEA relevance [2014] OJ L 330/1
The EU Takeover Directive	Directive 2004/25/EC of the European Parliament and of the Council of 21 April 2004 on takeover bids [2004] OJ L 142/12

Of the U.K.

CA 2006	Companies Act 2006
EA 2002	Enterprise Act 2002
Media Merger Guidance	Guidance on the Operation of the Public Interest Provisions relating to Newspaper and Other Media Mergers
The Cadbury Report	Report on Financial Aspects of Corporate Governance
The City Code	The City Code on Takeovers and Mergers
The U.K. Security Act 2021	National Security and Investment Act 2021
The U.K. Security Bill 2020	National Security and Investment Bill 2020
The 2017 Green Paper	National Security and Infrastructure Investment Review—The Government's review of the national security implications of foreign ownership or control
The 2018 U.K. CG Code	The 2018 U.K. Corporate Governance Code
The 2018 U.K. Guidance	The 2018 Guidance on Board Effectiveness
The 2018 White Paper	Security and Investment—A consultation on proposed legislative reforms

Of Germany

AktG	The Stock Corporation Act
AWG	The Foreign Trade and Payments Act
AWV	The Foreign Trade and Payments Ordinance
BHO	The Federal Budget Code
GWB	Act against Restraints of Competition
HGB	The German Commercial Code
The First Amendment to the AWG	The First Law to amend the Foreign Trade Act and other Laws
The 2020 German CG Code	The 2020 German Corporate Governance Code
WpÜG	The Securities Acquisition and Takeover Act

Of China

AML	The Anti-Monopoly Law
Amendment 2022	Amendment to the Anti-Monopoly Law (2022)
Catalogue of Industries	Catalogue of Industries for Guiding Foreign Investment
Implementing Regulation	Regulation on Implementing the Foreign Investment Law
Interim Provisions on Assessing the Impact	The Interim Provisions on Assessing the Impact of Concentration of Undertakings on Competition
Measures for Foreign Strategic Investment	Measures for the Administration of Strategic Investment in Listed Companies by Foreign Investor
Measures for the Security Review	Measures for the Security Review of Foreign Investment
Notice 2011	Notice of the General Office of the State Council on the Establishment of the Security Review System for Mergers and Acquisitions of Domestic Enterprises by Foreign Investors
Provisions on Foreign Mergers and Acquisitions (2009)	Provisions on Mergers and Acquisitions of Domestic Enterprises by Foreign Investors) (2009 Revision)
Provisions 2011	Provisions of the Ministry of Commerce on the Implementation of the Security Review System for Mergers and Acquisitions of Domestic Enterprises by Foreign Investors
The Company Law	2005 PRC Company Law
The Securities Law	2005 PRC Securities Law
The 2006 Takeover Measures	Measures for the Administration of the Takeover of Listed Companies
The 2018 Chinese CG Code	Corporate Governance Code for Listed Companies
The 2018 FI Negative List	Special Administrative Measures for the Access of Foreign Investment (2018)
The 2019 FI Negative List	Special Administrative Measures for the Access of Foreign Investment (2019)
The 2020 FI Negative List	Special Administrative Measures for the Access of Foreign Investment (2020)
The 2021 FI Negative List	Special Administrative Measures for the Access of Foreign Investment (2021)

Institutions

Of the EU

CJEU	European Court of Justice
The EC	The European Commission

Of the U.K.

FRC	Financial Reporting Council
MMC	Monopolies and Mergers Commission
MOD	Ministry of Defence
OFT	Office of Fair Trading
The CMA	Competition and Markets Authority
The Panel	The Panel on Takeovers and Mergers

Of Germany

BaFin	The Federal Financial Supervisory Authority
BKartA	Federal Cartel Office
BMWi (Renamed as BMWK after December 2021)	Federal Ministry for Economic Affairs and Energy
BMWK	Federal Ministry for Economic Affairs and Climate Action
GCGC Commission	Government Commission on the German Corporate Governance Code
The Minister	The Minister of the Federal Ministry for Economic Affairs and Energy

Of China

CC	Competition Commission
CPC	The Communist Party of China
CSRC	China Securities Regulatory Commission
Enforcement Department II	The Anti-monopoly Enforcement Department II
Joint Conference	Joint Ministerial Conference of China
MOFCOM	The Ministry of Commerce of China

National Bureau	The National Anti-monopoly Bureau
NDRC	The National Development and Reform Commission of China
SAIC	The State Administration for Industry and Commerce of China
SAMR	The State Administration for Market Regulation of China
SAMR Bureau	The Anti-monopoly Bureau of the State Administration for Market Regulation
SASAC	State-owned Assets Supervision and Administration Commission of the State Council
Security Review Office	The Office of the Foreign Investment Security Review Working Mechanism
SSE	Shanghai Stock Exchange
SZSE	Shenzhen Stock Exchange

Others

AG	The stock corporation
China CSR	China South Locomotive & Rolling Stock Corporation Limited
CNR	China CNR Corporation Limited
CRRC	China CRRC Corporation Limited
CSR	Corporate social responsibilities
EIN	European intervention notice
ESG	Environmental, Social and Governance
FDI	Foreign direct investment
I&C	Information and consultation
PIIN	Public Interest Intervention Notice
R&D	Research and Development
SPIN	Special public interest intervention notice
SRA	Self-regulatory agencies
UN PRI	Principles for Responsible Investment launched by the United Nations

Contents

About the Author

Huizi Ai Doctor of Law (Maastricht University), Lecturer at Law School, Beijing Normal University, Email: huizi.ai@bnu.edu.cn. This book is a result of the Ph.D. research project of Huizi Ai, which is sponsored by the China Scholarship Council. The author gratefully acknowledges very valuable comments and suggestions regarding the content of this book from Professor Niels Philipsen and Professor Mieke Olaerts.

List of Figures

List of Tables

Chapter 1
Introduction

Abstract This Chapter provides preliminary definitions of the crucial terms in this research and makes the presumption that takeovers may have varied effects on the relevant stakeholders and societal interests. By setting forth the detailed research questions and introducing the research methodology and structure of this book, it initiates the exploration of "what effects takeovers may have on different societal interests" and "how the relevant societal interests are protected under the current regulatory frameworks of the U.K., Germany and China" in later chapters.

1.1 Introduction

Corporate takeovers may have positive as well as negative effects on the different stakeholders involved. On the one hand, the combination of the acquirer[1] with the target company[2] may create synergies which are likely to enhance social welfare; and empirical studies have consistently found that target shareholders could gain significant positive returns from a takeover.[3] On the other hand, the synergy effect of takeovers and gains for the target shareholders may be generated at the expense of other stakeholders. For example, the incumbent management and the employees of the target company may lose their jobs after the change of control of the company; the creditors may find the face value of their claims suddenly deflated by the target's having taken on a heavy debt burden to finance the takeover or subsequent restructuring.[4] In addition, in a takeover where the acquirer is a foreign investor and the target company operates in security-sensitive sectors, a threat to the national security interest may occur. Where, after the takeover, the company changes its previously

[1] The expressions "acquirer" and "bidder" used in this research refer to the investor who attempts to acquire control of a company by means of a takeover.

[2] The expressions "target company" and "target" used in this research refer to the company which is likely to be taken over by a bidder. The board of such a company is referred to as the "target board"; the shareholders of it as the "target shareholders"; and the management of it as the "target management".

[3] Armour and Skeel (2007), pp. 1739–1740.

[4] Ibid.

H. Ai, *Protecting Societal Interests in Corporate Takeovers*,
https://doi.org/10.1007/978-981-19-7546-2_1

environmental-friendly production strategies, the environment and local community may also suffer negative consequences.

Traditionally, the takeover regulation worldwide has focused on addressing two main issues pertinent to the target shareholders[5]: the first issue is how to protect the shareholders from the management of the target company where there are no controlling shareholders[6]; and the second issue is how to ensure an equal treatment of the shareholders of the target company where there are controlling shareholders.[7] Since the early 2000s, discussions on rethinking the purposes of companies and the definition of contemporary corporate governance massively increased, particularly after the 2008 global financial crisis, which challenged the idea that shareholders were the only focal points in corporate activities.[8] It has gradually become a consensus that companies should also consider other stakeholders' interests and the legally recognized public interest when making decisions in takeovers; therefore, protection mechanisms were introduced into the takeover regulation in different jurisdictions.[9]

Against this background, this book aims to identify those who are the relevant stakeholders and what are the societal interests that may be affected by the manifold effects of takeovers and explore how they are protected under the current regulatory

---

[5] Davies and Worthington (2016), pp. 918–919; Kraakman et al. (2017), pp. 207–208.

[6] See Kraakman et al. (2017), p. 208. In this situation, regulation needs to prevent the target management from taking any steps to discourage a potential acquirer from putting an offer to its shareholders or from discouraging the shareholders from accepting it. There might also exist an opposite situation where the target shareholders may not view the takeover bid as wealth-enhancing but the incumbent management may have an incentive to promote it to the shareholders considering the gains they may get (for example, by reaping significant compensation for loss of office). See further discussions in Sect. 2.2.2.2.

[7] Ibid. In that situation, regulation needs to address the agency relationship between the controller and other shareholders.

[8] See Du Plessis et al. (2018), pp. 4–6: "Issues of corporate governance first gained international prominence in the late 1990s and early 2000s in the wake of a series of corporate accounting scandals, most notably Enron in the US and HIH in Australia; and the focus on corporate governance increased after 2008, in the aftermath of the global financial crisis". Other discussions in this field include, for example, Hillman A. J., & Keim, G. D. (2001). Shareholder value, stakeholder management, and social issues: what's the bottom line? *Strategic Management Journal, 22*(2), 125–139; Freeman, R. E., Wicks, A. C., & Parmar, B. (2004). Stakeholder theory and "the corporate objective revisited". *Organization Science, 15*(3), 364–369; Kacperczyk, A. (2009). With greater power comes greater responsibility? Takeover protection and corporate attention to stakeholders. *Strategic Management Journal, 30*(3), 261–285; Davies, P., & Hopt, K. J. (2018). Non-Shareholder Voice in Bank Governance: Board Composition, Performance and Liability. *European Corporate Governance Institute (ECGI)-Law Working Paper*. Available at: https://doi.org/10.2139/ssrn.3226244 (accessed 12 May 2022).

[9] See Griffin (2006), pp. 364–365: "In the context of companies, legislation and other regulatory powers are deemed as essential instruments in seeking to protect the wellbeing and stability of both the economy and the general public interest"; Nyombi et al. (2015), p. 164: the author mentioned that "one of the biggest drivers for 'stakeholderism' under takeover law is the issue of investor short-termism, which refers to corporate and investment decision-making based on short-term earnings expectations rather than long-term value creation for all stakeholders". See also the discussions as concluded in Schwarcz, 2016: the author analysed why corporate governance law should, and showed how it feasibly could, take public interest into account.

frameworks in the U.K., Germany and China. Section 1.2 of this chapter will explain the critical concepts in this thesis; Sect. 1.3 will set forth the detailed research questions and introduce the research methodology; Sect. 1.4 will present the research structure; Sect. 1.5 will clarify the societal relevance of this thesis.

1.2 Clarification of Critical Concepts

1.2.1 "Takeovers"

As one form of control transactions,[10] a takeover as discussed in this book refers to "a public offer from the acquirer (usually another company) made to the target shareholders to acquire all or some of those shares with the objective of gaining control of the target".[11] The public offer may be either "friendly" (i.e. supported by the target management) or "hostile" (i.e. made over the heads of the target management to the shareholders of the target).[12]

The potential shift of control in the target company is expected to have a disciplinary effect on its incumbent management, which makes takeovers often seen as a necessary corporate governance tool. The classic argument for this view also includes the following points: (i) ordinary corporate governance of the target company is not effective; (ii) the stock price reflects the true value of the target company under the relevant management (either the incumbent one or the new one after the takeover); (iii) concentrated shareholdings will bring strong incentives for the new owner to run the company well; (iv) gains for selling shareholders demonstrate the value of takeovers.[13] Contrary to this argument, others doubt the role of takeovers as a corporate governance tool. They hold that not all takeovers are good for the target company.[14] In fact, when takeovers first emerged in the U.S., the bidders were described as raiders and black knights, and members of the target company were often portrayed as unfortunate and unwilling pawns in the early literature.[15] Such

[10] Kraakman et al. (2017), p. 206. According to Kraakman et al., "control transactions may be structured in a variety of ways: (i) private contracts with a single or a small number of important shareholders ('sale of control'); (ii) purchases of shares on the market; or (c) a general and public offer to all the shareholders of the target company".

[11] See Article 2 (1)(a) of Directive 2004/25/EC of the European Parliament and of the Council of 21 April 2004 on takeover bids [2004] OJ L 142/12 (The EU Takeover Directive); Davies and Worthington (2016), p. 917.

[12] Kraakman et al. (2017), p. 206.

[13] Cahn and Donald (2018), pp. 928–929. See Clark, R. C. (1986). *Corporate Law*: Boston and Toronto: Little, Brown and Co, pp. 533–535; Easterbrook, Frank H., & Fischel, D. R. (1996). *The economic structure of corporate law*: Harvard University Press, pp. 171–174.

[14] Ibid, p. 930.

[15] Schneper and Guillén (2004), p. 265. See Hirsch, P. M. (1986). From ambushes to golden parachutes: Corporate takeovers as an instance of cultural framing and institutional integration. *American journal of Sociology*, *91*(4), 800–837; Schneider, S. C., & Dunbar, R. L. (1992). A

concerns usually exist in hostile takeovers where the acquirer may just intend to make quick profits by purchasing and selling off undervalued companies with no interest in improving the corporate governance of the target at all.[16] In addition, the expected effects of takeovers in bringing strong incentives for better corporate governance through concentrated shareholdings are also doubted. In practice, a takeover usually only temporarily concentrates voting rights for efficient use before releasing them once again to safely diversified (for investment risk purposes) but inefficient (for governance purposes) dispersed holdings.[17]

1.2.2 "Stakeholders" and "Relevant Societal Interests"

The above discrepancy in the ideas about the role of takeovers as a corporate governance tool indicates the intricacy of takeovers' effects on different stakeholders.

Companies are sometimes described as "institutions which are characterized by the intersecting interests of various stakeholders, including not only the shareholders and management, but also, for example, employees, banks, and the surrounding community".[18] Corporate governance, correspondingly, was traditionally defined as "the system by which a company is directed and controlled" and as "a set of relationships between the company's management, its board, its shareholders and other stakeholders".[19] Considering the fact that the acquirer "normally does not expend large resources to obtain control of the target company to just run it in the same way as previously",[20] it is reasonable to expect that a takeover would also have wide consequences for non-shareholder stakeholders who have interests in the target.

The definition and scope of "stakeholders" vary according to the different circumstances. Freeman (1984) defined "stakeholders" as "any group or individual who can

---

psychoanalytic reading of hostile takeover events. *Academy of Management Review, 17*(3), 537–567; Palmer, D., & Barber, B. M. (2001). Challengers, elites, and owning families: A social class theory of corporate acquisitions in the 1960s. *Administrative Science Quarterly, 46*(1), 87–120.

[16] Cahn and Donald, 2018, p. 930: The Delaware court in the U.S. has explained this position on takeovers repeatedly in its decisions. For example, in the *Blasius* case, two heavily indebted financiers attempted to acquire control of a gold mining company for the sole purpose of having it use gold to collateralize a massive loan and pay out the proceeds to them, which would push the target toward bankruptcy. See *Blasius Industries, Inc.* v. *Atlas Corp.*, 564 A 2d 651, 659 (Del. Ch. 1988).

[17] Ibid.

[18] Schneper and Guillén (2004), p. 263.

[19] European Commission (2011). Green paper: The EU corporate governance framework (COM(2011) 164 final). Available at: https://eur-lex.europa.eu/LexUriServ/LexUriServ.do?uri=COM:2011:0164:FIN:EN:PDF (accessed 12 May 2022). See ECGI.GLOBAL (1992). Report of the Committee on the Financial Aspects of Corporate Governance (The Cadbury Report). Available at: https://ecgi.global/sites/default/files//codes/documents/cadbury.pdf (accessed 12 May 2022); OECD.ORG (2004). OECD Principles of Corporate Governance. Available at: http://www.oecd.org/corporate/ca/corporategovernanceprinciples/31557724.pdf (accessed 12 May 2022).

[20] Davies and Worthington (2016), p. 918.

affect or is affected by the achievement of the organization's objectives" and depicted the modern companies from the stakeholders' view, which include the owners, consumer advocates, customers, competitors, suppliers, employees, Governments, local community organizations, environmentalists, media, and SIG.[21] He argued that each of these groups have a stake in the company and play a vital role in the success of the company.[22] Similarly, some scholars provided that "actors who have either a legal or a moral claim over the actions of the company can be counted as stakeholders".[23]

Contrary to this view, others have argued for a narrower scope of corporate stakeholders. For example, the agency theorists hold that "while too many stakeholders exist, not all of their inputs are critical, and their synchronous participation may lead to deadlocks in corporate decision-making".[24] Some scholars maintain that "only stakeholders with a significant firm-specific investment should enjoy influence in discussions about corporate control".[25] Others even contend that stakeholder is an "essentially contested concept, rather than merely ambiguous, which renders the quest to seek a singular definition unfeasible".[26]

It should be admitted that even with Freeman's explanatory map of a firm's stakeholders, the exact outside boundary of the stakeholder groups in a takeover can still be hard to predict. Freeman also acknowledged that the examples of stakeholders he gave were "enormously oversimplified", as each category of stakeholder groups could be broken down into several useful smaller categories.[27] The potential problems in defining the "stakeholders" in takeovers explain to some extent why non-shareholder stakeholders are often neglected in the existing literature. Nevertheless, the difficulty in delimiting this term does not justify the underestimation of their interests; on the contrary, it reveals, from another perspective, the necessity to reconsider and attach importance to these groups.

---

[21] See EXIHIBIT 1.5 at Freeman (1984), p. 25. EXIHIBIT 1.5 listed eleven types of stakeholder groups of a firm. Freeman pointed out that the groups listed were just examples of the categories of stakeholders. Among the listed stakeholders, "SIG" referred to "special interest groups". The idea behind SIGs is that "a group or individual can use the political process to further a position on a particular issue such as gun control, abortion, women's rights... or any of hundreds of other issues". The problems which SIGs represent for the manager is that "one can never be sure that an ad hoc group will not form to oppose the company on any particular issue". See Freeman (1984), p. 21.

[22] Ibid.

[23] Schneper and Guillén (2004), p. 263. See Carroll, A. B. (1989). *Business and Society: Ethics and Stakeholder Management*. Cincinnati, OH South Western.

[24] Aguilera and Jackson (2010), p. 500. See Jensen, M. C. (2001). Value maximization, stakeholder theory, and the corporate objective function. *European Financial Management Review, 14*(3), 47–63; Sternberg, E. (1997). The defects of stakeholder theory. *Corporate Governance: An International Review, 5*(1), 3–10; Tirole, J. (2000). Corporate governance. *Econometrica, 69*(1), 1–35.

[25] Schneper and Guillén (2004), p. 270. See Blair, M. M. (1995). *Ownership and control: rethinking corporate governance for the twenty-first century*. Brookings Institution; Aguilera, R. V., & Jackson, G. (2003). The cross-national diversity of corporate governance: Dimensions and determinants. *Academy of management Review, 28*(3), 447–465.

[26] Miles (2012), p. 295.

[27] Freeman (1984), p. 25.

This research presumes that the "stakeholders whose interests may be affected in a takeover include not only those who normally have a contractual relationship with the acquirer or the target company (such as investment contracts, employment contracts, and supply contracts); there may also be other stakeholders that are usually not directly related to the acquirer or target company but bear the consequences of the takeover". This research will refer to the first type of stakeholders as "corporate stakeholders"[28] and the second type as "other societal stakeholders"; put together, they will be referred to as "the relevant stakeholders" and their interests will be referred to as "the relevant societal interests" in takeovers. In later chapters, this book will explore what the relevant societal interests include, what the consequences of a takeover may mean for them, and how they are protected (or not protected) in the regulatory frameworks of the U.K., Germany and China.

1.2.3 "Regulatory Framework of Takeovers", "Government Regulation", "Private Regulation"

The "regulatory framework of takeovers" in the U.K., Germany and China consists of both "government regulation" and "private regulation" of takeovers in the jurisdictions. "Government regulation" refers to "all the rules formulated by the government (laws and other legal instruments), including both public laws (for example, the competition law) of which the enforcement can be via administrative or criminal law[29] and private laws (for example, the company law) which can be enforced through claims filed by private parties in court".[30] In contrast, "private regulation" refers to "private forms of regulation, which means that the regulatory design and enforcement tasks of the regulation are delegated to private actors, and the forms may include, for example, contractual agreements, private standard setting, private certification systems and self-regulation".[31] As one form of private regulation, self-regulation is formulated and enforced by self-regulatory agencies ("SRA" hereinafter), such as the association of a professional occupation or an industry.[32]

In this book, the government regulation under the regulatory framework of takeovers includes the national competition law, the laws and regulations for reviewing foreign direct investment (the "FDI" hereinafter), the takeover law, the corporate law in the three jurisdictions. The private regulation as examined in this book mainly refers to the self-regulatory instruments of takeovers, including the

---

[28] In this book, the author uses the term "corporate stakeholders" in a way which also includes shareholders. For a similar use of "corporate stakeholders", see for example, Kraakman et al. (2017), pp. 5, 23, 80; Marcoux (1998), p. 89.

[29] Philipsen (2018), p. 541.

[30] Ogus (2004), pp. 2, 26–28.

[31] Ibid, p. 539.

[32] For detailed discussion about the nature of "regulation" and "self-regulation" and their differences, see Sect. 2.3.1.

national corporate governance code and other important instruments issued by the self-regulatory agencies (such as the stock exchanges).

1.3 Research Questions and Structure

1.3.1 Research Questions

The central research question of this book is:

What are the societal interests that may be affected by a takeover, are these protected under the current regulatory frameworks of the U.K., Germany and China; (and if so) how are they protected and what recommendations can be made for future reforms in the three jurisdictions?

To answer this research question, this book will explore the following sub-questions:

(1) What market failure(s) can be caused by a takeover and what kinds of societal interests are affected?
(2) What are the relevant societal interests that are currently regulated in the three jurisdictions and which protection mechanisms are used?
(3) What are the similarities and differences between the regulatory frameworks of the three jurisdictions, and what are the strengths and weaknesses of them in addressing the relevant market failure(s) and protecting societal interests in takeovers?
(4) Based on the strengths and weaknesses of the current regulatory frameworks and protection mechanisms, what recommendations can be made for future reforms in the three jurisdictions?

1.3.2 Research Structure

This book consists of seven chapters and its structure is developed according to the above-mentioned research sub- questions.

This Chapter defines the crucial terms in this research and makes the presumption that "takeovers may have varied effects on the relevant stakeholders and societal interests". It initiates the exploration of "what effects takeovers may have on different societal interests" and "how the relevant societal interests are protected under the current regulatory frameworks" in later chapters.

Chapter 2 continues the exploration by answering sub-question 1. It analyses the potential market failure(s) which takeovers may cause and identifies how they affect the relevant societal interests. Following that, it introduces the theoretical role of government regulation and private regulation in addressing the market failure(s).

Chapters 3, 4 and 5 then answer sub-question 2. The three chapters examine the regulatory frameworks in the U.K., Germany and China in sequence to explore what societal interests are currently protected by government regulation and private regulation mechanisms in each jurisdiction. The three chapters also analyse the specific protection mechanisms as provided in different regulatory regimes, particularly the aims of the mechanisms, the responsible authorities and procedures for implementing the mechanisms (where they are of relevance to the public laws).

Following that, Chapter 6 answers sub-question 3. It makes a comparison of the protection mechanisms in the three jurisdictions to elucidate the similarities and divergences in both the substantive aspects (for example, the scope of the relevant societal interests they protect) and the procedural aspects of the protection mechanisms (for example, the responsible authorities and implementation procedures for the public law mechanisms). It also makes an evaluation of the protection mechanisms by identifying their respective strengths and weaknesses in addressing market failures as examined in Chapter 2.

Finally, Chapter 7 responds to sub-question 4. It draws final conclusions of the whole research and provides recommendations for future reforms in the three jurisdictions in the field of takeover regulation.

1.4 Methodology

To explore the above research questions, this book mainly relies on the following research methods: (1) doctrinal legal research; (2) comparative research; (3) law and economics analysis.

1.4.1 Doctrinal Legal Research

Defined in simple terms, doctrinal legal research is "research which asks what the law is in a particular area by collecting and then analysing any relevant legislation (so-called primary sources) and a body of case law".[33] The starting point of doctrinal legal research is to "determine the existing law in the particular research area". This may be done from a historical perspective and the search process may also include secondary sources such as journal articles and other written commentaries on the relevant legislation and case law.[34] The aim is to provide a systematic structuring of the texts of the relevant laws and lay a basis for a systemic interpretation of the laws.

---

[33] McConville (2017), pp. 20–21.

[34] Ibid.

This book uses doctrinal legal research to identify the regulatory frameworks of takeovers in the U.K., Germany and China, particularly laws in the government regulation regime and self-regulatory instruments in the corporate governance regime.[35] As specified in Sect. 1.2.3 of this chapter, the laws in the government regulation regime include competition law, FDI screening regulations, takeover law, corporate law; and the self-regulatory instruments mainly refer to the national corporate governance code. In addition, important policies issued by the administrative authorities pertaining to takeovers (which is of particular importance in China), representative takeover cases, journal articles and other written commentaries explaining the content and changes of the regulation will also be analysed.

1.4.2 Comparative Research

This book compares the regulatory frameworks of takeovers in the U.K., Germany and China. The reasons for choosing the three jurisdictions for this research are as follows.

Firstly, the prevalent shareholding structures of the companies in a country may have a deep impact on the vibrancy of its takeover market, particularly the market for hostile takeovers. It is observed that countries where concentrated shareholding structure prevails are often less reliant on takeovers as a corporate governance device since managerial monitoring can be performed by the corporate block holders.[36] In contrast to the U.K. where the companies are predominantly widely-held, companies with large block holders are more prevalent in Germany and China.[37] In line with

[35] It should be noted that the formal sources of law in China consist of *the Constitution,* the laws, regulations, administrative measures, and international law. See Liu (2019), pp. 106–112: (1) the term "laws" (in Chinese it is called "*fa lv*") has different meanings in the context of the Chinese legal system, and in a narrow sense, "laws" refers to the body of legislation enacted by the National people's Congress and its standing Committee; (2) the term "regulations" (in Chinese "*fa gui*") should be enacted by the State Council of the People's Republic of China or certain local people's congresses in accordance with *the Constitution* and laws ("*fa lv*"); (3) "administrative measures" (in Chinese "*gui zhang*") can be categorized into ministerial administrative measures (in Chinese "*bu men gui zhang*") and local administrative measures (in Chinese "*di fang xing gui zhang*"); the former should be enacted by ministerial departments within the Central Government, while the latter should be enacted by certain local governments. For the purpose of this book, "laws" (*fa lv*), "regulations" (*fa gui*) and "administrative measures" (*bu men gui zhang*) will form the discussion focus of the Chinese legal systems.

[36] Kraakman et al. (2017), p. 238; Martynova and Renneboog (2008), p. 2173.

[37] Martynova and Renneboog (2008), p. 2173; Huang (2014), p. 252; Ringe (2015), pp. 495, 508–516. According to Ringe (2015), Germany was traditionally viewed as a block holder system and the ownership of major German corporations was considered to be in the hands of strong block holders who de facto control their dependent companies' strategy. Ringe also found out that "in recent years the corporate ownership is becoming more dispersed and the old presumption of Germany as a closed system of strong networks dominated by block holders thus may no longer hold true. However, in comparison with the U.K., the ownership concentration overall in Germany is still relatively high".

this, takeover activities in Germany and China emerged at a much later stage and the number of hostile takeovers in the two countries has also been notably lower than that in the U.K. in the past two decades.[38] The different development stages of their takeover market imply divergences in the forms, content and focus of the takeover regulation in the three jurisdictions, which can provide a good basis for comparison.

Secondly, the corporate governance tradition of protecting non-shareholder groups and the tradition of employing private regulation may affect the design of the protection mechanisms for different stakeholders in a country. The corporate governance system in the U.K. has featured the "shareholder primacy" tradition for a long time. Germany is often mentioned as an example of the "stakeholder-centered" model, meaning that "to discipline managers, companies place greater emphasis on internal mechanisms such as representation from labour, creditors, and regulatory agencies in Germany, and the corporate control depends on the support of the various stakeholders".[39] In China, the administrative authorities often have a strong regulatory role in its fast-growing capital market and sometimes companies are required to pursue the "public interest" in their corporate activities. These diversified corporate governance traits provide an interesting perspective for comparing the focuses of the regulatory frameworks in the three jurisdictions. As to the tradition of employing self-regulation on the markets, it seems that the U.K. is in a much more advanced position, especially when considering the initial self-regulatory nature of its takeover law (The City Code on Takeovers and Mergers) and the responsible takeover authority (the Panel on Takeovers and Mergers).[40] By comparison, the role of peer-pressure, on which self-regulation largely depends, is much less developed in Germany and China, so are the self-regulatory instruments and agencies.[41]

Thirdly, the political interests and choices of the State in takeovers, particularly in foreign takeovers in strategic sectors, may significantly affect the three jurisdictions' regulatory frameworks of takeovers. Traditionally, the U.K. was more takeover-friendly towards foreign investors; by comparison, Germany and China had a more conservative stance towards foreign takeovers. In recent years, the Government's

[38] Martynova and Renneboog (2008), pp. 2149–2152; Huang (2014), pp. 251–253. According to Huang (2014), "takeovers in the U.K. and continental Europe were not well documented until the early 1960s and the early 1980s respectively; the U.K. saw a boom of hostile takeovers during the 1980s while the same happened a decade later in continental Europe; in China, the takeover market began to develop in the early 1990s, but the hostile takeovers have rarely been seen in the past two decades before 2014".

[39] Schneper and Guillén (2004), p. 268. See Guillén, M. F. (2000). Corporate governance and globalization: is there convergence across countries? *Advances in International Comparative Management, 13*, 175–204; Charkham, J. P. (1995). *Keeping good company: A study of corporate governance in five countries*. Oxford University Press; Prowse, S. D. (1995). Corporate governance in an international perspective. *Financial Markets, Institutions and Instruments, 4*, 1–63; Lazonick, W., & O'Sullivan, M. A. R. Y. (1996). Organization, finance and international competition. *Industrial and Corporate Change, 5*(1), 1–49; Dore, R. P. (2000). *Stock market capitalism: Welfare capitalism: Japan and Germany versus the Anglo-Saxons*. Oxford University Press.

[40] Hopt (2011), p. 64. For detailed discussion about the City Code on Takeovers and Mergers and the role of the Panel on Takeovers and Mergers, see Sects. 3.4.2 and 3.4.3.

[41] Ibid.

stances in the three jurisdictions towards foreign investors underwent a series of substantial changes. Reforms in this field indicate that their regulatory framework of takeovers may change over time and depending on the international environment.

It should be noted that some rules on takeovers and soft laws of corporate governance at the European Union (EU) level may also be of relevance to the national laws and self-regulation instruments in the U.K. (before Brexit) and Germany.[42] As the relevant rules at the EU level have either been embedded into or implemented by the national laws of the U.K. (before Brexit) and Germany, and the rules of corporate governance usually can be reflected from their national corporate governance code, they will not be the discussion focus of this book. As an exception, the recent reforms of the EU's FDI screening regulation have significant implications for the Member States' future stances towards foreign takeovers, and they will be discussed in combination with the reforms of the FDI screening regulation in Germany in Chap. 4.

1.4.3 Law and Economics Analysis

Economic analysis of law usually "takes a utilitarian view and argues for the implementation of legal rules which generate the most social welfare or benefits".[43] In this book, a law and economics analysis will be employed in two ways. Firstly, it is used to explain the potential market failure(s) in takeovers and to demonstrate their implications for different societal interests. This analysis aims to specify the (potential) justifications for introducing government or private regulation to protect the relevant stakeholders in takeovers. Besides this, the law and economics analysis serves as a benchmark for assessing the strengths and weaknesses of the protection mechanisms in the three jurisdictions. The evaluation of the protection mechanisms is primarily

---

[42] Regulation rules of takeovers at the EU level include, for example, (a) The EU Takeover Directive (Directive 2004/25/EC of the European Parliament and of the Council of 21 April 2004 on takeover bids [2004] OJ L 142/12); (b) The EC Merger Regulation (Council Regulation (EC) No 139/2004 of 20 January 2004 on the control of concentrations between undertakings [2004] OJ L 24/1). Other regulation or soft laws of the EU in the corporate governance field include, for example, (a) Directive 2017/1132 (which plays a major role in the corporate governance field by incorporating rules regarding stakeholder protection in cross-border mergers, see Arts 89, 98–101, 121); (b) Directive 2006/46/EC (which aims at promoting the application of national corporate governance codes by requiring that listed companies refer in their corporate governance statement to a national code); (c) The 2011 Green Paper on the EU Corporate Governance Framework (COM(2011) 164 final) (which addresses three paramount subjects of good corporate governance: board effectiveness, shareholder rights and responsibilities, and the comply-or-explain approach); and (d) The OECD Principles of Corporate Governance (which have implications for the EU's stance in stakeholder protection in corporate governance and provide methods to improve non-shareholder stakeholders' participation in fundamental corporate decisions). For an introduction of the EU corporate governance framework and the relevant OECD Principles, see Du Plessis et al., 2018, pp. 406–419.

[43] Smits (2012), p. 62.

based on their roles in solving the relevant market failures(s) pertinent to the societal interests and their respective advantages and disadvantages in this process.

1.5 Impact Statement

The societal impact of this research is mainly embodied in the following three aspects.

Firstly, the societal impact of this research on academia. For a long time, the research focus of academia in the area of takeover regulation has been on shareholder protection and anti-takeover measures of the target company. Other non-shareholder stakeholders, in contrast, seem to have been neglected in the literature. This research tries to fill this gap by discussing the current protection mechanisms for different societal interests (the legally recognized public interest considerations, the interests of corporate stakeholders and other societal interests affected by a takeover) and providing recommendations for future reforms in the field of takeover regulation. By doing so, this book will provide academia with new perspectives for future research. For example, it illustrates how the market failure theory may be relied on to analyse the impact of a takeover as well as other corporate activities on different societal interests; how similar protection mechanisms may be implemented differently in two jurisdictions; and how public authorities and self-regulation agencies may work together to improve the compliance of a protection mechanism. I hope that discussions in this book on the abovementioned aspects will provide inspiration for other scholars who may be interested in carrying out further research into these areas.

Secondly, the societal impact of this research on policymaking. Previous research of takeover regulation usually studied laws in a specific regime in isolation (for example, competition law, takeover law, FDI screening laws or corporate law). An added value of this research lies in the integrative approach it adopts by studying laws of different regimes as well as the self-regulatory corporate governance mechanisms and comparing their roles in protecting different societal interests. In this way, this research aims to provide an overall picture of the regulatory framework of takeovers in the three jurisdictions. The findings in Chaps. 3, 4 and 5 present the status quo of protection for different societal interests in the current regulatory framework of takeovers in the three jurisdictions, and the comparison and evaluation in Chap. 6 provide the policymakers with an overview of the strengths and weaknesses (problems) of the current regulatory framework in each jurisdiction. More importantly, in Chap. 7, this book proposes recommendations on using the public law (the competition law and FDI screening laws) mechanisms to strengthen the protection of the legally recognized public interest considerations and on improving the takeover law and corporate governance mechanisms to enhance the protection of the interests of corporate stakeholders and other societal interests affected by a takeover, which will provide policymakers in the three jurisdictions with implications in future reforms.

Thirdly, the societal impact of this research on companies and the general public. This research is also of interest to the companies and the general public in the three countries or companies from other countries that are (potentially) interested in conducting takeovers in the three countries. For the companies, this research provides them with useful references to the laws, self-regulatory instruments, administrative procedures and representative cases of takeover regulation in the three jurisdictions, which will help reduce the information costs in their future activities. Moreover, this book, by discussing the market failures in takeovers and analysing how they affect different societal interests, illustrates to the companies and the general public the importance of protecting the legally recognized public interest considerations and the interests of other non-shareholder stakeholders in takeovers and other corporate activities. I hope that the arguments presented in this book will have an impact on some of the companies' original ideas of neglecting the interests of non-shareholder stakeholders in takeovers and other corporate activities, and that my recommendations (particularly these on improving the takeover law and corporate governance mechanisms to enhance the protection of non-shareholder stakeholders) will enhance the companies' corporate governance performance and their assumption of corporate social responsibilities in the future.

Chapter 2
Market Failures in Takeovers

Abstract This chapter employs a law and economics approach to identify the potential market failures in takeovers and outlines the regulatory framework of takeovers that will be discussed in detail in Part II of this book (Chaps. 3, 4 and 5). It finds that four types of market failures may arise as a result of takeovers: increase of market power (potential monopoly), severe information asymmetries, negative externalities, and undersupply of public goods. The market failure problems may affect three types of societal interests: (i) the interests of corporate stakeholders with whom target companies have a contractual relationship, (ii) the legally recognized public interest considerations, and (iii) other societal interests affected by a takeover. To address the market failures and protect the relevant societal interests, regulatory frameworks of takeovers are established in different jurisdictions, which consist of both government regulation and private regulation.

2.1 Introduction

Takeovers are often regarded as a corporate governance mechanism that can enhance managerial efficiency. The presumption is that "a high positive correlation exists between a company's share price and managerial efficiency", and that "companies which are badly managed will be undervalued relative to competitors that are better managed (when everything else is equal) and become attractive takeover targets".[1] Under this pressure, another presumption is that "the managers, to avoid potential takeovers, will seek to maximize the value of the company, which may in turn create enhanced shareholder value by providing shareholders with a premium upon selling

[1] Gerner-Beuerle and Schilling (2019), pp. 245–246. See also Manne (1965), p. 112; Martynova and Renneboog (2008), p. 2173.

H. Ai, *Protecting Societal Interests in Corporate Takeovers*,
https://doi.org/10.1007/978-981-19-7546-2_2

their shares".[2] In addition to this managerial efficiency, takeovers, as a resource-allocation mechanism in the market, may also benefit society through maximum returns by facilitating the acquisition of resources by more efficient companies and creating synergies.[3]

The above efficiency-creation functions of takeovers have been discussed by abundant literature[4] and will not be further explored in this chapter. On the contrary, this chapter aims to identify what market inefficiencies takeovers may cause and how they may affect the relevant societal interests. Takeovers may have varied implications for different stakeholders. For example, while the target shareholders gain profits from the share premiums, the incumbent management and the employees of the target may lose their jobs; the synergies created by merging the resources of the acquirer and the target may lead to increased market power and threaten effective competition; in some takeovers with foreign investors, national security may be put at risk; in other cases, the environment and local community may suffer losses where the acquirer changes the relevant corporate strategies subsequent to the takeover.

This chapter employs a law and economics approach to identify the potential market inefficiencies in takeovers and analyses how they may affect the relevant societal interests. Section 2.2 first briefly explains the four sources of market failures; then it examines the market failures that often occur in takeovers and specifies their impact on the relevant stakeholders and societal interests. Following that, Sect. 2.3 discusses the roles of regulation in takeovers: Sect. 2.3.1 sheds light on the "public interest approach" and "private interest approach" in explaining government regulation and private regulation; Sect. 2.3.2 then outlines the regulatory framework of takeovers and introduces the government regulation and private regulation mechanisms that will be discussed in Part II of this book (Chaps. 3, 4 and 5). Section 2.4 brings the conclusion of this chapter.

---

[2] Varottil and Wan (2017), p. 217. See e.g., Easterbrook, F. H., & Fischel, D. R. (1981). The Proper Role of a Target's Management in Responding to a Tender Offer. *Harvard Law Review, 94*, 1161-1204, p. 1169; Jensen, M.C. (1988). The Takeover Controversy: Analysis and Evidence. In Coffee, J. C. (1988). *Knights, Raiders, and Targets, The Impact of the Hostile Takeover*. Oxford University Press, p. 314 (stating that "takeovers benefit target shareholders: premiums in hostile offers historically exceed 30%, on average, and in recent times have averaged about 50%"); Jensen, M.C. & Ruback, R.S. (1983). The Market for Corporate Control: The Scientific Evidence. *Journal of Financial Economics, 11* (1-4), 5-50, pp. 9-16 (arguing that "target shareholders can benefit from takeover premiums"); Kraakman, R. (1988). Taking Discounts Seriously: The Implications of "Discounted" Share Prices as an Acquisition Motive. *Columbia Law Review, 88*, 891, p. 908 (observing that "target shareholders can be better off selling shares at a premium"); Martynova and Renneboog, 2008, p. 2173 (arguing that "the bulk of M&As are expected to improve efficiency and trigger substantial share price increases at the announcement, most of which are captured by the target shareholders").

[3] Ibid. See, e.g., Coffee. J. C. (1984). Regulating the Market for Corporate Control: A Critical Assessment of the Tender Offer's Role in Corporate Governance. *Columbia Law Review, 84*(5), 1145–1296, p. 1221; Easterbrook, F. H., & Fischel, D. R. (1982). Corporate Control Transactions. *Yale Law Journal, 91,* 698–738, p. 705; Jensen, M.C. (1988). Takeovers: Their Causes and Consequences. *Journal of Economic Perspectives, 2* (1), 21–48, p. 23.

[4] See for example, the literature referred to in *supra* notes 2 and 3.

2.2 Market Inefficiencies in Takeovers

This section analyses the market inefficiencies in takeovers and their impact on different societal interests. Section 2.2.1 will first explain the concept of market failure in general, followed by Sect. 2.2.2 which examines the application of the market failure theory to the case of takeovers.

2.2.1 *Market Failure Theory*

Modern microeconomics specifies "the general equilibrium", "a condition under which the independent decisions of utility-maximizing consumers and profit-maximizing firms will lead to a spontaneous establishment of an equilibrium in all markets".[5] This general equilibrium will be achieved only "when competitive forces have led to the equality of marginal benefit and marginal cost in the market for every single transaction, which is unlikely to be realized in the real world".[6] Market failures refer to "situations where the allocation of goods and services in a market is not efficient".[7] In practice, such market failures may occur when the market prices give false signals about the real value of goods and services.[8] Four main sources of market failures have been identified in the economic literature: market power, externalities, severe information asymmetry and public goods.[9]

Market Power

Market failure occurs where competition is seriously impaired by monopolies and anti-competitive practices.[10] A monopoly can arise and persist only where "there are barriers to entry that make it impossible for competing firms to appear".[11] When producers or service providers have a dominant market position, the price of the goods or services exceeds the marginal cost of production and in the end is too high, while the quantity supplied is too low, which jeopardizes the interests of consumers from the viewpoint of efficiency.[12]

---

[5] Cooter and Ulen (2016), p. 38.

[6] Ibid.

[7] Philipsen (2018), p. 541.

[8] Bozeman (2007), p. 17.

[9] Cooter and Ulen (2016), pp. 38–42; Ogus (2004), pp. 30–41.

[10] Ogus (2004), p. 30. A "natural monopoly" is a special kind of monopoly which calls for different treatment. It occurs where it is less costly to society for production to be carried out by one supplier rather than by several or many. Therefore, the remedy for a "natural monopoly" lies not in competition. Public utilities, such as local water, telecommunications, cable and power companies are often natural monopolies. See Ogus (2004), pp. 30–31; Cooter and Ulen (2016), p. 29.

[11] Cooter and Ulen (2016), p. 29. In general, such barriers may arise from two sources: (i) from statutory and other legal restrictions on entry; and (ii) from technological conditions of production known as "economies of scale".

[12] Ibid, p.38.

Externalities

The presence of externalities may also lead to market failure. In a nutshell, "externalities" refer to "the side effects of production or consumption that are imposed on third parties".[13] Externalities happen when "there is a shift between the private costs and the social costs of an activity, both in the sense of a bigger social cost (negative externality) and in the sense of a bigger private cost (positive externality)".[14] The air or water pollution imposed by an industrial polluter on the neighbourhood is an often-cited example of negative externality[15]; the pollination that a beekeeper provides to his neighbour who runs an apple orchard is an example of positive externality.[16] The market fails in the presence of externalities because, "while the producer's activity imposes on third parties additional costs, such costs are not reflected (or "internalized") in the prices the producer charges for his products, and the purchasers of the product do not pay for its true social cost".[17] As a result, the producer would exercise too little self-restraint,[18] and more units of the product would be supplied than is socially appropriate and a misallocation of resources would occur.[19]

Information Asymmetry

Traditional economic analysis of the markets, particularly the theory of allocative efficiency, often assumes "perfect information" in the market: the decision-makers have adequate information on the alternatives available and they can process that information and behave rationally in a way that maximizes their expected utility.[20] Nevertheless, these assumptions do not always match situations in the real world. Most economists accept that human behaviour is constrained by "bounded rationality", which means that the capability of individuals to receive, store, and process information is limited.[21] Furthermore, information asymmetries may exist among the market players (for example, between sellers and consumers), severe ones of which may impede efficient transactions and thus lead to market failure. More specifically, such information asymmetry may lead to the problems of moral hazard or adverse selection.[22]

---

[13] Philipsen (2018), p. 542.

[14] Mattei (1997), pp. 30, 47. See also Cooter and Ulen (2016), pp. 39, 166–167.

[15] Ogus (2004), p. 35; Cooter and Ulen (2016), p. 39.

[16] Cooter and Ulen (2016), p. 39.

[17] Ibid, p. 35.

[18] Ibid, p. 39.

[19] Ibid, p. 35.

[20] Ogus (2004), p. 38.

[21] Ibid, p. 41.

[22] The terms "moral hazard" and "adverse selection" are usually used to refer to the problems faced by the insurance companies. "Moral hazard" arises when "the behaviour of the insured person or entity changes after the purchase of insurance so that the probability of loss or the size of the loss increases". "Adverse selection" arises because of the high cost to the insurers (insurance companies) of "accurately distinguishing between the insured persons with high risks and low risks"; to make a selection, the insurance companies often increase the insurance premiums, which, as a result, drives

Public Goods

Public goods are "commodities the benefit of which is shared by the public as a whole, or by some group within it".[23] It has two closely related characteristics: "non-rivalrous consumption" (meaning that "the consumption of public goods by one person does not leave less for any other consumer") and "non-excludability" (meaning that "it is impossible or too costly for the supplier to exclude those who do not pay from the benefit").[24] The often-cited example of public goods is the system which provides collective national (or local) security (the armed forces and the police). The consumers have a strong inducement to be free-riders of an aspect of public goods, from which they can benefit at no cost to themselves but the costs are covered from the payment of others.[25] As a result, the willingness to pay cannot be used to measure the demand and fails to provide incentives for the profit-maximizing suppliers to produce.[26] Thereby, "it is likely that too little of that particular public good will be provided, if private companies are the only providers of the public good".[27]

2.2.2 *Market Failures in Takeovers*

The four ssources of market failures are also observed in takeovers, which could cause negative consequences to the relevant societal interests.

2.2.2.1 Market Power

The synergy effects of takeovers often result from an increase in the market power of the acquirer. The presumption is that the acquirers, through takeovers, intend

out potential insured persons with good risks while retaining those with bad risks. For detailed discussions on "moral hazard" and "adverse selection" in the insurance area, see Akerlof (1970), pp. 493–494; Cooter and Ulen (2016), pp. 48–49, 240. The two problems may arise because of the information asymmetries between the buyer and seller (or provider of services) outside the insurance area. In Akerlof (1970), the author also used the example of the market for used cars to specify the essence of the "adverse selection" problem. Information asymmetries usually exist between the seller of a used car and the buyer, where the seller has more knowledge about the quality of a car (whether it is a good one, or a bad one which is often referred to as a "lemon"). Since it is impossible for a buyer to tell the difference between a good and a bad car, good cars and bad cars must still sell at the same price; as a result, the bad cars (lemons) tend to drive out the good ones. See Akerlof (1970), pp. 489–492.

[23] Ogus (2004), p. 38.

[24] Ibid. See also Cooter and Ulen (2016), pp. 40–41.

[25] Cooter and Ulen (2016), p. 41.

[26] Ogus (2004), p. 33.

[27] Cooter and Ulen (2016), p. 41.

to achieve "economies of scale" and build strength to compete with the dominant companies in their industries.[28] According to Gugler et al. (2003), the term "market power" connotes the ability to control price; therefore "takeovers which increase a company's market power must increase its ability to control (raise) the price of its products".[29] Based on this, Gugler et al. (2003) interpreted their findings which showed a subsequent increase in profits and decline in sales after takeovers as evidence of market power expansion of the acquirer subsequent to takeovers.[30] Where the expansion of the market power reaches the extent that creates barriers for competing companies to enter into the market, monopolies may occur. In such a situation, the competition interests (free and effective competition in the market), as a crucial part of the public interest, would be jeopardized and the welfare of the consumers would be harmed.

In addition to the competition interest and consumer welfare, the expanded market power of the acquirer may at the same time pose a threat to other societal interests. Among others, when the acquirer and the target both operate in the media area (for example, the newspaper sector and broadcasting sector), the establishment of a monopoly position of the acquirer through the takeover may negatively bear on the plurality for the range of information and views available to the citizens (media plurality), which is recognized as an important public interest in many jurisdictions.[31]

2.2.2.2 Information Asymmetry

Some scholars believe that takeovers may work as a channel to alleviate the information asymmetries between the companies and the market, given that "the announcements of a takeover usually result in the dissemination of a large quantity of information of the acquirer or target company".[32] Nevertheless, although in principle the

---

[28] Martynova and Renneboog (2008), p. 2149. "Economies of scale" refer to a condition of production in which the greater the level of output, the lower the average cost of production. "Economies of scale" is regarded as a source of barriers to market entry which may lead to the problem of monopoly. See Cooter and Ulen (2016), p. 29. For more about the "economies of scale" theory, see also Stigler, G. J. (1958). The economies of scale. *The Journal of Law and Economics, 1*, 54–71. In a nutshell, the theory of the "economies of scale" studies "the relationship between the scale of use of a properly chosen combination of all productive services and the rate of output of the enterprise".

[29] Gugler et al. (2003), p. 627.

[30] Martynova and Renneboog (2008), p. 2168. See Gugler et al. (2003).

[31] For example, in the BSkyB's takeover of ITV in the U.K., the Competition Commission of the U.K. stated that "media plurality is an important public interest consideration in a healthy and informed democratic society". See Competition Commission (14 December 2007). Acquisition by British Sky Broadcasting Group Plc of 17.9% of the Shares in ITV Plc. Available at: https://webarchive.nationalarchives.gov.uk/20140402234126/http:/www.competition-commission.org.uk/assets/competitioncommission/docs/pdf/non-inquiry/rep_pub/reports/2007/fulltext/535.pdf (accessed 16 May 2022). See Paras 5.8, 5.9 of the report. For more discussion about takeovers' impact on the media plurality, see Sect. 3.2.4.2 of this book.

[32] See Borochin et al., 2019; Draper and Paudyal, 2008; Officer et al., 2006. Borochin et al. (2019) confirmed the prediction that "because takeover announcements are accompanied by the release of

announcements of a takeover will attract the attention from the market (for example, the investors, the market regulators, the analysts and sometimes the media) and may reveal secrets concerning the acquirer and the target to some extent, information asymmetries could still exist and remain significant for the relevant stakeholders.

(1) Between the Acquirer and Target Company

Information asymmetries[33] between the acquirer and target company can be evident when the target company operates in areas which bear crucial national interests, for example, the areas of high technologies, infrastructure manufacturing or other security-sensitive areas. Where the acquirer comes from a foreign country, such information asymmetries can be more prominent and problematic, and the targets are often in an advantaged information position. Previous studies suggested that "the extent of information asymmetries foreign acquirers face is an important determinant of their post-takeover governance activities in the target: compared with domestic investors, foreign investors who have greater information disadvantages are less likely to engage in post-takeover governance activities in the target".[34] It is not surprising that target companies may lack the incentive to reduce such information asymmetries and sometimes they even employ them as a bargaining power against foreign acquirers. For example, in the high technology area, information asymmetries often exist between the target which has the innovation capability and the acquirer which pursues such a technological capability.[35] The incumbent management of the target can use its information advantage to bargain for certain autonomy after the

a large amount of information about the target firm, takeovers serve as a channel to alleviate the degree of the target's information asymmetry and significant announcement-period value gains are associated with the acquisition of target with high information asymmetry". Draper and Paudyal (2008) showed that "undervalued companies that have high information asymmetry between the company (the management) and the market (investors) may announce takeover bids to attract the attention of investors and analysts with a view to increase the share price through revaluation; bidders characterized by undervaluation and high information asymmetry earn more from bid announcement than other bidders". Officer et al. (2006) examined the information asymmetry in takeovers and showed that "acquirers' gains increase with the level of information asymmetry between the acquirer and the target about the target's value.".

[33] The numerous proxies that have been developed by scholars to measure the information asymmetry level of a target company include, for example, the company's age, size, the tangible assets, the average bid-ask spread, the abnormal accruals, the return volatility and so forth. See Borochin et al. (2019), pp. 45–46. It should be noted that scholars also admit that there is a lack of consensus with respect to which proxy best captures the true level of the information asymmetries.

[34] Kang and Kim (2010), pp. 1417, 1434. In this paper, the authors examined how the information asymmetries that foreign block acquirers face in the US affect their post-acquisition governance activities in US targets. Their findings also give implications regarding the relationship between the information asymmetries faced by foreign acquirers and their post-takeover corporate governance activities in other jurisdictions.

[35] See Gentile-Ludecke, S. (2013). What motivates German companies to agree to be sold to Chinese investors? The case of Chinese acquisitions in the German automotive sector. Available at: http://www.chinagoesglobal.org/wp-content/uploads/2013/08/Gentile_What_motivates_German_companies_to_agree_to_be_sold_to_Chinese_investors.pdf (accessed 16 May 2022).

takeover, such as the retention of the name and the center of innovations in the country.[36]

Moreover, information asymmetries also exist between the acquirer and the target shareholders concerning the value of the target, which may lead to the "adverse selection" and "free-rider" problems.[37] The acquirer usually has informational superiority concerning the value of the target compared with the target shareholders, particularly when the target has dispersed shareholdings and various institutional shareholders and the exchange of information between them is difficult. Such informational superiority of the acquirer may cause the skepticism of the target shareholders about the adequacy of the offer in comparison with the post-offer value the acquirer can generate.[38] The shareholders, in such situations, will doubt if the price the acquirer offers is high enough to reflect the target value. They will consider the potential results of tendering their shares to the acquirer, which may not only increase the post-offer value of the target company but also the wealth of other shareholders who stay in the company. In that situation, shareholders may prefer to free-ride on the benefits (i.e. an increase of the target value) after other shareholders first tender their shares.[39] Shareholders are thus incentivized to retain their shares; and when all or most of the shareholders choose to do so and hesitate to accept the offer, the acquirer will have to make a higher offer and the acquirer's costs will be increased.[40] In extreme cases, it would be impossible for the acquirer to capture any of the takeover surplus.[41]

(2) Between the Shareholders and the Management of the Target

In the context of corporate governance, agency problems can be observed in different relationships: (i) management acts as an agent of the shareholders; (ii) majority shareholders act as agents in relation to minority shareholders in voting on shareholder resolutions that are binding on the minority; (iii) the company, when entering into contracts with other stakeholders (for example, employees, customers, or creditors), affects the welfare of the stakeholders and acts as their agent.[42]

---

[36] Ibid, p. 12: It is observed that the possibility of maintaining autonomy due to the information asymmetry is a major driver for the German companies to pursue a Chinese investor in preference to other investors in many cases.

[37] For detailed explanation of "free-rider", see Cooter and Ulen (2016), pp. 103–104.

[38] Hirschleifer (1995), p. 879.

[39] Ibid, p. 878.

[40] Ibid, p. 862. The costs associated with revising an offer may include, for example: "the costs in the extension of the period during which managers must devote to the takeover contest; costs of obtaining further financing; where the takeover will be associated with restructuring of the acquirer and the target, then real investment and operating decisions of the acquirer may continue to be influenced by uncertainty over whether the takeover will occur; and the costs in the repetition of some mandated filings".

[41] Ibid, p. 878.

[42] Kraakman et al. (2017), pp. 29–30; Gerner-Beuerle and Schilling, 2019, p. 241. According to Kraakman et al., an "agency problem" or "principal-agent" problem arises whenever one party (the "principal"), relies upon actions taken by another party (the "agent"), which will affect the principal's welfare. It should be noted that Gerner-Beuerle and Schilling also discussed the fourth

As the agency theory suggests, "the agent commonly has better information than the principal about the relevant facts".[43] In a takeover, the agency problems between the shareholders and the incumbent management of the target can be important. In a company with no controlling shareholders, the board and the incumbent management are usually in actual control of the daily operation and have superior information concerning the value of the company. Consequently, there would be a disjunction between the parties to the dealings which bring about the transfer of control (the acquirer and target shareholders) and the parties to the control shift itself (the acquirer and target board).[44] The conflict of interests may incentivize the management, as the agent, to employ their information advantages to act opportunistically, which can also lead to the "moral hazard" problem.[45] In one situation, the incumbent board and management fear the risk of being ousted and try to defend the target from a potential takeover while the shareholders see a takeover as a wealth-enhancing mechanism. The board and the management may exploit their information about the target value and take actions to make the target less attractive to potential bidders (for example, by placing a block on the target's shares in the hands of persons not likely to take a hostile bid, or by placing strategic assets outside the reach of a successful bidder),[46] or they may increase the difficulty and costs for a successful bid (for example, by encouraging another company to make a competing friendly offer).[47] These defensive measures are likely to shift the acquirer's valuation of the target or the takeover and negatively affect the interests of the shareholders.[48]

In a contrary situation, the shareholders may be unwilling to accept the offer while the incumbent board and management actively facilitate the takeover as they will reap significant compensation after leaving office or become part of the bidding consortium afterwards. To persuade the shareholders, the incumbent management may provide misleading information or conceal important information with respect

type of agency problem where the other contractual constituencies are regarded as the agents in so far as their performance of the contract has a bearing on the welfare of the company (for instance, the company's revenue and thus profit depend on the productivity of its employees).

43 Kraakman et al. (2017), pp. 29–30.

44 Ibid, p. 207.

45 This means that "the agent may conduct self-interested behaviour that involves some element of guile, deception, misrepresentation, or bad faith". See explanation on the term "opportunism" in Kraakman et al. (2017), p. 29. Kraaakman here follows the usage of Oliver Williamson, see Williamson, O. (1985). *The economic institutions of capitalism.* Free Press, pp. 47–49.

46 Kraakman et al. (2017), p. 208. See also Hirschleifer (1995), p. 851: a value-reducing strategy, a defensive activity that reduces the post-takeover value of the target, such as sale of the asset of the target ("sale of the crown jewels"), can either reduce or increase information asymmetries between the bidder and the target shareholders.

47 Hirschleifer (1995), p. 881.

48 Ibid, p. 868. Some scholars show that even a defensive strategy that is good for the shareholders can reveal bad news; Hirschleifer argued that "a defensive strategy can be good for shareholders given the arrival of a bid, and yet undesirable ex ante because it deters investigation; and the negative average stock reactions associated with various kinds of defensive measures suggest that these actions are often undesirable for target shareholders.".

to the acquirer (for example, the true intention of the acquirer or the highly-leveraged funding for the takeover).

(3) Between the Takeover Companies and Other Non-shareholder Stakeholders

Information asymmetries are also observed as being between the acquirer, target, and other non-shareholder stakeholders (both corporate stakeholders and other societal stakeholders[49]), particularly in the post-takeover period. To gain clearance from the takeover authority, the acquirers, especially in foreign takeovers, often make promises concerning post-offer arrangements of the target company. This may include, for example, promises to continue environmental-friendly production strategies, to provide equal treatment to the employees and to maintain key factories and a high ratio of employment in the local community and to continue supporting the research and development ("R&D" hereinafter) in specific areas.[50] Usually, the acquirers have superior information about the details of such promises and the possibility of fulfilling them. The relevant stakeholders who bear an interest in these promises usually have limited access to the information after the change of control of the target and have limited capability to supervise the acquirer's fulfilment of the promises.[51] As a result, such information asymmetries may increase the risks of breach of commitments, which cause further negative externalities to the relevant stakeholders.

---

[49] See the definition of the "corporate stakeholders" and "other societal stakeholders" in Sect. 1.2.2 of this book.

[50] For example, The City Code on Takeovers and Mergers in the U.K. stipulates the "post-offer undertakings" and "post-offer intention statements" to encourage the takeover parties to make such promises. In the Melrose/GKN takeover in the U.K., Melrose made post-offer undertakings, including "to maintain the Melrose Group headquarters in the U.K.; to spend at least 2.2% of GKN's aggregate sales in R&D over the next five years". See WEDLAKEBELL.COM (23 April 2018). Melrose's Takeover of GKN Provides Another Instance of Post-offer Undertakings. Available at: https://wedlakebell.com/melroses-takeover-gkn-provides-another-instance-post-offer-undertakings/ (accessed 17 May 2022). In Fox's takeover of Sky, Fox made post-offer intention statements which include "to maintain Sky's U.K. headquarters at Osterley; to continue investment in U.K. content creation; to continue support of technology innovation, local communities, and young people in the U.K." See LEXOLOGY.COM (2 July 2021). Sky Takeover – Post-offer Undertakings. Available at: https://www.lexology.com/library/detail.aspx?g=2b3ebae4-522f-4370-a85e-f9872a6eacf8 (accessed 17 May 2022). For detailed discussion of the "post-offer undertakings" and "post-offer intention statements", see Sect. 3.4.3.1 of this book.

[51] For example, The City Code on Takeovers and Mergers prescribes that "the (Takeover) Panel may require a document to be sent to the offeree company's shareholders and persons with information rights and made readily available to its and the offeror's employee representatives…" The use of the word "may" indicates that the acquirer is not obliged to provide the information to all the relevant stakeholders. It also stipulates that the Takeover Panel "may require a party to an offer which has made a post-offer undertaking to appoint a supervisor to monitor compliance by that party with that undertaking," and further requires that the supervisor must be independent of the party to the offer concerned. Nevertheless, as the supervisor is appointed by the party, there is an implied conflict of interests. The supervisor may lack the incentive to solve the information asymmetry between the party who makes the undertaking and the stakeholders who bear an interest in the undertaking. See Rules19.5, 19.6, Rule 19 Continued 4 of The City Code on Takeovers and Mergers.

2.2.2.3 Negative Externalities

In essence, a takeover is a dealing between the acquirer and the target shareholders, through which the acquirer takes control of the target and shareholders take the premium and tender their shares. In addition to the two parties to this control transaction, a wide range of third parties may also bear the negative externalities of a takeover, including both corporate stakeholders and other societal stakeholders of the target.The negative externalities are often closely associated with the information asymmetries the relevant stakeholders may encounter and are reflected in the companies' breach of commitments subsequent to the takeover. The Kraft/Cadbury takeover in the U.K. provides good examples in specifying how a takeover may negatively affect different stakeholders and will be discussed in this section where it is of relevance.[52]

(1) On Corporate Stakeholders: Employees and Creditors

Among the non-shareholder corporate stakeholders, the negative externalities bearing on the employees and creditors are particularly evident.[53]

In the Kraft/Cadbury takeover, for instance, when the US company Kraft first announced its intention of taking over the U.K. food giant Cadbury in 2009, the employees of Cadbury who sensed deep insecurity came together and protested against the takeover.[54] In the run-up to the successful bid, Kraft gave public statements on the future of Cadbury, including a promise to keep open the Somerdale factory and an assurance that "there will be no further compulsory redundancies amongst manufacturing employees and no additional plant closures in the U.K. for the next two years".[55] Nevertheless, soon after the deal was done, Kraft announced the closure of the Somerdale factory which employed 400 staff members; and nearly two years later, the company announced a further 200 job cuts.[56]

With regard to creditors, their risks of insolvency may massively increase in a leveraged takeover which is financed with debt, particularly debt secured by the assets of the target company or assumed by the target when it is merged into a successful bidder.[57] In such leveraged takeovers, as the target eventually takes on the

---

[52] More other takeover cases in the U.K., Germany and China that are also of relevance will be discussed in Chaps. 3, 4 and 5 respectively.

[53] Kraakman et al. (2017), p. 209; Armour and Skeel Jr, 2007, p. 1739.

[54] THEGUARDIAN.COM (27 January 2010). Cadbury Workers Protest against Takeover. Available at: https://www.theguardian.com/business/2010/jan/27/cadbury-workers-takeover-protest (accessed 17 May 2022).

[55] House of Commons (6 April 2010). Mergers, acquisitions and takeovers: the takeover of Cadbury by Kraft—Ninth Report of Session 2009–10. Available at: https://publications.parliament.uk/pa/cm200910/cmselect/cmbis/234/234.pdf (accessed 17 May 2022). See Para. 32.

[56] BBC.COM (8 December 2011). Kraft and Cadbury: How Is It Working Out? Available at: https://www.bbc.com/news/uk-england-birmingham-16067571 (accessed 17 May 2022).

[57] Cahn and Donald (2018), p. 980. Such a leveraged takeover is usually referred to as a "leveraged buyout" or "LBO", which has been defined as "a shorthand expression describing a business practice wherein a company is sold to a small number of investors, typically including members of the

debt burden to finance the takeover or subsequent restructuring, there would be an increase in the proportion of fixed obligations (debt) in its capital structure and its creditors may find the face value of their claims suddenly deflated.[58] The increased risks bearing on the creditors reflect the agency problem between the controller of the target and its creditors, where the former may load the company with a heavy additional debt burden and threaten the interests of the latter.[59] While the shareholders can gain benefits by tendering their shares with a price that greatly outweighs the market price, and the managers, in a management buyout, own the controlling shares, the unsecured creditors often find that the value of their debt falls significantly and suffer the loss.[60] In some situations, the long-term lenders of the target, as the ones most at risk, may protect themselves through contractual provisions such as "event risk" covenants in loans; nevertheless, such covenants may not always provide full protection for them.[61] Research found that in some cases, the supplier contracts are not renewed due to a need to cut costs after a takeover, and financial providers face a higher risk of non-repayment of loans after the takeover of a debtor company.[62]

(2) On Other Societal Stakeholders

National Interests

Sometimes the negative externalities can reach far and bear on important national interests, particularly when the acquirer is a foreign investor and the target operates in sectors that have crucial impacts on people's daily life in the country. Among other societal interests, national security, the sufficient access to information through diversified media channels and the stability of the financial market usually have fundamental impacts on the security and quality of people's life and often give rise to public concerns in takeovers.

In a foreign takeover in the defence infrastructure area, the national security interest may be threatened after the foreign acquirer comes into control and captures high technologies. In the media sector, as the ranges, policies and aims of the media enterprises tend to converge under the same controller, takeovers may lead to insufficiency of media plurality. As a result, people's access to diverse sources of information is jeopardized. In the financial sector, the ultimate objectives of a financial service institution, whether it be a bank, insurance company, or securities company, usually include: "(i) to be financially safe and sound; (ii) to obtain the confidence of

---

company's management, under financial arrangements in which there is a minimum amount of equity and a maximum amount of debt"; where the target's own management buys out the company's public shareholders, it is referred to as a "management buyout" or "MBO".

58 Armour and Skeel Jr, 2007, p. 1739; Cahn and Donald (2018), p. 981.

59 Cahn and Donald (2018), p. 982. In a management buyout, the controller of the company would be the management, and the agency problem exists between the management and the creditors.

60 Ibid, pp. 981–982.

61 Kraakman et al. (2017), p. 210. See analysis on the "event risk" covenants in Bratton, W. W. (2006). Bond covenants and creditor protection: Economics and law, theory and practice, substance and process. *European Business Organization Law Review, 7*(1), 39-87, pp. 58-62.

62 Nyombi et al. (2015), p. 178.

the users and show fairness of its financial services to them; and (iii) to be efficient and effective".[63] Contrary to these objectives, a takeover of a too-big-to-fail bank may impose systemic risks on the whole national financial market, and a takeover between two rivalry banks may lead to anti-competitive behaviour in the market (such as more restrictive lending), which can harm investors' interests.[64]

Local Community and the Environment

The change of control after a takeover may also lead to changes in the target's strategies and fulfilment of its corporate social responsibilities and cause negative consequences to the local community and environment. For example, the closure of key factories subsequent to a takeover will not only affect the interests of the individual employees; when the unemployment problem becomes prevalent in a district, the economic development and social stability of the local community will also be harmed. In the Kraft/Cadbury case, the U.K. village Bournville used to be Cadbury's historic base. Before the takeover, Cadbury's long-term support for the local community (mainly through its support to local education and employment in Bournville) and its commitment to use Fairtrade products earned it an excellent reputation for pursuing goals of corporate social responsibility alongside corporate success.[65] After the announcement of the offer, whether the company would continue its support to the community and follow its previous commitments raised great attention in the U.K. To relieve public concerns, Kraft confirmed that it would uphold Cadbury's existing agreement to support the Cadbury Foundation, which gave grants to projects and partner organizations mainly in the fields of education and employment, and would "absolutely stand behind the Cocoa Partnership" and would stick to Cadbury's commitment to using Fairtrade cocoa beans to produce its chocolate.[66] Nevertheless, after the takeover, in 2017, the company moved some of its production sites from Bournville to Poland, which ignited fury in the local community and was regarded as a betrayal of its promise.[67] In November 2016, Cadbury also

---

63 Marcus (2000), p. 1.

64 Hankir et al.(2011), p. 2343. See also Berger, A. N., Goldberg, L. G., & White, L. J. (2001). The effects of dynamic changes in bank competition on the supply of small business credit. *Review of finance, 5*(1–2), 115–139.

65 House of Commons (6 April 2010). Mergers, acquisitions and takeovers: the takeover of Cadbury by Kraft – Ninth Report of Session 2009–10. See p. 17. Environmental protection is a key element of Fairtrade's view of sustainability. "Fairtrade" standards require smallholder farmer and larger hired labour production set-ups to comply in key areas; they also promote training for farmers, which include advice on switching to environmentally sustainable production and guide producers in adapting to climate change and mitigate their impact. See further introduction to Fairtrade at: http://www.fairtrade.org.uk/What-is-Fairtrade/Fairtrade-and-sustainability (accessed 17 May 2022).

66 Ibid, pp. 18–19.

67 BIRMINGHAMMAIL.CO.UK (15 January 2017). Anger as Cadbury makes Dairy Milk bars in Poland instead of Bournville. Available at: https://www.birminghammail.co.uk/news/midlands-news/anger-cadbury-makes-dairy-milk-12457521 (accessed 18 May 2022). Cadbury then clarified that this move was just a temporary measure aiming at improving the production condition in Bournville.

confirmed that it was no longer working with Fairtrade.[68] The above changes illustrate that the acquirer may breach its promises concerning social responsibilities by changing corporate strategies after the takeover and indicate the corresponding negative externalities to the sustainable development of the environment and local community.

2.2.2.4 Public Goods

Given the non-rivalrous consumption and non-excludability nature of public goods and the potential free-rider problem, government provision is seen as a primary solution to the underproduction of public goods.[69] The concern is often raised that provision of the public goods (for example, national defence, energy supply) by private companies will lead to under-investment.[70] Based on such understanding and presumption, public ownership played a key role in providing public goods such as defence infrastructure, energy supply and public transport in various jurisdictions in the post-war period.[71] In the late twentieth century, a mass process of privatization took place, which allowed private companies to replace the government in the production and supply of public goods in many sectors,[72] and provision of resources such as gas, water, and utilities such as city sewerage by private companies became common in many countries henceforth. Nevertheless, in some countries (such as China), even after the privatization reforms, the belief that national resources such as oil, gas, and strategic industries and services such as defence-related infrastructure and media should be managed by the government has never been completely abandoned.[73]

Against this background, sometimes takeovers may result in risks of undersupply of certain public goods where the target is a State-owned company that provides defence-related goods (such as defence armament) or supplies resources (such as

[68] INDEPENDENT.CO.UK (29 November 2016). In a Final Betrayal of the Cadbury Brand, Kraft Has Quietly Abandoned Its Promise to Stick With Fairtrade. Available at: https://www.independent.co.uk/voices/cadburys-chocolate-fairtrade-fair-trade-mark-farmers-kraft-american-brand-abandoned-promise-a7445826.html (accessed 18 May 2022).

[69] Cooter and Ulen (2016), p. 41. The government may "(i) undertake to subsidize the private provision of the public goods, either directly or indirectly through the tax system; (ii) undertake to provide the public goods itself and to pay the costs of providing the service through the revenues raised by compulsory taxation". See also Bernier et al. (2020), p. 223.

[70] See for example, Block (1983), pp. 29–30: it challenged the "under-investment" problem in private provisions of some public goods and contended that "the arguments on public goods could not justify the government operation or intervention in providing such goods". He also contended that "national defence does not fit well with the definition of public good", see pp. 12–13.

[71] Bernier et al. (2020), p. 91. It should be noted that in these jurisdictions, state intervention in the economy went beyond correcting market failures such as public goods to promote social goals that free markets may not achieve spontaneously.

[72] Ibid, pp. 91–92. For more discussion on the privatization process of State-owned economy in the U.K., Germany and China, see Chaps. 3, 4 and 5.

[73] Ibid, p. 92.

water, gas and oil), and the acquirer is a private-owned company. When the acquirer comes from another country, such risks are drastically increased as there is often concern that after the foreign acquirer takes control, it may threaten or oppress the home country by discontinuing or undersupplying the public goods.[74] In this situation, the problem of undersupply of public goods is closely associated with the takeovers' negative externalities to the national security interests.

2.3 The Role of Government Regulation and Private Regulation in Solving Market Failures

The above discussions about market failures specify that takeovers may cause inefficiencies which bear on the relevant societal interests. To solve such inefficiencies and protect the relevant societal interests, market intervention is needed. Among others, government regulation and private regulation are two common intervention forms. This section will employ two explanatory approaches as provided by microeconomics, namely the "public interest approach" and "private interest approach", to probe the nature of government regulation and private regulation. The aim of this section is to provide a theoretical basis for analysing the role of the regulatory frameworks of takeovers in the three jurisdictions in later chapters.

2.3.1 The Public Interest Approach and Private Interest Approach of Government Regulation and Private Regulation

2.3.1.1 Regulation[75]

The "public interest approach" uses the concept of "public interest" to explain the rationale for regulation.[76] It regards regulation as a possible remedy for market failures and a measure to protect the benefit of the public at large.[77] Scholars supporting this theory propose that "when the market fails, regulation should intervene to maximize social welfare"[78]; and "the regulatory intervention is directed towards gaining

---

[74] Ibid, p. 224.

[75] It should be noted that the term "regulation" in this section actually equates to the "government regulation" as discussed in other parts of this book, which means "rules formulated by the government (laws and other legal instruments). See the definition in Sect. 1.2.3 of this book.

[76] Hantke-Domas (2003), p. 165.

[77] See for example, Stigler (1971), p. 3.

[78] Hantke-Domas (2003), pp. 165, 168, 183.

an improvement in the social welfare".[79] This approach also acknowledges that it is not easy to choose the right form of regulation for curing market failures, considering the costs which regulation may generate.[80] To achieve the optimal form of regulation, the costs of correcting market failure by regulation have to be smaller than the benefits gained from the regulation.[81] Moreover, the form of regulation needs to be proportionate to the extent of market failure and should not go further (in limiting market entry or restricting competition) than necessary.[82] Furthermore, it is noteworthy that regulation is not always necessary nor is it the best way to solve market failures; in fact, private regulation or other market-based instruments (for example, taxation) may sometimes work better than regulation.[83]

The "private interest approach" focuses on the danger of the rent-seeking behaviour of the interest groups and holds that instead of protecting the public at large, "regulation only serves the interests of certain groups".[84] The "public choice theory" considers regulation as "the product of supply and demand on a political market: on the demand side, there are various interest groups formed by political entrepreneurs who demand favourable regulation; and on the supply side, there are wealth-maximizing politicians who wish to favour the interest groups that provide them with political support".[85] It argues that "the demand for favourable regulation by the interest groups is likely to cause the government actions to diverge from its originally beneficial objectives for society".[86] To that extent, "the public interest is merely a shield for the group interests and regulation becomes the result of the lobbying competition among many different interest groups".[87]

2.3.1.2 Private Regulation

The regulatory design and enforcement tasks of regulation are sometimes delegated to private actors or agencies.[88] As one form of private regulation, self-regulation can

---

[79] Philipsen (2007), p. 114.

[80] Ibid.

[81] Ibid, p. 116.

[82] Ibid.

[83] Philipsen (2018), pp. 542, 547.

[84] Hantke-Domas (2003), p. 165. The "private interest approach" originated from the "public choice theory", the "capture theory" and the so-called "economic (Chicago) theory of regulation", see Philipsen (2007), p. 116.

[85] Faure (2001), p. 127.

[86] Stearns (2017), p. 45.

[87] Philipsen (2007), p. 117. See Becker, G. S. (1983). A theory of competition among pressure groups for political influence. *The Quarterly Journal of Economics, 98*(3), 371–400.

[88] See the definition of "private regulation" in Sect. 1.2.3 of this book.

serve as a principal controlling device for a wide range of activities such as "financial services, advertising, and the practice of a large variety of professional occupations".[89] Self-regulatory rules also play an important role in regulating corporate activities, including for example, the listing rules and disclosure requirements set out by the stock exchanges governing its members, the national corporate governance code for listed companies; and in jurisdictions such as the U.K., the takeover law which was originally in a self-regulation form.[90] As Ogus (1995) argued, "there is no clear dichotomy concerning autonomy between private regulation and government regulation"; instead, "there is a spectrum containing different degrees of legislative constraints, outsider participation in relation to rule formulation or enforcement (or both), and external control and accountability".[91] The varied forms of self-regulation can be further divided into four types according to their legal force: "(i) self-regulation instruments that are formally binding, and non-compliance of which leads to public law or private law sanctions; (ii) codes of practice which presumptively apply unless an alleged offender can show that some alternative conduct was capable of satisfactorily meeting the regulatory goals; (iii) norms the breach of which leads to non-legal sanctions, such as ostracism; or (iv) standards compliance with which is purely voluntary".[92] Concerning the degree of autonomy from the government in the rule-making process, the varied self-regulatory instruments range from those "private to a firm, association or organization which are totally absent from government intervention" towards those "that have to be approved by a government ministry or some independent public authority".[93]

From the public interest approach, self-regulation is justified in a particular context where "there is some form of market failure (notably externalities or information asymmetries) but other private regulation instruments (for example, contractual agreements, private standard setting, private certification systems) are inadequate or too costly and public regulation is inferior (or also more costly) for solving the market failures".[94] According to the private interest approach, nevertheless, delegation of the regulatory powers to the SRAs may increase the possibilities of rent-seeking by interest groups when "there is relative absence of accountability and external constraints".[95]

---

[89] Ogus (1995), p. 97.

[90] The takeover law in the U.K. (The City Code on Takeovers and Mergers) will be discussed in Sect. 3.4 of this book. For more forms of self-regulation in the field of corporate governance, see Kershaw, D. (March 2015). Corporate Law and Self-Regulation (LSE Legal Studies Working Paper No. 5/2015). Available at: https://ssrn.com/abstract=2574201 (accessed 18 May 2022). For more forms of self-regulation in the securities market, see Carson, J. (January 2011). Self-Regulation in Securities Markets (World Bank Policy Research Working Paper No. 5542). Available at: https://ssrn.com/abstract=1747445 (accessed 18 May 2022).

[91] Ogus (1995), pp. 99–100.

[92] Philipsen (2003), p. 35. See Ogus, 2000, pp. 588–589.

[93] Ogus (1995), p. 100.

[94] Ibid, p. 97.

[95] Ibid, p. 98.

2.3.2 Government Regulation and Private Regulation for Takeovers

In practice, one can often observe a mix of government regulation and private regulation in the jurisdictions which provides for mechanisms to deal with the market failures in takeovers.[96] The government regulation consists of laws and other regulatory documents which are formulated by the government or its affiliated public agencies in different regimes. The national competition law in the merger control regime mainly regulates anti-competitive takeovers and mergers and may play a prominent role in addressing the monopoly problem. The FDI screening laws often provide for extra requirements to takeovers launched by foreign investors and are expected to reduce potential information asymmetries, negative externalities and undersupply of public goods in specific sectors. The national takeover law and corporate law which prescribe rules on the allocation of powers between different corporate organs may also play a role in dealing with the relevant market failure problems.

In the private regulation regime, self-regulatory national corporate governance code usually complements the corporate law by providing for corporate governance recommendations and mechanisms, which may also touch on the market failure problems in takeovers. Moreover, self-regulatory agencies such as the stock exchanges sometimes formulate mechanisms which are particularly targeted at their members' behaviour in takeovers and may also help address the relevant market failures.

The above government regulation and private regulation constitute the regulatory framework for protecting relevant societal interests in takeovers. As the aims of the laws and the self-regulatory mechanisms may differ, the scope of the stakeholders and societal interests that are protected as well as the specific protection mechanisms under the government regulation and private regulation also diverge.

2.4 Conclusion

According to microeconomic theory, the market fails when problems such as increase of market power, severe information asymmetries, externalities and public goods occur. According to the public interest approach, regulation is formulated to work as an intervention form to solve the market failures and protect the public interest. This regulation does not necessarily have to consist of (only) government regulation; private regulation, the formulation and enforcement of which are delegated to private actors or agencies, can sometimes be more efficient (e.g., less costly or more flexible) to address market failures than government regulation. The private interest approach, on the contrary, illustrates the risks that government regulation and private regulation

[96] It should be noted that in addition to regulating the market inefficiencies, the regulatory instruments adopted by the government concerning takeovers may have other objectives, such as "ensuring the distributive fairness or may be put in place for paternalistic objectives". See Philipsen (2003), p. 10.

can be dominated and exploited by interest groups (and politicians themselves) to pursue private interests rather than protecting the public at large.

Takeovers may create or enhance efficiencies by exerting disciplinary effects on the management and providing premiums to the shareholders, or through its resource-allocation role and synergy effects. Meanwhile, takeovers may cause inefficiencies in the market. The synergy effects usually result from an increased market power of the company, which may turn into a dominant position and even become a monopoly. Severe information asymmetries may exist between the acquirer and target shareholders, the shareholders and management of the target company, and the takeover parties and other societal stakeholders (such as the employees and creditors of the target, the public regulators, etc.) pending, during or after the takeover. Closely connected to the information asymmetries, some of the relevant stakeholders may suffer negative externalities while others gain. In specific industries or areas, privatization of the target company through a takeover may lead to undersupply or under-investments of public goods. These problems generate a wide impact on the relevant societal interests, which therefore may necessitate and justify the introduction of takeover regulation.

The regulatory framework of takeovers consists of both government regulation and private regulation. Government regulation is usually composed of national competition law, FDI screening laws, takeover law, and corporate law. The private regulation in this field includes rules in the national corporate governance code and instruments with respect to takeovers issued by the stock exchanges and other SRAs. In Part II of this book, Chaps. 3, 4 and 5 will respectively examine the regulatory frameworks of takeovers in the U.K., Germany and China to determine: (i) what are the societal interests that are currently protected under the national regulatory framework; and (ii) what are the specific protection mechanisms for different societal interests.

Chapter 3
The Regulatory Framework of the U.K.

Abstract Following the analysis of the market failure problems in takeovers in Chap. 2, this chapter continues by examining what societal interests are currently protected within the regulatory framework of takeovers in the U.K. and what the protection mechanisms are for these societal interests. To provide a panoramic view, it examines the competition law, the FDI screening regulation, the takeover law, the corporate law and the self-regulatory corporate governance code in the U.K. in sequence.

3.1 Introduction

As the legal instrument regulating the merger control in the U.K., the Enterprise Act 2002 provides for rules allowing the Government to intervene in takeovers and mergers to protect some "public interest" considerations in addition to protecting effective competition and the consumers' interests. Reforms to the Enterprise Act 2002 in recent years consecutively lowered the thresholds for reviewing certain takeovers and mergers and added a new public interest consideration, which further expanded the Government's power to protect the "public interest". In Sect. 3.2, the relevant considerations that have been recognized in previous cases by the U.K. Government as belonging to the "public interest" will be discussed in detail.

Section 3.3 sheds light on the FDI screening regulation in the U.K. and explores how the relevant regulation for reviewing foreign takeovers has evolved in recent years. The focus of the discussion will be placed on the reforms that have taken place in this field since 2016, particularly on the promulgation of The National Security and Investment Act 2021. The changes brought by the new regime under the National Security and Investment Act will be examined, with a particular focus on how these changes may affect the protection of the relevant societal interests in takeovers.

H. Ai, *Protecting Societal Interests in Corporate Takeovers*,
https://doi.org/10.1007/978-981-19-7546-2_3

The City Code on Takeovers and Mergers in the U.K. is well-known for its mechanisms for ensuring the target shareholders' decision-making power in a takeover. After Kraft's takeover of Cadbury in 2010[1] and Pfizer's attempted takeover of AstraZeneca in 2014,[2] there were fierce debates on whether the City Code on Takeovers and Mergers should be overhauled to make it more difficult for foreign firms to succeed in acquiring the U.K. companies,[3] and whether more attention should be given to protect non-shareholder stakeholders in a hostile takeover context.[4] In the corporate governance regime, the corporate law—Companies Act 2006 and the self-regulatory corporate governance code for listed companies provide for rules for protecting both the shareholders and other stakeholders in corporate activities. Such corporate governance rules lay a basis for the stakeholder-protection mechanisms in the takeover law regime (The City Code on Takeovers and Mergers). Thus, Sect. 3.4 will discuss the Companies Act 2006 and the corporate governance code of the U.K. in combination with the relevant mechanisms for stakeholder protection under the City Code on Takeovers and Mergers.

Section 3.5 provides a conclusion of this chapter.

---

[1] See the background of the Kraft/Cadbury takeover in Patrone (2011), p. 64: In August 2009, the management of the British chocolate manufacturer Cadbury first received the takeover proposal from the U.S. company Kraft, it dismissed it; nevertheless, the shareholders of Cadbury ultimately agreed on the deal and the Cadbury Board then revised its position and negotiated a friendly sale to Kraft in January 2010.

[2] House of Commons Library (17 October 2018). Contested mergers and takeovers. Available at: https://commonslibrary.parliament.uk/research-briefings/sn05374/ (accessed 18 May 2022). In May 2014, the debate on the public interest test under the U.K. regulation of takeovers and mergers was rekindled by the plans of U.S. pharmaceuticals company Pfizer to make a bid for the U.K. company AstraZeneca. Concerns were that the bid would risk the closure of R&D facilities in the U.K., with a knock-on impact on the country's science base.

[3] See e.g., Armour et al. (2011), p. 238. See also Nyombi (2015), p. 237: The Board Neutrality Rule (Non-frustration rule) under the City Code on Takeovers and Mergers was under criticism after the Kraft/Cadbury case.

[4] Patrone (2011), pp. 64–65. In the months following the takeover, Kraft revised its stance against closing Cadbury plants in the U.K. and announced that it would close the Somerdale chocolate plant, despite widespread protests and resistance. Economic nationalism and job losses are the foundation of the public criticism surrounding the Kraft/Cadbury takeover. See The Wall Street Journal (8 March 2010). Kraft Faces Probe on Cadbury. Available at: https://www.wsj.com/articles/SB10001424052748703915204575104002100336526 (accessed 18 May 2022). Facing the mounting public pressure, in February 2010, the Takeover Panel commenced a review of the City Code on Takeovers and Mergers with particular focus on the regulations that govern the unsolicited takeovers of U.K. Companies. See The Takeover Panel (1 June 2010). Consultation Paper Issued by the Code Committee of the Panel: Review of Certain Aspects of the Regulation of Takeover Bids. Available at: https://www.thetakeoverpanel.org.uk/wp-content/uploads/2008/11/PCP201002.pdf (accessed 18 May 2022).

3.2 Competition Law—Enterprise Act 2002

3.2.1 Background to the Public Interest Protection

A key objective of the Enterprise Act 2002 (the "EA 2002" hereinafter) is "to remove the decision-making from the political arena for the vast majority of takeovers".[5] To achieve this aim, it empowers the Competition and Markets Authority (the "CMA" hereinafter) to review and focus on the effect of "substantial lessening of competition" of a relevant merger situation.[6] In the meantime, it allows the Secretary of State to intervene based on specific public interest considerations in Sect. 58 in a relevant merger situation and a special merger situation.[7]

The criteria in the EA 2002 for determining whether a merger constitutes a "relevant merger situation" and a "special merger situation" as well as the specified public interest considerations both varied a lot in recent years, particularly after 2020, against the background of the COVID-19 pandemic and the introduction of the National Security and Investment Act 2021 (the "U.K. Security Act 2021" hereinafter).[8] A "relevant merger situation" is regarded as having been created if (a) two or more enterprises have ceased to be distinct enterprises at a time or in circumstances falling within Sect. 24, and (b) the turnover value threshold or the share of supply threshold as stipulated in Sect. 23 is met.[9] In 2018, the U.K. Government published two Orders to lower the turnover value and share of supply thresholds within the EA 2002 where the enterprise being taken over (or part of it) constitutes a "relevant enterprise".[10] In 2020, two other Orders came into force and added three more categories

---

[5] Parker & Majumdar (2016), p. 34. It should be noted that the relevant rules of Enterprise Act 2002 as discussed in this section use the word "merger"; as Enterprise Act 2002 does not distinguish "mergers" from "takeovers", the relevant rules apply to takeovers as well.

[6] Sections 22, 33 of the EA 2002. See the website of the CMA at: https://www.gov.uk/government/organisations/competition-and-markets-authority (accessed 20 May 2022).

[7] Section 42 of the EA 2002.

[8] In November 2020, the U.K. Government published the National Security and Investment Bill 2020 (the "U.K. Security Bill 2020" hereinafter), which became the National Security and Investment Act 2021 (the U.K. Security Act 2021) after receiving Royal Assent on 29 April 2021 and entered into force on 4 January 2022. For the content of this Act, see LEGISLATION.GOV.UK. National Security and Investment Act 2021. Available at: https://www.legislation.gov.uk/ukpga/2021/25/contents/enacted (accessed 19 May 2022).

[9] Section 23 of the EA 2002. The "turnover value threshold" is met where the annual U.K. turnover of the enterprise being acquired exceeds £70 million. The "share of supply threshold" is satisfied if the merged enterprises both either supply or acquire goods or services of a particular description in the U.K., and will, after the merger, supply or acquire 25% or more of those goods or services in the U.K. or in a substantial part of it. For detailed criteria on assessing whether a merger meets the turnover value threshold and the share of supply threshold, see Competition and Markets Authority (CMA) (4 January 2022). Mergers: Guidance on the CMA's jurisdiction and procedure. Available at:https://assets.publishing.service.gov.uk/government/uploads/system/uploads/attachment_data/file/1044636/CMA2_guidance.pdf (accessed 20 May 2022), paras 4.52–4.66.

[10] The two orders were The Enterprise Act 2002 (Share of Supply Test) (Amendment) Order 2018 and The Enterprise Act 2002 (Turnover Test) (Amendment) Order 2018. The Enterprise Act 2002

of businesses "the relevant enterprise" is active in: artificial intelligence, advanced materials, and cryptographic authentication, to which the lowered share of supply and turnover value thresholds applied.[11] Such provisions relating to the "relevant enterprise" were then removed by the U.K. Security Act 2021.[12] A "special merger situation", whilst it does not satisfy the turnover and the share of supply thresholds as stipulated in Sect. 23 for a "relevant merger situation", still falls within the scope of a relevant merger situation as long as it meets the other requirements. Previously, a special merger situation includes two types of mergers: (i) certain media mergers; and (ii) mergers involving government contractors in certain defence industry.[13] The U.K. Security Act 2021 then removed the type of mergers in the defence industry from the special merger situation category. Currently, a special merger situation may arise if it involves a supplier or suppliers of at least 25% of any description of newspapers or broadcasting in the U.K. or in a substantial part of it.[14]

Moreover, before 31 December 2020, Article 21(4) of the EC Merger Regulation applied to the U.K., which entitles the national authorities of the Member States of the EU to take appropriate measures to protect "legitimate interests" in a concentration with a Community dimension. At that time, according to Sects. 67 and 68 of the EA 2002, the Secretary of State had the power to intervene in a "European relevant merger situation", meaning that a relevant merger situation with a Community dimension (that is, it satisfies the turnover threshold requirements in Article 1 of the EC Merger Regulation). Because of the Brexit,[15] the EC Merger Regulation no longer applied to the U.K. since 31 December 2020, neither did the Secretary of State's public interest intervention apply in such European relevant merger situation.[16] This section, nevertheless, will still discuss the defined public interest considerations for such

(Share of Supply Test) (Amendment) Order 2018 inserted a Sect. 23A into the EA 2002 which defined a "relevant enterprise". The definition covered enterprises which are involved in specified activities in connection with: (i) military or dual-use goods which are subject to export control, (ii) computer processing units, and (iii) quantum technology. According to Sect. 23A, for mergers which involve the takeover of a relevant enterprise, the U.K. Government may intervene where (i) the target has a U.K. turnover of over £1million (rather than £70 million) or (ii) the target or parties combined have a U.K. share of supply of at least 25%.

[11] The two Orders were The Enterprise Act 2002 (Share of Supply Test) (Amendment) Order 2020 and The Enterprise Act 2002 (Turnover Test) (Amendment) Order 2020.

[12] The previous Sect. 23A of the EA 2002 was omitted by Sect. 58 of the U.K. Security Act 2021.

[13] The previous subsections 59(3B) and 59(8) of the EA 2002 stipulated the conditions of a special merger situation that involves government contractors in certain defence industry. These provisions were removed by Sect. 58 of the U.K. Security Act 2021.

[14] Subsections 59(3C)(3D), 59A of the EA 2002. For more analysis of a special merger situation, see Competition and Markets Authority (CMA) (4 January 2022). Mergers: Guidance on the CMA's jurisdiction and procedure, paras 16.14–16.18.

[15] Following the U.K.'s departure from the EU on 31 January 2020, the U.K. entered a transition period due to end on 31 December 2020, see the specification of EU-UK relationship concerning the Brexit at https://eur-lex.europa.eu/content/news/Brexit-UK-withdrawal-from-the-eu.html (accessed 22 May 2022).

[16] The previous Sects. 67 and 68 were omitted by virtue of The Competition (Amendment etc.) (EU Exit) Regulations 2019 (S.I. 2019/93).

European relevant merger situations under the EA 2002 (before 31 December 2020) and the EC Merger Regulation, given that the explanation of these considerations at that time was closely related to the explanation of the public interest considerations in other relevant merger situations.

In addition to the changes in the scope of merger situations in which the Secretary of State may intervene for public interest reasons, the scope of the defined public interest reasons in a relevant merger situation also experienced major changes after 2020. A new public interest consideration was added into Sect. 58 in June 2020: the need to maintain in the U.K. the capability to combat and mitigate the effects of public health emergencies. Following that, the "national security" interest, which was the only public interest consideration on the coming into force of the EA 2002, was removed from Sect. 58 by virtue of the U.K. Security Act 2021. These changes will also be discussed in this section.

3.2.2 Protection of the Public Interest in a Relevant Merger Situation

3.2.2.1 Recognized Public Interest Considerations in a Relevant Merger Situation

There is no doubt that the competition interest, among others, constitutes one crucial public interest consideration that the EA 2002 intends to protect in takeovers and mergers. Any anti-competitive outcome of a relevant merger situation according to the EA 2002 should be treated as being adverse to the public interest, unless it is justified by one or more than one public interest consideration which is relevant.[17] The CMA is responsible for reviewing the anti-competitive outcome of a relevant merger situation (the result of "a substantial lessening of competition" within the market in the U.K.) and decides on the actions that need to be taken to cure the anti-competitive outcome.[18] In a relevant merger situation, the Secretary of State also takes into account the "substantial lessening of competition" when it decides whether to make a reference to the CMA (before 2014, the Competition Commission).[19] However, whether the "substantial lessening of competition" exists does not affect the Secretary of State's final decision on whether the relevant merger situation operates against the public interest; what play a crucial role in the decision-making process are the public interest considerations listed in Sect. 58.[20]

---

[17] Subsection 45(6) of the EA 2002.

[18] Subsections 22(1), 33(1), 35(1)(2), 36(1)(2) of the EA 2002.

[19] The Competition Commission closed on 1 April 2014. Its functions were transferred to the CMA. See the archived website of the Competition Commission at: https://webarchive.nationalarchives.gov.uk/20140402141250/http://www.competition-commission.org.uk/ (accessed 23 May 2022).

[20] Subsections 45(2)(3)(4)(5) of the EA 2002. See also Parker & Majumdar (2016), p. 176. The Secretary of State may decide to make a reference to the Phase II investigation taking into account

Under the previous regime of the EA 2002, the Secretary of State may give a public interest intervention notice ("PIIN") to the CMA (before 2014, it was the "Office of Fair Trading", the "OFT" hereinafter)[21] in a relevant merger situation based on the following public interest consideration(s): (i) national security; (ii) public interest considerations in the media area; (iii) stability of the financial system of the U.K.; and (iv) the need to maintain in the U.K. the capability to combat and mitigate the effects of public health emergencies.[22] The U.K. Security Act 2021 removed the national security consideration from the public interest reasons under the EA 2002 and establishes a separate national security review regime, which comes into force on 4 January 2022.[23] There is no minimum turnover or share of supply threshold for the Secretary of State to intervene for the national security reason under the new regime, which applies to investors from any country.[24] This section will still discuss the definition of the national security consideration and the relevant public interest cases subject to the EA 2002 prior to the introduction of the U.K. Security Bill 2020 (the initial form of the U.K. Security Act 2021[25]). New changes introduced by the U.K. Security Act 2021 with regard to the application of a national security review (such as the scope of the "trigger events") and the intervention procedure in a national security review (such as the dual notification systems) will be analysed in detail together with other FDI screening regulations in Sect. 3.3 of this book.

Additionally, the EA 2002 allows the Secretary of State to specify a new public interest consideration, or to remove or amend any consideration specified in this section in the form of an order.[26] In fact, the financial stability consideration and the

---

the relevant public interest consideration(s) concerned and the substantial lessening of competition resulted from (or that may be expected to result from the relevant merger situation), or taking into account *only* the relevant public interest consideration(s) concerned.

[21] The Office of Fair Trading (OFT) was responsible for protecting consumer interests throughout the U.K. Its responsibilities have been passed to a number of different organizations. In April 2014, the CMA took over the OFT's functions in competition and consumer protection. See its archived website at: https://webarchive.nationalarchives.gov.uk/20140525130048/http://oft.gov.uk/ (accessed 20 May 2022).

[22] Sections 58 of the EA 2002.

[23] Sections 58, 62 of the U.K. Security Act 2021. Any merger which has previously been subject to a national security intervention under the EA 2002 (either through an intervention notice, a special intervention notice, or a European intervention notice) cannot be called in again under the U.K. Security Act 2021. See Department for Business, Energy and Industrial Strategy (4 January 2022). Guidance: The National Security and Investment Act alongside regulatory requirements. Available at: https://www.gov.uk/government/publications/the-national-security-and-investment-act-alongside-regulatory-requirements/the-national-security-and-investment-act-alongside-regulatory-requirements (accessed 23 May 2022).

[24] The Secretary of State may "call-in" any transaction if (s)he reasonably suspects that the transaction constitutes a "trigger event" and may conduct an in-depth national security assessment. See Sect. 1 of the U.K. Security Act 2021.

[25] For the detailed timeline of the enactment of the U.K. Security Act 2021, see Parallel Parliament. National Security and Investment Act 2021. Available at: https://www.parallelparliament.co.uk/bills/2019-21/nationalsecurityandinvestment (accessed 19 May 2022).

[26] Subsection 58 (3) of the EA 2002. The Secretary of State has the power to issue an intervention notice whilst simultaneously seeking the Parliament's approval for the recognition of a further

new consideration related to public health emergencies were added by the Secretary of State in this way against the changing background of the market environment.

National Security

The national security interest was listed as the only public interest consideration at the time when the EA 2002 came into force.[27] In the past years, by contrast, the Secretary of State has intervened in mergers under the national security consideration more frequently than under any other public interest consideration.[28]

As of 31 December 2020 when the EC Merger Regulation still applied to the U.K., the "national security" consideration under the EA 2002 included public security, which has the same meaning as in Article 21(4) of the EC Merger Regulation.[29] The European Commission interpreted "public security" in two ways: "(i) it refers to the national defence interest, which allows a Member State to intervene in a merger which is contrary to the essential interests of its security and is connected with the production of or trade in arms, munitions and war material; (ii) in addition to the defence interest in the strict sense, it could also cover, as interpreted by the European Court of Justice (the "CJEU" hereinafter), security of supplies to the country in question of a product or service considered of vital or essential interest for the protection of the population's health".[30] The CJEU once provided indications of the sectors related to public security in relevant cases and stated that "public security may be relied on only if there is a genuine and sufficiently serious threat to a fundamental interest of society".[31] With regard to the energy sector, the CJEU acknowledged that

category of public interest consideration (as exercised in the Lloyds/HBOS merger case which will be discussed later in this section).

[27] Parker, J., & Majumdar, A. (2016), p. 15. See the historical evolution of the Enterprise Act 2002 at pp. 6–18.

[28] For example, up to June 2020, the U.K. Government had intervened 12 times under the national security consideration, 7 times under media plurality and once under financial stability. See Department for Business, Energy and Industrial Strategy (June 2020). Enterprise Act 2002: Changes to the public interest grounds for intervention in merger cases (Guidance 2020). Available at: https://assets.publishing.service.gov.uk/government/uploads/system/uploads/attachment_data/file/924368/enterprise-act-2002-guidance-merger.pdf (accessed 24 May 2022).

[29] Subsection 58(2) of the EA 2002. Because of the Brexit, subsection 58(2) was first modified by virtue of The Competition (Amendment etc.) (EU Exit) Regulations (S.I.2019/93) on 31 December 2020. It was then omitted by Sect. 58 of the U.K. Security Act 2021 on 4 January 2022.

[30] European Commission (1998). Notes on Council Regulation (EEC) 4064/89. Available at: https://ec.europa.eu/competition/mergers/legislation/notes_reg4064_89_en.pdf (accessed 23 May 2022).

[31] Competition Policy International (CPI) (December 2017). Merger Control and the Public Interest: European Spotlight on Foreign Direct Investment and National Security. Available at: https://www.competitionpolicyinternational.com/wp-content/uploads/2017/12/Europe-Column-December-Full.pdf (accessed 23 May 2022). See Case C-503/99 *Commission v Belgium* [2002], para 47; C-483/99, *Commission v France* [2002], para 48; and Case C-463/00 *Commission v Spain* [2003], para 72; COMP/M.4685-ENEL ACCIONA/ENDESA, paras 57–58.

"measures necessary to ensure a minimum level of energy supplies in the event of a crisis may fall under the notion of public security".[32]

It is noteworthy that the lowering of the thresholds for certain mergers involving a "relevant enterprise" under the EA 2002 after 2018, which has been discussed earlier in this section, was principally intended to enable the Secretary of State to intervene on the grounds of national security in takeovers and mergers in specified areas (artificial intelligence and the development or production of items for military or military and civilian use).[33]

Public Interest Considerations in Newspaper and Media Mergers

The public interest considerations in the media area were inserted into Sect. 58 by the Communications Act 2003.[34] The considerations cover the standards objectives of the content of newspapers and broadcasting, the availability of broadcasting, and the plurality of the suppliers of the media enterprises in the U.K.[35]

In newspaper mergers, accurate presentation of news, free expression of opinion, a plurality of views in each newspaper market should be taken into account to decide whether the merger is contrary to the public interest.[36] In other media mergers, the plurality of media ownership, the availability of a wide range of high quality broadcasting throughout the U.K., and the attainment of certain standards for program content are the basis for deciding whether the merger is contrary to the public interest.[37] It should be noted that, although there is often an overlap between the competition concern and at least the media plurality concern in media mergers, according to the Guidance on the Operation of the Public Interest Provisions relating to Newspaper and Other Media Mergers (the "Media Merger Guidance" hereinafter),[38] the review of the public interest considerations in the media merger must be separated from the competition assessment.[39]

---

[32] Ibid. See Case C-503/99 *Commission v Belgium* [2002] ECR I-4809, paragraphs 46 and 48; and Case C-463/00 *Commission v Spain* [2003] ECR I-4581, paras 71, 73; Case 72/83 Campus Oil [1984] ECR 2727, paras 34 and following.

[33] Competition and Markets Authority (CMA) (4 January 2022). Mergers: Guidance on the CMA's jurisdiction and procedure (see footnote 23 at p. 14). The lowered thresholds also enabled the CMA to review a merger involving changes of control of relevant enterprises on competition grounds.

[34] See the content of Communications Act 2003 available at: https://www.legislation.gov.uk/ukpga/2003/21/contents (accessed 24 May 2022).

[35] Subsections 58 (2A)(2B)(2C) of the EA 2002.

[36] Subsections 58 (2A) (2B) of the EA 2002; Subsection 375 (1) of Communications Act 2003.

[37] Subsection 58 (2C) of the EA 2002; Subsection 375 (1) of Communications Act. See also Parker & Majumdar (2016), pp. 158–161, 164–171.

[38] See Department for Trade and Industry (DTI) (May 2004). Guidance on the Operation of the Public Interest Provisions relating to Newspaper and Other Media Mergers. Available at: https://assets.publishing.service.gov.uk/government/uploads/system/uploads/attachment_data/file/595816/file14331__1_.pdf (accessed 24 May 2022). The guidance was published by the then Department of Trade and Industry (DTI) in May 2004, which is now replaced by the Department for Business, Energy and Industrial Strategy.

[39] Parker & Majumdar (2016), p. 164. See Department for Trade and Industry (DTI) (May 2004). Guidance on the Operation of the Public Interest Provisions relating to Newspaper and Other Media Mergers, paras. 5.15, 7.3.

Stability of the Financial System of the U.K.

Maintaining the stability of the U.K. financial system was acknowledged as a public interest consideration in 2008 against the background of the proposed Lloyds/HBOS merger.[40]

At the beginning of the proposed Lloyds/HBOS merger, the OFT submitted a report to the Secretary of State stating that this anticipated merger would result in a substantial lessening of competition in relation to personal current accounts, banking services for small and medium enterprises in Scotland, and mortgages.[41] This report also contained a special resolution report which provided details on "maintaining financial stability".[42] It emphasized that "the special resolution regime would enable the Authorities to deal with banks that get into financial difficulty in a manner that supports the public interest in financial stability, continuity of banking services and depositor protection".[43] In the end, the Secretary of State considered that "... the merger will result in significant benefits to the public interest as it relates to ensuring the stability of the U.K. financial system and that these benefits outweigh the potential for the merger to result in the anti-competitive outcomes identified by the OFT".[44]

This case provides basic understandings of "the stability of the U.K. financial system". Among other things, the continuity of banking services and the protection of depositors are regarded as the founding pillars of the U.K. financial system, which are of crucial importance in takeovers and mergers in the financial domain.

---

[40] It was inserted into Sect. 58 of the EA 2002 by The Enterprise Act 2002 (Specification of Additional S.58 Consideration) Order. Before 31 December 2020, this consideration was only to be taken into account in a "relevant merger situation" and a "special merger situation", but was not relevant in a "European relevant merger situation".

[41] Parker & Majumdar (2016), pp. 171–172. See Office of Fair Trading (24 October 2008). Anticipated acquisition by Lloyds TSB plc of HBOS plc: Report to the Secretary of State for Business Enterprise and Regulatory Reform. Available at: https://assets.publishing.service.gov.uk/media/5592bba440f0b6156400000c/LLloydstsb.pdf_jsessionid_4EBCDA0A4B36535AF8355B90D18E00A2.pdf (accessed 24 May 2022).

[42] Bank of England, HM Treasury and and FSA (July 2008). Financial stability and depositor protection: special resolution regime. Available at: https://assets.publishing.service.gov.uk/government/uploads/system/uploads/attachment_data/file/238704/7459.pdf (accessed 24 May 2022).

[43] Ibid. See Chap. 2 of the report: SRR objectives, roles and governance.

[44] Parker & Majumdar (2016), p. 172. See Department for Business, Enterprise & Regulatory Reform (31 October 2008). Decision by Lord Mandelson, the Secretary of State for Business, not to refer to the Competition Commission the merger between Lloyds TSB Group plc and HBOS plc under Sect. 45 of the Enterprise Act 2002 dated 31 October 2008. Available at: http://data.parliament.uk/DepositedPapers/Files/DEP2008-2685/DEP2008-2685.pdf (accessed 24 May 2022). See para 12.

Maintaining in the U.K. the Capability to Combat and Mitigate the Effects of Public Health Emergencies

In June 2020, the Secretary of the State, in exercise of the powers conferred by the EA 2002, made an Order to add a new public interest consideration in Sect. 58: the need to maintain in the U.K. the capability to combat and mitigate the effects of public health emergencies.[45]

The U.K. Government considers this new consideration as a "necessary" and "proportionate" measure to allow it to scrutinize and take actions in takeovers and mergers which may pose risks to the country's capability to respond to the COVID-19 pandemic or future public health emergencies.[46] Based on this consideration, the Government may, for example, impose conditions on a merger prohibiting any diminution of critical capabilities or even blocking the merger where appropriate.[47] In practice, the relevant capability to combat public health emergencies can be found in companies that are normally active in the public health sector, such as vaccine researchers, drug manufactures and medical supply companies.[48] Moreover, companies in other areas which are usually not directly related to the public health sector may also fall within the scope of the new consideration. For example, the U.K. Government may intervene in an engineering company that designs and makes parts for cars considering its potential capability to produce ventilators during a public health emergency based on the engineering know-how and machinery it possesses;[49] it may also intervene in companies providing internet services or in the food supply chain or in the delivery sector given that goods and services in these sectors may be increasingly demanded in a lockdown time during a public health emergency.[50] It is expected that the Government would have to act reasonably in making such a link between the relevant capability with companies in these "far" areas; and it is not anticipated that intervention on these grounds would be frequent.[51]

---

[45] The Enterprise Act 2002 (Specification of Additional Sect. 58 Consideration) Order 2020 (S.I. 2020/627).

[46] The Department for Business, Energy and Industrial Strategy (BEIS) issued a Guidance for this change. See Department for Business, Energy and Industrial Strategy (June 2020). Enterprise Act 2002: Changes to the public interest grounds for intervention in merger cases (Guidance 2020). Available at: https://assets.publishing.service.gov.uk/government/uploads/system/uploads/attachment_data/file/924368/enterprise-act-2002-guidance-merger.pdf (accessed 24 May 2022), para 13.

[47] Ibid, para 9.

[48] Ibid, para 32.

[49] Ibid, para 30.

[50] Ibid, para 27.

[51] Ibid, para 30.

3.2.2.2 The "Public Interest Intervention" Procedure in a Relevant Merger Situation

The intervention steps based on public interest considerations in a relevant merger situation subject to the EA 2002 are as follows.[52]

First of all, the Secretary of State may give an intervention notice to the CMA, which identifies the relevant public interest consideration(s), if it believes that it is or it may be the case that public interest consideration(s) as listed is of relevance to the merger situation concerned.[53]

The CMA must within such period as the Secretary of State may require, give an advisory report to the Secretary of State setting forth its advice and recommendations on the public interest considerations mentioned in the intervention notice concerned.[54] In the case of media mergers, the Office of Communications (Ofcom), which is the regulator and competition authority for the U.K. communications industries, must give an additional report containing its advice and recommendations on the media public interest considerations mentioned in the intervention notice to the Secretary of State.[55] In practice, sometimes after the Secretary of State has referred the proposed deal to the CMA for investigation, the CMA appoints an inquiry group of independent panel members with a variety of backgrounds to investigate, decide and report on the question set out in the referral.[56]

After receiving the report from the CMA, the Secretary of State may make a referral to the CMA, taking into account the following considerations: (i) if a substantial lessening of competition within any market or markets in the U.K. was the result of, or is expected to be the result of the creation of the merger situation; and (ii) if the public interest consideration(s) mentioned in the intervention notice is relevant to the

---

[52] For detailed conclusion of the public interest intervention procedure in a relevant merger situation, see also Competition and Markets Authority (CMA) (4 January 2022). Mergers: Guidance on the CMA's jurisdiction and procedure, paras 16.6–16.12. These steps also applied to public interest intervention in takeovers and mergers with national security concerns that were completed before 12 November 2020, prior to the introduction of the U.K. Security Bill 2020.

[53] Sections 42, 43 of the EA 2002 stipulate the "Public interest intervention notice (PIIN)" in relevant merger situations.

[54] Sections 44, 61 of the EA 2002.

[55] Sections 44A, 61A of the EA 2002. See the website of the Ofcom at: https://www.ofcom.org.uk/. Except for the investigation report from the Ofcom in the case of newspaper and media mergers, the CMA may also contact other governmental departments and other sectoral regulators for their views on public interest issues where appropriate. The sectoral regulators include, for example, the Ministry of Defence (MOD) in mergers of the defence sectors, the Gas and Electricity Markets Authority (Ofgem) for mergers of the energy sectors, the Financial Conduct Authority (FCA) and Bank of England for mergers relevant to the stability of the U.K. financial system, and National Health Service Improvement (NHSI) for National Health Service (NHS) mergers. See Competition and Markets Authority (CMA) (4 January 2022). Mergers: Guidance on the CMA's jurisdiction and procedure, paras 2.11, 9.24, 9.26, 16.6.

[56] See the example of the Fox/Sky deal. Competition and Markets Authority (CMA) (23 January 2018). CMA provisionally finds Fox/Sky deal not in the public interest. Available at: https://www.gov.uk/government/news/cma-provisionally-finds-foxsky-deal-not-in-the-public-interest (accessed 24 May 2022).

merger situation.[57] The Secretary of State may make a decision that the merger situation concerned operates against the public interest and make a referral to the CMA in two situations: (i) there is a substantial lessening of competition, and the public interest consideration(s) in the intervention notice is relevant to the merger situation; or (ii) there is no substantial lessening of competition, but the public interest consideration(s) mentioned in the intervention notice is relevant to the merger situation, and the Secretary of State makes such decision taking account only of the public interest consideration(s).[58]

Correspondingly, the CMA will look into different questions according to the different situations of the Secretary of State's referral and give its answers in a report to the Secretary of State.[59] For a referral which finds there are both a substantial lessening of competition resulted from the merger situation and relevant public interest consideration(s), the CMA should decide on whether both of the two aspects exist, and based on the two aspects, whether the merger situation goes against the public interest; for a reference which finds only relevant public interest consideration(s), but no substantial lessening of competition, the CMA will then only take account of the relevant public interest consideration to make such a decision.[60]

In the end, the Secretary of State, after receiving the report from the CMA, will decide whether to make an adverse public interest finding in relation to the relevant merger situation concerned (if, taking into account the likelihood of a substantial lessening of competition and/or the relevant public interest considerations, the merger operates or may be expected to operate against the public interest),[61] or whether to make no finding at all in the matter (if he decides that no public interest consideration is relevant to the merger situation concerned).[62]

In summary, the public interest intervention steps in a relevant merger situation subject to the EA 2002 are illustrated as the flows in Fig. 3.1.

Among the above procedural steps, the period up to the making of a reference in stage (iii) is commonly referred to as "Phase 1", whereas the stages following the making of a reference are referred to as "Phase II".[63]

---

57 Subsections 45(2)(3)(4)(5) of the EA 2002.

58 Ibid.

59 Sections 47, 50 of the EA 2002.

60 Section 47 of the EA 2002.

61 Subsections 54(2)(3) of the EA 2002.

62 Subsections 54(2)(4) of the EA 2002.

63 CAT's judgment in *Lebedev Holdings Limited and Another v Secretary of State for Digital, Culture, Media and Sport* [2019] CAT 21.

Fig. 3.1 Public interest intervention steps in a relevant merger situation[64]

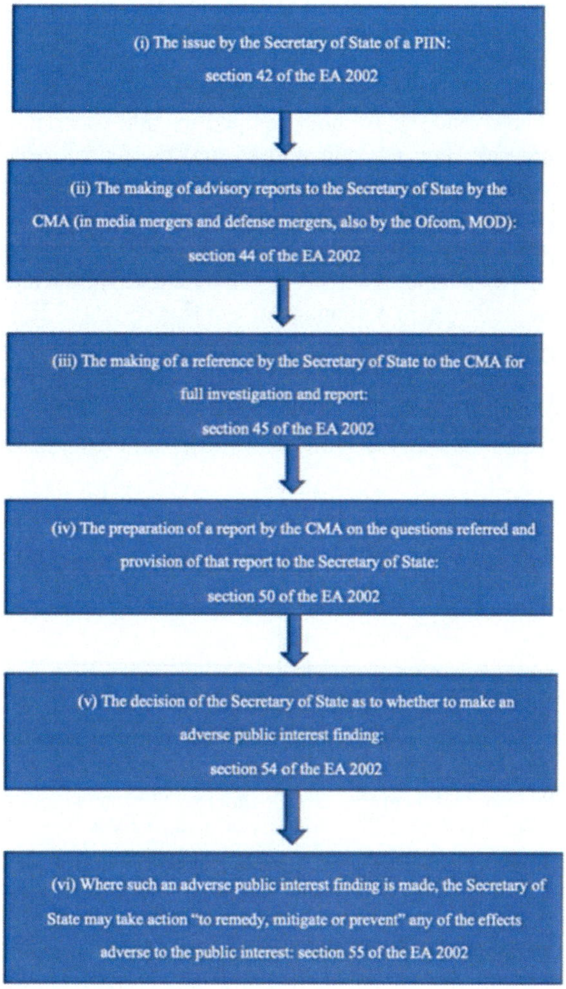

[64] The procedure flow in Fig. 3.1 is formulated by the author based on the conclusion about public interest intervention in media mergers in the CAT's judgment in *Lebedev Holdings Limited and Another v Secretary of State for Digital, Culture, Media and Sport* [2019] CAT 21, available at: https://www.catribunal.org.uk/sites/default/files/2019-08/1328_Lebedev_Judgment_160819.pdf (accessed 25 May 2022). In this judgment, the Competition Appeal Tribunal (CAT) found that a public interest intervention notice cannot be issued later than four months from the Secretary of State receiving notice of the "material facts" relating to a completed transaction.

Under the new regime established by the U.K. Security Act 2021,[65] the national security review is separate from the merger control review and a takeover or merger may qualify for both reviews.[66] Where there are grounds for a takeover or merger to be considered for both competition and national security reasons, the Investment Security Unit, which is part of the Department for Business, Energy and Industrial Strategy, will work closely with the CMA to manage the case[67]: the CMA solely assesses the competitive effects of the transaction,[68] whilst the Investment Security Unit operates the national security regime. The Secretary of State for Business, Energy and Industrial Strategy, may scrutinize and intervene in such cases and decides the outcome of the national security review.[69] In the cases being investigated in parallel, the Secretary of State may direct the CMA to do, or not to do, anything under the merger part of the EA 2002, as long as (s)he reasonably considers that the direction is necessary and proportionate for the purpose of preventing, remedying or mitigating a risk to national security.[70]

3.2.3 Protection of the Public Interest in a European Relevant Merger Situation and a Special Merger Situation

3.2.3.1 Recognized Public Interest Considerations in a European Relevant Merger Situation and a Special Merger Situation

Before 31 December 2020, the EC Merger Regulation applied to the U.K. which entitles the national authorities of the Member States to take appropriate measures to protect "legitimate interests" in a concentration with a Community dimension. Among others, the "public security", "plurality of the media" and "prudential rules"

---

[65] According to Sect. 62(1) of the U.K. Security Act 2021, the new regime applies to takeovers or mergers that are in process, contemplation or have been contemplated on and after 12 November 2020, and these that were completed before 12 November 2020 were exempt from the new regime. See Department for Business, Energy and Industrial Strategy (14 April 2022). Guidance: Check if you need to tell the government about an acquisition that could harm the UK's national security. Available at: https://www.gov.uk/guidance/national-security-and-investment-act-guidance-on-acquisitions (accessed 27 May 2022).

[66] See Competition and Markets Authority (CMA) (4 January 2022). Mergers: Guidance on the CMA's jurisdiction and procedure, para 17.3.

[67] Department for Business, Energy and Industrial Strategy (4 January 2022). Guidance: The National Security and Investment Act alongside regulatory requirements.

[68] With regard to the interaction of the new national security regime with the CMA functions, see Sect. 31 of the U.K. Security Act 2021.

[69] See Competition and Markets Authority (CMA) (4 January 2022). Mergers: Guidance on the CMA's jurisdiction and procedure, para 17.3. The Secretary of State's call-in power in such takeovers and mergers will be discussed in detail in Sect. 3.3.2.

[70] Section 31 of the U.K. Security Act 2021. The Secretary of State must consult the CMA and such other persons prior to issuing any direction where appropriate.

are the three recognized legitimate interests, for which national authorities do not need to communicate with the European Commission before taking appropriate measures.[71] At the national level, the EA 2002 repeated that the Secretary of State may intervene in a "European relevant merger situation" to protect "legitimate interests",[72] but it did not stipulate specific considerations for the "legitimate interests". Thereby, at that time, the public interest grounds on which the Secretary of State may intervene in a European relevant merger situation included those that were applicable in a relevant merger situation under the EA 2002 (other than "maintaining the stability of the U.K. financial system").[73] Meanwhile, they should also coincide with the "public security", "plurality of the media" and "prudential rules" as specified under the EC Merger Regulation.[74] As a result, before 31 December 2020, the public interest considerations for a European relevant merger situation include two aspects: (i) national security; and (ii) the newspaper and media public interest considerations. As discussed in the previous section, the sectors related to "national security" must not be explained beyond the scope as defined by the European Commission and CJEU. The "public interest considerations related to newspaper and media mergers" contained not only "plurality of the media", but also other aspects such as standards objectives of the media service, and newspaper content. In practice, the Secretary of State for Culture, Media and Sport sometimes issued a European Intervention Notice on the grounds of media plurality and commitment to broadcasting standards.[75]

Before the introduction of the U.K. Security Act 2021, a special merger situation included certain media mergers and mergers involving government contractors.[76] In

---

[71] Article 21 (4) of The EC Merger Regulation. For considerations other than the three acknowledged ones, the Secretary of State must first communicate to the Commission and wait for the latter's decision before taking any measures. "Prudential rules" refer to EU rules of prudential requirements, which mainly concern the amount of capital and liquidity that banks hold. The goal of these rules is to strengthen the resilience of the EU banking sector so that it can better absorb economic shocks, while ensuring that banks continue to finance economic activity and growth. For the explanation by the European Commission and the relevant EU legislation, see European Commission. Prudential Requirements. Available at: https://ec.europa.eu/info/business-economy-euro/banking-and-finance/financial-supervision-and-risk-management/managing-risks-banks-and-financial-institutions/prudential-requirements_en (accessed 26 May 2022).

[72] The previous Sects. 67, 68 of the EA 2002, which have been omitted by virtue of The Competition (Amendment etc.) (EU Exit) Regulations 2019 (S.I. 2019/93).

[73] The previous Sect. 58 (2D) of the EA 2002 specified that the interest of "maintaining the stability of the U.K. financial system" did not apply to a concentration with a Community dimension. This part of Sect. 58(2D) has been omitted by virtue of The Competition (Amendment etc.) (EU Exit) Regulations 2019 (S.I. 2019/93).

[74] As the scope of the "prudential rules" under the EC Merger Regulation may overlap with the considerations related to "maintaining the stability of the U.K. financial system" in the EA 2002, the Secretary of State's discretion in this area in a European relevant merger situation at that time was indeed made more difficult by the exception rule under the EA 2002.

[75] See for example, OFCOM (20 June 2017). Public interest test for the proposed acquisition of Sky plc by 21st Century Fox, Inc. Available at: https://assets.publishing.service.gov.uk/government/uploads/system/uploads/attachment_data/file/623244/Public_Interest_Test_report_-_non_confidential_-_For_publication.pdf (accessed 29 May 2022).

[76] Section 59 of the EA 2002.

a special media merger situation, the Secretary of State can intervene to protect the considerations listed under the newspaper and media mergers in Sect. 58. In mergers involving "relevant government contractor",[77] as this term may suggest, the sectors were often related to national defence, and the Secretary of State intervened on the grounds of national security. Currently, mergers involving government contractors have been removed from the special merger situation by virtue of the U.K. Security Act 2021.

3.2.3.2 The "Public Interest Intervention" Procedure in a European Relevant Merger Situation and a Special Merger Situation

The general intervention procedure in a European relevant merger situation (as of 31 December 2020) and a special merger situation is similar to that in a relevant merger situation. Meanwhile, some major differences can still be observed as follows.

First and foremost, the considerations taken into account by the Secretary of State to make the intervention notice are different. Both the European intervention notice (EIN) and special intervention notice (SIN) exclude the judgment of a substantial lessening of competition resulting from the merger situation and only focus on the relevant public interest considerations.[78] Accordingly, the reference and decision made by the Secretary of State and the report made by the CMA do not cover the aspect of the substantial lessening of competition either.[79]

Besides, in a special media merger situation, an additional investigation and report are also required from the Ofcom after it receives the intervention notice from the Secretary of State. In a European relevant merger situation before 31 December 2020, after the Secretary of State issued an EIN, a reference to the CMA was not possible due to the fact that the Commission, and not the U.K. authorities, had the jurisdiction in such a situation.[80]

Last, the Secretary of State may take actions at different stages in different merger situations. The Secretary of State may by Order provide for the taking of action, where an EIN has been given, to remedy, mitigate or prevent effects adverse to the

[77] According to the previous subsection 59(8) of the EA 2002, which has been omitted by virtue of the U.K. Security Act 2021, a relevant government contractor means (a) government contractor (i) who has been notified by or on behalf of the Secretary of State of information, documents or other articles relating to defence and of a confidential nature which the government contractor or an employee of his may hold or receive in connection with being such a contractor; and (ii) whose notification has not been revoked by or on behalf of the Secretary of State; or (b) a former government contractor who was so notified when he was a government contractor and whose notification has not been revoked by or on behalf of the Secretary of State.

[78] Subsections 59(2) and 60(1) of the EA 2002 stipulate the "Special public interest intervention notice (SPIN)" in special merger situations; the previous subsections 67(2)(3), 68(3) stipulated the "European intervention notice (EIN)" in European merger situations.

[79] Subsections 62 (2)(3), 65, 66, and the previous subsections 68(1)(4) of the EA 2002.

[80] The previous subsection 67 (1)(b) of the EA 2002. See Parker & Majumdar (2016), p. 184.

"legitimate interests" resulting from the merger situation concerned.[81] By contrast, in a relevant merger situation without an EU dimension (including the special merger situation), the Secretary of State may take such action where it has been decided to make an adverse public interest finding and has published his decision within the period so required.[82]

3.2.4 *Analysis of Cases with a Public Interest Intervention*

This section analyses the cases that took place before 31 December 2020 in the U.K. where the Secretary of State intervened based on the public interest considerations, particularly on the national security interest and the public interest considerations in the media merger areas.[83] The discussion focus is on how the Secretary of State and the CMA explained the relevant public interest considerations in individual cases.

3.2.4.1 Cases with a National Security Concern

As of 31 December 2020, the Secretary of State intervened in twelve cases in total under the national security interest[84]: (1) General Dynamics/Alvis ("EIN" issued by the Secretary of State in April 2004); (2) Finmeccanica/AgustaWestland ("EIN" issued by the Secretary of State in August 2004); (3) Finmeccanica/BAE ("EIN" issued by the Secretary of State in February 2005); (4) Lockheed Martin/Insys ("SIN" issued by the Secretary of State in August 2005); (5) General Electric/Smith ("EIN" issued by the Secretary of State in March 2007); (6) Atlas Elektronik UK/QinetiQ("SIN" issued by the Secretary of State in May 2009); (7) Hytera/Sepura ("PIIN" issued by the Secretary of State in April 2017)[85]; (8) Gardner Aerospace

[81] The previous subsection 68 (1) of the EA 2002.

[82] Subsections 55(1)(2), 66(5)(6) of the EA 2002.

[83] The Lloyds/HBOS merger (2008) is the only case reviewed under the public interest consideration of "stability of the U.K. financial market" to date. See the discussion on it in Sect. 3.2.1.1. As of 31 December 2020, there has not been any transaction reviewed by the Government on the newly added public interest consideration relating to the public health areas.

[84] The Intervention Notice given by the Secretary of State to the OFT and the Report given by the OFT to the Secretary of State concerning the national security concerns in mergers prior to June 2009 can be found on the archived website of the Department for Business Innovation & Skills (BIS), available at: https://webarchive.nationalarchives.gov.uk/20090609022327/http://www.berr.gov.uk/whatwedo/businesslaw/competition/mergers/public-interest/national-security/index.html (accessed 29 May 2022). Since April 2014, as the CMA took over the responsibilities from the OFT in this area, the Intervention Notice given by the Secretary of State to the CMA and the Report by the CMA to the Secretary of State in cases after 2014 can be found on the current website of the CMA, available at: https://www.gov.uk/cma-cases.

[85] See the "PIIN" issued by the Secretary of State in Hytera/Sepura available at: https://assets.publishing.service.gov.uk/government/uploads/system/uploads/attachment_data/file/607762/sepura-hytera-public-interest-intervention-notice.pdf (accessed 29 May 2022); see more introduction of

Holdings/Northern Aerospace ("PIIN" issued by the Secretary of State in June 2018)[86]; (9) Connect Bidco/Inmarsat plc ("PIIN" issued by the Secretary of State in July 2019)[87]; (10) Gardner Aerospace Holdings/Impcross Ltd ("PIIN" issued by the Secretary of State in December 2019)[88]; (11) Advent International/Cobham ("EIN" issued by the Secretary of State in September 2019)[89]; (12) Aerostar/Mettis Aerospace ("PIIN" issued by the Secretary of State in December 2019).[90] The above cases can be categorized into two groups: those taking place before 2018 and those after 2018 when the "relevant enterprise" provisions were added into the EA 2002 and the thresholds for the Secretary of State to intervene in these relevant enterprises were lowered. In these cases, the Secretary of State's concerns towards the national security issue include "the maintenance of strategic capabilities" and "the protection of classified information and technology".[91]

The seven mergers before 2018 were all closely related to the defence sector, and the target companies in these cases are active in the supply of products or services relating to the military interest or the fundamental infrastructure of the U.K.: (1) the Hytera/Sepura merger took place in the sector of communications devices, such as the radio devices used by emergency services and other agencies in the U.K.; (2) the General Dynamics/Alvis merger in the sector of armoured fighting vehicles and military land systems; (3) Finmeccanica/AgustaWestland in the sector of civil

---

this case available at https://www.gov.uk/government/consultations/proposed-acquisition-of-sepura-plc-by-hytera-communications-corporation-ltd-draft-undertakings (accessed 29 May 2022).

[86] See the "PIIN" issued by the Secretary of State in Gardner Aerospace Holdings/Northern Aerospace available at: https://assets.publishing.service.gov.uk/government/uploads/system/uploads/attachment_data/file/717303/Northern-Gardner_PII_Notice_-_17_June_2018_v1.pdf (accessed 29 May 2022); see more introduction of this case available at: https://www.gov.uk/cma-cases/gardner-aerospace-holdings-northern-aerospace-merger-inquiry (accessed 29 May 2022).

[87] See the "PIIN" issued by the Secretary of State in Connect Bidco/Inmarsat plc available at: https://assets.publishing.service.gov.uk/government/uploads/system/uploads/attachment_data/file/819668/Inmarsat-_Public_Interest_Intervention_Notice.pdf (accessed 29 May 2022); see more introduction of the case available at: https://www.gov.uk/government/publications/proposed-acquisition-of-inmarsat-plc-by-connect-bidco-ltd-public-interest-intervention (accessed 29 May 2022).

[88] See the "PIIN" from the Secretary of State in Gardner Aerospace Holdings/Impcross Ltd available at: https://www.gov.uk/government/publications/proposed-acquisition-of-impcross-limited-by-gardner-aerospace-holdings-limited (accessed 29 May 2022); see more introduction of the case available at: https://www.gov.uk/cma-cases/gardner-aerospace-holdings-limited-impcross-limited-merger-inquiry (accessed 29 May 2022).

[89] See the "EIN" from the Secretary of State in Advent International/Cobham available at: https://assets.publishing.service.gov.uk/government/uploads/system/uploads/attachment_data/file/832152/Cobham-Advent_European_Intervention_Notice__-_17th_September_2019__002_.pdf (accessed 29 May 2022); see more introduction of the case available at: https://www.gov.uk/cma-cases/advent-international-cobham-merger-inquiry (accessed 29 May 2022).

[90] See the "PIIN" from the Secretary of State in Aerostar/Mettis Aerospace available at: https://assets.publishing.service.gov.uk/government/uploads/system/uploads/attachment_data/file/854549/20191220_Mettis-Aerostar_PII_Notice.pdf (accessed 29 May 2022); see more introduction of the case available at: https://www.gov.uk/government/publications/proposed-acquisition-of-mettis-aerospace-by-aerostar (accessed 29 May 2022).

[91] Parker & Majumdar (2016), p. 152.

and military helicopters; (4) Finmeccanica/BAE in the sector of military avionics and communications business; (5) General Electric/Smith in the sector of aerospace systems and equipment; (6) Lockheed Martin/Insys in the sector of defence engineering and allied armed forces; and (7) Atlas Elektronik UK/QinetiQ in the sector of underwater systems. The OFT (in the Hytera/Sepura case, it was the CMA) in these cases prepared a report for the Secretary of State which contained the national security concerns as identified by the Ministry of Defence (the "MOD" hereinafter) (in the Hytera/Sepura case, it was the Home Office). The reports also set out undertakings in lieu of reference that were negotiated or suggested by the MOD (in the Hytera/Sepura case, the Home Office) to remedy or prevent any adverse public interest impact of the transaction concerned.[92] In the end, the Secretary of State accepted the undertakings made by the parties in the merger concerned, and none of these mergers was referred for a Phase II investigation.[93]

In 2018, along with the growing concerns about inward foreign investments in the infrastructure sectors of the U.K., the thresholds under the EA 2002 were lowered for the Secretary of State to review "a relevant enterprise" engaged in three specified areas; in 2020, the specified areas for "a relevant enterprise" were further enlarged.[94] In line with this change, the Secretary of State issued national security intervention notices more frequently between 2018 and December 2020. Most of the cases after 2018 were related to the aerospace sector, which is also closely linked to the defence interest.

In the Gardner Aerospace Holdings/Northern Aerospace merger (in the sector of supply of parts used in the manufacture of aircraft), the Secretary of State decided that there was no public interest consideration which he was able to consider as relevant to the merger and did not refer the case to a Phase II investigation.[95] In Connect Bidco/Inmarsat plc case (the target Inmarsat plc provides satellite communications services, including for military purposes and the acquirer involved a consortium of US and Canadian equity investors), the Secretary of State accepted the undertakings proposed by Connect Bidco and Inmarsat to ring-fence and limit access to sensitive information and secure ongoing supply.[96] In the takeover of Impcross Ltd (a U.K.

---

[92] See the "undertakings in lieu of reference" ("UIL") in Sects. 22, 33, 73(2) of the EA 2002. See also Parker & Majumdar (2016), pp. 711–715: "Following its Phase I investigation, if the CMA concludes that a relevant merger situation has resulted, or may be expected to result, in a substantial lessening of competition (SLC), the CMA is under a duty to refer the merger in question to Phase II; however, the CMA may, instead of making such a reference and for the purpose of remedying, mitigating or preventing the SLC concerned or any adverse effect that has or may have resulted from it (or may be expected to result from it), accept from the merging parties such UILs as it considers appropriate".

[93] Parker & Majumdar, 2016, p.152.

[94] See Sect. 3.2.1 "Background to the Public Interest Protection".

[95] See WWW.GOV.UK (20 July 2018). Gardner Aerospace Holdings/Northern Aerospace merger inquiry. Available at: https://www.gov.uk/cma-cases/gardner-aerospace-holdings-northern-aerospace-merger-inquiry (accessed 29 May 2022).

[96] See the Government's decision to accept the undertakings available at: https://assets.publishing.service.gov.uk/government/uploads/system/uploads/attachment_data/file/843009/Enterprise_Act_2002_Undertakings__1_.pdf (accessed 29 May 2022).

manufacturer of aerospace parts for the U.K. military) by Gardner (a Chinese owned aerospace company), the Secretary of State raised concerns about the protection of the U.K.'s aerospace capability and the safeguarding of sensitive information and skills in the aerospace area; although the acquirer Gardner abandoned the transaction later, the Secretary of State still required it to give undertakings that it would not acquire shares in Impcross for one year without written consent from the Secretary of State.[97] In Advent International/Cobham, the acquirer Advent is a US-based private equity investor and the target Cobham is a supplier in the defence and aerospace sector in the U.K. The Secretary of State in this case was mainly concerned about insufficient security controls after the takeover which might further result in unauthorized access to sensitive defence and security data held by Cobham.[98] In the end, the Secretary of State accepted the undertakings from the two companies, including for example, commitments to continue and strengthen the existing security arrangements after the takeover, notification to the MOD in the event of a material change to Cobham's ability to supply key services.[99] In the Aerostar/Mettis Aerospace case, the target Mettis is also a U.K. company in the aerospace area and the acquirer Aerostar is a Chinese company which abandoned the transaction following the Secretary of State's intervention.[100]

It could be concluded from the above cases that, before 31 December 2020, the major concerns with regard to "the strategic capabilities" were that, following the takeovers, the essential U.K. capabilities to develop, operate and maintain such military/defence-related product "could be either run down, sold off or transferred abroad", or "there would also be profound implications for U.K. security of supply, as well as the timely delivery of advice or systems".[101] The main concerns about "the classified sensitive information and technology" at that time lied in that, after the takeover by foreign companies, the sensitive information and technology in the specific fields would "be combined with foreign information and technology without U.K. knowledge or approval", or would "be subject to foreign countries' export control".[102]

---

[97] Ibid. See the undertakings made in this case available at: https://assets.publishing.service.gov.uk/government/uploads/system/uploads/attachment_data/file/915954/gardner-undertakings.pdf (accessed 29 May 2022).

[98] See Department for Business, Energy and Industrial Strategy. Anticipated Acquisition of Cobham plc by AI Convoy Bidco ltd: Notice of Proposed Undertakings Offered by the Parties. Available at: https://assets.publishing.service.gov.uk/government/uploads/system/uploads/attachment_data/file/847149/Tue_19112019_Cobham_Advent_consultation_notice_FINAL_FOR_GOV.UK.pdf (accessed 29 May 2022).

[99] Ibid.

[100] For more details of this case, see WWW.GOV.UK (26 February 2020). Proposed acquisition of Mettis Aerospace by Aerostar. Available at: https://www.gov.uk/government/publications/proposed-acquisition-of-mettis-aerospace-by-aerostar-decision-notice (accessed 29 May 2022).

[101] See conclusions of the concerns in Parker & Majumdar (2016), pp. 152–157. The concerns about "the strategic capabilities" and "the classified sensitive information and technology" can be easily detected from the presentations made by the Ministry of Defence in the OFT/CMA reports to the Secretary of State in the selected mergers.

[102] Ibid.

3.2.4.2 Cases with a Public Interest Concern in Newspaper and Media Mergers

The public interest considerations in the newspaper merger cases differ from these in the broadcasting and cross-media cases.

(1) Public Interest Considerations in a Newspaper Merger

The public interest considerations in a newspaper merger are set out as follows: (a) accurate presentation of news in newspapers; (b) free expression of opinion in newspapers; (c) a sufficient plurality of views in newspapers.[103] According to the Media Merger Guidance, the newspaper public interest considerations were derived from concerns that were identified in particular cases examined by the Competition Commission (the "CC" hereinafter) and the Monopolies and Mergers Commission (the "MMC" hereinafter) under the newspaper merger regime of the Fair Trading Act 1973.[104] After the new regime came into force, it was also expected that there would be considerable continuity between the analysis of cases under the Fair Trading Act 1973 and under the EA 2002.[105]

The representative newspaper mergers in recent years where the Secretary of State issued a PIIN on the grounds of public interest concerns include: (1)Trinity Mirror/ Northern & Shell Media Group (in May 2018)[106]; (2) Scalable/Independent Digital News and Media (IDNM) (in June 2019)[107]; (3) International Media Company (IMC)/Lebedev Holdings Limited (LHL) (in June 2019)[108]; (4) Daily Mail and

[103] Subsections 58 (2A)(2B) of the EA 2002.

[104] Parker & Majumdar (2016), p. 157. See para 5.3 of Media Merger Guidance. Prior to the EA 2002, the U.K. mergers were reviewed under the Fair Trading Act 1973, which set a broader public interest test. Under Sect. 84, the Competition Commission, and its predecessor, the Monopolies and Mergers Commission, were required to take into account "all matters which appear to them in the particular circumstances to be relevant".

[105] Para 5.3 of Media Merger Guidance.

[106] See the PIIN given by the Secretary of State in Trinity Mirror/Northern & Shell Media Group available at: https://www.gov.uk/government/publications/letter-from-dcms-to-trinity-mirror-plc-and-northern-shell-media-group-limited-1-may-2018 (accessed 29 May 2022). See more introduction to this case available at: https://www.gov.uk/cma-cases/trinity-mirror-northern-shell-media-group-merger-ingury (accessed 29 May 2022).

[107] See the PIIN by the Secretary of State in two cases: (i) Scalable/Independent Digital News and Media (IDNM), (ii) International Media Company (IMC)/Lebedev Holdings Limited (LHL), available at: https://assets.publishing.service.gov.uk/government/uploads/system/uploads/attachment_data/file/812972/REDACTED-20190627_-_PIIN_LHL_27_June_2018pdf__1__Redacted.pdf (accessed 29 May 2022).

[108] Ibid. See more introduction to this case available at: https://www.gov.uk/cma-cases/minority-acquisition-by-imc-of-lebedev-holdings-limited-and-scalable-lp-of-idmn-merger-inquiry. In the PIIN of this case, the Secretary of State required the CMA and the Ofcom to submit their reports by 23 August 2019. However, on 5 July 2019, IDNM and LHL made an application to the Competition Appeal (the "CAT") seeking annulment of the PIIN and the public interest intervention process as "the Secretary of State's PIIN is legally flawed since (i) it was issued after the statutory time-limit, and (2) it sets a time period for reports from the CMA and Ofcom which means that no reference under Phase 2 could be made because that would be past the statutory deadline for a reference".

General Trust (DMGT)/JPI MEDIA publications limited (in January 2020).[109] The Secretary of State in the end found relevant public interest considerations as established in none of these cases.

In Trinity Mirror/Northern & Shell Media Group, the Secretary of State intervened based on concerns about "free expression of opinion in newspapers" and "sufficient plurality of views in newspapers"; after receiving the investigation report from the Ofcom, it then decided not to refer the merger to a Phase II investigation on the grounds that no public interest consideration to which he was able to have regard was relevant to the merger. In the two mergers in 2019—Scalable/Independent Digital News and Media (IDNM) and International Media Company (IMC)/Lebedev Holdings Limited (LHL), the acquirers—Scalable and IMC are both Cayman Islands companies of which 50% of the shares are held by an investment fund, and the targets IDNM and IMC have significant footprints in the newspaper market of the U.K.[110] The Secretary of State issued a PIIN in the two mergers on the basis of "accurate presentation of news" and "free expression of opinion". In its report to the Secretary of State, the Ofcom concluded that it did not consider a reference was warranted on the grounds of "accurate presentation of news" or "free expression of opinion" in the two transactions.[111] It held that "it is not always necessarily contrary to the public interest for newspaper proprietors to take an interest in the content of their newspaper, or for newspapers to express strong or controversial views"; besides, the Ofcom considered it important "in the light of the challenging market context for newspapers in the U.K., that investment in the industry is generally encouraged, as this will help to sustain a plurality of news providers".[112] In Daily Mail and General Trust (DMGT)/JPI MEDIA publications limited, the Secretary of State also intervened on the grounds of "sufficient plurality of views" in newspapers, but finally

The CAT gave its judgment which did not quash the PIIN, but gave a declaration that "the time limit for the Secretary of State to make a reference, under Sect. 45 of the EA 2002, to the CMA expired on 1 July 2019". See OFCOM (21 August 2019). Public interest test on the completed acquisitions by International Media Company of shares in Lebedev Holdings Limited and by Scalable Inc of shares in Independent Digital News and Media Limited. Available at: https://assets.publishing.service.gov.uk/government/uploads/system/uploads/attachment_data/file/831826/Ofcom_report_to_DCMS_LHL_and_IDNM_-_21_August_2019_Redacted.pdf (accessed 29 May 2022), para 2.5; see the CAT's judgment in *Lebedev Holdings Limited and Another v Secretary of State for Digital, Culture, Media and Sport* [2019] CAT 21, available at: https://www.catribunal.org.uk/sites/default/files/2019-08/1328_Lebedev_Judgment_160819.pdf (accessed 29 May 2022).

[109] See the PIIN by the Secretary of State in Daily Mail and General Trust (DMGT)/JPI MEDIA available at: https://assets.publishing.service.gov.uk/government/uploads/system/uploads/attachment_data/file/859705/PIIN_DMGT_i_Redacted.pdf (accessed 29 May 2022). See more introduction to this case available at: https://www.gov.uk/cma-cases/dmg-media-limited-jpimedia-publications-limited-merger-inquiry (accessed 29 May 2022).

[110] See OFCOM (21 August 2019). Public interest test on the completed acquisitions by International Media Company of shares in Lebedev Holdings Limited and by Scalable Inc of shares in Independent Digital News and Media Limited.

[111] Ibid, see para 8.8.

[112] Ibid, see paras 8.5, 8.6.

accepted the Ofcom's conclusions that the merger did not reduce the plurality of views provided across newspaper groups in the U.K.[113]

To further understand the "accurate presentation of news", "free expression of opinion" and "sufficient plurality of views", in addition to the recent cases, the Media Merger Guidance can be relied on as it summarized the fifty newspaper cases that were referred to the CC between 1973 and 2004, and in ten of these cases adverse public interest findings were observed.[114] The following parts discuss the essentials of the relevant public interest considerations in the newspaper mergers as provided by the Media Merger Guidance.

(a) *Accurate Presentation of News*

The impact of a relevant merger situation on accurate presentation of the news is likely to be assessed by reference to evidence of the past behaviour of the enterprises in question, or by the persons with control of such enterprises, in relation to that or other enterprises, including but not limited to newspapers.[115] In the merger case of *David Sullivan/Bristol Evening Post* (1990), the MMC concluded that David Sullivan's connection with the Daily Star suggested that he would seek to influence editorial policy and the character and content of the newspapers in a manner which would harm both the accurate presentation of news and the free expression of opinion.[116]

(b) *Free Expression of Opinion*

In considering the impact of a newspaper merger on free expression of opinion, the CC (and before the CC, the MMC)'s focus is on the potential impact on editorial decision-making of the transfer of newspapers in question, that is the extent to which the transaction would affect the freedom of editors to operate without interference from the proprietor.[117] The MMC highlighted the case of *George Outram & Company Ltd/The Observer* (1981), where the concern was that the sale of The Observer to George Outram, whose parent company Lonrho had wide-ranging commercial interests would influence The Observer's editorial independence.[118]

(c) *Plurality of views*

The test of a sufficient plurality of views is intended to enable not only a sufficient number of views to be expressed and a variety of these views, but also a variety of outlets and publications in which they can be expressed.[119] When making such assessment, the size and nature of the relevant area, and the extent to which other newspapers in the same area contribute to the level of plurality of views are expected

---

[113] See the notice by the Secretary of State available at: https://assets.publishing.service.gov.uk/government/uploads/system/uploads/attachment_data/file/876110/Remittal_Notice_DMGT_purchase_of_JPIMedia.pdf (accessed 29 May 2022).

[114] Paras 5.3–5.15 of Media Merger Guidance.

[115] Para 5.5 of Media Merger Guidance.

[116] Para 5.6 of Media Merger Guidance.

[117] Para 5.7 of Media Merger Guidance.

[118] Para 5.9 of Media Merger Guidance. See also Parker & Majumdar (2016), pp. 159–160.

[119] Para 5.11 of Media Merger Guidance.

to be taken into account.[120] Besides, where the merger would result in the newspaper companies being owned by one entity, it is likely that the Secretary of State might raise the concerns about the plurality of views. For example, in the *Century Newspapers/TRN* case (1989), the then Secretary of State concluded that the merger could be expected to operate against the public interest as it would have resulted in the News Letter and the Belfast Telegraph being owned by the same entity and refused to consent this merger in the end.[121] The same concern also arose in the *Trinity plc/Mirror Group plc* and *Regional Independent Media Holdings Ltd/ Mirror Group plc* (1999).[122]

(2) Public Interest Considerations in Broadcasting and Cross-media Mergers

The public interest considerations in a broadcasting merger or cross-media merger include the following: (a) plurality of persons with control of media enterprises; (b) range of broadcasting; and (c) commitments to the broadcasting standards objectives.[123] The Media Merger Guidance, together with the relevant cases in which the Secretary of State intervened with concerns, sheds light on the meaning of these public interest considerations.

(a) *Plurality of Persons with Control of Media Enterprises*[124]

The Media Merger Guidance interpreted this public interest consideration as primarily concerned with ensuring that the control of media enterprises is not overly concentrated in the hands of a limited number of persons.[125] To assess the impact of a merger on this consideration, the Secretary of State may consider: (i) the number of persons controlling media enterprises serving the relevant audiences in any given area of the U.K.; and (ii) the combined audience shares of the media enterprises resulting from the transaction.[126]

The leading case pertinent to this consideration is the *Sky/ITV* merger in 2007. In this case, the Secretary of State issued a PIIN which specified that the "sufficient plurality of persons with control of the media enterprises" may be relevant to the assessment of the merger.[127] The Ofcom, in its report to the Secretary of State,

---

[120] Para 5.12 of Media Merger Guidance.

[121] Para 5.13 of Media Merger Guidance. See also Parker & Majumdar (2016), p. 161. News Letter is a Northern Irish newspaper with a largely rural readership expressing strong Unionist views; the Belfast Telegraph is a newspaper with a much larger readership focused on Greater Belfast offering both Protestant and Roman Catholic views.

[122] Para 5.14 of Media Merger Guidance. The then Secretary of State gave a consent to this merger with condition. See also Parker & Majumdar (2016), p. 161.

[123] Subsection 58(2C) of the EA 2002.

[124] An enterprise is a media enterprise if it "consists of or is involved in broadcasting". See subsection 58A (1) of the EA 2002.

[125] Para 7.7 of Media Merger Guidance.

[126] Paras 7.9, 7.10 of Media Merger Guidance. See also Parker & Majumdar, 2016, p. 165.

[127] See the PIIN given by the Secretary of State to the OFT and the report from the CC in this case available at: https://webarchive.nationalarchives.gov.uk/20090609022325/http://www.berr.gov.uk/whatwedo/businesslaw/competition/mergers/public-interest/broadcasting/index.html (accessed 30 May 2022).

concluded that as a result of the merger, there may not be a sufficient plurality of persons with control of the media enterprises serving the cross-media audience for national news and the TV audience for national news in the U.K.[128] The CC, on the contrary, found that this merger was unlikely to have an adverse effect on the plurality of news. In its report to the Secretary of State, the CC explained the "plurality of persons with control of media enterprises" in a way as referring both to the range of and the number of persons with control of media enterprises.[129] The CC thought it was important to draw two distinctions: "one is between the plurality of persons with control of media enterprises and the implications of that plurality for the range of information and views made available to audiences; the other is between the range of information and views that are provided across separate independent media groups (external plurality) and the range that are provided within individual media groups (internal plurality)".[130] To assess the sufficiency of the plurality, the CC looked qualitatively at sufficiency, as well as the change in plurality that arose as a result of the acquisition, in relation to both internal and external plurality.[131] Regarding the external plurality aspect, the CC held that both ITV and Sky were significant news providers, and their links to related companies (ITN and News International) increased the potential significance of their contribution to the plurality of news;[132] as to the internal plurality aspect, media owners had limited ability to influence the news content, and it was the editorial staff that determined the day-to-day content of their programming.[133] Considering the extent of the influence conferred on BSkyB by its acquisition of a 17.9% shareholding in ITV, the regulatory mechanisms, combined with the strong culture of editorial independence within television news production, the CC did not expect that BSkyB's ability would materially influence ITV and create an adverse effect on the plurality of news.[134] Therefore, the CC concluded that the acquisition would not materially affect the sufficiency of plurality of persons with control of media enterprises serving audiences for news.[135]

[128] Ibid. See also Parker & Majumdar (2016), p. 166.

[129] Ibid. See para 30 of the CC's report.

[130] Ibid.

[131] Ibid, see para 32.

[132] Ibid, see para 5.52. See also Parker & Majumdar (2016), p. 167.

[133] Ibid, see paras 5.52–5.57. See also Parker & Majumdar (2016), p. 167.

[134] Ibid, see para 5.75.

[135] Ibid. In a more recent case Global Radio Holdings/GMG Radio Holdings Limited in 2012, the Secretary of State, in its PIIN intervention was also concerned about the media plurality arising from the merger. In the end it accepted the Ofcom's recommendation that the merger should not be referred to the Competition Commission on media plurality grounds. See the PIIN in Global Radio Holdings/GMG Radio Holdings Limited available at: https://webarchive.nationalarchives.gov.uk/20121204123324/http://www.culture.gov.uk/images/publications/media_merger_Intervention_Notice.pdf (accessed 30 May 2022); see more introduction to Global Radio Holdings/GMG Radio Holdings Limited available at: https://www.gov.uk/government/news/global-radio-and-guardian-media-group-radio-merger-not-to-be-considered-on-media-plurality-grounds--2 (accessed 30 May 2022).

Another case in this field is the acquisition by News Corporation of British Sky Broadcasting plc in 2010. In this case, News Corporation owned 39.14% of Sky and intended to acquire all the remaining shares in Sky. The European Commission concluded that "the transaction constitutes a concentration with a Community dimension, but that it would not significantly impede effective competition in the European Economic Area (EEA) or any substantial part of it."[136] The Secretary of State issued an EIN on the grounds of media plurality in this case.[137] In its report to the Secretary of State, the Ofcom first analysed the "static" effects of this transaction: the effects of the proposed acquisition on plurality immediately after the transaction in terms of range and number of persons controlling media enterprises including their ability to influence opinions.[138] To assess the "static" effects, the Ofcom had regard to the "external plurality", "internal plurality" and the multi-sourcing and online news provision.[139] Then it analysed the "dynamic effects" of this transaction: how the proposed acquisition could result in changes to the level of media plurality over a long period of time.[140] Based on these analyses, the Ofcom advised that this proposed acquisition "may be expected to operate against the public interest since there may not be a sufficient plurality of persons with control of media enterprises providing news and current affairs to U.K.-wide cross-media audiences".[141] In the end, the Secretary of State accepted undertakings from News Corporation in lieu of reference.[142]

---

136 Office of Fair Trading (30 December 2010). A Report to the Secretary of State for Culture, Olympics, Media and Sport in response to the European intervention notice issued on 4 November 2010 in relation to the anticipated acquisition by News Corporation of British Sky Broadcasting Group plc. Available at: https://assets.publishing.service.gov.uk/media/555de323ed915d7ae2000067/report-newscorp-30dec10.pdf (accessed 30 May 2021), see para 20. See European Commission (21 December 2010). Case No COMP/M.5932–News Corp/BskyB: Notification of 3 November 2010 pursuant to Article 4 of Council Regulation No 139/2004. Available at: https://ec.europa.eu/competition/mergers/cases/decisions/m5932_20101221_20310_1600159_EN.pdf (accessed 30 May 2022), see para 310: In the end, the European Commission decided not to oppose the transaction and to declare it compatible with the internal market and with the EEA Agreement.

137 Parker & Majumdar (2016), p. 168. See Office of Fair Trading (30 December 2010). A Report to the Secretary of State for Culture, Olympics, Media and Sport in response to the European intervention notice issued on 4 November 2010 in relation to the anticipated acquisition by News Corporation of British Sky Broadcasting Group plc.

138 See OFCOM (31 December 2010). Report on public interest test on the proposed acquisition of British Sky Broadcasting Group plc by News Corporation. Available at: https://webarchive.nationalarchives.gov.uk/20121204120049/http://www.culture.gov.uk/publications/7737.aspx (accessed 30 May 2022), see para 5.1.

139 Ibid, see para 5.2.

140 Ibid, see para 6.1.

141 Ibid, see para 7.1.

142 WWW.GOV.UK. (30 June 2011). News Story: News Corporation/BskyB merger. Available at: https://www.gov.uk/government/news/news-corporation-bskyb-merger (accessed 30 May 2022).

In a more recent case of the acquisition by 21st Century Fox of Sky (2016–2018),[143] the CMA took the Ofcom's definition of plurality as the starting point for its assessment and explained this consideration from two aspects: (i) ensuring that there is a diversity in the viewpoints that are available and consumed, across and within media enterprises; and (ii) preventing any one media owner, or voice, having too much influence over public opinion and the political agenda.[144] The CMA found in this case that the Murdoch family, through the MFT (Murdoch Family Trust), would be able to exercise a significantly increased level of control over Sky and Sky News as a result of the transaction, which would enable the MFT to exercise materially greater influence over public opinion and the political agenda through Sky and Sky News.[145] It then concluded that the Transaction may be expected to result in an insufficient plurality of persons with control of media enterprises serving audiences in the U.K.[146]

(b) *Range of Broadcasting*

According to the Media Merger Guidance, this consideration relates to the impact of a merger on broadcasting content in the U.K. and refers to the need for the availability, throughout the U.K., of a wide range of television and radio services which (taken as a whole) are both of high quality and calculated to appeal to a variety of tastes and interests.[147] The primary focus of this consideration is on the assessment of the future plans of the acquirer; the proposals for program organization, program content, genre or style of programming, as well as the overall innovation and ambition of the media owner's plans might all be considered as relevant.[148] Moreover, the media owner's past compliance with requirements on his other broadcasting enterprises to deliver a sufficient range and/or quality of broadcasting services in the U.K. would also be taken into account.[149]

(c) *Commitments to the Broadcasting Standards Objectives*

In the Secretary of State's view, the intention behind this consideration is to assess whether persons controlling or carrying on media enterprises post-merger are likely

---

[143] See more introduction to this case available at: https://www.gov.uk/government/collections/proposed-merger-between-twenty-first-century-fox-inc-and-sky-plc (accessed 30 May 2022).

[144] See Competition and Markets Authority (CMA) (1 May 2018). A report on the anticipated acquisition by 21st Century Fox, Inc of Sky Plc. Available at: https://assets.publishing.service.gov.uk/government/uploads/system/uploads/attachment_data/file/713920/CMAFoxSky_report_nonconfidential.pdf (accessed 30 May 2022), see para 23.

[145] Ibid, see para 11.142.

[146] Ibid, see para 12.22. In the end, on 5 June 2018, the Secretary of State accepted the CMA's recommendation that the anticipated acquisition was not in the public interest due to media plurality concerns and accepted the CMA's recommendation that the most effective and proportionate remedy is for Sky News to be divested to a suitable third party. See WWW.GOV.UK (5 June 2018). 21st Century Fox/Sky merger inquiry. Available at: https://www.gov.uk/cma-cases/twenty-first-century-fox-sky-merger-european-intervention-notice (accessed 30 May 2022).

[147] Ibid, see para 7.17.

[148] Ibid, see para 7.19.

[149] Ibid, see para 7.20.

to comply with the spirit as well as the letter of the broadcasting standards set down in the Communications Act 2003.[150] In assessing the effect of a merger on a person's commitment to these standards, the Secretary of State may take into account, among other considerations, the following factors: (i) the likelihood that there will be a genuine commitment to broadcasting standards by the person who will control the media enterprise; (ii) a past compliance of any other broadcasting enterprises controlled by the proposed purchaser with the broadcasting standards (based on a qualitative assessment rather than focusing on the number of infringements, and taking into account the due impartiality and accuracy of news offered); (iii) the compliance of any broadcasting media enterprises controlled by the purchaser with broadcasting standards in other geographic regions or jurisdictions; (iv) the record of the compliance of any non-broadcasting media enterprises owned by the purchaser with standards applicable to those media enterprises.[151]

In the 21st Century Fox/Sky case, the CMA also relied on the above factors to review the transaction on the grounds of "a genuine commitment to broadcasting standards". The CMA first looked into the "genuine commitment to the attainment of the broadcasting standards objectives". It considered the extent to which the media enterprises controlled by the MFT, the one that would control these enterprises following the transaction, demonstrated such a genuine commitment.[152] Then it assessed the records of both Sky and Fox's approach to the broadcasting standards in the U.K. (e.g., their compliance arrangements, and compliance records),[153] their approach to the broadcasting standards outside the U.K.,[154] a wider regulatory compliance and corporate governance of the two, which may indicate if the two media enterprises' policies, systems and procedures are nominal or ineffective in terms of supporting and promoting a culture of compliance with regulatory standards.[155] Taking all these aspects into account, the CMA concluded that Fox, Sky, and the MFT had a genuine commitment to the attainment of the broadcasting standards objectives.[156]

In addition to the above detailed considerations in assessing a newspaper merger or a media merger, the Media Merger Guidance also points out that the plurality concerns

---

[150] Ibid, see para 7.22. These standards objectives relate to, for example, "the protection of minors; the prohibition of material likely to encourage crime or disorder; the due impartiality and accuracy of television and radio news services, and impartiality requirements more generally; the exercise of responsibility with respect to the content of religious programs; the protection of the public from offensive and harmful material; the exclusion of prohibited political advertising; the prevention of misleading, harmful or offensive advertising and unsuitable sponsorship; the fulfilment of the international obligations of the United Kingdom in respect of broadcast advertising; the prevention of undue discrimination between advertisers; and the prohibition of broadcasts of subliminal material". See Sect. 319(2) of Communications Act 2003.

[151] Ibid, see para 7.24. See also the conclusion in Parker & Majumdar (2016), pp. 170–171.

[152] See Competition and Markets Authority (1 May 2018). A report on the anticipated acquisition by 21st Century Fox, Inc of Sky Plc, para 13.30.

[153] Ibid, see Sect. 14.

[154] Ibid, see Sect. 15.

[155] Ibid, see Sect. 16.

[156] Ibid, see para 17.1.

in a newspaper merger, broadcasting and cross-media merger "may be more likely to arise in relation to mergers between existing newspaper proprietors".[157] However, when assessing such mergers, the public interest test and the test on the competition concerns must be applied separately, the latter of which should be conducted by the competition authorities where appropriate. The aspects of the substantial lessening of competition test will not be replicated or imported in the public interest test.[158]

3.2.5 Intermediate Conclusion

The analysis in this section illustrates that in the competition law regime, the EA 2002 protects both the competition interest and other public interest considerations. The CMA, in its control of a takeover or merger, is required only to consider the competition effect of the transaction; meanwhile, the Secretary of State has the power to intervene if (s)he believes that one or many of the public interest considerations listed under the EA 2002 may be relevant to the takeover or merger concerned. Before the coming into force of the U.K. Security Act 2021, the non-competition public interest considerations that were recognized by the EA 2002 included: (i) the national security interest; (ii) the stability of the financial market of the U.K.; (iii) public interest considerations in media mergers (such as free expression of views, media plurality, and retaining the standards objectives of different media, etc.); and (iv) the capability of the U.K. to combat and mitigate public health emergencies. The national security interest was replaced by virtue of the U.K. Security Act 2021, which establishes a separate national security review regime in takeovers and mergers operated by the Investment Security Unit.

In the public interest intervention process, the CMA provides the Secretary of State with a report and its opinions on the public interest concerns in the takeover or merger; the relevant government department or public body may also provide advice to the CMA and the Secretary of State in a takeover or merger in specific industries and areas. In the end, the Secretary of State independently decides that: (i) no public interest consideration is relevant in the takeover or merger; (ii) the public interest benefits of the takeover or merger outweigh its potential harms and the transaction can be approved (such as in the Lloyds/HBOS merger); or (iii) there are adverse public interest findings in the takeover or merger which prohibit it or clear it by accepting the remedies from the parties concerned.

The previous cases show that the national security interest and the media-related public interest considerations are the most common grounds that have led to a public interest intervention in the U.K. The reforms to the EA 2002 that took place between 2018 and 2020 lowered the thresholds for the CMA to review a takeover or merger and strengthened the power of the Secretary of State to protect the "strategic capabilities" and "classified sensitive information and technology" of the U.K., which are

[157] Para 5.15 of Media Merger Guidance.

[158] Ibid, see paras 5.15, 7.3.

often closely linked to the national security interest. The newly added public interest consideration in healthcare-related areas has further enlarged the Secretary of State's intervention power in the post-pandemic period. Under the new regime of the U.K. Security Act 2021, the Government's intervention power in takeovers and mergers with national security concerns is further enhanced as there is no longer minimum turnover or share of supply threshold for the Secretary of State to intervene. The new national security review regime will be discussed together with other FDI screening regulation of the U.K. in Sect. 3.3.

3.3 Regulations in the FDI Screening Regime

Another eye-catching change after 2020 in the regulatory framework of takeovers in the U.K. is in its FDI screening regime. As discussed in Sect. 3.2, the U.K. Security Act 2021, which was first introduced by the U.K. Government in Bill form (the U.K. Security Bill 2020) in November 2020 and finally came into force as Act of Parliament in January 2022, provides a major overhaul of the FDI screening regime of the U.K. and largely expands the U.K. Government's power to scrutinize and intervene in foreign takeovers to protect national security in the post-pandemic world.[159]

3.3.1 The FDI Screening Regime Before 2020

Traditionally, the U.K. has held a welcoming stance towards foreign investments and has recognized the benefits for the economy and citizens brought by its openness.[160] Based on this stance, prior to 2017, the U.K. did not have in place separate regulations for reviewing inward foreign investments on the grounds of protecting societal interests, particularly the national security interest. The public interest considerations stipulated in the EA 2002 applied irrespective of the nationality of investors,[161]

[159] As mentioned earlier in this chapter, the U.K. Security Act 2021 applies to investors from any country. The author puts the detailed discussion about the application of this Act under this section as the U.K., through this Act, established a standalone FDI screening regime which contrasts sharply with the previous regime.

[160] For example, the Government in 2018 recognized that "the FDI into the U.K. leads to tangible and considerable benefits: almost 76,000 new jobs were created by inward investment projects in 2017/18; and foreign direct investment can boost domestic labour productivity through bringing new technology, skills, and managerial best-practice to the U.K." See Department for Business, Energy and Industrial Strategy (July 2018). National Security and Investment—A consultation on proposed legislative reforms (The 2018 White Paper). Available at: https://assets.publishing.service.gov.uk/government/uploads/system/uploads/attachment_data/file/728310/20180723_-_National_security_and_investment_-_final_version_for_printing__1_.pdf (accessed 29 May 2022).

[161] Competition Policy International (CPI) (December 2017). Merger Control and the Public Interest: European Spotlight on Foreign Direct Investment and National Security. There are broad powers within the Industry Act 1975 entitling the Government to intervene in the event of a transfer of

and ad hoc investment review was led by the responsible government ministry for the sector in question.[162] Against this background, between 2007–2017, on average, the U.K. was one of the world's top FDI destinations, ranking third among the G20 nations for flows of inward FDI.[163]

Meanwhile, the increasing national security risks arising from foreign hostile takeovers of U.K. companies have also gradually attracted the U.K. Government's attention. In 2017, the U.K. Government published a Green Paper (the "2017 Green Paper" hereinafter) highlighting the Government's limited power in reviewing FDI in an increasingly complex and interconnected international landscape.[164] In 2018, it published a White Paper (the "2018 White Paper" hereinafter) setting out the Government's proposed reforms (both for short-term and longer-term), and seeking views from businesses, investors and other groups about how to implement these reforms in the most suitable way.[165] In the proposed reforms in this period, the U.K. Government committed to implementing a transparent, proportionate and wholly national-security focused regime.[166] The new regime would only target the economy areas which present heightened risks to national security and restrict any potential impact on FDI into the U.K.

The 2017 Green Paper sought the public's views on three potential options for reforms to address the challenges on national security: (i) to expand the Government's call-in power under the EA 2002 to allow it to scrutinize a broader range of transactions for national security concerns; (ii) to introduce a mandatory notification regime for foreign investment in key parts of the U.K. economy; and (iii) a combination of both of the above.[167] Having considered the consultation responses and undertaken further analysis, the Government decided to pursue an expanded call-in power with a voluntary notification regime instead of a mandatory notification regime.[168] The expanded call-in power of the Government at that time was achieved by lowering the

---

control of manufacturing firms to foreign owners "*where that change of control would be contrary to the interests of the United Kingdom*", but until 2017 these powers have never been used and remained untested.

[162] For example, the Department for Business, Energy and Industrial Strategy has the responsibility for reviewing investments in the energy sector; and the Department for International Trade prepares market information for a variety of industries.

[163] UNCTAD.ORG (June 6 2018). World Investment Report 2018. Available at: https://unctad.org/system/files/official-document/wir2018_en.pdf (accessed 30 May 2022). As of 2017, the U.K. had the third highest inward FDI stock ($1.6 trillion), only behind the United States ($7.8 trillion) and China ($3.5 trillion).

[164] Department for Business, Energy and Industrial Strategy (October 2017). National Security and Infrastructure Investment Review—The Government's review of the national security implications of foreign ownership or control (The 2017 Green Paper). Available at: https://assets.publishing.service.gov.uk/government/uploads/system/uploads/attachment_data/file/652505/2017_10_16_NSII_Green_Paper_final.pdf (accessed 29 May 2022).

[165] Department for Business, Energy and Industrial Strategy (July 2018). National Security and Investment—A consultation on proposed legislative reforms (The 2018 White Paper).

[166] Ibid.

[167] Para 2.04 of the 2018 White Paper.

[168] Paras 2.14–2.16 of the 2018 White Paper.

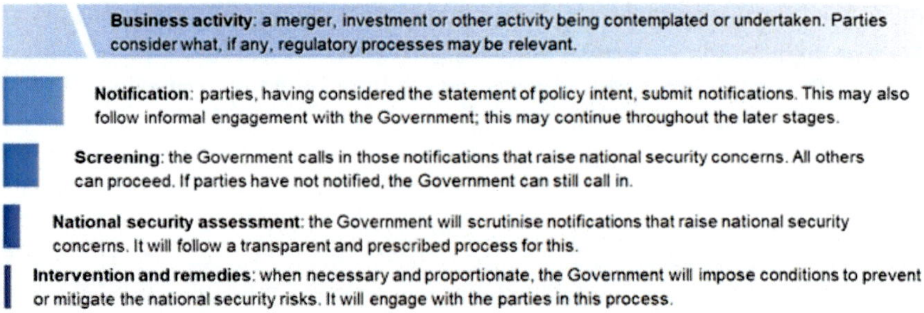

Fig. 3.2 The proposed voluntary notification regime by the 2018 white paper[171]

thresholds for a relevant merger situation concerning a "relevant enterprise", which has been discussed under the EA 2002 in Sect. 3.2. With regard to the voluntary notification, the Government encouraged the parties to make notifications voluntarily when they consider that their transaction may raise national security concerns; in the event where the parties choose not to notify the Government, the Government still reserved the right to intervene to protect national security.[169] The 2018 White Paper also explained the trigger events that may give rise to national security risks and permit Government intervention and stressed that the Government may only act when necessary and proportionate.[170] The FDI screening regime as proposed under the 2018 White Paper is summarized in Fig. 3.2.

3.3.2 The New FDI Screening Regime Introduced by the U.K. Security Act 2021

Even after the revisions to the thresholds for a "relevant enterprise" in the EA 2002 in 2018 and 2020, the U.K. Government still regarded that the sectors that allow for the Secretary of State's national security interventin were largely limited; and as of the publication of the U.K. Security Bill 2020, there only have been twelve public interventions on national security grounds since 2002.[172] The provisions in the final form of the U.K. Security Bill 2020—the U.K. Security Act 2021, respond to the proposed reforms in the 2018 White Paper and set out a new FDI screening regime in the U.K. which significantly expands the Government's existing powers to review and intervene in potentially hostile FDI for the national security purpose. Compared

---

[169] Para10 of the 2018 White Paper.

[170] Chapters 3, 6 of the 2018 White Paper.

[171] Figure 3.2 originates from Fig. 3.1 in the 2018 White Paper.

[172] WWW.GOV.UK (11 November 2020). New powers to protect U.K. from malicious investment and strengthen economic resilience. Available at: https://www.gov.uk/government/news/new-powers-to-protect-uk-from-malicious-investment-and-strengthen-economic-resilience (accessed 30 May 2022).

with the FDI screening regime under the EA 2002, the new landscape under the U.K. Security Act 2021 presents major changes in several aspects.

3.3.2.1 A Standalone FDI Screening Regime in the U.K.

The U.K. Security Act 2021 introduces a standalone FDI screening in the U.K. for the first time. The Secretary of State's power to intervene in takeovers and mergers with national security concerns was largely restricted by the thresholds for a relevant merger under the EA 2002. The new regime under the U.K. Security Act 2021 does not include a minimum turnover value or share of supply threshold; instead, the Secretary of State may "call-in" any transaction if (s)he reasonably suspects that the transaction constitutes a "trigger event" and may conduct an in-depth national security assessment.[173]

Until the coming into force of the U.K. Security Act 2021, the Government's intervention power based on the national security interest in the EA 2002 continued, and where the foreign takeovers do not meet the thresholds in the EA 2002, the Government could intervene based on the powers conferred by the U.K. Security Act 2021.[174] Under the new regime, as has been discussed in Sect. 3.2, the national security review is separate from the merger control review under the EA 2002 and the CMA will no longer be involved in the national security assessment. The Secretary of State for Business, Energy and Industrial Strategy, along with the Investment Security Unit, undertakes the national security assessment and decides on the outcome of the

[173] Section 1 of the U.K. Security Act 2021. For the definition of "trigger event", see Sects. 5, 7, 8, 9 of the U.K. Security Act 2021: A "trigger event" is a acquisition that was not completed before 12 November 2020 and that falls within scope of the following prescribed categories: (a) Acquisitions of shares/voting rights, including: (i) an acquisition of control which results in a holding of more than 25%, 50% or 75% retrospectively of the votes of shares in a qualifying entity (representing three different threshold categories of control), (ii) an acquisition of voting rights that enable or prevent the passage of any class of resolution governing the affairs of the qualifying entity; (b) Acquisitions of material influence over a qualifying entity's policy; (c) Asset acquisition: an acquisition of a right or interest in, or in relation to, a qualifying asset, providing the ability to use the asset, or use it to a greater extent than prior to the acquisition; or to direct or control how the asset is used, or direct or control how the asset is used to a greater extent than prior to the acquisition. The assets in scope of the U.K. Security Act 2021 are land, tangible moveable property, and idea, information, or technique with industrial, commercial or other economic value. See conclusion of a "trigger event" in ROPESGRAY.COM (1 December 2020). The National Security and Investment Bill. Available at: https://www.ropesgray.com/en/newsroom/alerts/2020/12/The-National-Security-and-Investment-Bill (accessed 30 May 2022).

[174] WWW.GOV.UK (11 November 2020). New powers to protect U.K. from malicious investment and strengthen economic resilience.

review,[175] whose role thereby has a "quasi-judicial" feature, meaning that (s)he will act independently and is not subject to any improper influence.[176]

3.3.2.2 The Mandatory Notification and Voluntary Notification Requirements in Foreign Takeovers

The U.K. Security Act 2021 intentionally does not give an explicit definition of "national security" or set out the circumstances in which national security is, or may be, considered at risk.[177] In contrast with the voluntary notification design proposed by the 2018 White Paper, the U.K. Security Act 2021 introduces a mandatory notification requirement for seventeen areas of the economy which are more likely to give rise to risks to national security. Investors and businesses for transactions involving these areas must submit a formal notification to the Investment Security Unit, providing as much relevant information as possible for clearance of the acquisition.[178] The transaction will not be permitted to complete until clearance is given by the Secretary of State; where the transaction that is subject to mandatory notification completes prior to obtaining clearance, it will be void.[179] The seventeen areas of the economy include: (a) advanced materials, (b) advanced robotics, (c) artificial intelligence, (d) civil nuclear, (e) communications, (f) computing hardware, (g) critical suppliers to Government, (h) cryptographic authentication, (i) data infrastructure, (j) defence, (k) energy, (l) military and dual use, (m) quantum technologies, (n) satellite and space technologies, (o) suppliers to the emergency services, (p) synthetic biology, and (q) transport.[180]

---

175 The Investment Security Unit sits within the Department for Business, Energy and Industrial Strategy and notifies the government about transactions; it will also coordinate cross-government activity to identify, assess and respond to national security risks arising through market activity. See WWW.GOV.UK (11 November 2020). New powers to protect U.K. from malicious investment and strengthen economic resilience.

176 Department for Business, Energy and Industrial Strategy (24 July 2018). Consultation outcome – National Security and Investment: Proposed Legislative Reforms. Available at: https://www.gov.uk/government/consultations/national-security-and-investment-proposed-reforms (accessed 30 May 2022).

177 Department for Business, Energy and Industrial Strategy (2 November 2021). National Security and Investment Act 2021: Statement for the purposes of Sect. 3. Available at: https://www.gov.uk/government/publications/national-security-and-investment-statement-about-exercise-of-the-call-in-power/national-security-and-investment-act-2021-statement-for-the-purposes-of-section-3 (accessed 30 May 2022).

178 Section 14(1) of the U.K. Security Act 2021. See also Department for Business, Energy and Industrial Strategy (3 March 2021). The National Security and Investment (NSI) Regime: process for businesses factsheet. Available at: https://www.gov.uk/government/publications/national-security-and-investment-bill-2020-factsheets/the-national-security-and-investment-nsi-regime-process-for-businesses-factsheet (accessed 30 May 2022).

179 Section 13(1) of the U.K. Security Act 2021.

180 Department for Business, Energy and Industrial Strategy (2 November 2021). National Security and Investment Act 2021: Statement for the purposes of Sect. 3. For a detailed description of target entities and activities with regard to these seventeen areas, see The National Security and Investment

The government may amend the scope of transactions subject to a mandatory notification.[181] In fact, in the process of introducing the U.K. Security Bill 2020, the Government once launched an eight-week consultation which closed in January 2021 to work out the final parts of the economy sectors that would be finalized to be subject to the mandatory notification.[182] The concerns and suggestions shared by businesses and investors during the consultation suggested that many of the proposed sector definitions at that time were still very broad in scope and needed to be further specified.[183] The Government, in its response to this consultation, significantly narrowed the definitions of the acquisitions within the seventeen sectors to ensure that the new FDI screening regime is targeted and proportionate.[184] For example, in adjusting the definition, the Government changed one of the proposed sectors—"engineering biology" to "synthetic biology" to narrow down the scope of entities subject to the mandatory notification.[185] This effort reflects the U.K. Government's longstanding policy to be open to foreign investment and to ensure that national security powers are sufficiently flexible to protect the nation.[186] In accordance with this policy, the mandatory notification requirement under the U.K. Security Act 2021 is backed up by a voluntary notification option for other sectors in the economy and the "call-in" power of the Secretary of State.

The voluntary notification regime runs in parallel to the mandatory notification regime. Investors and businesses for transactions that do not involve the specified seventeen sectors are encouraged to also submit a notification if the transaction constitutes "trigger events" and could raise national security risks. The Secretary of State may "call in" a takeover for assessment if (s)he reasonably suspects that it meets the criteria to be a trigger event (a "qualifying acquisition") and that it has already

Act 2021 (Notifiable Acquisition) (Specification of Qualifying Entities) Regulations 2021 available at: https://www.legislation.gov.uk/ukdsi/2021/9780348226935.

181 Section 6(5) of the U.K. Security Act 2021.

182 Department for Business, Energy and Industrial Strategy (November 2020). National Security and Investment: Sectors in Scope of the Mandatory Regime (Consultation on secondary legislation to define the sectors subject to mandatory notification in the National Security and Investment Bill 2020). Available at: https://assets.publishing.service.gov.uk/government/uploads/system/uploads/attachment_data/file/935774/nsi-consultation.pdf (accessed 30 May 2022).

183 In March 2021, the U.K. Government published a document which provided an overview of the response to the consultation on the sectors in scope of the mandatory notification under the U.K. Security Bill 2020. See Department for Business, Energy and Industrial Strategy (March 2021). National Security and Investment: Sectors in Scope of the Mandatory Regime (Government Response to the consultation on mandatory notification in the specific sectors under the National Security and Investment Bill). Available at: https://assets.publishing.service.gov.uk/government/uploads/system/uploads/attachment_data/file/965784/nsi-scope-of-mandatory-regime-gov-response.pdf (accessed 30 May 2022).

184 Ibid, see para 27.

185 Ibid, see para 28.

186 Department for Business, Energy and Industrial Strategy (2 November 2021). National Security and Investment Act 2021: Statement for the purposes of Sect. 3.

given rise to, or may give rise to, a risk to national security.[187] The Secretary of State will assess each qualifying acquisition on a case-by-case basis, taking account of all the relevant considerations, inter alia of three risk factors—target risk, acquirer risk, and the control risk.[188] The Secretary of State can call in a review within six months from "becoming aware" of the trigger event, subject to an overall period of five years beginning with the day on which the trigger event took place.[189] Nevertheless, where the non-notified transaction falls within a mandatory notification requirement, the "five-year" deadline does not apply.[190] This retrospective "call-in" power, together with the relevant civil and criminal sanctions for the non-notified transactions that have been completed without a clearance from the Secretary of State will push investors to be cautious when making notification decisions.[191]

The new regime also sets out the timeline for the national security assessment of a takeover. After the Secretary of State receives a mandatory or voluntary notice, (s)he must first decide whether to reject or accept it.[192] Where the Secretary of State accepts the notification notice, (s)he will then decide on whether to further give a "call-in" notice in relation to the transaction or notify the relevant person that no further action will be taken within a review period of 30 working days.[193] On the day the Secretary of State gives a "call-in" notice to the acquirer, the "assessment period" begins, which requires the Secretary of State to complete its initial screening of the national security risks of the transaction within 30 working days (with the possibility

[187] Section 1 of the U.K. Security Act 2021. See the scope of a "qualifying acquisition" at Department for Business, Energy and Industrial Strategy (14 April 2022). Guidance: Check if you need to tell the government about an acquisition that could harm the UK's national security.

[188] See Department for Business, Energy and Industrial Strategy (2 November 2021). National Security and Investment Act 2021: Statement for the purposes of Sect. 3. The "target risk" concerns whether the target of the qualifying acquisition (the entity or asset being acquired) is being used or could be used in a way that raises a risk to national security; the "acquirer risk" concerns whether the acquirer has characteristics that suggest there is or may be a risk to national security from the acquirer having control of the target; the "control risk" concerns the amount of control that has been, or will be, acquired through the qualifying acquisition, and a higher level of control may increase the level of national security risk.

[189] Section 2 (2) of the U.K. Security Act 2021.

[190] Sections 2 (3), 13 (1). Moreover, the five-year retrospective call-in power will not apply to transactions which took place prior to the introduction of the U.K. Security Bill 2020 to Parliament. See WWW.GOV.UK (11 November 2020). New powers to protect U.K. from malicious investment and strengthen economic resilience.

[191] Sections 39, 40 of the U.K. Security Act 2021.

[192] Sections 14 (5), 18 (5) of the U.K. Security Act 2021.

[193] Sections 14 (8)(9), 18 (8)(9) of the U.K. Security Act 2021. Besides, the review period for the Secretary of State to decide on whether to give a call-in notice or to give a validation notice to the acquisition subject to mandatory notification but has been completed without approval of the Secretary of State is also 30 working days. See Sects. 15, 16 of the U.K. Security Act 2021.

of an extension for an additional 45 working days).[194] The Secretary of State needs to decide within this time whether to approve the transaction, to approve it subject to conditions or to prohibit the transaction. During the assessment period, the Secretary of State may make interim orders to prevent or reverse pre-emptive action or mitigate its effects.[195] Before the end of the assessment period, the Secretary of State must make a final order or give a final notification.[196] Under the U.K. Security Act 2021, the parties to the transaction will have the right to appeal to the courts for certain decisions of the Secretary of State.[197]

3.3.3 Intermediate Conclusion

Compared with the FDI screening regime under the EA 2002, the U.K., after the publication of the U.K. Security Act 2021, for the first time has a standalone FDI screening regime, which largely expands the Government's powers of screening inward foreign takeovers.[198] Under the new regime, takeovers taking place in seventeen areas of economy are considered as most likely to give rise to national security risks and are therefore subject to the mandatory notification requirement. For takeovers in other sectors, a voluntary notification option runs in parallel with the mandatory notification which also gives the Government a "call-in" power to proactively intervene. The seventeen areas subject to the mandatory notification give an overview of the broad scope of the sectors and activities that may be intervened by the Government on the national security basis. Meanwhile, the U.K. Government emphasizes that it will remain firmly open to investment and will not use the call-in power to interfere arbitrarily with investment.[199] Instead, the U.K., through the introduction of the new national security regime, aims to take a targeted, proportionate approach to ensure that the Government can scrutinize, impose conditions on or block a deal in any sector where there is an unacceptable risk to national security.[200]

[194] Section 23 (1)(2)(3) of the U.K. Security Act 2021.

[195] Section 25 (1) of the U.K. Security Act 2021.

[196] Section 26 (1) of the U.K. Security Act 2021.

[197] Sections 49, 50, 51 of the U.K. Security Act 2021.

[198] WWW.GOV.UK (11 November 2020). New powers to protect U.K. from malicious investment and strengthen economic resilience.

[199] Department for Business, Energy and Industrial Strategy (2 November 2021). National Security and Investment Act 2021: Statement for the purposes of Sect. 3.

[200] WWW.GOV.UK (11 November 2020). New powers to protect U.K. from malicious investment and strengthen economic resilience.

3.4 Takeover Law, Corporate Law and Self-Regulatory Corporate Governance Code

3.4.1 Background

Apart from the aforementioned public interest considerations in the competition law and the FDI screening regulation, government regulations in the takeover law field and corporate law field in the U.K. provide for mechanisms for corporate stakeholders and other societal stakeholders. The City Code on Takeovers and Mergers (the "City Code" hereinafter),[201] through the "non-frustration" requirement on the board of directors, focuses on protecting the target shareholders in takeovers; meanwhile, it sets out mechanisms such as "post-offer undertakings" and "post-offer intention statements" to provide opportunities for other important stakeholders to be considered by the acquirer and the target in a takeover.In the corporate governance field, the Companies Act 2006 (the "CA 2006" hereinafter)[202] provides for basic corporate governance rules for companies which feature the so-called "enlightened shareholder value" theory.[203] Based on these rules, the board of directors should not only consider the shareholder interest, but should also "have regard to" other stakeholders in making decisions. In the field of private regulation, the corporate governance code for listed companies—the 2018 U.K. Corporate Governance Code ("The 2018 U.K. CG Code" hereinafter)[204] continues this "enlightened shareholder value" stance and provides for mechanisms to engage non-shareholder stakeholders, particularly employees in the corporate governance of listed companies. In the event of a takeover, the target company may employ these mechanisms to protect both shareholders and other stakeholders.

This section discusses the relevant rules in the City Code, the CA 2006 and the 2018 U.K. CG Code. The objective of this discussion is to explore what stakeholders and societal interests are protected, what protection mechanisms are there for them, and how these mechanisms could be employed in takeovers.

---

[201] See the content of the City Code available at: https://www.thetakeoverpanel.org.uk/the-code/download-code (accessed 1 June 2022).

[202] See the content of the Companies Act 2006 available at: https://www.legislation.gov.uk/ukpga/2006/46/contents (accessed 1 June 2022).

[203] See detailed analysis on the "enlightened shareholder value" theory in Sect. 3.4.2.1.

[204] See the content of the 2018 U.K. CG Code available at: https://www.frc.org.uk/getattachment/88bd8c45-50ea-4841-95b0-d2f4f48069a2/2018-UK-Corporate-Governance-Code-FINAL.pdf (accessed 1 June 2022).

3.4.2 Protection of the Shareholders

3.4.2.1 The Focus of Protecting Shareholders in the CA 2006

(1) The "Shareholder Value" Tradition of Corporate Governance

The focus of directors on maximizing shareholder value has been particularly dominant in the U.K. since the 1980s.[205] The "shareholder value" largely originated from the English partnership law in the nineteenth century, when the shareholders were considered to be "the company" (i.e. the joint stock company) and the conception of "the company" was not separated from its shareholders.[206] Under the "shareholder value" doctrine, the board's power derives from the company's charter, which is wholly under the control of the shareholders, and directors can be removed at any time by ordinary shareholder vote.[207] Correspondingly, directors under this model are imposed with an ultimate duty to promote the success of their company for the benefit of its members; in most cases, this is explained as the value of shareholders.[208] Under the perspective of the "shareholder value", in takeovers, the interests of the target shareholders are of paramount importance, and it is difficult to fit into that structure a mechanism to protect other stakeholders.[209]

The "shareholder value doctrine" could be discerned from the corporate governance designs in the CA 2006. The CA 2006 does not decide between the one-tier or two-tier board, and companies are permitted to structure their boards as they wish in the articles of association.[210] The Model Articles for Public and Private Companies

---

205 Rühmkorf (2015), p. 45. See Omran, M., Atrill, P., & Pointon, J. (2002). Shareholders versus stakeholders: corporate mission statements and investor returns. *Business Ethics: A European Review, 11*(4), 318–326.

206 Ibid. For a historical overview, see Ireland, P. (2010). Limited liability, shareholder rights and the problem of corporate irresponsibility. *Cambridge Journal of Economics, 34*(5), 837–856.

207 Kraakman et al. (2017), p. 12. For the definition of the "shareholder value" (also called as "shareholder primacy"), see Kraakman, et al. (2017), pp. 98–99 (in footnote 115): "The most famous articulation of the 'shareholder primacy' ideal comes from the case of *Dodge v Ford Motor Company*, 170 NW 668 (Mich. 1919), in which it is explained as 'it is not within the lawful powers of a board of directors to share and conduct the affairs of a corporation for the merely incidental benefit of shareholders and for the primary purpose of benefiting others'; in *eBay Domestic Holdings, Inc. v Newmark*, 16 ATLANTIC REPORTER 3d 1, 33 (Del. Ch. 2010), the shareholder primacy' was articulated as 'promoting, protecting, or pursuing non-stockholder considerations must lead at some point to value for stockholders'".

208 Department for Business, Energy and Industrial Strategy (November 2016). Corporate Governance Reform: Green Paper. Available at: https://assets.publishing.service.gov.uk/government/uploads/system/uploads/attachment_data/file/584013/corporate-governance-reform-green-paper.pdf (accessed 17 January 2022), see p. 69.

209 Kraakman et al. (2017), p. 209.

210 Gerner-Beuerle and Schilling (2019), pp. 304, 308. Companies Act 2006 only requires that "a private company must have at least one director" and "a public company must have at least two directors". See Sects. 154, 156 of the CA 2006.

are based on the one-tier board model.[211] Apart from the general meeting, the CA 2006 does not set out any other separate organ under the CA 2006 to control the board of directors.[212] It is also the Model Articles for Public and Private Companies that provide rules to furnish the shareholders to remove the directors at any time with or without any cause.[213]

This prevailing "shareholder value" doctrine was subject to criticism in the U.K. for a while, and there was a considerable debate about corporate theory in the Company Law Review Steering Group when they prepared the 2006 reform of the company law.[214] In its Consultation Paper, the Company Law Review Steering Group explained the background for introducing an "enlightened shareholder value" in the company law[215]:

> There will inevitably be situations in which the interests of the shareholders and other participants will clash, even when the interests of shareholders are viewed as long-term ones. Examples include a decision whether to close a plant, with associated redundancies, or to terminate a long-term supply relationship, when continuation in either case is expected to make a negative contribution to shareholder returns. In such circumstances the law must indicate whether shareholder interests are to be regarded as overriding, or some other kind of balance should be struck.

Against this reform background, Sect. 172 of the CA 2006 introduced the "enlightened shareholder value" by stipulating the directors' duty to "promote the success of the company" and to "have regard to" a number of non-shareholder stakeholders in their decisions and to value the building up of a long-term relationship with them.[216] Moreover, it also imposed on the directors a reporting requirement concerning these stakeholder matters.[217]

(2) The "Enlightened Shareholder Value" in the CA 2006

One explanation of the statutory statement of directors' duty under Sect. 172 of the CA 2006 is that it simply codifies the existing common law obligations of the

---

[211] Ibid, see p. 308. See Model Articles for Private Companies Limited by Shares, Model Articles for Private Companies Limited by Guarantee, Model Articles for Public Companies, available at: https://www.gov.uk/guidance/model-articles-of-association-for-limited-companies (accessed 30 May 2022).

[212] Ibid, see pp. 304, 308.

[213] Ibid. See Art 4(1) of Model Articles for Public Companies; Art 4 of Model Articles for Private Companies; Sect. 168 of the CA 2006.

[214] Rühmkorf (2015), p. 32. See WEBARCHIVE.NATIONALARCHIVE.GOV.UK (February 1999). Modern Company Law for a Competitive Economy—The Strategic Framework (A Consultation Document from the Company Law Review Steering Group). Available at: https://webarchive.nationalarchives.gov.uk/20121101191957/http:/www.bis.gov.uk/files/file23279.pdf (accessed 30 May 2022). See paras 5.1.4–5.1.7 of the Consultation Paper.

[215] WEBARCHIVE.NATIONALARCHIVE.GOV.UK (February 1999). Modern Company Law for a Competitive Economy—The Strategic Framework (A Consultation Document from the Company Law Review Steering Group). See para 5.1.15 of the Consultation Paper; see also Du Plessis et al. (2018), p. 50.

[216] Section 172 of the CA 2006.

[217] Sections 414A, 414B, 414C of the CA 2006.

directors.[218] Prior to the CA 2006, directors' duties were based on the common law,[219] which are to be understood as the rules and principles developed by case law and remain of utmost importance for interpreting the statutory provisions in the U.K.[220] Apart from the employees and the creditors' interests, having regard to the long-term consequences of corporate decisions and acting fairly as between members of the company, according to some scholars, were all recognized as the interests a director needs to consider in the old common law.[221] Section 172 reaffirms these issues and provides for a non-exhaustive list of the considerations directors must "have regard to" in order to promote the "success of the company", including:

i. The interests of the company's employees,
ii. The need to foster the company's business relationships with suppliers, customers and others,
iii. The impact of the company's operations on the community and the environment.[222]

In addition, Sect. 172 also reiterates that "the duty imposed by this section has effect subject to any enactment or rule of law requiring directors, in certain circumstances, to consider or act in the interests of creditors of the company".[223] Indeed, as the considerations listed are not exhaustive, the directors may owe a wide range of duties to their companies in addition to the general duties as listed.[224] More impor-

[218] Department for Trade and Industry (DTI) (June 2007). Companies Act 2006: Duties of Company Directors (Ministerial Statements). Available at: https://webarchive.nationalarchives.gov.uk/20070628230000/http://www.dti.gov.uk/files/file40139.pdf (accessed 30 May 2022). Minister Margaret Hodge argued that Sect. 172 continued the existing duties established by the case law, the only major exception being the new procedures for dealing with conflicts of interest. See also Gerner-Beuerle & Schilling (2019), p. 76: The authors pointed out that "the general duties in Sects. 170 to 177 are all derived from case law"; and "the statutory law in England in general, builds on concepts and terminology elaborated by the body of existing case law, constantly interacts with the case law and can only be properly comprehended against the background of the case law".

[219] Rühmkorf (2015), p. 40. See also Payne (2002), p. 91: The fiduciary duties of directors are part of the common law in the U.K., which include firstly, the duty to act in good faith in what the directors consider to be the best interests of the company (the duty of loyalty); and, secondly, the requirement that directors must exercise their powers for a proper purpose.

[220] Gerner-Beuerle & Schilling (2019), p. 76.

[221] Rühmkorf (2015), p. 41. For the protection of employees, see for example, Sect. 309 of Companies Act 1985; for the protection of creditors, see for example, *West Mercia Safetywear Ltd v Dodd* [1988] BCLC 250; for acting fairly between members of the company, see for example, *Mutual Life Insurance Co of New York v Rank Organization Ltd* [985] BCLC 11; for having regard to the likely consequences of any decision in the long-term, see for example, *Gaiman v National Association for Mental Health* [1971] Ch 317.

[222] Section 172(1) of the CA 2006.

[223] Section 172(3) of the CA 2006.

tantly, some terms under this provision still call for further explanations, such as "act in the way he considers, in good faith", "the success of the company", and "have regard to".

(a) *"In Good Faith"*

As to the interpretation of the more subjective "*he considers, in good faith*", corresponding common law rules and equitable principles are applied.[225] The duty "to act in good faith" can be understood as corresponding to the "duty of loyalty" of directors.[226] It is likely the courts will refer to the common law duty "to act bona fide" for the company when interpreting the "good faith" provision.[227] After the enactment of the CA 2006, in the case *Cobden Investments Ltd v RWM Langport Ltd,* the judge held that "the old-fashioned phrase acting '*bona fide in the interests of the company*' is reflected in the statutory words acting 'in good faith in a way most likely to promote the success of the company for the benefit of its members as a whole'".[228] The term "acting 'bona fide'" was interpreted in the case *Re Smith and Fawcett Ltd* in the way that "directors of a company must act '… bona fide in what they consider—not the court may consider—is in the interests of the company, and not for any collateral purpose'".[229] Based on this stand, the courts are not likely to judge the merits of the directors' decisions as long as they exercised reasonable care, skill and diligence in discharging the Sect. 172 duty.[230] The exception merely exists in very clear cases where the commercial issues and the directors' subjective judgments would prevail.[231] This leads to the result which encourages judicial deference to directors in corporate decisions.[232] And it would often be difficult to find directors

---

224 Department for Trade and Industry (DTI) (June 2007). Companies Act 2006: Duties of Company Directors (Ministerial Statements). See pp. 5–6.

225 Subsection 170 (4) of the CA 2006 requires that "The general duties shall be interpreted and applied in the same way as common law rules and equitable principles, and regard shall be had to the corresponding common law rules and equitable principles in interpreting and applying the general duties". See also Rühmkorf (2015), p. 42.

226 Nyombi (2015), p. 245.

227 Rühmkorf (2015), p. 42. See also Tate (2012), p. 112.

228 Ibid, p. 43. See *Cobden Investments Ltd v RWM Langport Ltd, Southern Counties Fresh Foods Limited, Romford Wholesale Meats Limited* [2008] EWHC 2810 (Ch) [52].

229 Ibid. *Re Smith and Fawcett Ltd* [1942] Ch 304 [306].

230 Nyombi (2015), p. 245. Nyombi argues that the common law duty of loyalty relates to the internal management rules, which was explored by Lord Eldon LC in *Carlen v Drury* [1812] 1 Ves & B 154, stating that: "court is not required on every occasion to take the management of every playhouse and Brewhouse in the Kingdom.".

231 Rühmkorf (2015), p. 43. See *Iesini v Westrip Holdings Ltd* [2009] EWHC 2526. See also Kraakman et al. (2017), p. 98.

232 Kraakman et al. (2017), p. 98.

to be in breach of this duty as long as they can convince the judge that they acted in good faith in the decision-making process.[233]

(b) *"The Success of the Company for the Benefit of Its Members as a Whole"*

Courts in the U.K. traditionally found that the interests of the company were best understood as the aggregate of the shareholder interests.[234] Under Sect. 172(1), directors are required to promote the success of the company "for the benefit of its members as a whole". The term "members as a whole" thus forms a crucial factor in judging the objective of the directors' decision-making. In *Gaiman v National Association for Mental Health*, the court explained this term as including "present and future shareholders",[235] a stand which is in line with the shareholder value theory. Based on this understanding, the other stakeholders' interests may only be taken into account if they ultimately benefit the shareholders.

The term also stipulates "for the benefit of its members as a whole". The Ministerial Statement in 2007 illustrated that the starting point for interpreting the directors' duty is that "it is essential for the members of the company to collectively define the objective they wish to achieve"; and the duty is to promote the success for the members as a collective body, rather than only to benefit the majority shareholders, or any particular shareholder or section of shareholders.[236] It also articulated that in principle, the success of a commercial company was interpreted as a long-term increase in the value; for certain companies, such as charities and community interest companies, it would mean the attainment of the objectives for which the company has been established.[237] Above all, it is still for the directors to form a good faith judgment about what is success for the members as a whole.[238]

(c) *"Have Regard to"*

In the Ministerial Statement, "have regard to" was explained in the way of "giving proper consideration to…"[239] This requirement seeks to "capture cultural change

---

[233] Rühmkorf (2015), p. 44. See also Nyombi (2015), p.245. Nyombi also argued that without judicial inspection, directors only have to show a rational basis for the decision and they would have complied with the duty.

[234] Cahn & Donald (2018), p. 396. See e.g. *Heron International Ltd v Lord Grade* [1983] BCLC 244, 5.11 (CA); *Brady v Brady [1988]* BCLC 20, 40 (CA); Ferran (1999: 134); Davies (2003: 372).

[235] Rühmkorf (2015), p. 45. *Gaiman v National Association for Mental Health* (1971) Ch [317], [330].

[236] Department for Trade and Industry (DTI) (June 2007). Companies Act 2006: Duties of Company Directors (Ministerial Statements), see pp. 7–8: "Duty to promote the success of the company".

[237] Ibid, p. 7. See also Du Plessis et al. (2018), p. 51. Under the Companies (Audit, Investigations and Community Enterprise) Act 2004, a new type of company called the "community interest company" can be established. The community interest company is a limited liability business form designed for enterprises that wish to use their profits and assets for the "public good". See LEGISLATION.GOV.UK. Companies (Audit, Investigations and Community Enterprise) Act 2004. Available at: https://www.legislation.gov.uk/ukpga/2004/27/section/26 (accessed 31 May 2022).

[238] Ibid, p. 8.

[239] Ibid. p. 9.

in the way companies conduct their businesses".[240] Some scholars regarded this requirement as a symbol that for the first time "the U.K. company law has formally recognized the residual risk borne by the listed stakeholders and so requires attention to be paid thereto", and "to that extent, it represents a development from the common law's narrow focus on shareholder interests".[241]

Nevertheless, other scholars also pointed out that in terms of protection of the creditors and employees, the new requirement in essence is just a restatement of the existing law and no actual development was made. According to them, the list of stakeholders under Sect. 172(1) does not include creditors, although two potential categories, suppliers and employees, are listed; although Sect. 172(3) provides that the directors' duty is subject to "any enactment or rule of law" requiring directors to consider creditor interests in certain circumstances, it is only a reiteration of the existing statutory provisions which protect directors against, for example, wrongful trading.[242] With regard to employees, some scholars argued that the inclusion of employees in Sect. 172(1) is actually a weakening of the employees' governance position, as previously directors were required to have regard to the interests of employees in the performance of their duties, but under the new regime, they are only required to consider the employee interests to the extent that it would promote the success of the company for its members' benefit.[243] Thus, the scholars pointed out that under the new regime, the shareholder interests remain paramount and the interests of non-shareholder stakeholders are only to be considered insofar as it is desirable to promote "the success of the company" for the benefits of its members.[244] To that extent, the other stakeholders' interests do not enjoy an independent value in the directors' decisions, but rather, they are only in an affiliated position to promote the overall success of the company, which is subject to the judgment of the directors and sometimes may be over-ruled by majority shareholders.

(d) *The Enforceability of Sect. 172: "A Right Without a Remedy"?*

Some scholars argue that the way Sect. 172 has been drafted is the principal reason for the lack of enforcement of this provision.[245] The use of the subjective judgment of "good faith", the vague gist of "success of the company", the implicit prioritization of shareholder value, and the lack of instruction as to how to deal with a conflict of the listed considerations, may turn these stakeholder considerations to a mere "right without remedy".[246]

---

[240] Ibid, p. 2.

[241] Tate (2012), p. 113.

[242] Ibid. See the protection rule of creditors against wrongful trading in Sect. 214 of Insolvency Act 1986. Tate in this paper also argued that Sect. 172 (3) recognizes the common law position which imposed on directors a duty towards creditors' in times of financial distress, as in *Gwyer v London Wharf (Limehouse) Ltd* [2003] 2 BCLC 153.

[243] Ibid. See the protection rule of employees in the previous regime in Sect. 309 of Companies Act 1985.

[244] Ibid, p. 114. See Davies & Worthington (2008), p. 509.

[245] Rühmkorf (2015), p. 49.

[246] Ibid. See also Fisher (2009), p. 15.

There are few cases to date which address the duty under Sect. 172.[247] The courts normally will not intervene with the board's decision concerning the duty to promote the success of the company unless the decision is one that no reasonable director would have considered to be in the company's best interest.[248] As Davis et al. (2012) explained, it would be very difficult to show that the directors, when making a decision, have breached this duty, except in egregious cases or cases where the directors have, obligingly, left a clear record of their thought processes leading up to the challenged decision.[249] In exceptional cases where the courts do step in to interfere, the standard of conduct as required of directors under Sect. 172, which is subjective, is not subject to the courts' second review.[250]

More importantly, in practice, the stakeholders cannot bring a claim where they think the directors breach their duties under Sect. 172; such a law suit can only be initiated either by the board on behalf of the company against the delinquent directors or by shareholders in derivative proceedings pursuant to Sect. 260(3) of the CA 2006.[251] Thus, the effectiveness of enforcing the directors' duties under Sect. 172 through a court's intervention depends largely on the willingness and ability of shareholders to launch such a claim against delinquent directors.[252] Scholars found that such private litigation by shareholders against directors is not prevalent in the U.K.; rather enforcement by public authorities provides an obvious alternative or supplement to the private enforcement, which is particularly the case in the takeover regime as can be reflected in the public enforcement by the Panel on Takeovers and Mergers.[253] Based on the number of cases in which the Panel on Takeovers and Mergers offers guidance, scholars argue that the public enforcement may be a substitute for civil litigation concerning the directors' breach of duties.[254]

---

[247] See the conclusion of the existing cases in Tsagas, G. (2017). Section 172 of the Companies Act 2006: Desperate Times Call for Soft Law Measures. In N. Boeger, & C. Villiers (Eds.), *Shaping the Corporate Landscape*: *Towards Corporate Reform and Enterprise Diversity* (pp: 131–150): Hart Publishing. Available at: https://papers.ssrn.com/sol3/papers.cfm?abstract_id=2996090 (accessed 31 May 2022).

[248] Lim, E (2017). Judicial Intervention in Directors' Decision-Making Process: Sect. 172 of the Companies Act 2006. *Journal of Business Law 169*. Available at: https://ssrn.com/abstract=3103345 (last visited: January 17 2021).

[249] Ibid. See Davies, P. L., Worthington, S., & Micheler, E. (2012). *Gower and Davies' principles of modern company law* (Vol. 20,088). London: Sweet & Maxwell, p. 543.

[250] Ibid.

[251] Ibid. See also Rühmkorf (2015), pp. 48–49.

[252] Ibid. The author argued that because of the restrictive standing rules governing derivative actions, the "loser pays fees" rule and the absence of class actions, suing miscreant directors may not always be the best course of action for shareholders.

[253] Armour et al. (2009), pp. 692, 695: The authors analysed the reasons for the reduced occurrence of the private litigation by shareholders in the U.K. compared with the U.S., and held that while the U.K. directors face numerous regulatory and administrative obligations under companies legislation, these obligations generally do not provide a legal foundation for civil suits.

[254] Ibid, p. 717: The authors also held that as the City Code often imposes tighter constraints on directors than directors' fiduciary duties under corporate law, compliance with the former will necessarily imply compliance with the latter. Also, as the Panel normally bars parties from engaging

To conclude, it seems that the "stakeholder protection" content under Sect. 172 of the CA 2006 does not really make any difference from the previous "shareholder value" tradition. Altogether, the subjective elements of this requirement (such as "in good faith", "have regard to"), the ambiguity in the "success of the company", the lack of instructions for coordinating different interests, and lack of liability rules in the case of breach of the duty make it hard to enforce. In takeovers, it is likely that the stakeholders' interests under Sect. 172 are still in a subordinated position and would only be considered by the directors when they can promote the shareholder interests.

3.4.2.2 Shareholders' Decision-Making Power Under the City Code

(1) Background: The "Shareholder Value" Nature of the City Code

Not until the end of the 1950s, did the battle for corporate control yield a concrete regulatory development in the U.K.[255] In July 1959, the Governor of the Bank of England secretly invited a committee consisting of trade groups representing merchant banks, institutional investors, the largest commercial banks, and the London Stock Exchange, to devise a code of conduct to regulate takeover bids.[256] The committee then adopted the *Notes on Amalgamation of British Business*, which was primarily themed as protecting shareholders in takeovers, and the principles of "shareholder value" (or "shareholder primacy") and the correlative "board neutrality" in takeovers were established at that time.[257] In the late 1960s, the Working Party of the Bank of England drafted a new set of takeover rules, and the City Code was developed during this period which continued the shareholder-oriented spirit.[258]

At its initiation, the City Code followed a self-regulatory route.[259] In 1968, the Panel on Takeovers and Mergers (the "Panel" hereinafter) was set up to oversee the application of the City Code.[260] The London business community then agreed to impose sanctions in the case of failure to adhere to the City Code; in the end, a mix of a self-regulatory system and an informal enforcement mechanism was put in place in the takeover regime.[261] Following the implementation of the EU Takeover Directive by virtue of the CA 2006, the rules set out in the City Code and the Panel both have

in any litigation (apart from a reference to the antitrust authorities) that might frustrate an actual or potential takeover bid, there is consequently little litigation surrounding takeovers in the U.K.

[255] Armour et al. (2011), p. 235.

[256] Ibid, p. 236.

[257] Ibid. p. 207. For more of the "board neutrality rule", see Nyombi (2015), pp. 241–242.

[258] Armour et al. (2011), pp. 236–237.

[259] Nyombi (2015), p. 238. See also Gerner-Beuerle & Schilling (2019), p. 76.

[260] The Panel on Takeovers and Mergers is the supervisory authority to carry out certain regulatory functions in relation to takeovers pursuant to the EU Takeover Directive, and to regulate takeovers and other matters to which the City Code applies. See its website available at: https://www.thetakeoverpanel.org.uk/ (accessed 30 May 2022). See also Button (2018), pp. 10–11, 367–371.

[261] Nyombi (2015), p.238.

a statutory basis.[262] After the Brexit, the U.K. no longer has a legal obligation to transpose the EU Takeover Directive, but the Panel's statutory basis to make rules relating to takeover supervision in the U.K. remains unchanged.[263] The Panel has both the obligation and the authority to promulgate rules governing the conduct of takeovers.[264] It enforces the City Code and can give any direction that, for example, appears to it to be necessary to restrain any person from acting (or continuing to act) in breach of the City Code; it can also order compensation to be paid in certain cases and can seek enforcement of the City Code and its rulings by the courts.[265]

One of the main focuses of the City Code is on ensuring the decision-making rights and fair treatment of the shareholders of the target company.[266] The "non-frustration" requirement in Rule 21.1, as a reflection of the "board neutrality" principle, provides the target shareholders with an exclusive power to make decisions during the takeover process. According to this rule, any actions by the board of the target that have the effect of frustrating any offer or bona fide possible offer or preventing the shareholders from deciding on the merits of the offer cannot be taken without either general meeting approval or dispensation from the Panel.[267]

In addition to the "non-frustration" rule, the "mandatory bid" requirement in Rule 9 provides extra protection for minority shareholders and promotes equal treatment among the shareholders of the target company. According to this requirement, anyone purchasing (taken together with shares in which persons acting in concert with him are interested) 30 per cent or more of the voting rights in the target's share capital must make an offer ("mandatory bid") for the remainder of the target's share capital.[268]

---

[262] Directive 2004/25/EC of the European Parliament and of the Council of 21 April 2004 on takeover bids [2004] OJ L 142/12 (The EU Takeover Directive). Article 4(1) of the EU Takeover Directive requires that Member States should "designate the authority or authorities competent to supervise bids", and the designated authorities "may be private bodies recognized by national law". In line with this, Sect. 942 of Companies Act 2006 confers the Panel with certain statutory powers while it does not seek to regulate the constitution of the Panel. See also Davies & Worthington (2016), p. 921; Gerner-Beuerle & Schilling (2019), p. 76.

[263] The U.K. Government, by virtue of The Takeovers (Amendment) (EU Exit) Regulations 2019 (S.I. 2019/217) made changes to Part 28 of the CA 2006. It also made an Explanatory Memorandum to explain the amendments (see it available at: https://www.legislation.gov.uk/uksi/2019/217/pdfs/uksiem_20190217_en.pdf, accessed 31 May 2022), which mainly removed references in the CA 2006 to EU law (including the EU Takeover Directive) (e.g. Section 943 of the CA 2006) to ensure legal clarity and to effect a freestanding domestic takeover regime.

[264] Sections 943–945 of Companies Act 2006. See also Gerner-Beuerle & Schilling (2019), p. 77.

[265] See the details of the Panel's information, enforcement and disciplinary powers in "Introduction: Sects. 9–11" of the City Code. Nevertheless, some scholars argued that whilst the City Code reinforces the Panel's decision-making and regulation over takeovers, it does not change the self-regulatory nature of it, and the Panel "remains firmly rooted in the private sector, both in composition and in practice." See Varottil & Wan (2017), p. 56.

[266] See "Introduction: Sect. 2(a)" of the City Code. The City Code also aims to promote the integrity of the financial market in the U.K.

[267] Rule 21.1(a) of the City Code. Rule 21.1(c) provides the situations where the Panel normally agrees to disapply this "non-frustration" requirement.

[268] See Rule 9.1 of the City Code. It should be noted that, a partial bid in the U.K. requires the consent of the Panel, which would normally be granted if the bid would not result in the acquisition of

The mandatory bid requirement is expected to chill some potential offers by forcing the acquirers to raise enough money to acquire the entire company rather than just a controlling stake and to ensure that all shareholders get the opportunity to share the control premium.[269]

Both the "non-frustration" rule and the "mandatory bid" rule reflect the focus of the City Code on protecting the shareholder group in takeovers and the underlying "shareholder primacy" orientation. The two rules also greatly influence the designs of the EU Takeover Directive.[270]

(2) Restriction on the Anti-takeover Actions of the Board of Directors

Rule 21.1 also exemplifies the actions that the board of directors cannot launch without shareholder approval or the Panel's dispensation. While not exhaustive, the examples cover most of the ways in which a board can use the corporate power to create defences, including, for example, the issuance of new shares, the acquisition or disposal of significant assets, leveraging the capital structure or entering into substantial contracts other than in the ordinary course of business.[271] The board, however, under this rule, may still take actions such as searching for an alternative friendly acquirer to compete with the existing one (the "white knight").[272] Moreover, the "non-frustration" rule only restricts the proposed actions by the target board during the course of an offer or where the board believes that a bona fide offer might be imminent. To that extent, it leaves room for the board to take pre-offer "embedded defences", such as the "poison pill" or shareholder rights plan, a "staggered board"

---

more than 30% of the target's voting rights (see Rule 36.1 of the City Code). Besides, dispensations from the obligation to make a mandatory bid under Rule 9 are available from the Panel in certain circumstances (see Appendix 1 to the City Code).

[269] Armour & Skeel (2007), p. 1737. Under the City Code, acquiring a "controlling stake" is defined as acquiring "an interest, or interests, in shares carrying in aggregate 30% or more of the voting rights...of a company, irrespective of whether such interest or interests give de facto control". See "Definitions" at C7 of the City Code.

[270] Ibid, p. 1787. According to Amour & Skeel (2007), the EU Takeover Directive "takes as its starting point many aspects of the British model of takeover regulation, both as to substance (the "board neutrality" rule" and the "mandatory bid" rule) and as to procedure (oversight of takeovers to be through a regulator rather than courts).".

[271] Rule 21.1(b) of the City Code. See analysis of these measures in Kraakman, et al. (2017), p. 212; Kershaw, D. (2016). Hostile Takeovers and the Non-Frustration Rule: Time for a Re-Evaluation. Available at: https://ssrn.com/abstract=2875772 or http://dx.doi.org/10.2139/ssrn.2875772 (last visited: January 12 2021), p. 5.

[272] See more introduction to the "white knight" strategy at Kraakman et al. (2017), pp. 214–215.

mechanism or the use of "golden shares" or "golden parachute" provision.[273] Nevertheless, the takeover practice in the U.K. shows that these embedded defences by the board are also difficult to conduct, which is partly owing to the U.K.'s corporate governance designs in various aspects.[274] For example, the CA 2006 requires directors to first seek approval from the general meeting for authority to issue new shares, and in listed companies this usually will only be granted subject to guidelines formalized by institutional investors.[275] The "staggered board" mechanism may be pale confronted with the rule that shareholders may remove directors at any time by ordinary resolution;[276] and the relevant rules which require that the public company must, at the accounts meeting, approve the directors' remuneration report also make it hard for the board members to design too generous "golden parachute" clauses for self-protection.[277]

The use of "golden shares" as a pre-bid anti-takeover measure was also largely restricted in the U.K. before the Brexit. "Golden shares" refer to "certain prerogatives maintained by Member States after the privatization of a State-owned company".[278] Such "golden shares" first emerged in the U.K. during privatizations in the 1980s, and then spread to other European countries such as France, Germany and Italy.[279] Through the "golden shares", a privatized company does not give the Government a general right to intervene in its day-to-day activities, but it could grant the Government disproportionately powerful decision rights, such as the veto rights over certain fundamental corporate decisions such as takeovers and mergers, dissolutions, and

---

[273] Armour & Skeel (2007), p. 1736. For "poison pill", see Armour & Skeel (2007), p. 1734; Kraakman et al. (2017), p. 216. A "poison pill" plan refers to the design adopted by the target company in issuing a series of convertible preference shares to the original shareholders and establishing certain conditions for the exercise of such shares; the conditions are usually triggered when the acquirer's shareholding of the target company reaches a certain standard (usually 10 or 15%) in a hostile takeover; and in that situation, the preference shares would be inflated to dilute the shareholding of the acquirer. For a "staggered board" and "golden parachute", see Huang (2014), pp. 296–306. A "staggered board" design stipulates different terms of the office for the directors, and requires that only a fraction of the board members is to be replaced each time at a board re-election. A "golden parachute" clause refers to the special compensation agreement signed between a listed company and its directors, supervisors and other senior management, according to which when these people resign after the acquirer gets the control of the target, the company must pay compensation to them; and the standard of compensation is usually far above their normal remuneration. For "golden shares", see Kraakman et al. (2017), p. 96.

[274] Ibid.

[275] Ibid. See Sects. 549–551 of the CA 2006.

[276] Ibid, p. 1737. See Sect. 168 of the CA 2006.

[277] Ibid. See Sects. 420–422, 439–440 of the CA 2006. For "accounts meeting" in relation to a public company, see Sect. 437(3) of the CA 2006: an "accounts meeting" means a general meeting of the company at which the directors of a public company must lay the company's annual accounts and reports.

[278] Papadopoulos (2021), pp. 56–57: "More specifically, golden shares are defined as a tool that governments use to retain control over certain decisions in privatized companies and are often justified by Member States on the grounds that they are necessary to achieve certain policy objectives of a public interest nature".

[279] Kraakman et al. (2017), p. 96.

sales of assets, disproportionately to, or sometimes irrespective of, any ownership interest in the company.[280] The "golden share" clauses increase the difficulty for potential acquirers to get control of the target company; and the Government and the board of the company may employ these clauses as an effective pre-bid anti-takeover defence to drive away hostile takeovers and to protect the public interest at large.[281] In practice, some privatized companies in public utility sectors are still subject to scrutiny by the specific sector regulators;[282] and they are usually required to pursue public policy objectives such as security of supply and environmental sustainability (for example, the privatized energy companies).[283] In the event where the Government keeps a "golden share" in these companies, it often utilizes the rights conferred by such share to prevent hostile takeovers by foreign acquirers in strategic sectors.[284] The oversized shareholder rights conferred to the Government may constitute restrictions on the rights of new shareholder(s) (the potential acquirer) and breach the rules of free movement of capital or the freedom of establishment under the EU law.[285]

In previous cases, the European Commission criticized the situation where "golden shares impeded the competition of the internal market; and the limitation of control rights for private shareholders deterred investors, particularly foreign investors, from acquiring shares of companies which embed such golden shares, and thereby constitutes a restriction of the free movement of capital".[286] The CJEU in the case law ruled that such golden shares "indeed restrict the free movement of capital"; only in exceptional cases,[287] the CJEU accepted such measure when (1) it was justified on the basis of overriding reasons of general interest,[288] (2) effective to achieve its objective pursued,[289] (3) applies equally to nationals of the Member

[280] Ibid.

[281] Ibid.

[282] European Commission (July 2016). State-owned Enterprises in the EU: Lessons Learnt and Ways Forward in a Post-crisis Context. Available at: https://ec.europa.eu/info/sites/info/files/file_import/ip031_en_2.pdf (accessed 18 January 2021), see p. 95. For instance, Network Rail Limited is regulated by the Office of Rail and Road. Other key regulators are the Office of Gas and Electricity Markets (Ofgem), the Office of Communications, the Water Services Regulation Authority, and the Financial Conduct Authority. These bodies set standards, promote competition and ensure consumer protection.

[283] Ibid.

[284] Ibid.

[285] Consolidated version of the Treaty on the Functioning of the European Union (TFEU) [2016] OJ C 202/1. See Articles 63 (free movement of capital) and 49 (freedom of establishment).

[286] Werner (2017), p. 993. See for example, Case C-58/99 *Commission v Italy* [2000]; Case C-463/00 *Commission v Spain* [2003]; Case C-98/01 *Commission v United Kingdom* [2003].

[287] Ibid. For example, between 2000 and 2013, the CJEU reviewed eighteen infringement proceedings with golden share initiated by the European Commission, and only in two cases (C-503/99 *Commission v Belgium* in 2002 and C-95/12 *Commission v Germany* in 2013) permitted the national measures.

[288] Ibid.

[289] Ibid.

State concerned and of other EU Member States and complies with the principle of proportionality.[290]

In the U.K., the Government once retained such "golden shares" in the privatized company British Airport Authority (BAA) when it was privatized in 1987. The rights conferred to the Government through "golden share" were once denied by the CJEU in the *Commission v United Kingdom* in 2003.[291] At that time, BAA owned seven of the most important international airports of the U.K.[292] To protect the "general interest", the Government created a "special share" (golden share) through the articles of association of the BAA in 1987 which prevented any person from acquiring more than 15% of the voting shares in the company's capital and required the Government's consent for certain operations by the company.[293] Moreover, to achieve "public interests", the U.K. Government, through the Civil Aviation Authority, also "set strict price limits on how much BAA could charge customers".[294] In the *Commission v United Kingdom* in 2003, the CJEU held that the national provisions of golden share "could create obstacles to the right of establishment of nationals of other Member States as well as to the free movement of capital within the Community".[295] Meanwhile, the CJEU acknowledged that "by reason of exceptions provided for by the Treaty, the Member States may impose restrictions on those freedoms in certain circumstances linked to the exercise of official authority, public policy, public security and public health; but such exceptions must be restrictively interpreted, pass the proportionality test, and be in conformity with the principle of legal certainty, and must not be implemented for purely economic ends".[296] Nevertheless, in the case at issue, the U.K. Government "has not even argued that there is any general interest so far as it is concerned", and "expressly stated that it did not wish to rely on any justification based on possible overriding requirements relating to the general interest".[297] Thus in the end, the CJEU held that "there is no need to examine whether the rules can be justified on that basis" and decided that the golden share rules at issue "constitute a restriction on the free movement of capital".[298]

Based on this stance of the CJEU, the board's use of "golden share" provisions (sometimes in concert with the Government) as a pre-bid takeover defence is restricted in practice.

---

290 Ibid.

291 Case C-98/01 *Commission v United Kingdom* [2003], Judgment of the Court of 13 May 2003.

292 Werner, 2017, p. 997.

293 Ibid. See also Case C-98/01 *Commission v United Kingdom* [2003], Judgment of the Court of 13 May 2003, paras 8–11.

294 Ibid, p. 998.

295 Case C-98/01 *Commission v United Kingdom* [2003], Judgment of the Court of 13 May 2003, para 20.

296 Ibid, see para 21.

297 Ibid, see papas 22, 49.

298 Ibid, see para 49.

3.4.3 *Protection of Other Stakeholders*

3.4.3.1 "Post-Offer Undertaking" and "Post-Offer Intention Statement" in the City Code

(1) Background and Definition

A "post-offer intention statement" refers to a statement made by a takeover party relating to "any particular course of action that the party intends to take, or not take, after the end of the offer period"; a "post-offer undertaking" in essence is an intention statement which is also made by the takeover party in relation to the offer and is pertinent to any particular course of action that the party commits to take, or not take, after the end of the offer period; the difference is that it is clearly described by that party as a "post-offer undertaking".[299] By comparison, actions specified in a post-offer intention statement are not legally binding, and the takeover party does not need to consult the Panel for making such statement[300]; but the terms in a post-offer undertaking are legally binding for the period specified in the undertaking and consent of the Panel is required before the takeover party makes any such undertakings.[301] The Panel is also entitled to require the party making such undertakings to provide periodic written reports (at not more than 12 months' intervals) to the Panel, and require that party to appoint an independent supervisor to monitor the compliance.[302] In case of breach, the Panel is able to obtain an order from the court to seek for compliance,or to use its disciplinary power such as issuing a statement of censure.[303]

Prior to 2014, the City Code did not distinguish a voluntary commitment made by the takeover party in which it states what actions it "commits" to take or not take from a statement of intention in which the takeover party "states" to take or not take any actions.[304] Based on the "shareholder value" ("shareholder primacy") orientation, for a long time, the City Code did not deem it as its major task to protect other stakeholders in takeovers.[305] In consistency with this absence of attention, takeover parties, particularly the target company, are likely to be merely obsessed with the

---

[299] See "Definitions: Post-offer undertaking, Post-offer intention statement", Rules 19.5 (post-offer undertakings), 19.6 (post-offer intention statements) of the City Code.

[300] The party making such statements must, at the end of the 12 months from the end of the offer period or such period specified in the statement, confirm in writing to the Panel whether it has complied with its stated intention. See Rule 19.6 (c) of the City Code; see also Button (2018), p. 356.

[301] Rule 19.5 (e)(f) of the City Code.

[302] Rule 19.5 (h)(i) of the City Code.

[303] Rules 10(d), 11 of the City Code.

[304] BURGES-SALMON.COM (February 2015). Briefing: UK Takeover Code. Available at: https://www.burges-salmon.com/-/media/files/publications/open-access/uk_takeover_code.pdf (accessed 30 May 2022).

[305] In 2011, the Panel emphasized again that it was neither responsible for the financial and commercial merits of takeovers, nor the competition policy or wider questions of public interest. See The Takeover Panel (21 July 2011). Review of Certain Aspects of the Regulation of Takeover Bids: Response Statement by the Code Committee of the Panel following the Consultation on PCP

shareholder interests without having regard to other stakeholders' situation when making decisions in takeovers. This may aggravate the agency problems between the company and non-shareholder stakeholders, leaving a sour taste in the mouths of the latter who stand to lose their jobs or see the company become highly leveraged while the former gains premiums and leaves.[306] In 2014, Pfizer's proposed offer to AstraZeneca led to great debate and concerns in society.[307] In this case, Pfizer stated that subject to successful completion of its combination with AstraZeneca, it would make a series of significant commitments for a minimum of five years, including, for example, "to establish the combined company's corporate and tax residence in England, to base key scientific leadership in the U.K., to integrate the operations of the combined company so as to employ a minimum of 20 per cent of the combined company's total R&D workforce in the U.K. going forward".[308] The Panel noted that Pfizer's statements were unusual in that a bidder would normally express such statements as "statements of intention" rather than as "commitments" and the commitments made in this case were long-term.[309] Triggered by this offer, the Panel proposed a document to amend the City Code to introduce a new framework for the regulation of statements made by the acquirer and target, which further distinguished the binding "undertakings" from the "intention statements".[310] In practice, post-offer intention statements have been more widely used by the acquirers than post-offer undertakings. The statements often cover the key aspects of the target's future after the takeover, specifically the R&D functions, the balance of the skills and functions of the target's employees and management, and the location and functions of the target's headquarters.

(2) Relevant Cases of Post-offer Undertakings

Although the City Code does not oblige the takeover parties to make such undertakings, the political environment often leaves a foreign acquirer with few other

---

2011/1. Available at: http://www.thetakeoverpanel.org.uk/wp-content/uploads/2008/11/RS201101.pdf (accessed 30 May 2022), see Sects. 1.6, 1.7. According to the Panel, these tasks are the responsibility of Government and other bodies, for example, the Competition Commission, the Office of Fair Trading and the European Commission.

[306] Nyombi (2015), p. 258.

[307] Concerns were that the bid would risk the closure of R&D facilities in the U.K., with a knock-on impact on the country's science base. See the backgrounds of the debates in this takeover at: FT.COM (4 May 2014). Political row intensifies over Pfizer bid for AstraZeneca. Available at: https://www.ft.com/content/c4157c5c-d36c-11e3-b0be-00144feabdc0 (accessed 17 January 2021); THE GUARDIAN.COM (May 5 2014). Pfizer's AstraZeneca bid under scrutiny by MPs amid fears over industry future. Available at: https://www.theguardian.com/business/2014/may/05/pfizer-astrazeneca-mps-investigation-science-industry (accessed 17 January 2021).

[308] BURGES-SALMON.COM (February 2015). Briefing: UK Takeover Code.

[309] Button (2018), p. 353.

[310] See The Takeover Panel (15 September 2014). Consultation paper issued by the Code Committee of the Panel—Post-offer Undertakings and Intention Statements (PCP 2014/2). Available at: https://www.thetakeoverpanel.org.uk/wp-content/uploads/2008/11/PCP201402.pdf (accessed 13 January 2021).

options.[311] In practice, the takeover party often uses post-offer undertakings as a means to address public, political or regulatory concerns in the target company's business, employees, locations, as well as its R&D investment, the sustainable development of the environment, and the prosperity of the local community following the completion of the offer.[312]

The first ever post-offer undertakings were entered into by Softbank Corporation in 2016 in relation to its offer for ARM Holding.[313] In this case, SoftBank, a Japanese company made a £24.3 billion acquisition offer for ARM Holdings, a technology company in the U.K. To relieve the public concerns from the media and Government about the risks of losing important U.K. technology, the Japanese acquirer made several post-offer undertakings, including, for example, at least doubling the total number of employees of ARM in the U.K. within five years, increasing the number of employees of ARM outside the U.K. within five years, and maintaining ARM's global headquarters in Cambridge for five years.[314]

In Melrose's takeover of GKN in 2018, GKN was one of U.K.'s oldest engineering companies and Melrose specialized in turning around troubled manufacturing businesses and selling them on. The Secretary of State raised several concerns about the effect of this takeover on the economy, including the effect on employment (as GKN was regarded as a valuable employer in the U.K.) and the U.K.'s industrial strategy (in the light of the importance of GKN's R&D activities).[315] The fact that GKN benefited from government-sponsored contracts and participated in a sector that enjoyed active engagement from government-sponsored R&D and that a large number of pensioner stakeholders depended on GKN's ability to fund its pension schemes further increased the concerns.[316] In response, Melrose made post-offer undertakings, including, for example, maintaining Melrose's headquarters and listing in the U.K. for at least five years from completion of its offer, maintaining a board comprising of a majority of U.K. residents, and continuing supporting the R&D development of the GKN.[317]

As illustrated by the above cases, the legally-binding post-offer undertakings and other more-commonly-adopted post-offer intention statements provide the non-shareholder stakeholders with the possibilities to be considered by the takeover parties. Such undertakings and statements often cover the interests of the employees

---

311 WEDLAKEBELL.COM (23 April 2018). Melrose's Takeover of GKN Provides Another Instance of Post-offer Undertakings. Available at: https://wedlakebell.com/melroses-takeover-gkn-provides-another-instance-post-offer-undertakings/ (accessed 17 January 2021).

312 Button (2018), p. 355.

313 Ibid, p. 354.

314 Ibid. See also LONDONSTOCKEXCHANGE.COM (4 October 2019). SoftBank Group Post-offer undertakings (Appendix A). Available at: https://www.londonstockexchange.com/news-article/market-news/softbank-group-post-offer-undertakings/14255122 (accessed 13 January 2021).

315 HANSARD.PARLIAMENT.UK (27 March 2018). GKN: Proposed Takeover by Melrose. Available at: https://hansard.parliament.uk/commons/2018-03-27/debates/6FC2E74F-344E-455A-9EA7-E3A3EA2CA1BC/GKNProposedTakeoverByMelrose (assessed 2 June 2022).

316 Ibid.

317 Ibid. See also Button (2018), p. 355.

of the target, the local community and the environment; and the content usually includes, for example, sustaining the employment of the target and assuring an equal treatment of the employees, supporting the local community (through maintaining of the headquarters or key parts of the target in the local community), keeping on the R&D research investment, and sometimes continuing the environmental-friendly policies.

3.4.3.2 Disclosure of Non-financial Stakeholder Information Under the City Code and the CA 2006

The City Code incorporates rules that stipulate the duties of the acquirer to publish its intentions with regard to the business, employees and pension scheme(s) in its offer document,[318] and the duties of the target board to give its opinion (as well as the reasons) of the takeover offer.[319] These rules implemented the relevant provisions under the EU Takeover Directive.[320] Article 6 of the EU Takeover Directive stipulates that "the Member States shall ensure that an acquirer is required to make public an offer document"; among other information of the takeover offer, the document should contain "the acquirer's intentions with regard to the future business of the target company, in so far as it is affected by the bid, the offeror company and with regard to safeguarding of the jobs of their employees and management".[321] Such information includes the acquirer's intentions concerning "any material change in the conditions of employment, and in particular its strategic plans for the two companies and the likely repercussions on employment and the locations of the companies' places of business".[322] Article 9 of the EU Takeover Directive further requires that the target board (for a company with a two-tier board, meaning both the management board and the supervisory board) should make public a document specifying its opinion of the offer as well as the reasons for this opinion.[323] This document should include the board's views on "the effects of implementation of the bid on all the company's interests and specifically employment" and "the acquirer's strategic plans for the

---

318 Rules 24.1, 24.2 of the City Code.

319 Rules 25.1, 25.2 of the City Code.

320 In 2006, the U.K. issued The Takeovers Directive (Interim Implementation Regulations) 2006 (2006 No. 1183) to implement The EU Takeover Directive. See its official version available at: https://www.legislation.gov.uk/uksi/2006/1183/contents/made (accessed 20 May 2021). For a conclusion of the substantive provisions implementing the EU Takeover Directive, see "Part 22" at pp. 28–34 in Explanatory Memorandum to The Takeovers Directive (Interim Implementation Regulations) 2006 (2006 No. 1183), available at: https://www.legislation.gov.uk/uksi/2006/1183/pdfs/uksiem_20061183_en.pdf (accessed 21 May 2021). Because of the Brexit, on 12 November 2020, the Panel published a Statement 2020/11 with various amendments to the City Code that took effect at the end of the transition period (31 December 2020). See Statement 2020/11 available at: https://www.thetakeoverpanel.org.uk/download/2020-11?wpdmdl=8797 (accessed 2 June 2022).

321 Article 6(2), (3)(i) of the EU Takeover Directive.

322 Ibid.

323 Ibid, Article 9(5).

target and their likely repercussions on employment and the locations of the target as set out in the offer document in accordance with Article 6(3)(i)".[324]

In the corporate governance regime, the CA 2006 stipulates a "strategic report" mechanism which completes the directors' duty to non-shareholder stakeholders under Sect. 172 and may also be employed to reduce the information asymmetries the target stakeholders encounter in a takeover. As a complement to the directors' duty in Sect. 172 of the CA 2006 and another reflection of the "enlightened shareholder value" doctrine, Sect. 414(A) of the CA 2006 requires the directors to prepare a strategic report for each financial year of the company, of which the purpose is to inform the company members and help them assess how directors have performed their duty under Sect. 172.[325] This strategic report must include a statement which describes how the directors have had regard to the matters as set out in Sect. 172(1)(a) to (f) when performing their duty under that section.[326] In addition to this statement, the strategic report must also contain a review of the company's business, including an analysis concerning both financial information and certain non-financial matters.[327] With regard to the non-financial matters, a quoted company is required to include the following information in its strategic report:

i. Environmental matters (including the impact of the company's business on the environment),
ii. The company's employees, and
iii. Social, community and human rights issues.[328]

This non-financial reporting requirement under the CA 2006 is influenced by the EU Non-financial Reporting Directive (Directive 2014/95/EU).[329] To finalize

---

324 Ibid.

325 Subsection 414(B) of the CA 2006. This strategic report requirement does not apply if the company is entitled to the small companies exemption.

326 Subsection 414CZA (1) of the CA 2006. Subsection 414CZA (2) stipulates that this "Sect. 172(1) statement" requirement does not apply if the company qualifies as medium-sized in relation to that financial year.

327 Subsection 414(C)(2)(4) of the CA 2006. Subsection 414(C)(6) stipulates that the requirements of subsection (4) relating to non-financial information do not apply if the company qualifies as medium-sized in relation to that financial year.

328 Subsection 414(C)(7) of the CA 2006. See the definition of "quoted company" in Subsection 385(2) of the CA 2006. Information about any policies of the company in relation to the above matters and the effectiveness of these policies must be included in the report.

329 Directive 2014/95/EU of the European Parliament and of the Council of 22 October 2014 amending Directive 2013/34/EU as regards disclosure of non-financial and diversity information by certain large undertakings and groups Text with EEA relevance [2014] OJ L 330/1 (The EU Non-financial Reporting Directive). Directive 2014/95/EU amends the EU Accounting Directive (Directive 2013/34/EU) (by inserting an Article 19a into the original Article 19) and requires large public-interest companies with more than 500 employees to include a "non-financial statement" in the management report. Under Directive 2014/95/EU, large companies have to publish reports on the policies they implement in relation to: (i) environmental protection; (ii) social responsibility and treatment of employees; (iii) respect for human rights; (iv) anti-corruption and bribery; (v) diversity on company boards (in terms of age, gender, educational and professional background). See introduction to the EU "Non-financial

the transposition of Directive 2014/95/EU, Sects. 414CA and 414CB of the CA 2006 impose a reporting obligation on some large companies with more than 500 employees, such as traded companies, banks, insurance undertakings and other companies, to incorporate the non-financial information statement in their strategic report. In addition to this non-financial information statement, in January 2022, a "sustainability information statement" was further inserted into the CA 2006 as part of the strategic report, which came into force on 6 April 2022.[330] Currently, the CA 2006 requires that both the non-financial and sustainability information statement should contain the climate-related financial disclosures of the company;[331] and for some large companies with more than 500 employees (such as traded companies, banks, insurance undertakings and other companies), their non-financial and sustainable information statement should contain information relating to: (i) environmental matters; (ii) the company's employees; (iii) social matters; (iv) respect for human rights; and (v) anti-corruption and anti-bribery matters.[332]

The non-financial statement[333] from the board may provide relevant stakeholders with information about how their interests are (or will be) affected by corporate activities and clues about whether the directors have considered their interests in their decisions. The "duty" to incorporate the non-financial and sustainability information statement under the CA 2006 is implemented on a "comply or explain" basis,[334] different from the implementation of other financial information in the board's strategic report. In cases where the report does not contain the above non-financial or sustainability information in the strategic report, it must state which kinds of information it does not contain.[335]

To some extent, the requirement on reporting non-financial matters may compensate for the lack of direct enforceability of the directors' duties under Sect. 172, given that companies who value their reputations may not refuse to provide information on the stakeholders' issues and leave the public with the impression that they do not respect or consider broad stakeholders in their activities.[336] Empirical study found that compliance with the provisions of the strategic report is very high.[337] Nevertheless, it is also observed that the quality of non-financial reporting still needs to be improved: companies often do not report how they have regard to the non-financial

reporting" available at: https://ec.europa.eu/info/business-economy-euro/company-reporting-and-auditing/company-reporting/non-financial-reporting_en (accessed 15 January 2021).

330 The "sustainability information statement" was inserted into Sect. 414(C)(2) of the CA 2006 by virtue of The Companies (Strategic Report) (Climate-related Financial Disclosure) Regulations 2022 (S.I. 2022/31).

331 Section 414CB(A1) of the CA 2006. Section 414CB(2A) of the CA 2006 defines the climate-related financial disclosures in detail.

332 See Sects. 414CA(1), 414CB(1) of the CA 2006. See the analysis on the non-financial information statement in the CA 2006 in Esser & MacNeil, 2019.

333 And the "sustainability information statement" after 6 April 2022.

334 See subsections 414(C)(7), 414 CB(4), 414CB(4A) of the CA 2006.

335 Ibid.

336 Tate, 2012, p. 118.

337 See Esser, MacNeil, & Chalaczkiewicz-Ladna, 2018.

matters; and the relevant type of information is not always available in the report (for example, information on labour issues such as the types of contracts and the issue of workforce voice).[338] Moreover, the reports the companies give often do not concentrate sufficiently on the long-term prospects: although they have long-term plans, they may not be willing to disclose them.[339]

Besides, according to Esser and MacNeil (2019), the logic underlying the difference between the mandatory application basis of the financial reporting and the "comply or explain" basis of the non-financial information disclosure is that the financial strands of strategic reporting are a *sine qua non* for the emergence of informed shareholders who can effectively engage in corporate decisions (directly through the general meeting and indirectly through the appointment or dismissal power of directors, and the legal remedies to them in the event that directors do not comply with their duties).[340] By comparison, the disclosure of stakeholder issues does not play such a central role in the corporate governance framework, particularly owing to the fact that the stakeholders lack formal channels to engage in corporate decisions even with the information they need.[341] This argument illustrates that the role of this non-financial stakeholder statement in protecting other stakeholders is restricted, given that under the CA 2006 these stakeholders have no engagement mechanisms to directly participate in corporate decisions such as takeovers.[342] In the event of a takeover, the offer document which specifies the acquirer's intentions pertinent to the future businesses of the target company (in particular the employment and the locations) and the board's opinion on the takeover offer as required by the City Code may provide the relevant stakeholders with essential information about how their interests would be affected. Nevertheless, even with the relevant information, the stakeholders may still have no channel to engage in the board's decisions and make their voice (pros or cons of the takeover) heard. The 2018 U.K. CG Code,

[338] Chalaczkiewicz-Ladna & MacNeil, 2020: it was found that in an interview of the FTSE 100 companies, many participant companies were confused as to the application of Sect. 172 (especially regarding where and how they should be reported) and directors' awareness in this regard was perceived to be inadequate.

[339] Ibid.

[340] See Esser and MacNeil, 2019.

[341] Ibid.

[342] Employees at larger companies (those with more than fifty employees) in the U.K. have the right to information about the development of corporate activities and economic situation of the company and right to consultation about major corporate changes, particularly redundancies. See Sect. 20 of Information and Consultation of Employees Regulations 2004 (Statutory Instrument 2004 No. 3426) of the U.K. This document followed and implemented the General Framework for Informing and Consulting Employees (Directive 2002/14/EC) at the EU level and provides employees in large companies with rights to be informed and consulted on a wide range of business issues. According to Directive 2002/14/EC, the information and consultation ("I&C" hereinafter) right of employees covers data on a company's "recent and probable development of activities and economic situation, employment structure and probable development, especially if there is a threat to jobs, and decisions that could lead to substantial changes in the way work is organized or in contractual relations". See EUR-LEX.EUROPA.EU. EU General Rules on Employee Information and Consultation. Available at: https://eur-lex.europa.eu/legal-content/EN/TXT/?uri=LEGISSUM%3Ac10817 (accessed 2 June 2022). See also Kraakman et al. (2017), p. 91.

as a complement to the CA 2006 and the City Code, provides some engagement mechanisms for the stakeholders in corporate activities, in particular for employees, which will be discussed in the following section.

3.4.3.3 The Stakeholder Engagement Mechanisms Under the 2018 U.K. CG Code

Corporate governance came to prominence in the U.K. after the Cadbury Committee released the Report on Financial Aspects of Corporate Governance ("The Cadbury Report" hereinafter) in 1992.[343] The Cadbury Report contained recommendations and is widely accepted as the first "comply or explain" governance code.[344] It laid the foundation for the U.K. corporate governance system since then and significantly influenced corporate governance developments throughout the world.[345] At the heart of the Cadbury Report was a Code of Best Practice designed for all listed companies to achieve the necessary high standards of corporate behaviour.[346] The listed companies registered in the U.K., as a continuing obligation of being listed, are required to state whether they are complying with the Code of Best Practice and to give reasons for any areas of non-compliance.[347] This "comply or explain" principle can be classified as a "market-based" or "self-regulatory" approach to promote good corporate governance,[348] and it is observed that this principle remains important as part of a strong corporate governance framework in the U.K.[349] The Code of Best Practice and the "comply or explain" principle form the basis for the current U.K. Corporate Governance Code, the application of which is overseen by the independent regulator—the Financial Reporting Council.[350]

In 2016, the U.K. government launched a Green Paper Consultation to seek views on how to improve its corporate governance framework.[351] Based on the feedback

---

[343] Du Plessis et al., 2018, p. 259. The Cadbury Committee was established by the Financial Reporting Council, the London Stock Exchange, and the accountancy profession in May 1991 to focus particularly on the control and reporting functions of board of directors and the role of auditors. See The Cadbury Report available at: https://ecgi.global/sites/default/files/codes/documents/cadbury.pdf (accessed 18 January 2021).

[344] Ibid, p. 260.

[345] Ibid.

[346] See para 1.3 of The Cadbury Report.

[347] Ibid.

[348] Du Plessis et al., 2017, p. 561. See also Du Plessis et al., 2018, p. 263 (the authors classified the "comply or explain" rule as a "soft-law" approach).

[349] See Financial Reporting Council (January 2017). Developments in Corporate Governance and Stewardship 2016. Available at: https://www.frc.org.uk/getattachment/ca1d9909-7e32-4894-b2a7-b971b4406130/Developments-in-Corporate-Governance-and-Stewardship-2016.pdf (accessed 18 January 2021), see p. 4.

[350] Du Plessis et al., 2018, p. 261. See the homepage of the Financial Reporting Council (FRC) at: https://www.frc.org.uk/ (accessed 21 January 2021).

[351] See Department for Business, Energy and Industrial Strategy (November 2016). Corporate Governance Reform: Green Paper.

received from interested parties, the Government made the Response to the green paper consultation in 2017, which set out a package of measures to enhance corporate performance in the U.K.[352] In 2018, the Financial Reporting Council published the 2018 U.K. CG Code, which is applicable to all companies with a premium listing, whether incorporated in the U.K. or elsewhere, and applies to accounting periods beginning on or after 1 January 2019.

The 2018 U.K. CG Code emphasizes building positive relationships between the company and its stakeholders and strengthening stakeholders' voice at the board level.[353] It requires the board to "understand the views of the company's other key stakeholders" and to "describe in the annual report how their interests and the matters set out in Sect. 172 of the CA 2006 have been considered". To this extent, the content of the 2018 U.K. CG Code reinforces the "enlightened shareholder value" stance under the CA 2006 and complements the general provisions concerning the directors' duty under Sect. 172.

Under the CA 2006, the disclosure of non-financial stakeholder information has evolved to meet the needs of stakeholders; meanwhile, it seems that there has been less focus on the stakeholders' role in engaging in corporate decision-making.[354] The 2018 U.K. CG Code goes further than Sect. 172 of the CA 2006 by setting out mechanisms for workforce engagement on the board; and instead of enumerating a set of rigid rules, it offers flexibility through the application of principles and the continuation of the "comply or explain" approach. It requires that "the board should keep engagement mechanisms under review so that they remain effective"; and among other stakeholders, it sets out mechanisms for the workforce engagement, requiring the board to use one, or a combination, of the following methods: (i) a director appointed from the workforce; (ii) a formal workforce advisory panel; and (iii) a designated non-executive director.[355] In the event in which the board has not chosen one or more of them, it should explain what alternative arrangements are in place and why it considers that they are effective.[356]

As another complement, the 2018 Guidance on Board Effectiveness ("The 2018 U.K. Guidance") gives examples of the key stakeholders with which the company has to build and maintain good relationships.[357] Those include the workforce, customers, suppliers, regulators, government, bondholders, banks and other creditors, trade

---

[352] See Department for Business, Energy and Industrial Strategy (August 2017). Corporate Governance Reform: The Government response to the green paper consultation. Available at: https://assets.publishing.service.gov.uk/government/uploads/system/uploads/attachment_data/file/640631/corporate-governance-reform-government-response.pdf (accessed 17 January 2021).

[353] Financial Reporting Council (2018). Revised U.K. Corporate Governance Code 2018 highlights. Available at: https://www.frc.org.uk/getattachment/524d4f4b-62df-4c76-926a-66e223ca0893/2018-UK-Corporate-Governance-Code-highlights.pdf (accessed 2 June 2022). See p. 1.

[354] See Esser & MacNeil, 2019.

[355] See Provision 5 of the 2018 U.K. CG Code.

[356] Ibid.

[357] Financial Reporting Council (July 2018). Guidance on Board Effectiveness. Available at: https://www.frc.org.uk/getattachment/61232f60-a338-471b-ba5a-bfed25219147/2018-Guidance-on-Board-Effectiveness-FINAL.PDF (accessed 2 June 2022).

unions and community groups.[358] It should be noted that the 2018 U.K. Guidance is not mandatory. Although boards are encouraged to refer to the 2018 U.K. Guidance alongside the 2018 U.K. CG Code, it is for the individual company to decide on the governance arrangements based on the company's circumstances. Nevertheless, the 2018 U.K. Guidance still sheds light on the relevant societal interests which the companies are encouraged to consider and protect in corporate activities such as takeovers.

Where the listed companies implement the workforce engagement mechanisms as listed in the 2018 U.K. CG Code, the employees who can participate in the board decisions in a takeover may consider the interests of non-shareholder stakeholder groups, particularly the interests of the employee group, based on the information they get from the non-financial statement. To that extent, the strategic report, particularly the non-financial stakeholder statement, when combined with the stakeholder engagement mechanisms, may also provide protection to non-shareholder stakeholders in a takeover situation.

3.4.4 Intermediate Conclusion

In the takeover law regime, the City Code provides for mechanisms to protect the interests of target shareholders and other stakeholders, with the focus dedicated on shareholder protection. The "non-frustration rule" aims at restricting the board of directors' anti-takeover actions and ensuring that shareholders have the power to decide on the merit of an offer. The mechanisms of "post-offer undertaking" and "post-offer intention statement" may incentivize acquirers to make promises and arrangements for other stakeholders (such as the employees, environmental protection, the development of local community, etc.). The disclosure requirement on the acquirer with regard to how the offer would affect the business, employees and other stakeholders (such as stakeholders of the pension scheme(s)) and requirement for the target board to give its opinion on the takeover offer also take into account the interests of other non-shareholder stakeholders.

In the corporate governance regime, the CA 2006 features an "enlightened shareholder value" by requiring the directors to consider non-shareholder stakeholders in their decisions and publish strategic reports on stakeholder matters. Given the fact that the stakeholders still lack an engagement mechanism in a takeover, to what extent this "enlightened shareholder value" could really make a difference in protecting other stakeholders in takeovers is open for further debate. The U.K. CG Code, as a complement to the CA 2006 in this field, does provide for some stakeholder engagement mechanisms, particularly for employees in corporate decisions. Nevertheless, such mechanisms are implemented on a "comply or explain" basis, meaning that listed companies can still decide in individual takeover situations whether to engage other stakeholders in the board's decision.

---

358 Ibid.

3.5 Conclusion

The analysis in this chapter illustrates that currently the regulatory framework of the U.K. covers some legally recognized public interest considerations, the interests of corporate stakeholders and other societal interests affected by a takeover. The protection mechanisms vary with regard to the different stakeholders and societal interests.

Protection of the Legally Recognized Public Interest Considerations

The EA 2002 and the U.K. Security Act 2021 recognize some public interest considerations in takeovers. Among others, the national security interest was of first concern in the EA 2002 before it was replaced by virtue of the U.K. Security Act 2021. According to the cases as of December 2020, national security concerns often arise in foreign takeovers in sectors closely related to the defence area and involve risks to "the maintenance of the U.K.'s strategic capabilities" and "the protection of classified information and technology". In addition to the national security interest, the EA 2002 also recognized effective competition, accurate presentation of news, free expression of opinion in newspapers, media plurality and some standards objectives of broadcasting and stability of the financial system as public interest considerations. The cases as discussed in this chapter shed light on the detailed meaning of these considerations. Against the background of the COVID-19 pandemic, a new consideration of the country's capability to combat public health emergencies was added into the public interest category under the EA 2002 in 2020, the meaning of which still needs to be explored in combination with future cases in this area. With regard to the protection mechanisms, the EA 2002 sets out a "public interest intervention" mechanism which allows the Secretary of State to intervene in takeovers based on the recognized public interest reasons. The public interest intervention process runs parallel with the merger control process. In previous cases, most of the public interest interventions were launched by the Secretary of State under the national security reason. With the coming into force of the U.K. Security Act 2021, the U.K. enters into a new FDI screening regime, where takeovers in certain areas of the economy are considered as bearing high risk(s) to national security and therefore are subject to mandatory notification obligation. The mandatory notification is backed up with the Government's call-in power, meaning that the Secretary of State may intervene in and assess takeovers and mergers which (s)he reasonably believes (may) give rise to national security risks. The new regime largely expands the power of the Government in reviewing both foreign and domestic takeovers to protect the national security interest.

Protection of the Interests of Corporate Stakeholders and Other Societal Interests Affected by a Takeover

In the takeover law regime, protecting target shareholders is the main task of the City Code. Through the "non-frustration rule", the City Code restricts the board of directors' actions during a takeover. The CA 2006, in the corporate law regime, introduced the so-called "enlightened shareholder value" doctrine. Under the CA 2006, directors are required to "have regard to" other stakeholders (such as employees, creditors, suppliers, environment, etc.), which in principle, may promote the protection for these stakeholders in corporate activities such as takeovers. Nevertheless, the ambiguity in the current provisions still casts doubt on the extent to which this "enlightened shareholder value" could really play a role in protecting the interests of these stakeholders in a takeover.

Another reflection of the "enlightened shareholder value" is the board of directors' duty to provide a strategic report which contains a statement with non-financial information and sustainability information. Such non-financial and sustainability statement may provide the stakeholders with information on how corporate activities affect their interests and whether and how directors have considered their interests in their decisions. In the event of a takeover, the City Code further requires the acquirer company to disclose its intentions concerning the future businesses of the target and the target board to provide its opinion on the offer. Such information may play a role in reducing the information asymmetries between non-shareholder stakeholders and the parties to the takeover. To this extent, it may provide protection to these stakeholders. Nevertheless, the CA 2006 and the City Code do not provide relevant stakeholders with direct mechanisms to engage in the board's decisions in a takeover. As a complement, the 2018 U.K. CG Code stipulates workforce engagement mechanisms for listed companies. In takeovers, such mechanisms may promote the board to really consider the interests of other stakeholders, particularly of the employees. Moreover, the City Code allows the takeover parties to make commitments on the arrangement of non-shareholder stakeholders and societal interests through the "post-offer undertakings" and "post-offer intention statement". Previous cases show that the takeover parties, to relieve public concerns, often make commitments such as providing equal treatment for employees, sustaining the key factories in the local community, continuing the R&D investment and supporting the environmental-friendly production strategies.

Chapter 4
The Regulatory Framework of Germany

Abstract This chapter explores the regulatory framework of Germany to answer two questions: (1) what are the relevant societal interests that are protected under the German framework; and (2) what are the protection mechanisms. It first examines the competition law and FDI screening regulation in the German regulatory framework to conclude the public interest considerations that are recognized and protected in takeovers. Following that, it analyses the takeover law, corporate law and the self-regulatory corporate governance code of Germany to detect what other stakeholders are protected and how are their interests regulated in the current regulatory framework of Germany.

4.1 Introduction

The Act against Restraints of Competition (GWB) provides for rules regulating the merger control regime in Germany. In addition to this, it stipulates rules allowing for a separate responsible authority, through a separate procedure, to review and recognize the public interest considerations in an anti-competitive takeover and to give exemption to the takeover based on such considerations. Section 4.2, by analysing the relevant rules in the GWB and discussing the past decisions in this field, concludes what kinds of societal interests have been recognized as the crucial public interest considerations.

In the FDI screening regime, the Foreign Trade and Payments Act (AWG) and the Foreign Trade and Payments Ordinance (AWV) incorporate rules on reviewing foreign takeovers. In recent years, the Government has been issuing several amendments to the two regulations to enhance its power in this field. Section 4.3 explores recent reforms in this area and analyses how such reforms affect the protection of the relevant societal interests in foreign takeovers.

Section 4.4 discusses the relevant rules in the takeover law regime in conjunction with those in the corporate governance regime. In the takeover law regime, the Securities Acquisition and Takeover Act (WpÜG) prescribes rules concerning the decision-making power to take anti-takeover actions in the target. Such rules

H. Ai, *Protecting Societal Interests in Corporate Takeovers*,
https://doi.org/10.1007/978-981-19-7546-2_4

are closely linked to the basic corporate governance mechanisms (such as the two-tier board and co-determination system) under the corporate law for German stock corporations—the Stock Corporation Act (AktG). The WpÜG also provides for rules to ensure the disclosure of information on stakeholder issues in takeovers, which reflect the requirements on the management to provide a non-financial statement in the German Commercial Code (HGB) and the AktG. To avoid repetition in the discussion, Sect. 4.4 thus examines the relevant mechanisms under the WpÜG in combination with the AktG and HGB. In the corporate governance area, the German Corporate Governance Code complements the AktG by providing for principles, recommendations and suggestions of acknowledged good corporate governance standards, some of which cover the protection of stakeholders in corporate activities. To the extent where it is of relevance, Sect. 4.4 also discusses the private regulation under the German Corporate Governance Code. Section 4.5, based on the discussions in previous sections, makes conclusions of this chapter.

4.2 Competition Law—The Act Against Restraints of Competition

The Act against Restraints of Competition (the "GWB" hereinafter) is the applicable regulation in the merger control regime of Germany.[1] The objective of the GWB is to preserve and safeguard undistorted competition by combatting any anti-competition effects caused by market players.[2] Under the GWB, this "public interest exemption" mechanism is designed as a safety valve in outstanding cases where non-competition public interests trump the harms on competition that a takeover or merger may

[1] Act against Restraints of Competition (Gesetz gegen Wettbewerbsbeschränkungen) (GWB) (Issued on 26 August 1958. The German official version of the GWB was published on 26 June 2013 (BGBI. I S. 1750, 3245), which incorporates recent amendments in 2021 and 2022, see it available at: https://www.gesetze-im-internet.de/gwb/BJNR252110998.html (accessed 3 June 2022); the official English version available online has not incorporated the new amendments in 2022, see it available at: https://www.gesetze-im-internet.de/englisch_gwb/englisch_gwb.html#p0759 (accessed 3 June 2022). Under the new regime introduced by this amendment, the merger control authority will be able to prohibit very specific anti-competitive behaviour by platform companies with outstanding cross-market importance in digital markets. The amendment also raises the national turnover thresholds for merger control: mergers will be subject to merger control review only if, among other conditions, one of the companies concerned achieves an annual turnover in Germany of at least 50 million euros (previously 25 million euros) and if another company participating in the merger achieves an annual turnover in Germany amounting to at least 17.5 million euros (previously five million euros). See more introduction to this amendment at: https://www.bmwi.de/Redaktion/DE/Pressemitteilungen/2021/01/20210118-altmaier-mit-dem-gwb-digitalisierungsgesetz-schaffen-wir-ein-modernes-wettbewerbsrecht-fuer-das-digitale-zeitalter.html (accessed 25 February 2021).

[2] Vieweg and Fischer (2019), p. 195. The original description in German is "Kartellrecht (GWB) Schutz der Freiheit des Wettbewerbs gegen Beschränkungen (Quantität) Ziel des Kartellrechts ist die Erhaltung und Sicherung eines unverfälschten Wettbewerbs durch Bekämpfung von Wettbewerbsbeeinträchtigungen durch Wirtschaftssubjekte."

cause.[3] This section mainly explores what societal interests have been recognized as "public interest" reasons in past decisions of the GWB and what is the procedure for implementing this "public interest exemption" mechanism.

4.2.1 Background to the "Public Interest Exemption" Mechanism: The Recognized Public Interest Considerations and Relevant Procedure

When reviewing a takeover or merger, the Federal Cartel Office ("Bundeskartellamt", the "BKartA" hereinafter) considers only the competitive concerns of a concentration to decide if it would significantly impede effective competition and should be prohibited.[4] A decision based on the competition criteria closes the merger control proceedings before the BKartA.[5] To protect the BKartA from being subject to political pressure, the GWB provides for a "public interest exemption" mechanism to allow some important societal interests, if recognized as a "public interest" to be protected in takeovers. The "public interest exemption" mechanism empowers the Minister of the Federal Ministry for Economic Affairs and Climate Action (BMWK)[6] (the Minister) upon application, to issue a Ministerial Authorization to permit a takeover or merger on two grounds: (1) "the restraint of competition is outweighed by the advantages to the economy as a whole resulting from such concentration", (2) or "the concentration is justified by an overriding public interest".[7]

Put together, the two grounds for a Ministerial Authorization—"advantages to the economy" ("gesamtwirtschaftlichen Vorteilen") and "an overriding public interest" ("ein überragendes Interesse der Allgemeinheit") are referred to as "non-competition public interest" in this Chapter. Only after the BKartA makes the decision to prohibit the concentration, can the parties of the takeover or merger concerned apply in writing

---

[3] BUNDESKARTELLAMT.DE (10 June 2016). Working Party No. 3 on Co-operation and Enforcement—Public interest considerations in merger control (Note by Germany). Available at: https://www.bundeskartellamt.de/SharedDocs/Publikation/EN/Diskussions_Hintergrundpapiere/2016/OECD_2016_Public_interest_considerations_in_merger_control.pdf?__blob=publicationFile&v=2h (accessed 3 February 2021). See p. 2.

[4] Section 36 of the GWB. See Busche and Röhling (2014), p. 330.

[5] BUNDESKARTELLAMT.DE (10 June 2016). Working Party No. 3 on Co-operation and Enforcement—Public interest considerations in merger control (Note by Germany). See p. 2.

[6] Before December 2021, the responsible authority was the "Federal Ministry for Economic Affairs and Energy (BMWi)". With the change of responsibilities subject to Organisationserlass des Bundeskanzlers Olaf Scholz, the Federal Ministry for Economic Affairs and Energy (BMWi) was renamed "Federal Ministry for Economic Affairs and Climate Action (BMWK)" in December 2021. See Bundesministerium für Wirtschaft und Klimaschutz (BMWK) (1 February 2022). "Bundesministerium für Wirtschaft und Energie (BMWi)" heißt jetzt "Bundesministerium für Wirtschaft und Klimaschutz (BMWK)". Available at: https://www.exist.de/EXIST/Redaktion/DE/Aktuelles/Nachrichten/Wichtige-Mitteilung-fuer-alle-EXIST-Projekte.html (accessed 28 April 2022).

[7] Section 42 of the GWB.

to the BMWK for a Ministerial Authorization.[8] The Ministerial Authorization thus serves as a "public interest exemption" to takeovers that have anti-competitive effects. The Minister, through a separate procedure from the BKartA's merger control, should decide whether the harms to competition which have been recognized by the BKartA can be outweighed by the non-competition public interest reasons.[9] In this way, the BKartA is confined to consider purely competitive criteria, and the Minister of the BMWK, based on the opinions from the Monopolies Commission, could make an independent decision on the non-competition public interest considerations.[10] The two-stage procedure is regarded as a compromise between the proponents for a merger control regime based on purely competitive concerns and the supporters for a merger control regime based on wide-ranging industrial policies.[11]

The GWB does not provide for specific considerations or criteria for interpreting the "advantages to the economy" or "an overriding public interest". It only requires that the authorization may be granted only if the scope of the restraint of competition does not endanger the market economy ("marktwirtschaftliche Ordnung nicht gefährdet wird").[12] As the political circumstances are often unknown during the decision-making procedure, it is not easy to predict whether a Ministerial Authorization can be granted in an individual case.[13] In the Ministerial Authorization review, opinions from the Monopolies Commission prior to the Minister's decision provide the public with an overview of the weight of the relevant societal interests in takeovers. Where the Minister's decision deviates from the Monopolies Commission's opinion, it should state the reasons for the deviation in its decision.[14] The Minister has a maximum of eight months to decide on an application for the Ministerial Authorization.[15] During the decision-making process of the Minister, the relevant undertakings as well as the Monopolies Commission have a right to a public hearing.[16] After the decision is made, the undertakings concerned may file an appeal against the Minister's decision at the Düsseldorf Higher Regional Court; third parties

[8] Subsection 42(3) of the GWB.

[9] Subsection 42(1) of the GWB.

[10] The Monopolies Commission ("Monopolkommission") is a permanent, independent expert committee which advises the German government and legislature in the areas of competition policymaking, competition law, and regulation. It publishes occasion-related Special Reports ("Sondergutachten") in the Ministerial Authorization proceedings. See the mission of the Monopolies Commission available at: https://monopolkommission.de/en/monopolies-commission.html (accessed 3 February 2021).

[11] Busche and Röhling (2014), p. 331.

[12] Subsection 42(1) of the GWB.

[13] Busche and Röhling (2014), p. 333.

[14] Subsection 42(1) of the GWB.

[15] Subsection 42(4) of the GWB.

[16] Section 56(7) of the GWB.

may also appeal against the decision by which an authorization is granted pursuant to Section 42 if they claim that the decision infringed their rights.[17]

In practice, it is very difficult to obtain a Ministerial Authorization. Until December 2021, the Ministerial approval was only granted 10 times (some with conditions) in 23 applications.[18] The past decisions by the Minister provide practical guidance on what societal interests in takeovers are normally protected under this public interest exemption mechanism. In some cases, the Minister's authorization gave rise to considerable criticism, even the challenge to abolish this mechanism.[19]

4.2.2 Analysis of Previous Ministerial Authorization Decisions

This section studies fifteen out of the twenty-three previous applications for a Ministerial Authorization.[20] The fifteen cases are listed in Table 4.1 and include all of the ten applications which were finally granted with a Ministerial Authorization (some were granted with conditions or partly granted).[21] In the fifteen cases, the "overriding public interest" or "advantages to the economy as a whole" reasons put forward by the applicants cover a wide range of societal aspects. After examining the Monopolies Commission's Special Reports ("Sondergutachten zur Ministererlaubnis")[22] and the Minister's decisions, this section divides the relevant arguments as submitted by the

[17] Subsections 73(2)(4) of the GWB. For more procedural details of the Ministerial Authorization, see the policy introduction published by the BMWK (in English), available at: https://www.bmwk.de/Redaktion/EN/Dossier/competition-policy.html (accessed 3 February 2021).

[18] See the list of the 23 applications at Bundesministerium für Wirtschaft und Klimaschutz (BMWK). Übersicht über die bisherigen Anträge auf Ministererlaubnis nach § 24 Abs.3/§ 42 GWB, available at: https://www.bmwk.de/Redaktion/DE/Downloads/Wettbewerbspolitik/antraege-auf-ministererlaubnis.pdf?__blob=publicationFile&v=9 (accessed 27 April 2022).

[19] Vieweg and Fischer (2019), p. 234.

[20] The choice of the fifteen cases from the twenty-three applications is based on the discussions in three significant German books in this area: (1) Busche and Röhling (2014); (2) Vieweg and Fischer (2019); (3) Bechtold and Bosch (2018). The choice mainly considers the case relevance (the frequency of relevant discussions) to "the public interest consideration" under Section 42, the final results of the Ministerial Authorization and the case significance on the market.

[21] The other eight cases which are not discussed in this section include: (1) SACHS/GKN (21.03.78, Not granted by the Monopolies Commission; Withdrawn by the applicant), (2) BURDA/SPRINGER (17.11.81, Not granted by the Monopolies Commission; Withdrawn by the applicant), (3) KLÖCKNER/SEN (08.11.84, Not granted by the Monopolies Commission; Withdrawn by the applicant), (4) VEW/SIDECHAR (19.07.85, Not granted by the Monopolies Commission, Not granted by the Minister), (5) RHEINMETALL/WMF (23.07.85, Withdrawn by the applicant), (6) DAIMLER-BENZ/MAN/ENASA (14.08.90, Withdrawn by the applicant); (7) BAYWA/WLZ (29.01.92, Not granted), (8) POTASH CORP./KALI UND SALZ (27.03.97, Not granted by the Monopolies Commission, Not granted by the Minister).

[22] See the list of the Monopolies Commission's Special Reports on Ministerial Approval ("Sondergutachten zur Ministererlaubnis") available at: https://monopolkommission.de/de/gutachten/sondergutachten/sondergutachten-ministererlaubnis.html (accessed 26 April 2022).

Table 4.1 The fifteen cases of ministerial authorization under Section 42 GWB[23]

No.	Case	Application time	Monopolies commission's opinion	Minister's decision
1	VEBA/GELSEN BERG	09.01.74	Not granted	Granted (01.02.74)
2	VAW/KA1SER/PREUSSAG	24.01.75	Not granted	Not granted (26.06.75)
3	BABCOCK/ARTOS	28.04.76	Not granted	Granted with conditions (17.10.76)
4	THYSSEN/HÜLLER-HILLE	27.01.77	Partly granted	Partly granted (01.08.77)
5	VEBA/BP	04.10.78	Not granted	Granted with conditions (05.03.79)
6	IBH/WIBAU	07.08.81	Granted	Granted (09.12.81)
7	DAIMLER-BENZ/MBB	02.05.89	Granted with conditions	Granted with conditions (06.09.89)
8	MAN/SULZER	20.09.89	Not granted	Not granted (24.01.90)
9	E.ON/RUHRGAS	15.02.02, 04.03.02	Not granted	Granted with conditions (05.07.02, 18.09.02)
10	HOLTZBRINCK/BERLINER VERLAG	13.01.03	Not granted	Withdrawn by the applicant (29.09.03)
11	Landkreis Rhön-Grabfeld/Rhön Klinikum AG	16.01.06	Not granted	Not granted (22.05.06)
12	Asklepios Kliniken Hamburg/Krankenhaus Mariahilf	28.09.07	Not granted	Withdrawn by the applicant (28.02.08)
13	Uniklinikum Greifswald /Kreiskrankenhaus Wolgast	07.12.07	Granted	Granted (17.04.08)
14	EDEKA/Kaiser's Tengelmann	29.04.15	Not granted	Granted with conditions (09.03.16)
15	Miba/Zollern	18.02.19	Not granted	Granted with conditions (19.08.19)

[23] Table 4.1 originates from Bundesministerium für Wirtschaft und Klimaschutz (BMWK). Übersicht über die bisherigen Anträge auf Ministererlaubnis nach § 24 Abs.3/§ 42 GWB. The original Table listed the 23 applications and was in German.

applicants in the fifteen cases into two categories: (1) arguments that were recognized by the Monopolies Commission or the Minister as "in principle satisfying the 'public interest exemption'"; (2) arguments that were regarded by the Monopolies Commission and the Minister as "in principle not satisfying the 'public interest exemption'" (nevertheless, in exceptional cases, such arguments might be recognized together with other considerations). The first category further includes two types: (i) recognized public interest arguments the establishment of which has been proven by the applicant in the selected cases; (ii) recognized public interest arguments the establishment of which has not been sufficiently proven by the applicant in the cases. The second category also consists of two types: (i) arguments in principle considered as not belonging to public interest but were recognized in exceptional cases (mainly because of political policies at that time); (ii) arguments in principle not belonging to public interest and were denied in the individual cases. The following part will discuss the four types of arguments against individual cases in sequence.

4.2.2.1 Arguments in Principle Satisfying the "Public Interest Exemption" Mechanism

(1) Type 1: Arguments the Establishment of Which Has Been Proven in the Fifteen Cases

Six arguments were recognized as the public interest considerations, the establishment of which was proven by the takeover parties in the fifteen cases.

(a) *Maintaining Important Know-how and Innovation Potential in Specific Areas*

The takeover or merger's effect on maintaining the know-how in specific areas was submitted by the applicant as a public interest argument in four cases: (1) THYSSEN/HÜLLER-HILLE (in the special machine manufacturing area),[24] (2) IBH/WIBAU (in the asphalt mixing plant area),[25] (3) MAN/SULZER (in the mechanical and plant engineering area),[26] (4) Miba/Zollern (in the slide bearing production area).[27] In all of the four cases, the Monopolies Commission assessed the submitted proof and concluded that the know-how effect of the merger and takeover

[24] See the special report (in German): Sondergutachten der Monopolkommission (Band 4–6): Zusammenschlußvorhaben der Thyssen Industrie AG mit der Hüler Hille GmbH. Nomos Verlagsgesellschaft, Baden-Baden 1977 (ISBN 3-7890-0311-5).

[25] See the special report (in German): Sondergutachten der Monopolkommission (Band 10 und 12): Zusammenschlußvorhaben der IBH Holding AG mit der WIBAU AG. Nomos Verlagsgesellschaft, Baden-Baden 1982 (ISBN 3-7890-0768-4).

[26] See the special report (in German): Sondergutachten der Monopolkommission (Band 19): Zusammenschlußvorhaben der MAN Aktiengesellschaft und der Gebrüder Sulzer Aktiengesellschaft. Nomos Verlagsgesellschaft, Baden-Baden 1982 (ISBN 3-7890-2170-9).

[27] See the online special report (in German): MONOPOLKOMMISSION.DE (2019). Sondergutachten 81: Zusammenschlussvorhaben der Miba AG mit der Zollern GmbH & Co. KG (Sondergutachten der Monopolkommission gemäß § 42 Abs. 5 Satz 1 GWB). Available at: https://monopolkommission.de/images/PDF/SG/s81_volltext_oeffentlich.pdf (accessed 25 May 2022).

failed to satisfy the public interest exemption criteria. However, in Miba/Zollern, the Minister overthrew the Monopolies Commission's recommendation by holding that the "know-how and innovation potential for energy transition and sustainability is sufficient in the case and goes significantly further than the restriction of competition brought about by the merger".[28] It recognized this argument and permitted the merger in the end.

In principle, the Monopolies Commission held that, to be recognized as a public interest, the preservation of the know-how caused by the merger must have a particularly high value for society[29]; and in terms of quality of technology, it must have macroeconomic growth effects.[30] In its assessment, the Monopolies Commission considered whether the know-how belonged to the high-technology area and was easily accessible in the area, and whether the preservation effect was specific to the merger. For example, in IBH/WIBAU, the Monopolies Commission believed that the know-how in the field of control technology for asphalt mixing plants can be owned or procured by any company operating close to the market quickly without much effort, and therefore denied this argument.[31] In THYSSEN/HÜLLER-HILLE, the Monopolies Commission found that the technological know-how of HÜLLER-HILLE GmbH, the leader in the special purpose machinery industry, has not increased as a result of the merger with THYSSEN, so the securing of the know-how does not require the merger nor justifies the merger.[32]

(b) *Strengthening of International Competitiveness*

Section 42 of the GWB explicitly provides that the international competitiveness of the merging entity is a public interest consideration that has to be taken into account in the Ministerial Authorization.[33] In the following cases, the applicants claimed this argument: (1) VAW/KAISER/PREUSSAG (in the aluminium area),[34] (2) THYSSEN/HÜLLER-HILLE, (3) IBH/WIBAU, (4) DAIMLER-BENZ/MBB (in the arms production area),[35] (5) MAN/SULZER, (6) E.ON/RUHRGAS (in the energy

[28] See para 50 of the Ministerial Authorization decision (in German): Bundesministerium für Wirtschaft und Klimaschutz (BMWK) (August 2019). DER BUNDESMINISTER FÜR WIRTSCHAFT UND ENERGIE (Gesch.-Z.: I B 2—20302/14-02). Available at: https://www.bmwi.de/Redaktion/DE/Downloads/V/verfuegung-verwaltungsverfahren-miba-zollern.pdf?__blob=publicationFile&v=6 (last visited: January 26 2021).

[29] See para 147 of the Special Report of Miba/Zollern.

[30] See para 55 of the Special Report of MAN/Sulzer.

[31] See para 53 of the Special Report of IBH/Wibau.

[32] See para 57 of the Special Report of THYSSEN/HÜLLER-HILLE.

[33] Subsection 42(1) of the GWB.

[34] See the special report (in German): Sondergutachten der Monopolkommission (Band 3): Zusammenschlußvorhaben der Kaiser Aluminium & Chemical Corporation, der Preussag AG und der Vereinigte Industrie-Unternehmungen AG. Nomos Verlagsgesellschaft, Baden-Baden 1975 (ISBN 3-7890-0159-7).

[35] See the special report (in German): Sondergutachten der Monopolkommission (Band 18): Zusammenschlußvorhaben der DAIMLER-BENZ AG mit der MESSERSCHMITT-BÖLKOW-BLOHM GmbH. Nomos Verlagsgesellschaft, Baden-Baden 1989 (ISBN 3-7890-1847-3).

supply area),[36] (7) Miba/Zollern. Only in IBH/WIBAU, the Monopolies Commission and the Minister recognized that the merger would strengthen WIBAU AG's competitive position in foreign markets.[37] In the other six cases, this public interest was considered as not established by the merger.[38]

In VAW/KAISER/PREUSSAG, the Monopolies Commission admitted that "by means of rationalization effects, the concentration may indirectly improve the competitiveness of the undertakings involved in international markets".[39] However, it also posited that "even without the merger, the companies involved have reached a size that enables them to compete in the international markets, and it is not clear why further growth in size is necessary for the competitiveness of the companies".[40] To this extent, the Monopolies Commission questioned whether the international competitiveness effect based on the rationalization advantages of the merger could justify the proposed concentration.[41] In THYSSEN/HÜLLER-HILLE, the Monopolies Commission held that "the company size is not a prerequisite for international competition."[42] Consistent with this opinion, it also emphasized that "the leading position of the German machine tool industry on the world market in the past was achieved by a large number of small and medium-sized independent companies."[43]

In E.ON/RUHRGAS, the Monopolies Commission went further to specify that "the primary protection objective of the GWB is domestic competition and therefore improving international competitiveness should, in principle, be regarded as secondary."[44] It clearly illustrated that "improving the international competitive position of a company is to be interpreted restrictively by the law, i.e., it must be demonstrated in concrete terms that the company cannot survive in the long term without the merger on international markets".[45] This position highlights a prerequisite for recognizing this argument as public interest, i.e., the merger must be indispensable for the parties' participation in international competition.[46] In the most recent case—Miba/Zollern, the Monopolies Commission held a similar position that this argument could be recognized if it was definitively proven that "the merger creates economies

[36] See the online special report (in German): MONOPOLKOMMISSION.DE. Sondergutachten 34: Zusammenschlussvorhaben der E.ON AG mit der Gelsenberg AG und der E.ON AG mit der Bergemann GmbH (Sondergutachten der Monopolkommission gemäß § 42 Abs. 4 Satz 2 GWB). Available at: https://monopolkommission.de/images/PDF/SG/s34_volltext.pdf (accessed 26 January 2021).

[37] See paras 55–63 of the Special Report of IBH/WIBAU.

[38] It should be noticed that, while the Monopolies Commission did not recognize the international competitiveness effect in E.ON/RUHRGAS, the Minister finally granted this merger based on the improvement of the international competitiveness and on the security of the German gas supply. See Peyer (2012), pp. 121–144.

[39] See para 109 of the Special Report of VAW/KAISER/PREUSSAG.

[40] Ibid, para 102.

[41] Ibid, para 103.

[42] See para 53 of the Special Report of THYSSEN/HÜLLER-HILLE.

[43] Ibid.

[44] See para 192 of the Special Report of E.ON/RUHRGAS.

[45] Ibid.

[46] Ibid.

of scale which leads to the company's permanent participation in markets outside Germany, or allows or opens access to foreign markets in the first place".[47]

(c) *Retention and Creation of Jobs*

The takeover or merger's effect on preserving and creating jobs was the most frequently submitted public interest argument. Twelve out of the fifteen applications used this employment argument: (1) VAW/KAISER/PREUSSAG, (2) THYSSEN/HÜLLER-HILLE, (3) BABCOCK/ARTOS (in the technology and engineering area),[48] (4) IBH/WIBAU, (5) MAN/SULZER, (6) E.ON/RUHRGAS, (7) HOLTZBRINCK/BERLINER VERLAG (in the newspaper/publishing area),[49] (8) Landkreis Rhön-Grabfeld/Rhön Klinikum AG (in the healthcare and hospital area),[50] (9) Asklepios Kliniken Hamburg/Krankenhaus Mariahilf (in the healthcare and hospital area),[51] (10) Uniklinikum Greifswald/Kreiskrankenhaus Wolgast (in the healthcare area),[52] (11) EDEKA/Kaiser's Tengelmann (in the area of food retailing),[53] (12) Miba/Zollern.

The employment effect of the takeover or merger was interpreted in a very strict way in the twelve cases, and the Minister only recognized this argument in four

[47] See para 192 of the Special Report of Miba/Zollern.

[48] See the special report (in German): Sondergutachten der Monopolkommission (Band 4–6): Zusammenschlußvorhaben der Deutsche Babcock AG mit der Artos-Gruppe. Nomos Verlagsgesellschaft, Baden-Baden 1977 (ISBN 3-7890-0311-5).

[49] See the online special report (in German): MONOPOLKOMMISSION.DE. Sondergutachten 36: Zusammenschlussvorhaben der Georg von Holtzbrinck GmbH & Co. KG mit der Berliner Verlag GmbH & Co. KG (Sondergutachten der Monopolkommission gemäß § 42 Abs. 4 Satz 2 GWB). Available at: https://monopolkommission.de/images/PDF/SG/s36_volltext.pdf (accessed 26 January 2021). See the supplementary special report: MONOPOLKOMMISSION.DE. Sondergutachten 36: Zusammenschlussvorhaben der Georg von Holtzbrinck GmbH & Co. KG mit der Berliner Verlag GmbH& Co. KG (Ergänzendes Sondergutachten der Monopolkommission gemäß § 42 Abs. 4 Satz 2 GWB). Available at: https://monopolkommission.de/images/PDF/SG/s38_volltext.pdf (accessed 26 January 2021).

[50] See the online special report (in German): MONOPOLKOMMISSION.DE. Sondergutachten 45: Zusammenschlussvorhaben der Rhön-Klinikum AG mit dem Landkreis Rhön-Grabfeld (Sondergutachten der Monopolkommission gemäß § 42 Abs. 4 Satz 2 GWB). Available at: https://monopolkommission.de/images/PDF/SG/s45_volltext.pdf (accessed 26 January 2021).

[51] See the online special report (in German): MONOPOLKOMMISSION.DE. Sondergutachten 52: Zusammenschlussvorhaben der Asklepios Kliniken Hamburg GmbH mit der Krankenhaus Mariahilf gGmbH (Sondergutachten der Monopolkommission gemäß § 42 Abs. 4 Satz 2 GWB). Available at: https://monopolkommission.de/images/PDF/SG/s52_volltext.pdf (accessed 26 January 2021).

[52] See the online special report (in German): MONOPOLKOMMISSION.DE. Sondergutachten 53: Zusammenschlussvorhaben des Universitätsklinikums Greifswald mit der Kreiskrankenhaus Wolgast gGmbH (Sondergutachten der Monopolkommission gemäß § 42 Abs. 4 Satz 2 GWB). Available at: https://monopolkommission.de/images/PDF/SG/s53_volltext.pdf (accessed 26 January 2021).

[53] See the online special report (in German): MONOPOLKOMMISSION.DE. Sondergutachten 70: Zusammenschlussvorhaben der Edeka Zentrale AG & Co. KG mit der Kaiser's Tengelmann GmbH (Sondergutachten der Monopolkommission gemäß § 42 Abs. 4 Satz 2 GWB). Available at: https://monopolkommission.de/images/PDF/SG/s70_volltext.pdf (accessed 26 January 2021).

applications: (1) VAW/KAISER/PREUSSAG (the merger was recognized as having the effect of preventing additional unemployment), (2) BABCOCK/ARTOS (the job retention effect in this case was at first rejected by the Monopolies Commission, but then was recognized by the Minister considering the merger's job securing effect in the region), (3) IBH/WIBAU, and (4) EDEKA/Kaiser's Tengelmann (the job retention effect in this case was disputable: at first this argument was rejected by the Monopolies Commission, then the Minister recognized that the merger helped safeguard about 16,000 workers' jobs and permitted the merger; afterwards, the Ministerial Authorization was suspended by the Düsseldorf Higher Regional Court).[54]

In the early cases, the Monopolies Commission admitted that "in principle, the achievement of full employment is a primary economic policy objective, and the general public has a special interest in maintaining and safeguarding jobs".[55] After the EDEKA/Kaiser's Tengelmann case, the Minister Sigmar Gabriel reiterated that "securing workers' rights is also a requirement of the social market economy".[56] In contrast with this position, the Monopolies Commission applied rigid criteria in interpreting and assessing this argument in individual cases.

First of all, it believed that employment security should be achieved primarily through employment policy instruments that do not materially affect the functioning of the market mechanism.[57] Instead of an anti-competitive merger, other socially and competitively viable solutions (such as funds from social, regional or structural policy) should first be sought in order to solve unemployment problems.[58] Secondly, it emphasized that "the public interest in full employment does not mean that jobs can be sustained in a particular enterprise".[59] Usually, it is not easy to predict and to prove in the specific case that the future job security or creation can be achieved by the merger.[60] Past experience showed that the capacity and job development after the

[54] The Minister Sigmar Gabriel expressed his disappointment on the Court decision and repeated again that the retaining of jobs was a crucial common good in this case. See Bundesministerium für Wirtschaft und Klimaschutz (BMWK) (13 July 2016). Pressestatement: Bundesminister Sigmar Gabriel zur Entscheidung des Oberlandesgerichts Düsseldorf im Ministererlaubnisverfahren EDEKA/Kaiser's Tengelmann. Available at: https://www.bmwk.de/Redaktion/DE/Reden/2016/20160713-gabriel-zur-entscheidung-des-oberlandesgerichts-duesseldorf-im-ministererlaubnisverfahren-edeka-tengelmann.html (accessed 2 June 2022).

[55] See e.g., para 43 of the Special Report of THYSSEN/HÜLLER-HILLE; para 52 of the Special Report of MAN/SULZER; para 130 of the Special Report of Uniklinikum Greifswald/Kreiskrankenhaus Wolgast.

[56] See Bundesministerium für Wirtschaft und Klimaschutz (BMWK) (13 July 2016). Pressestatement: Bundesminister Sigmar Gabriel zur Entscheidung des Oberlandesgerichts Düsseldorf im Ministererlaubnisverfahren EDEKA/Kaiser's Tengelmann.

[57] See para 43 of the Special Report of THYSSEN/HÜLLER-HILLE.

[58] See para 52 of the Special Report of MAN/SULZER.

[59] See para 42 of the Special Report of THYSSEN/HÜLLER-HILLE; para 52 of the Special Report of MAN/SULZER; para 152 of the Special Report of Miba/Zollern.

[60] See paras 95, 96 of the Special Report of VAW/KAISER/PREUSSAG. It predicted and compared the changes to the regional unemployment rate and average national rate in the situation of the merger and without the merger.

merger was permitted usually ran differently with what the companies had assumed.[61] Besides, it also assessed whether the employment effect brought by the merger would last in the long term or only temporarily. It held that restrictions on competition were justified by the preservation of jobs only if the latter could avoid long-term structural unemployment.[62] Experience showed that mergers were usually not suitable to secure endangered jobs in the long term.[63] Only in rare cases could the merger itself influence the employment in a positive way; usually, a market dominance resulting from the merger would threaten the jobs at the competitors.[64] Therefore, to avoid temporary economic unemployment cannot be used as a justification for an impairment of the economy.[65]

Moreover, the Monopolies Commission often compared the unemployment rate of the region affected by the merger with the average unemployment rate of a wider region (usually the average national rate) to assess the quantitative weight of the problem and the urgency to solve the problem with the merger.[66] In addition to the prevalence of unemployment in the geographic areas, in some cases, it also compared the prevalence of unemployment among certain occupational groups.[67] If in some occupational groups the structural causes of unemployment cannot be excluded in some places, the merger would then not be seen as a proper way to cure such a problem.

(d) *Securing Energy Supply*

Four out of the fifteen cases were conducted in the energy supply area, in which the applicants put forward the argument of securing the energy supply in Germany, including: (1) VEBA/GELSENBERG,[68] (2) VAW/KAISER/PREUSSAG, (3) VEBA/BP,[69] (4) E.ON/RUHRGAS. In VAW/KAISER/PREUSSAG, this argument was not recognized (given that "a macroeconomic interest in a largely self-sufficient aluminium industry is not apparent")[70]; in the other three cases, the Minister assessed the energy supply security and finally permitted the merger.

The long-term safeguarding of the energy supply of the Federal Republic of Germany was first recognized as part of the public interest ("advantages to the

61 See para 203 of the Special Report of E.ON/RUHRGAS.

62 See para 43 of the Special Report of THYSSEN/HÜLLER-HILLE.

63 See para 152 of the Special Report of Miba/Zollern.

64 Busche and Röhling (2014), pp. 335–336. See e.g. para 152 of the Special Report of Miba/Zollern.

65 See para 204 of the Special Report of E.ON/RUHRGAS.

66 See e.g., Table 10 (on page 80) in the Special Report of THYSSEN/HÜLLER-HILLE; Tables 17, 18 in the Special Report of the VAW/KAISER/PREUSSAG.

67 See para 49 of the Special Report of THYSSEN/HÜLLER-HILLE.

68 See the special report (in German): Sondergutachten der Monopolkommission (Band 2): Wettbewerbliche und strukturelle Aspekte einer Zusammenfassung von Unternehmen im Energiebereich (VEBA/Gelsenberg). Nomos Verlagsgesellschaft, Baden-Baden 1975 (ISBN 3-7890-0154-6).

69 See the special report (in German): Sondergutachten der Monopolkommission (Band 8): Zusammenschlußvorhaben der Deutschen BP AG und der VEBA AG. Nomos Verlagsgesellschaft, Baden-Baden 1979 (ISBN 3-7890-0489-8).

70 See para 107 of the Special Report of VAW/KAISER/PREUSSAG.

economy as a whole") in the VEBA/GELSENBERG case.[71] In VEBA/BP, the Minister considered that the merger would help to restructure the two companies' oil business without government aid, which would contribute to the German mineral oil industry and secure 3% of Germany's crude oil demand in the long term.[72] In E.ON/RUHRGAS, the Monopolies Commission pointed out that "the use of the word 'security of supply' for various situations carries the danger that the meaning of the word will be emptied".[73] Nevertheless, in principle, the Monopolies Commission still agreed that "the objective of security of supply should be recognized as a macroeconomic advantage, which, if the proposed merger contributes to its achievement, is capable of compensating for the restrictions of competition".[74]

(e) *Environmental Objectives of the Federal Government*

The environmental benefits created by the merger were discussed in two of the fifteen cases: (1) E.ON/RUHRGAS, and (2) Miba/Zollern. In the E.ON/RUHRGAS case, the environmental argument was not recognized; and in the Miba/Zollern, the Minister finally permitted the merger based on the environmental and the employment benefits the merger would create.

For a long time, the Monopolies Commission upheld that environment protection, as a general objective stipulated in Article 20a of the Basic Law ("Grundgesetz") belongs to the overriding public interest.[75] Nevertheless, the Monopolies Commission also posited that "while the German industries, associations, and companies sometimes made agreements aiming at environment protection, it should be noted that those were only voluntary commitments"; "as there is no explicit obligation of an individual company if the desired goals were not achieved, there is thus no possibility to assign responsibility to a company".[76] For this reason, "it is impossible to control the environment protection commitments at company level".[77] Besides, in the E.ON/RUHRGAS case, the Monopolies Commission found that "E.ON has not yet indicated that it intended to give particular support to the accelerated expansion of those power plant technologies which, in view of the CO_2 emissions target, are of central importance".[78] In the most recent Miba/Zollern case, the Minister recognized the potential environmental benefits due to the improved R&D ability, which would be a result of the preservation of the know-how and the synergies effect of the joint venture.[79]

---

[71] See para (2) on page 10 of the Special Report of VEBA/GELSENBERG.

[72] This case was referred to in para 158 of the Special Report of E.ON/RUHRGAS.

[73] See para 156 of the Special Report of E.ON/RUHRGAS.

[74] Ibid, para 158.

[75] Ibid.

[76] Ibid.

[77] Ibid.

[78] Ibid, para 210.

[79] See para 251 of Ministerial Authorization (in German): Bundesministerium für Wirtschaft und Klimaschutz (BMWK) (August 2019). DER BUNDESMINISTER FÜR WIRTSCHAFT UND ENERGIE (Gesch.-Z.: I B 2—20302/14-02).

(f) *Preservation of the Status as the University Hospital and Medical Faculty as Well as the Expansion of a Research Focus of the Faculty*

This argument is closely linked to the healthcare sector and was only presented and recognized as a public interest reason in Uniklinikum Greifswald/Kreiskrankenhaus Wolgast. In this case, the Monopolies Commission held that, with the merger, "the University Hospital will be able to steer patient flows in such a way that the number of cases at the Greifswald site will rise and thus not only maintain the number of beds in Greifswald, but also significantly increase them".[80] The long-term safeguarding of the university medical status of the hospital and the existence of the medical faculty in Greifswald were therefore considered as of considerable importance to the public interest.

(2) Type 2: Arguments the Establishment of Which Has Not Been Proven in the Fifteen Cases

In the fifteen cases, the Monopolies Commission and the Minister also recognized that in principle, the defence interest, the press diversity, and societal interests related to the medical care policies belonged to the "public interest exemption" reasons under Section 42 GWB. However, the applicants using the three arguments in the relevant cases failed to concretely prove that these considerations were (or would be) achieved as a result of the takeover or merger.

(a) *Defence Interest*

In the Miba/Zollern case, the Monopolies Commission recognized the public interest in preserving or strengthening industries relevant to national defence[81]; but it disagreed with the applicant and doubted that the slide bearing production must be based in Germany so that the important national defence armaments in Germany can be produced.[82] The Monopolies Commission pointed out that "the Federal Government is committed to intensified European and Euro-Atlantic armaments co-operations, which implement equipment and procurement projects jointly for all partner nations; against this background, as in this case, a national orientation of entire value-added chains, even in the key defence-relevant industries, does not appear to be in line with the goals of the Federal Government".[83] In addition, the Monopolies Commission also considered that it was not clear that the sliding bearings of the companies involved in this case belonged to the key national technologies of the German defence industry.

(b) *Press Diversity*

The protection of press diversity was discussed in HOLTZBRINCK/BERLINER VERLAG. In this case, the Monopolies Commission recognized the public interest

[80] See paras 152, 160 of the Special Report of the Uniklinikum Greifswald/Kreiskrankenhaus Wolgast.

[81] See para 151 of the Special Report of Miba/Zollern.

[82] Ibid.

[83] Ibid.

objective of promoting the diversity of the press.[84] Nevertheless, it did not see the proposed merger as necessary for achieving this objective.[85] It also put forward that press diversity is a concern of users and the community as a whole, which should not be assessed on the basis of the business figures of the individual publishers.[86] Instead, promotion of press diversity should focus on defining appropriate framework conditions which were predominantly based on the economic independence of competing suppliers of press products.[87]

(c) *Societal Interests in the Medical Care Area*

In the medical care area, except for the preservation of the university hospital and the status of the university medical faculty, and the expansion of the research focus of the faculty as discussed in the Uniklinikum Greifswald/Kreiskrankenhaus Wolgast case, other societal interests may also be affected by a takeover or merger. These include, for example, the societal interests in securing local medical care and improving the quality of healthcare,[88] in strengthening the research focus of the Community medicine, in improving the health policy benefits and promoting health tourism,[89] and in reducing hospital costs and the corresponding efficiency advantages.[90]

In principle, the Monopolies Commission admitted that the achievement of healthcare policy objectives, the expansion of the research focus of medicine, and the significant improvements of the level of the regional healthcare performance caused by the takeover or merger were possible common good advantages within the meaning of Section 42 GWB.[91] However, in the cases where the applicants put forward these considerations, the relationships between the takeover or merger and these benefits were not adequately demonstrated.

4.2.2.2 Arguments in Principle Not Satisfying the "Public Interest Exemption" Mechanism

In addition to the above arguments, the applicants of the fifteen cases also tried to use other reasons to gain Ministerial Authorization. In principle, the Monopolies Commission and the Minister did not recognize these arguments as satisfying the "public interest exemption" conditions under Section 42. Only in exceptional cases,

[84] See para 94 of the Special Report of HOLTZBRINCK/BERLINER VERLAG.

[85] Ibid.

[86] Ibid, para 98.

[87] Ibid, para 100.

[88] This consideration has been discussed in three cases: Landkreis Rhön-Grabfeld/Rhön Klinikum AG, Asklepios Kliniken Hamburg/Krankenhaus Mariahilf, and Uniklinikum Greifswald/Kreiskrankenhaus Wolgast.

[89] This consideration has been discussed in Uniklinikum Greifswald/Kreiskrankenhaus Wolgast.

[90] This consideration has been discussed in Landkreis Rhön-Grabfeld/Rhön Klinikum AG.

[91] See paras 113, 128 of the Special Report of Uniklinikum Greifswald/Kreiskrankenhaus Wolgast, para 99 of the Special Report of Asklepios Kliniken Hamburg/Krankenhaus Mariahilf.

for some political considerations, did they admit these arguments and give an exemption for the transaction. These arguments thus shed light on what societal interests are often affected by a takeover and may lead to public concerns in practice.

(1) Type 1: Arguments in Principle Not Recognized as of Public Interest and Not Admitted in the Previous Cases

(a) *Rationalization Benefits of Takeovers*

The rationalization ("Rationalisierungsfusion") effects of a takeover or merger were claimed in some cases as a public interest: (1) VAW/KAISER/PREUSSAG, (2) BABCOCK/ARTOS, (3) DAIMLER-BENZ/MBB, (4) MAN/SULZER, (5) E.ON/RUHRGAS, (6) Landkreis Rhön-Grabfeld/Rhön Klinikum AG, and (7) Asklepios Kliniken Hamburg/Krankenhaus Mariahilf. The results showed that, in principle, the Monopolies Commission and the Minister did not recognize the rationalization advantages of a takeover or merger as satisfying the two public interest exemptions.

First of all, the Monopolies Commission gave some examples of the rationalization advantages of a takeover or merger. Rationalization effects could be observed, for example, through lower prices and better quality of the products in the market (for the customers),[92] through a higher payment or improvement of the working conditions of the employees, and through a dividend increase at publicly traded companies and increased tax payments to the state.[93] It could also be discerned from the increase in the R&D, the improvement of sales and service (through savings in personnel), etc.[94] The Monopolies Commission pointed out that sometimes the economic benefits coming from the rationalization effect of the takeover and merger only meant a redistribution of incomes, rather than real macroeconomic benefits.[95]

The Monopolies Commission also emphasized that without effective competition in the market, it could not be guaranteed that the rationalization benefits be realized and passed on to customers.[96] It held that "the rationalization advantages could only be recognized in the event where the merger is necessary to ensure technical progress or to maintain an efficient export economy in the general interest of the economy".[97] To obtain Ministerial Authorization, the rationalization advantages of a merger would only be considered if the effects have reached the extent of macroe-

[92] See para 159 of the Special Report of Landkreis Rhön-Grabfeld/Rhön Klinikum AG.

[93] See para 75 of the Special Report of VAW/KAISER/PREUSSAG.

[94] See para 49 of the Special Report of MAN/SULZER. Such rationalization benefits of a takeover or merger are usually reflected as the internal cost savings coming from the fact that fewer actual production factors are needed for a given product, or a larger volume of product is produced with the same factor input.

[95] See para 75 of the Special Report of VAW/KAISER/PREUSSAG.

[96] Ibid, para 72.

[97] Ibid.

conomic benefits.[98] Specifically, under the Ministerial Authorization procedure, the applicants must prove that: "(1) the expected efficiency gains from the takeover or merger are high and are likely to materialize; (2) the efficiency gains not only benefit the owners of the company, but also the general public; (3) the takeover or merger must be necessary to realize the efficiency advantages".[99] Moreover, the temporary rationalization benefits would also be compared with the long-term restriction on competition and permanent damage to economy in the assessment.[100]

(b) *The Takeover or Merger's Reorganization Effect and Effect in Preventing the Financial Collapse of Companies*

The past decisions show that in principle the Monopolies Commission and the Minister did not recognize this argument as of public interest. In the VAW/KAISER/PREUSSAG case, the reorganization/restructuring effect was claimed by the applicant who argued that the company would be faced with a financial collapse without the merger, but was rejected by the Monopolies Commission.[101] In THYSSEN/HÜLLER-HILLE, the Monopolies Commission observed that before the merger, the existence of the HÜLLER-HILLE was threatened, and the company experienced a sharp drop in production in all branches of special purpose machinery.[102] The Monopolies Commission believed that "after the reorganization by Thyssen Industrie AG, there was a tangible improvement in the business situation of HÜLLER-HILLE, and this development was likely to continue in view of the improving economic outlook for special purpose machinery".[103] In IBH/WIBAU, the Monopolies Commission held that "the reorganization of a business cannot by itself be regarded as a macroeconomic advantage", and that "the preservation of a particular company can therefore only be significant for the decision of the Minister, if there are other concrete overall economic advantages that outweigh the competition harms".[104]

(c) *Benefits for Local Residents*

In Asklepios Kliniken Hamburg/Krankenhaus Mariahilf and EDEKA/Kaiser's Tengelmann, the applicants claimed benefits of the transaction for local residents. In Asklepios Kliniken Hamburg/Krankenhaus Mariahilf, the side effects of the merger on the housing development in the local region were denied by the Monopolies Commission as a common good.[105] In EDEKA/Kaiser's Tengelmann, the Monopolies Commission did not believe that regional supply bottlenecks might arise without the takeover.[106]

---

[98] See para 50 of the Special Report of MAN/SULZER.

[99] See para 159 of the Special Report of Landkreis Rhön-Grabfeld/Rhön Klinikum AG.

[100] See para 77 of the Special Report of VAW/KAISER/PREUSSAG.

[101] See paras 61, 62 of the Special Report of MAN/SULZER.

[102] See paras 61, 62 of the Special Report of THYSSEN/HÜLLER-HILLE.

[103] Ibid, see paras 61, 64.

[104] See para 48 of the Special Report of IBH/WIBAU.

[105] See para 128 of the Special Report of Asklepios Kliniken Hamburg/Krankenhaus Mariahilf.

[106] See paras 207, 236 of the Special Report of the EDEKA/Kaiser's Tengelmann.

(2) Type 2: Arguments in Principle Not Recognized as Public Interest but Admitted in Exceptional Cases

(a) *Improving the Efficiency of the German Industry*

The macroeconomic significance of the efficiency of German industry has been discussed in three cases. In DAIMLER-BENZ/MBB, the industrial policy objective of strengthening the German aerospace industry was considered by the Monopolies Commission. The Monopolies Commission argued that the improvement of the systemic capability, the industrial leadership, the German influence in the European Airbus Consortium, and the international cooperation could only be achieved through politics.[107] However, the Minister finally gave approval in this case considering the advantages arising from the combination of the air and space transport sectors and improvements in the relevant area of high technology research.[108] It could also be observed from this case that political considerations instead of economic benefits may sometimes be a decisive factor in the public interest assessment.

The improvement of the efficiency of the food retailing industry was discussed in the EDEKA/Kaiser's Tengelmann case; and the prevention of the structural crisis in the aluminium industry was discussed in the VAW/KAISER/PREUSSAG case. In both the two cases, the Monopolies Commission denied that this efficiency effect could be considered as a public interest. It held that while the merger might aim at solving temporary overcapacity of the industry, the short-term changes are not suitable as such to justify the permission of a merger, which would change the market structures permanently.[109] Similarly, it regarded that "the increase of the efficiency of the German food retailing through the merger and promotion of medium-sized structures does not count as benefit to the public good".[110]

(b) *Other Financial Benefits of the Takeover or Merger*

In some cases, the applicants also used the arguments of financial benefits of the takeover or merger. In principle, the financial benefits of the takeover or merger were rejected by the Monopolies Commission and the Minister as a public interest justification. For example, in EDEKA/Kaiser's Tengelmann, the applicant used the "tax benefits" created by the merger; in Landkreis Rhön-Grabfeld/Rhön Klinikum AG, the argument was "the relief of public budgets after the merger"; in E.ON/RUHRGAS, the financial benefit was put forward as "the dissolution of a shareholder blockade"; and in BABCOCK/ARTOS, it was the "prevention of the financial collapse". As to the tax benefits, the Monopolies Commission concluded that the actual tax effects of a single transaction could not be determined ex ante with sufficient certainty.[111] For the relief of public budgets, it argued that "it is the task of fiscal policy and not of competition policy, and in particular of the Ministerial approval procedure, to relieve

[107] See paras 294, 310 of the Special Report of DAIMLER-BENZ/MBB.

[108] Majone (1996), pp. 146–147.

[109] See para 66 of the Special Report of VAW/KAISER/PREUSSAG.

[110] See para 237 of the Special Report of EDEKA/Kaiser's Tengelmann.

[111] See para 235 of the Special Report of EDEKA/Kaiser's Tengelmann.

public budgets".[112] The dissolution of a shareholder blockade, in itself alone, was also denied as a common good advantage.[113] Only in one exceptional case of the DAIMLER-BENZ/MBB case, the Minister recognized the benefits in the reduction of subsidies as a result of the privatization of Airbus German from this merger and granted this case with conditions.[114]

4.2.2.3 Intermediate Conclusion

The "public interest exemption" mechanism under the GWB works as a major tool for protecting important societal interests (the recognized public interest considerations) in Germany. The arguments submitted by the applicants in the fifteen cases illustrate that the consequences of a takeover may bear on various stakeholders and societal interests. To decide whether the societal interests belong to the public interest and outweigh the competition restraints, the Monopolies Commission and the Minister should take into account a wide range of considerations and give detailed reasoning for their opinions or decisions.

In the fifteen cases, the arguments that were in principle recognized by the Minister as public interest exemption reasons under Section 42(1) GWB include: (i) the preservation of important know-how, (ii) improvement of the international competitiveness, (iii) retention of the employment rate in the region, (iv) security of the energy supply of the country, (v) achievement of the environmental objectives of the Federal Government, (vi) preservation of the university hospital and the R&D of the university medical faculty, (vii) defence interest of the country, (viii) press diversity, (ix) achievement of the healthcare policy objectives and improvement of the healthcare level. Whilst in principle not recognized as the public interest reasons, in exceptional cases, financial benefits in the reduction of subsidies from the privatization after the merger and the improved efficiency of a German industry were considered as in the public interest. In such exceptional cases, political policies at that time played an important role in the Minister's decision. The rationalization effect, the restructuring effect, other financial benefits and the benefits for the local residents created by the takeover or merger in the selected cases were not recognized as public interest exemption reasons under Section 42 GWB. In the assessment of such arguments, the Monopolies Commission considered the economic benefits of the transaction and did not believe that they could outweigh the competitive restrictions.[115]

---

[112] See para 154 of the Special Report of Landkreis Rhön-Grabfeld/Rhön Klinikum AG.

[113] See para 237 of the Special Report of E.ON/RUHRGAS.

[114] See Budzinski and Stöhr (2018). Die Ministererlaubnis Als Element Der Deutschen Wettbewerbsordnung: Eine Theoretische Und Empirische Analyse (The Public Interest Exception (Ministererlaubnis) in German Merger Control: A Theoretical and Empirical Analysis of the Instrument). Available at: https://papers.ssrn.com/sol3/papers.cfm?abstract_id=3226967 (accessed 3 June 2022).

[115] It should be noted that, in the other two cases which are not discussed in this section, "the privatization of state-owned enterprises" and, more generally, the "return of state influence to the private sector" were recognized as in the public interest (see BWM WuW/E 225 (230) Kali + Salz/PCS).

The Minister's decisions in these cases also indicate that the criteria for assessing the relevant arguments may be changeable and unpredictable in practice. Nevertheless, some consistent rules could still be drawn from past experience. Firstly, to serve as an overriding public interest, it is not enough that the takeover or merger only benefits the parties to the transaction. The benefits of the transaction should at least have a macroeconomic or socio-political impact.[116] Secondly, it should be borne in mind that the assessment of the public interest considerations is a trade-off process: the more restraints the takeover or merger has on competition, the higher are the requirements for proving the public interest or the macroeconomic benefits.[117] Besides, the facts to take into account in the assessment must in principle be present at the time of the decision; forecasts for future events must be made with reasonable probability, and circumstances that are subject to short-term changes are not likely to be proper evaluation factors.[118] Furthermore, in principle, the overriding public interest under Section 42 is restricted to the territory of the Federal Republic of Germany; public interest benefits in favour of the EU or in favour of other individual EU Member States are not eligible for recognition.[119]

4.3 Regulations in the FDI Screening Regime

In the FDI screening regime, the Foreign Trade and Payments Act (the "AWG" hereinafter)[120] and the Foreign Trade and Payments Ordinance (the "AWV" hereinafter)[121] are the two major regulations in Germany and the BMWK (before December 2021, called as the BMWi) is the responsible authority for reviewing takeovers of domestic companies by foreign investors on a case-by-case basis.[122] In

[116] Busche and Röhling (2014) p. 334.

[117] Ibid, see p. 337.

[118] Ibid, see p. 338.

[119] Ibid. See para 149 of the Special Report of Miba/Zollern. However, if the exchange relationships are roughly distorted on demand markets, which have a considerable Community importance, the Monopolies Commission assumes that the national market economy is in danger.

[120] Foreign Trade and Payments Act (Außenwirtschaftsgesetz) (AWG) (Issued on 6 June 2013 (BGBI. I S. 1482). It was last amended in May 2022, see the official German version available at: https://www.gesetze-im-internet.de/awg_2013/BJNR148210013.html (accessed 4 June 2022); the official English version only includes the recent amendments to the AWG in August 2021, see it available at: https://www.gesetze-im-internet.de/englisch_awg/index.html (accessed 4 June 2022).

[121] Foreign Trade and Payments Ordinance (Außenwirtschaftsverordnung) (AWV) (Issued on 2 August 2013 (BGBI. I S. 2865). It was last amended in May 2022, see the official German version available at: https://www.gesetze-im-internet.de/awv_2013/BJNR286500013.html (accessed 4 June 2022); the official English version only includes the recent amendments to the AWV in August 2021, see it available at: https://www.gesetze-im-internet.de/englisch_awv/index.html (accessed 4 June 2022).

[122] Bundesministerium für Wirtschaft und Klimaschutz (BMWK). Investment screening. Available at: https://www.bmwi.de/Redaktion/EN/Artikel/Foreign-Trade/investment-screening.html (accessed 4 June 2022).

the past few years, the Federal Government of Germany, by making amendments to the AWV and AWG, has taken consecutive steps to strengthen its FDI screening regulation to protect specific public interests in foreign takeovers. Among others, the reforms taking place in this field in 2020 particularly responded to the Covid-19 crisis and the newly formulated EU FDI screening framework. Sect. 4.3.1 first presents the relevant rules regulating FDI screening in Germany before 2020 and analyses the public interest considerations that were protected at that time; following that, Sect. 4.3.2 further discusses the new reforms since 2020 as well as the changes to the relevant public interest considerations under the new regime.

4.3.1 FDI Screening Regulation Before 2020

Both the AWV and the AWG encompass rules on cross-sector investment review and sector-specific review. The cross-sector investment review in principle applies to any foreign takeovers satisfying the threshold of the acquisition of shareholdings, regardless of the sectors where the takeover takes place, and decides whether a foreign takeover of the domestic company poses a threat to the public order or security of Germany. The sector-specific investment review, in comparison, applies solely to foreign takeovers of domestic companies that operate in security-sensitive areas and are closely connected to the security and defence interests of Germany. In 2017 and 2018, the Government adopted the Ninth Amendment and the Twelfth Amendment to the AWV respectively, which indicated the beginning of a tendency towards a stricter FDI screening regime and laid the basis for the rules of the current regime.

4.3.1.1 Reforms in 2017 and 2018

The first steps taken by the Government towards a much stricter approach of reviewing foreign takeovers were largely triggered by a series of takeovers of German industrial giants by foreign investors during 2015–2018, predominantly by investors from China.[123] For example, in 2015 alone, nearly 70 takeovers of German companies by Chinese investors were made with a total transaction volume of almost $ 13 billion.[124] The takeovers of this period, inter alia the Kuka case and Aixtron case, have raised great public concerns about the competence of the existing FDI screening regulation at that time, and the Government also acknowledged that the existing legal

[123] Bundesministerium für Wirtschaft und Klimaschutz (BMWK) (5 October 2017). Schlaglichter der Wirtschaftspolitik. Available at: https://www.bmwi.de/Redaktion/DE/Schlaglichter-der-Wirtschaftspolitik/2017/10/onlinemagazin-schlaglichter-10-17.html?cms_textId=626220&cms_artId=626206 (accessed 4 June 2022).

[124] Ibid.

instruments have reached their limits in view of the scope and complexity of the FDI screening as shown in the individual cases.[125]

For example, in the Midea/Kula takeover, in 2016, the Chinese company Midea took over 95% of the voting rights of Kuka, a German leading robotic group.[126] The BMWi, in this case, issued a certificate of non-objection after a preliminary examination, without entering into the second stage of the review procedure.[127] The announcement triggered a public debate on the influence of foreign investors on German companies and fueled the fears that Germany's most advanced industrial technologies and important know-how could be potentially transferred to its international competitors, such as China.[128] In another attempted takeover of Aixtron in 2016, the Chinese company Fujian Grand Chip Investment announced its intention to acquire 50.1% of the voting rights of the German electronics manufacturer Aixtron.[129] The Chinese investor had already successfully applied for a certificate of non-objection from BMWi. However, the BMWi then revoked the certificate in October 2016 based on "previously unknown security-related information".[130] This case led to debate over whether the government should do more to protect strategic technologies.[131]

Against this background, on 12 July 2017, the Federal Government adopted the Ninth Amendment to the AWV, introducing stricter rules for the review of takeovers by investors from countries outside the European Union.[132] Based on this, the German Government made a formal prohibition to foreign investment in the Leifeld case.[133] In 2018, the Chinese company Yantai Taihai aimed to take over the Leifeld Metal Spinning, a German company which produces sophisticated, seamless pipe-formed metal parts that are used in the aerospace as well as the nuclear sector.[134] The BMWi concluded that the takeover would endanger the German public order and security

---

[125] Ibid.

[126] LEXOLOGY.COM (8 January 2019). Foreign Investment Review in Germany. Available at: https://www.lexology.com/library/detail.aspx?g=bf8f2601-8db6-43a8-ad67-7ddf14c1c066 (accessed 3 February 2021).

[127] Ibid.

[128] Ibid. Kuka develops and produces robots for various industries, such as automotive, electronics, energy or healthcare. See also FT.COM (5 February 2019). German minister calls for fund to counter foreign takeovers. Available at: https://www.ft.com/content/e78e8452-2944-11e9-a5ab-ff8ef2b976c7 (accessed 3 February 2021).

[129] LEXOLOGY.COM (8 January 2019). Foreign Investment Review in Germany.

[130] REUTERS.COM (24 October 2016). Germany stalls Chinese takeover of Aixtron, citing security worries. Available at: https://www.reuters.com/article/us-aixtron-m-a-fujian-germany-idUSKCN12O13G (accessed 3 February 2021).

[131] Ibid.

[132] Bundesministerium für Wirtschaft und Klimaschutz (BMWK) (5 October 2017). Schlaglichter der Wirtschaftspolitik.

[133] LEXOLOGY.COM (8 January 2019). Foreign Investment Review in Germany.

[134] Ibid. Accordingly, the takeover qualified as subject to cross-sectoral review, on the basis that it "operates critical infrastructure".

in this case, which represented the start of a stricter stand in reviewing foreign investments in the future.

On 29 December 2018, the Twelfth Amendment to the AWV entered into force, which further expanded the competences of the BMWi in reviewing and potentially prohibiting (direct or indirect) investments from Non-EU investors in German companies.[135] The amendment lowered the threshold from 25 to 10% for screening the acquisitions of shareholdings in companies that carry out activities which are defined as being relevant for the security of Germany. The new 10% threshold applied to companies in particularly sensitive areas, inter alia, to those of critical infrastructure, other security-related infrastructure, and defence-related companies; and media companies were also included in this category.[136] According to this amendment, the screening procedure can commence at an earlier stage in particularly sensitive areas, which gave the Federal Government the chance to find out at an earlier stage whether the foreign takeover affects essential security interests.[137]

4.3.1.2 Public Interest Considerations in the FDI Screening Regime Before 2020

(1) Public Interest Considerations under Cross-sector Investment Review

Based on the two amendments in 2017 and 2018, with regard to cross-sector investment review, the AWV entitled the BMWi to examine whether the public order or security of Germany is endangered in cases where a non-EU resident acquires ownership of at least 25% of the voting rights of a domestic company, and 10% of the voting rights of a domestic company in particularly sensitive sectors.[138] Based on these two amendments, the AWV gave examples of the acquisitions which may particularly be deemed as a threat to public order or security, and where the 10% threshold instead of 25% applies, including acquisitions of companies which operate in sectors such as critical infrastructure, develop or modify software for critical infrastructure operation, or are active in telecommunications surveillance, render cloud computing services, have a licence for telematics infrastructure, or are in the media industry and are characterized by particular topicality and breadth of impact.[139]

---

[135] Bundesministerium für Wirtschaft und Klimaschutz (BMWK). Investment screening. See the Twelfth Amendment to the AWV (in German) available at: https://www.bmwi.de/Redaktion/DE/Downloads/XYZ/zwoelfte-verordnung-zur-aenderung-der-aussenwirtschaftsverordnung.pdf?__blob=publicationFile&v=4 (accessed 4 February 2021).

[136] Bundesministerium für Wirtschaft und Klimaschutz (BMWK) (19 December 2018). Strengthening our national security via improved investment screening. Available at: https://www.bmwi.de/Redaktion/EN/Pressemitteilungen/2018/20181219-staerkung-unserer-nationalen-sicherheit-durch-verbesserte-investitionspruefung.html (accessed 4 February 2021).

[137] Ibid.

[138] Ibid. See subsections 55(1), 56(1) of the AWV.

[139] Subsection 55a(1) of the AWV.

The considerations for a cross-sector investment review under the AWG were stipulated as the "public security and external interests of Germany".[140] The public interest aspects listed in the AWG as belonging to such considerations at that time included "the essential security interests of Germany", "the peaceful coexistence of nations", "foreign relations of Germany", "the public order or security of Germany within the meaning of Articles 36, 52(1) and 65(1) of the TFEU", and "the health and life of human beings in accordance with Article 36 of the TFEU".[141] Based on the cases of the CJEU, the BMWi regards that public security may be affected by acquisitions related to issues such as security of supply in the event of a crisis, telecommunications and electricity, or the provision of services of strategic importance.[142]

(2) Public Interest Considerations under Sector-specific Investment Review

Compared with the cross-sector investment review, the sector-specific investment review rules under the AWV and AWG apply solely to foreign takeovers of domestic companies that operate in security-sensitive areas and are closely connected to the security and defence interests of Germany. During this period, the AWV stipulated the security-sensitive sectors in which the essential security interests of Germany may be endangered in a foreign takeover, including for example, those relating to the manufacturing of military weapons or other military equipment, of products with IT security functions that are used for processing classified government information.[143] At that time, the threshold for the BMWi to initiate a sector-specific review was 10% of the voting rights by the foreign acquirer following the acquisition.[144] The sectors listed in the AWG at that time for sector-specific review were similar to those in the AWV, including also the manufacturer or developer of military weapons or other military equipment, and products with IT security functions.[145] In this context, relevant EU legislation and case law of the CJEU also need to be taken into account.[146]

[140] Section 4 of the AWG.

[141] Subsection 4(1) of the AWG. TFEU: Consolidated version of the Treaty on the Functioning of the European Union [2016] OJ C 202/1.

[142] Bundesministerium für Wirtschaft und Klimaschutz (BMWK). Investment screening.

[143] Subsection 60(1) of the AWV.

[144] Subsection 60a(1) of the AWV.

[145] Section 5 of the AWG.

[146] Bundesministerium für Wirtschaft und Klimaschutz (BMWK). Investment screening.

4.3.2 FDI Screening Regulation After 2020

4.3.2.1 Background: The New EU FDI Screening Framework and the COVID-19 Crisis

In March 2019, the EU adopted a regulation setting up a framework for the screening of investments from non-EU countries on the grounds of security or public order (the "EU FDI Screening Regulation" hereinafter).[147] This regulation came into force in October 2020 and established an EU-wide framework in which the European Commission (the "EC" hereinafter) and the Member States can coordinate their actions on foreign investments.[148] In March 2020, as part of measures taken in connection with the COVID-19 emergency, the EC issued guidance to Member States on FDI screening which identified the increased risk of attempts by non-EU acquirers to obtain healthcare capacities (such as the production of medical or protective equipment) or related industries (such as research establishments) in the EU via foreign direct investment in times of the public health crisis.[149] The guidance called on Member States to make full use of all the FDI screening mechanisms available at the Union and national level to protect its critical health infrastructures, supply of critical inputs, and other critical sectors.[150]

At the national level, to adapt to the new EU FDI screening framework and respond to the COVID-19 pandemic, Germany initiated several amendments to the AWV and the AWG in 2020, which extended the scope of industries and types of companies subject to a cross-sector investment review and a sector-specific investment review and introduced new assessment factors for the BMWK to take into account in its FDI screening.

---

[147] Regulation (EU) 2019/452 of the European Parliament and of the Council of 19 March 2019 establishing a framework for the screening of foreign direct investments into the Union [2019] OJ L 79 I/1. See the regulation in English available at: https://eur-lex.europa.eu/legal-content/EN/TXT/PDF/?uri=CELEX:32019R0452&from=EN (accessed 4 February 2021).

[148] See more background of the EU FDI Screening Regulation at: EC.EUROPA.EU (9 October 2020). EU foreign investment screening mechanism becomes fully operational. Available at: https://ec.europa.eu/commission/presscorner/detail/en/ip_20_1867 (accessed 4 June 2022).

[149] Communication from the Commission Guidance to the Member States concerning foreign direct investment and free movement of capital from third countries, and the protection of Europe's strategic assets, ahead of the application of Regulation (EU) 2019/452 (FDI Screening Regulation) (C(2020) 1981 final) [2020] OJ C 99 I/01.

See the guidance in English available at: https://eur-lex.europa.eu/legal-content/EN/TXT/?uri=celex%3A52020XC0326%2803%29 (accessed 4 June 2022).

[150] Ibid. For those Member States that do not have a screening mechanism or whose mechanisms do not cover all relevant transactions, it calls them to introduce fill-fledged screening mechanism to avoid risks in these sectors.

4.3.2.2 Relevant Amendments to the AWV and AWG

(1) Fifteenth Amendment to the AWV

To respond to the COVID-19 pandemic, the Federal Government of Germany published the Fifteenth Amendment to the AWV, which came into force on 3 June 2020 and expanded the range of transactions of cross-sector investment review.[151]

(a) *Expanded Cross-sector Investment Review of Takeovers in the Healthcare Sector*

The Fifteenth Amendment to the AWV focused on protecting the critical infrastructures in the healthcare sector. It added four types of companies in the healthcare area into the group of domestic companies under Section 55 (paragraph 1 sentence 2) AWV, the acquisitions of which by non-EU investors are subject to an investigation by the BMWK on the grounds for protecting public order or security.[152] In the future, acquisitions of these companies must be reported to the BMWK and the threshold of 10% of shares applies in these situations.[153] The new types of companies include those: (i) that develop or manufacture personal protective equipment (e.g. FFP2 and FFP3 masks); (ii) that develop, manufacture or place on the market medicinal products that are essential for ensuring the provision of healthcare to the population, or hold a corresponding marketing authorization; (iii) that develop or manufacture medical devices for the diagnosis, prevention, monitoring, prediction, prognosis, treatment or alleviation of life-threatening and highly contagious infectious diseases; or (iv) that develop or manufacture the in-vitro-diagnostic medical devices, used to provide information on physiological or pathological processes or conditions or to establish or monitor therapeutic measures in relation to life-threatening and highly contagious infectious diseases.[154]

(b) *Implementation of the Rules under the EU FDI Screening Regulation*

In reviewing the acquisitions of the above companies in the healthcare areas, Article 4(1) of the EU FDI Screening Regulation should be complied with, which specifies the factors the Member States may take into account when determining whether the

---

[151] Bundesministerium für Wirtschaft und Klimaschutz (BMWK) (29 October 2020). Außenwirtschaftsverordnung. Available at: https://www.bmwi.de/Redaktion/DE/Gesetze/Aussenwirtschaft/AWV.html (accessed 4 February 2021). The previous amendments to the AWV and AWG are also listed on this webpage.

[152] See the Fifteenth Amendment to the AWV in German available at: http://dipbt.bundestag.de/dip21/brd/2020/0315-20.pdf (accessed 4 February 2021). See "Zielsetzung und Notwendigkeit der Regelungen" (Objective of the regulations).

[153] Bundesministerium für Wirtschaft und Klimaschutz (BMWK) (29 October 2020). Änderungen im Investitionsprüfungscrecht. Available at: https://www.bmwk.de/Redaktion/DE/Artikel/Service/Gesetzesvorhaben/aenderungen-im-investitionspruefungsrecht.html (accessed 4 June 2022).

[154] See Article 1 para 1(a) (cc) No. 8–11 of the Fifteenth Amendment to the AWV. The English translation of these new types of companies referred to TWOBIRDS.COM (October 2020). Germany: foreign trade law—Modifications and their effects and impacts on M&A transaction. Available at: https://www.twobirds.com/en/news/articles/2020/germany/aenderungen-im-aussenwirtschaftsrecht-und-ihre-auswirkungen-auf-die-transaktionspraxis (accessed 4 February 2021).

foreign investment is likely to affect security or public order, including for example, the potential effects of the investment on critical infrastructure, critical technologies, supply of critical inputs, access to sensitive information, and the freedom and pluralism of the media.[155] The Fifteenth Amendment to the AWV also introduced other factors the BMWK may take into account when reviewing a foreign acquisition of the companies as listed in Section 55, which implemented the considerations as listed under Article 4(2) of the EU FDI Screening Regulation, including whether (i) the acquirer is directly or indirectly controlled by the government (including any other governmental agencies or armed forces) of a third country; (ii) whether the acquirer has already been involved in activities that had adverse effects on the public order or security of Germany or another EU Member State; or (iii) whether the acquirer was involved in an offence that is referred to in Section 123(1) GWB or a criminal offence or an administrative offence under the AWG and the War Weapons Control Act.[156]

(2) The First Law to Amend the Foreign Trade Act and Other Laws ("First Amendment to the AWG")

The First Law to amend the Foreign Trade Act and other Laws (the "First Amendment to the AWG" hereinafter) came into force on 17 July 2020 which particularly served to implement the requirements under the EU FDI Screening Regulation.[157] The amendment lowered the benchmark for a cross-sector investment review: whilst under the previous regime, an "actual risk" (both real and serious) of the acquisition on public order or security is decisive, in the future, it is only required that the public order or security is "likely to be affected" by the acquisition.[158] This change from "actual risk" to "probable impairment" aims to enable the BMWK to review acquisitions of critical companies more proactively.[159] In addition to the acquisitions' effects on Germany, the BMWK is also required to consider the effects of the acquisition on other EU Member States or programs of Union interest.[160] Moreover, under the new regime, all notifiable acquisitions are pending ineffective until the BMWK gives its

---

155 See "Zielsetzung und Notwendigkeit der Regelungen" of the Fifteenth Amendment to the AWV.

156 See Article 1(1b) of the Fifteenth Amendment to the AWV. The English translation of these new types of companies referred to TWOBIRDS.COM (October 2020). Germany: foreign trade law—Modifications and their effects and impacts on M&A transaction.

157 See the First Amendment to the AWG (in German) available at: https://www.bgbl.de/xaver/bgbl/start.xav?startbk=Bundesanzeiger_BGBl&jumpTo=bgbl120s1637.pdf#__bgbl__%2F%2F*%5B%40attr_id%3D%27bgbl120s1637.pdf%27%5D__1611827724468 (accessed 4 February 2021). See the consolidation version of the AWG after this amendment (in German) available at: https://www.bmwi.de/Redaktion/DE/Downloads/A/au%C3%9Fenwirtschaftsgesetz-awg.pdf?__blob=publicationFile&v=4 (accessed 4 February 2021).

158 Bundesministerium für Wirtschaft und Klimaschutz (BMWK) (29 October 2020). Änderungen im Investitionsprüfungscrecht. See Article 1(4) of the First Amendment to the AWG: it used the term "voraussichtlich beeinträchtigt", meaning "likely to be affected".

159 Ibid. In this introduction to this amendment by the BMWK, it used the word "Prüfmaßstab", which means "test standard".

160 See Article 1(4) of the First Amendment to the AWG.

approval.[161] Furthermore, the amendment also unified the deadline for the BMWK to review the acquisition in the AWV and the AWG.[162]

With regard to the sector-specific investment review, the First Amendment to the AWG extended the application of the review to domestic companies that "modify" or "have actual control over" weapons of war or other armaments, whilst under the previous rules, only companies "manufacture or develop" such goods were regulated.[163] To that extent, it further strengthened the protection of security interests in foreign investment.

(3) Sixteenth and Seventeenth Amendment to the AWV

Following the First Amendment to the AWG, to ensure Germany's full participation in the new EU-wide FDI screening framework, the Government took a further step in October 2020 and passed the Sixteenth Amendment to the AWV, which came into force on 29 October 2020.[164] This amendment introduced more adjustments to the AWV and emphasized that in the future, acquisitions which have potential adverse effects on the public order or security in other EU Member States or on certain projects and programs of Union interest will also be included into the catalogue subject to the FDI screening in Germany.[165]

In April 2021, Germany adopted the Seventeenth Amendment to the AWV to further implement the relevant requirements under the EU FDI Screening Regulation, which came into force on 1 May 2021.[166] This new amendment further defines the sectors and industries relevant to the "critical technologies" as stipulated in Article 4(1) of the EU FDI Screening Regulation.[167] The amendment extends the scope of the key sectors in which the acquisitions of companies are subject to a cross-sector review and fall under a mandatory filing requirement (by inserting a "Section 55a" after Section 55 of the AWV, which adds companies that operate in, for example, high-quality remote sensing systems, raw materials extractors, companies that are of

---

[161] Bundesministerium für Wirtschaft und Klimaschutz (BMWK) (29 October 2020). Änderungen im Investitionsprüfungscrecht. See Articles 1(6), 3 of the First Amendment to the AWG.

[162] TWOBIRDS.COM (October 2020). Germany: foreign trade law—Modifications and their effects and impacts on M&A transaction.

[163] See Article 1(4)(3) of the First Amendment to the AWG.

[164] See the Sixteenth Amendment to the AWV (in German) available at: https://www.bmwi.de/Redaktion/DE/Downloads/S-T/sechzehnte-verordnung-zur-aenderung-der-au%C3%9Fenwirtschaft-verordnung.pdf?__blob=publicationFile&v=8 (accessed 4 February 2021).

[165] Bundesministerium für Wirtschaft und Klimaschutz (BMWK) (29 October 2020). Änderungen im Investitionsprüfungscrecht. See also MORGANLEWIS.COM (24 November 2020). Germany further aligns foreign direct investment screening regime with EU Regulation. Available at: https://www.morganlewis.com/pubs/2020/11/germany-further-aligns-foreign-direct-investment-screening-regime-with-eu-regulation (accessed 4 February 2021).

[166] Ibid. See the Seventeenth Amendment to the AWV (in German) available at: https://www.bmwi.de/Redaktion/DE/Downloads/P-R/referentenentwurf-siebzehnte-verordnung-zur-aenderung-der-aussenwirtschaftsverordnung.pdf?__blob=publicationFile&v=10 (accessed 4 February 2021).

[167] See "Begründung—B. Besonderer Teil" of the Seventeenth Amendment to the AWV.

fundamental importance for food safety, etc.).[168] With regard to the sector-specific investment review, the amendment extends the scope of defence-related companies that are listed under Section 60 AWV and subject to mandatory filing requirements, and the new regime will cover all companies that manufacture, modify or have control of goods that are under the Export List or fall into the scope of protection of a secret patent.[169] It is noteworthy that this amendment does not transfer all sensitive activities listed in Article 4(1) of the EU FDI Screening Regulation into the AWV. For example, concerning the "access to" or "control" of "personal data" as listed under Article 4(1)(d) of the EU FDI Screening Regulation, the amendment concludes that since almost every company processes a substantial amount of personal date, introducing such a category would lead to unlimited notification obligations; concerning the activities in "biotechnology, nanotechnology, energy storage or defence" as listed under Article 4(1)(b), the amendment does not introduce them as new categories given that the existing categories under the AWV already cover these technologies.[170]

4.3.2.3 Intermediate Conclusion

The above consecutive reforms reformulate the AWV and AWG and establish a much more stringent FDI screening regime in Germany. Prior to 2017, the AWV and AWG mainly regulated foreign takeovers in the security-related areas and focused on protecting the security interest of Germany. The current regime, by introducing new categories of companies and activities subject to cross-sector and sector-specific investment review, significantly extends the scope of the relevant societal interests that are regulated in a foreign takeover. For example, under the new regime, the cross-sector investment review, as required by the new EU FDI screening framework, no longer only aims at protecting the public order and security of Germany, but also considers the takeovers' potential effects on the public order and security of other

[168] See Articles 3, 8 of the Seventeenth Amendment to the AWV. The current rules for cross-sector investment review are listed under Sections 55–59 of the AWV. The translation of examples discussed here referred to the analysis at: DLAPIPER.COM (25 January 2021). Germany Foreign Direct Investment (FDI) Control: Massive Extension of Scope (available at: https://www.dlapiper.com/zh-Hans/hongkong/insights/publications/2021/01/germany-foreign-direct-investment-control/, accessed 4 February 2021), and analysis at: COVCOMPETITION.COM (28 January 2021). Significant Revamp of German FDI Regime—German Government Presents New Rules on FDI Screening (available at: https://www.covcompetition.com/2021/01/significant-revamp-of-german-fdi-regime-german-government-presents-new-rules-on-fdi-screening/, accessed 4 February 2021).

[169] See Articles 3, 8 of the Seventeenth Amendment to the AWV. The current rules for cross-sector investment review are listed under Sections 60–62 of the AWV. See also COVCOMPETITION.COM (28 January 2021). Significant Revamp of German FDI Regime—German Government Presents New Rules on FDI Screening.

[170] See the specification of the reasons for not introducing these categories in "B. Besonderer Teil—Allgemeines/Vorbemerkung" of the Seventeenth Amendment to the AWV. See also COVCOMPETITION.COM (28 January 2021). Significant Revamp of German FDI Regime—German Government Presents New Rules on FDI Screening.

Member States. The extension of the scope of the industries, sectors and activities of companies subject to a review by the BMWK indicates the increasing complexity in explaining the "public order and security". Against the background of the COVID-19 pandemic, ensuring the country's capabilities of providing healthcare-related products and services and of combatting emergencies undoubtedly falls within the connotation of "public order and security". Moreover, protecting domestic companies that are active in industries of crucial infrastructures and technologies from potential acquisitions by non-EU investors is another main theme of protecting the "public order and security". It is also predictable that in the future, the categories of companies considered as relevant to the "crucial infrastructure and technologies" would be further enlarged and the powers of the BMWK would be enhanced to enable it to take more proactive measures in foreign investments.

4.4 Takeover Law, Corporate Law and Self-Regulatory Corporate Governance Code

4.4.1 Background

In Germany, the stock corporation (the "AG" hereinafter) accounts for a majority of all the takeover cases.[171] The Stock Corporation Act (the "AktG" hereinafter) is the corporate law applicable to the AGs.[172] It prescribes corporate governance mechanisms for the AGs such as the two-tier board and the co-determination system with employee participation on the supervisory board, which lay the basis for other protection mechanisms for different stakeholders and societal interests in corporate activities such as takeovers. In the takeover law regime, the Securities Acquisition and Takeover Act (the "WpÜG" hereinafter) provides for rules regulating the decision-making power in the target in a takeover.[173] The WpÜG also incorporates requirements on the disclosure of non-financial information in takeovers, which coincide with the non-financial reporting requirements on the management board under

[171] According to Stohlmeier (2015), p. 1, stock corporation accounts for more than 90% of the takeover cases in Germany.

[172] Stock Corporation Act (Aktiengesetz) (AktG) (Issued on 6 September 1965 (BGBI. I S. 1089). It was last amended on 10 August 2021. See the current official German version available at: https://www.gesetze-im-internet.de/aktg/BJNR010890965.html (accessed 4 June 2022); the official English version available online has not incorporated the new amendments in 2021, see it available at: http://www.gesetze-im-internet.de/englisch_aktg/ (accessed 4 June 2022).

[173] Securities Acquisition and Takeover Act (Wertpapiererwerbs- und Übernahmegesetz) (WpÜG) (Issued on December 20 2001 (BGBI. I S. 3822). It was last amended on 10 August 2021. See the current official German version available at: http://www.gesetze-im-internet.de/wp_g/Wp%C3%9CG.pdf (accessed 4 June 2022).

the German Commercial Code (the "HGB" hereinafter) and the AktG.[174] Such non-financial disclosure, in theory, provides non-shareholder stakeholders with access to learning the potential changes a takeover may bring. Besides, in the private regulation field, the German Corporate Governance Code (currently the 2020 German Corporate Governance Code still applies, the "2020 German CG Code" hereinafter) applies to listed companies and provides for principles, recommendations and suggestions which cover protection of various societal interests in corporate activities.[175]

To avoid repetition, this section discusses the government regulation under the AktG, the WpÜG and the HGB as well as the private regulation under the 2020 German CG Code with regard to protection of the relevant societal interests in a takeover. The discussion focus is on the relevant corporate governance mechanisms in these laws and self-regulatory instruments, inter alia the decision-making power and the co-determination system in the target company (to see which stakeholders may participate in the decision-making) and the non-financial disclosure requirement (to see which stakeholders may use this disclosure report to alleviate potential information asymmetries).

Moreover, in some takeovers where the State of Germany is a shareholder of the target, the Government may intervene and set obstacles for the acquirers to protect certain societal interests by collaborating with the employee representatives on the supervisory board and utilizing the co-determination system, such as the takeover battle between Porsche SE (the acquirer) and VW AG (the target) during 2007 and 2009.[176] This section will discuss the Porsche SE/VW AG case in detail to specify what anti-takeover measures the Government (as a shareholder) adopted, what role the employees and supervisory board played in the takeover as well as the CJEU's stance in this case.

---

[174] German Commercial Code (Handelsgesetzbuch) (HGB) (Issued on 10 May 1897). It was last amended on 10 August 2021. See the current official German version available at: https://www.gesetze-im-internet.de/hgb/BJNR002190897.html#BJNR002190897BJNG000300300 (accessed 4 June 2022). There is no official English translation of these sections (Sections 289b, 289c) available online, the translation of the relevant sections used in this part referred to Kessedjian and Rivera (2020), p. 410.

[175] The German Corporate Governance Code is published by the Federal Ministry of Justice and Consumer Protection (Bundesministerium der Justiz und für Verbraucherschutz bekannt gemacht). See the official version of the 2020 German CG Code available at: https://www.dcgk.de//files/dcgk/usercontent/de/download/kodex/191216_Deutscher_Corporate_Governance_Kodex.pdf (accessed 2 February 2021); see the official version in English available at: https://www.dcgk.de//files/dcgk/usercontent/en/download/code/191216_German_Corporate_Governance_Code.pdf (accessed 2 February 2021). On 21 January 2022, the Commission (Regierungskommission Deutscher Corporate Governance Kodex) adopted the draft of the German Corporate Governance Code 2022 (the "2022 German CG Code"), and the publication date of it in the Federal Gazette is still open; until then, the 2020 German CG Code will continue to apply. See more introduction to the German Corporate Governance Code at the website of REGIERUNGSKOMMISSION, available at: https://www.dcgk.de/en/code/code-2019.html (accessed 4 June 2022).

[176] See Case C-112/05 *Commission v Germany*, Judgment of the Court of 23 October 2007 (available at: http://curia.europa.eu/juris/liste.jsf?num=C-112/05, accessed 4 February 2021). This case will be discussed in Sect. 4.4.2.3.

4.4.2 Protection of the Shareholders and Employees

Corporate governance mechanisms of a two-tier board and employee co-determination in Germany are often characterized as barriers to hostile takeovers.[177] In the corporate law regime, rules on the two-tier board system (the board of directors and the board of supervisors)[178] and the co-determination by employees on the supervisory board under the AktG provide a legal basis for the employees to participate in the decision-making process of major corporate activities. In the takeover law regime, the WpÜG gives the supervisory board a prominent role in approving the management board's anti-takeover actions. Based on such designs, the interests of the shareholder group and employee group are primarily protected in a takeover.

4.4.2.1 The Two-tier Board and the Co-determination System Under the AktG

According to the AktG, it is mandatory for an AG to have a management board, a supervisory board and an annual general meeting of shareholders.[179] The resolutions of the general meeting of the AG are passed by a simple majority vote unless the law or the articles of association require differently.[180] In principle, each share grants one vote, while restrictions may apply to the non-voting shares and the articles of association of a non-listed AG may restrict the voting right of certain shares by setting a maximum amount.[181]

The AktG requires almost all types of German listed companies to have employee representatives on the supervisory board, whilst the number and process of appointing the employee representatives are determined by other Acts, depending on the size of the company and the industry in which it operates.[182] Basically, the employee

---

[177] Höpner and Jackson (2006), p. 144. Scholars posited that the German statutory regulations on co-determination have the effect of "poison pills" on foreign companies that consider taking them over peacefully. As a result, amicable mergers between German and non-German companies rarely take place. See also Du Plessis et al. (2017), p. 200.

[178] In this book, the "board of directors" is also called the "management board", and the "board of supervisors" is also called "supervisory board".

[179] Sections 76, 95,118 of the AktG.

[180] Section 133 of the AktG.

[181] Subsections 12(1), 134(1), 139(1) of the AktG. See Vieweg and Fischer (2019), p. 128.

[182] Sections 95, 96 of the AktG. See Gerner-Beuerle and Schilling (2019), p. 78. The other Acts include: (1) the *Montan-Mitbestimmungsgesetz* (the Act on the Co-Determination by Employees in the Supervisory Boards and Management Boards of Mining Enterprises and Enterprises, the "MontanMitgbestG") for the mining (coal), iron, and steel industry; (2) the *Mitbestimmungsgesetz* (the Employee Co-Determination Act, the "MitbestG") for companies with more than 2,000 employees and (3) the *Drittelbeteiligungsgesetz* (the Act on One-Third Employee Representation in the Supervisory Board, the "DrittelbG") for companies with more than 500 employees. According to subsection 96(1) AktG, the requirement that the members of the supervisory board representing the stockholders and the employees applies to companies subject to the MontanMitbestG, the MitbestG, and the DrittelbG, as well as the Gesetz über die Mitbestimmung der Arbeitnehmer bei

participation at the supervisory board has three forms: (1) for certain types of corporations, one third of the supervisory board must be appointed by the employees or their representatives and other two-thirds by the general meeting or in accordance with the articles of associations; (2) for other types, it is the "parity co-determination" which requires half of the supervisors to be appointed by employees and half by the general meeting, with one neutral member appointed by them both; (3) for the final group of corporations, it is the "quasi-parity co-determination" which entitles shareholders and employees to appoint equal numbers of representatives on the supervisory board, with the chairperson appointed by the shareholders and having a tie-breaking vote.[183] Under this co-determination system, employee representatives are accorded considerable power in corporate activities, considering that "formally they have a statutory right to veto nominees to the management board" and "informally they are in a position to disrupt the proceedings of the supervisory board".[184]

The 2020 German CG Code also incorporates provisions concerning the role of the supervisory board and the co-determination system. The 2020 German CG Code contains three kinds of rules: (i) rules in the form of "principles" which mainly reflect material legal requirements for responsible governance under the AktG and have a binding effect on the listed companies (meaning that they have to comply with these rules in their corporate governance); (ii) rules in the form of recommendations (the "shall provisions") and suggestions (the "should provisions"), which incorporate internationally and nationally acknowledged standards for good corporate governance.[185] Compliance with the recommendations is not mandatory, but deviations have to be explained (the "comply or explain" approach).[186] As to the suggestions (the "should provisions"), the listed companies may depart without disclosure.[187] In principle, it requires that the supervisory board of listed companies is involved in decisions of fundamental importance[188]; and it provides for recommendations as to the composition and independence of the members on the supervisory board.[189] As

einer grenzüberschreitenden Verschmelzung (the Act on Employee Co-Determination in the Case of a Cross-Border Merger, the "MgVG").

183 Du Plessis et al. (2018), p. 335. See also Cahn and Donald (2018), pp. 361–364, which categorizes the German co-determination system into five regimes.

184 Kraakman et al. (2017), p. 91: "The election to the management board is by a two-thirds majority vote of the supervisory board". See Section 31(2) of the *Mitbestimmungsgesetz* (the Employee Co-Determination Act, the "MitbestG").

185 Vieweg and Fischer (2019), p. 124. The Regierungskommission formulates these recommendations and suggestions and will review the code at least once a year in order to find out if it still describes the best practice of good corporate governance or if it should be adapted. See its website available at: https://www.dcgk.de/de/kodex.html (accessed 4 February 2022).

186 Section 161 of the AktG requires that the management board and supervisory board of listed companies need to submit an annual declaration on whether they adhere to the recommendations (not the suggestions) or name the recommendations that they have not implemented and explain why not. See also DCGK.DE. Deutscher Corporate Governance Kodex (available at: https://www.dcgk.de/de/kodex.html, accessed 4 February 2022).

187 See para 3 of the "Foreword" (at page 2) of the 2020 German CG Code.

188 See Principle 6 of the 2020 German CG Code.

189 See Principle 6, Recommendations C.1 to C.12 of the 2020 German CG Code.

to a takeover situation, the 2020 German CG Code only stresses the decision-making role of shareholders. It specifies that, in the form of suggestion, "the management board should convene an Extraordinary General Meeting at which shareholders will discuss the takeover offer and may decide on corporate actions".[190]

4.4.2.2 The Supervisory Board's Prominent Role Under the WpÜG

In the event of a takeover, the supervisory board has a prominent role in the decision-making process of the target company. In Germany, most of the anti-takeover actions the board is allowed to take are subject to approval from the supervisory board and general meeting of shareholders. This design mainly deals with the agency problems between board of directors and shareholders while at the same time providing protection to employees through the co-determination system on the supervisory board.

Germany opts out from the board neutrality rule under the EU Takeover Directive[191] by allowing the management board to take anti-takeover measures if these have been approved by the supervisory board which is co-determined in large corporations.[192] The WpÜG allows a potential target company to choose to abide by the stricter European restriction rules which in principle prohibit both the board of directors and the supervisory board from taking pre-bid anti-takeover actions (thus to "opt-in" the board neutrality rules under the EU Takeover Directive).[193] In such an "opt-in" situation, there are four exceptions which allow the management board to take the following actions: (i) actions to which the management board and the supervisory board have been authorized by the general meeting after publication of the decision to make an offer; (ii) actions taken in the normal course of business; (iii) actions taken outside the normal course of business, to the extent that they serve the realization of decisions that were made and partially realized prior to the decision to make an offer; and (iv) the search for competition offers ("the white knight").[194]

Where the target does not make such an "opt-in" choice by specifying in its articles of association, the less restrictive provisions concerning the anti-takeover measures under Section 33 WpÜG apply, which in principle prevent the management board

---

[190] See Suggestions A.5 of the 2020 German CG Code. In the 2017 version of the German Corporate Governance Code, Section 3.7 (para 2) required that "after the announcement of a takeover offer, the management board must not—until publication of the result – take any actions that could prevent the success of the offer, unless such actions are permitted under the applicable law; and in making their decisions, the management board and the supervisory board are also required to observe the best interests of the shareholders and the company". The 2020 German CG Code deleted this requirement.

[191] Directive 2004/25/EC of the European Parliament and of the Council of 21 April 2004 on takeover bids [2004] OJ L 142/12.

[192] Kraakman et al. (2017), p. 210.

[193] Subsections 33a(1)(2) of the WpÜG.

[194] Subsection 33a(2) of the WpÜG.

from taking post-bid anti-takeover actions.[195] Section 33 also provides for two types of exceptions to the restriction on the management boards' anti-takeover actions. The first type of exception targets actions taken during the pending takeover offer or a mandatory offer. It allows the management board at this stage to still take the following actions: (i) actions that a diligent and conscientious manager of a company not subject to a takeover offer would have taken; (ii) the search for a competing offer (the "white knight"); (iii) actions which have been specifically approved by the supervisory board.[196] The second type of exception applies to actions taken prior to the publication of the decision to make an offer. At that stage, for those actions falling within the competence of the general meeting of shareholders, the general meeting may authorize the management board to take such actions in order to prevent the success of takeover bids.[197] Actions based on such anticipatory authorization need to satisfy the following conditions: (i) the actions should be specified in detail in the authorization[198]; (ii) the authorization is subject to a maximum term of 18 months and should be achieved at the vote with at least 75% of the share capital; (iii) more importantly, any actions by the management board on the basis of the general meeting's authorization also require the consent of the supervisory board.[199] Furthermore, the management board, when taking actions, either pre-bid or post-bid, is always subject to the following cumulative restrictions: (i) it should follow the rules concerning the allocation of competences within an AG (for example, where according to the AktG or the articles of association or the supervisory board's by-laws, the management board's action may require the approval of the shareholders' meeting or the supervisory board)[200]; (ii) it should always observe the principle of equal treatment of all shareholders and act in the best interest of the company.[201]

Scholars argued that in practice there is little value to the shareholder meeting's anticipatory authorization for pre-bid anti-takeover actions, considering that this authorization also needs consent from the supervisory board, whilst according to subsection 33(1) AktG, the management board may take post-bid anti-takeover actions simply with the approval of the supervisory board (without shareholder

195 Subsections 33(1), 33a(1) of the WpÜG.

196 Subsection 33(1) of the WpÜG.

197 Subsection 33(2) of the WpÜG. For those that are not within the competence of the shareholder meeting, the board of directors do not need such anticipatory authorization (e.g., the "golden parachute" mechanism which entitles the members of the boards to create a prohibitively high compensation package in the event that an offeror reaches a defined threshold of voting rights or shares). See conclusion of the anti-takeover measures under the German law in Stohlmeier (2015), pp. 118–121.

198 Subsection 33(2) of the WpÜG. See Stohlmeier (2015), p. 116: "A general authorization to prevent the success of a takeover offer is not permissible. The anticipatory shareholders' resolution must specify the type of activities the management board is authorized to undertake, but a detailed description of the defence measures is not required".

199 Subsection 33(2) of the WpÜG.

200 Stohlmeier (2015), p. 117, see "Figure 9 Permissibility of Defensive Actions".

201 Ibid. See subsection 3(1)(3) of the WpÜG.

approval).[202] It is also observed that anti-takeover measures have only played a marginal role in Germany, partly owing to its historically low level of hostile takeover bids, and partly because of the rules that require the equal treatment of shareholders and concerning the pre-emptive rights for newly issued shares of stock under the AktG.[203] The current rules concerning the management board's anti-takeover actions illustrate the strong position of the supervisory board in a takeover, given that the supervisory board's approval is required for both pre-bid and post-bid anti-takeover actions. As put by Hopt (2009), "the permissibility of all kinds of defensive actions if the management board gets the consent of the supervisory board waters down the anti-frustration rule considerably".[204] Hopt (2009) argued that in practice, "the best allies for the target management board in hostile takeovers are the employee representatives on the supervisory board, considering that both of them may stand to lose if the takeover is successful (the former their jobs as directors and the latter their employment in case of restructuring and dismissals)".[205] This alliance is reflected in the famous Porsche SE/VW AG takeover battle which will be soon discussed in the following section. Pursuant to the required consent from the supervisory board and the co-determination of employee representatives, the management board's actions in a takeover will not only take into account the shareholder interests, but also the interests of employees. Furthermore, within the shareholder group, to ensure equal treatment of shareholders, the WpÜG also provides for a "mandatory bid" rule to protect minority shareholders, which requires that mandatory offers must be made by the acquirers to all other shareholders when they acquire control (holding 30% or more of the voting rights) of the target for the first time.[206]

4.4.2.3 The Porsche SE/VW AG Takeover Battle

The takeover battle between the Porsche SE (the acquirer) and VW AG (the target) during 2007 and 2009 sheds light on how the German Government, as a shareholder of the target, could utilize the role of the supervisory board and the co-determination

[202] See last sentence of subsection 33(1) of the WpÜG. See Kraakman et al. (2017), pp. 213, 219; see also Stohlmeier (2015), p. 118.

[203] Höpner and Jackson (2006), p. 146. See Article 3(1)(a) of the EU Takeover Directive. This article requires Member States to ensure that "all holders of the securities of an offeree company of the same class must be afforded equal treatment". See also Section 186(1) of the AktG, which requires that "Each stockholder must be allotted, upon his making the corresponding demand, a portion of the new shares of stock corresponding to his portion of the current share capital". As a result, the defensive measures in Germany are largely limited to share buy-backs, engaging in alternative acquisitions, and searching for a white knight.

[204] Hopt (2009), p. 382.

[205] Ibid, p. 383.

[206] Subsection 29(2), 35 of the WpÜG.

system to intervene to prevent potential takeover bids.[207] It also illustrates the important role of the employee representatives in a takeover, particularly when they are backed by trade unions and form an alliance with the State shareholder.[208]

(1) Background: The State's Participation in Privatized Companies and State-controlled Companies

Since the 1990s, the role of the State has changed from provider to guarantor of public services in Germany. The privatization process in Germany left the State with some interests but not necessarily controlling interests in some privatized companies, particularly in the areas such as infrastructure, transport, defence and science.[209] According to Section 65 of the Federal Budget Code ("Bundeshaushaltsordnung", the "BHO" hereinafter), the State should take part in the founding of a private-law enterprise or take a holding in an existing enterprise of this kind only if there is an important interest on the part of the Federation and the purpose intended by the Federation cannot be achieved better or more efficiently in any other way.[210]

In companies where the State directly or indirectly has a majority shareholding, Section 65 of the BHO requires that the responsible federal ministry should use its influence to ensure that the company does not acquire a shareholding of more than one quarter of the shares of another enterprise, increase such a shareholding or sell all or part of it without the consent of that ministry.[211] It is also required that the responsible federal ministry uses its influence to ensure that the members of the supervisory bodies of the companies in which the State has a majority shareholding take the special interests of the Federation into consideration in their activities.[212] Based on these requirements, in takeovers of such companies, it is likely that the State may intervene to protect specific societal interests, inter alia, the public interests such as the defence interest and securing of supply of the public services.

(2) The State's Intervention in the Porsche SE/VW AG Takeover

In this case, the state of Lower Saxony (with a capital participation of 20% in the VW AG) as well as the trade unions (which mainly acted through the employee representatives on the supervisory board of the VW AG) were close allies of the target VW AG.[213] To fend off the takeover attempt by Porsche, the VW AG mainly relied on three corporate governance tools which provide a glimpse of the "golden share" by the Government: (1) by virtue of a special statute (the "VW Law") to give each of the state of Lower Saxony and the Federal Government (on condition that they were shareholders in the company) the power to appoint two representatives on

---

207 See the details of this case in Du Plessis et al. (2017), pp. 215–221.

208 Ibid, p. 221.

209 Bernier et al. (2020), p. 310.

210 Ibid. See Section 65 of the BHO (in German) available at: https://www.gesetze-im-internet.de/bho/__65.html (accessed 4 June 2022).

211 See Subsection 65(3) of the BHO.

212 See Subsection 65(6) of the BHO.

213 Du Plessis et al. (2017), p. 215.

the supervisory board; (2) to apply a 20% voting cap according to the VW Law to all votes of shareholders at the shareholder meeting, meaning that even if a shareholder possessed more than 20% of shares of the VW, his/her votes would not count more than 20%; (3) by virtue of the VW Law, to require the favourable vote of more than four fifths of the share capital for resolutions of the general meeting, which under the normal corporate law only requires a favourable vote of at least three quarters of the share capital (thus shareholders with 20% of the shareholding would constitute a "blocking minority" to the resolutions of the shareholders' meeting).[214] In March 2005, the EC sued Germany for its violation of the EC Treaty on the grounds of its use of the three tools.[215]

With regard to the first tool—the appointment power of the state of Lower Saxony and the Federal Government, the background was that the supervisory board of the VW consisted of twenty members, ten of which were employee representatives. The CJEU held that the general company law restricted the rights of representation conferred on certain shareholders to one third of the number of the shareholders' representatives on the supervisory board; in this case, as ten out of the twenty members on the supervisory board were employee representatives, the shareholder representatives who may be appointed by the Federal State and the state of Lower Saxony may exceed a maximum of three.[216] Nevertheless, altogether, the VW Law entitled the Federal State and the state of Lower Saxony to each appoint two members on the supervisory board, that is, a total of four persons, which thus constituted a derogation from thegeneral company law.[217] It was presumed that, normally, both the trade unions and the Lower Saxony government pursued the same job-preserving goal; in the situation where the employee representatives and the state of Lower Saxony allied, they would hold the majority of votes on the supervisory board, which would enable them to oppose to takeovers that could lead to changes they were not anticipating, inter alia the potential reduction of jobs in the state or relocation of jobs to another country.[218]

The CJEU also pointed out that the supervisory board in Germany had significant powers, especially considering that its approval was necessary for a number of transactions, including investments and acquisition of other undertakings.[219] Thus, the power conferred on the Federal Government and the State of Lower Saxony to appoint four members on the supervisory board made it possible for them to exercise influence which exceeded their levels of investment and would restrict other shareholders' participation in the company; as a result this would deter direct investors

[214] Case C-112/05 *Commission v Germany*, Judgment of the Court of 23 October 2007. See paras 6 and 7. See also Du Plessis et al. (2017), pp. 215–221.

[215] Ibid, see para 9.

[216] Ibid, see paras 59–61.

[217] Ibid.

[218] Du Plessis et al. (2017), p. 217.

[219] Case C-112/05 *Commission v Germany*, Judgment of the Court of 23 October 2007. See para 65.

from other Member States from investing in the company's capital.[220] In its judgment, the CJEU found that this appointment power indeed violated the free movement of capital as stipulated in the TFEU.[221]

Concerning the voting cap, the CJEU admitted that the company was allowed to decide whether to follow the principle that "voting rights must be proportionate to the share of capital" which was laid down under the corporate law, or to amend this and impose limitations on the voting rights in certain cases.[222] Nevertheless, it also emphasized that there was a difference between a power made available to shareholders who were free to decide on this and a specific obligation imposed on shareholders by way of legislation as in this case by the VW Law.[223] Similarly, whilst the corporate law required a majority of at least 75% of the share capital for making certain resolutions (such as amendment of the company's articles of association, capital or financial structures), the company's articles of association may choose to increase and fix the percentage at a higher level; nevertheless, this choice of increasing the thresholds should also be made at the will of shareholders, rather than by a national measure.[224] The CJEU held that through the use of the voting cap, the Federal and state government could make a blocking minority, which enabled them to oppose important resolutions and exercise considerable influence on the basis of a lower level of investment than would be required under general company law.[225] The combination of the voting cap and the block minority would thus limit the possible effective participation of other shareholders in the company and deter direct investors from other Member States.[226] Thus the CJEU held that the combination use of the voting cap and the blocking minority was against the free movement of capital under the EC law; nevertheless, it omitted to state in clear terms that either of the two legal tools, when standing alone as such, would be unlawful as well.[227]

(3) Observations from the Takeover

In this case, the VW Law which set the above anti-takeover tools was formulated on the basis of an agreement between the trade unions, the government and the workers during the 1950s. Under this agreement, the workers and the trade unions, in return for relinquishing their claim to a right of ownership over the company, secured the assurance of protection against any large shareholder which might gain control of the company.[228] In the cases where the State is entitled with "golden share" rights,

[220] Ibid. See paras 64, 66.

[221] Ibid, see paras 66, 68. See Article 63 of the TFEU.

[222] Ibid, see para 39.

[223] Ibid, see para 40.

[224] Ibid, see para 45.

[225] Ibid, see paras 50–51.

[226] Ibid, see para 52.

[227] Ibid, see paras 44–56. See also Du Plessis (2017), pp. 220–221. In 2011, the EC started another attempt before the CJEU to have the 20% cap and the blocking minority of 20% enshrined in the VW Law of 1960 scrapped, but this claim was again dismissed in October 2013 in Case C-95/12 *European Commission v Federal Republic of Germany*, Judgment of the Court of 22 October 2013.

[228] Ibid, see para 22.

it often utilizes such rights to fend off potential acquirers to achieve certain public policy objectives (such as maintaining the employment rate in a certain region and ensuring the provision of public goods and services). As illustrated by this case, the State's intervention mechanisms should not violate the national laws and the relevant obligations under the EU laws. This case also reflected that the employee representatives of the target can have an important role in takeovers, particularly when they are backed by trade unions and formed an alliance with the State shareholder.[229] As approval from the supervisory board is required before the management board can take any anti-takeover actions, the stance of the employee representatives can be crucial: they may either choose to support the management board (and as in this case, the State shareholder) and approve the anti-takeover actions, or to reduce the impediment for the acquirer by not giving consent to the anti-takeover actions.

4.4.3 Protection of Other Stakeholders

4.4.3.1 Stakeholder-Orientation Embodied in the Corporate Governance System

The German system of corporate governance has often been described as stakeholder-oriented.[230] In the event of a takeover, the WpÜG, in its general principles, stipulates that "the management and supervisory board of the target company must act in the interests of the target company".[231] To understand the "interests of the target company", the foreword of the 2020 German CG Code may be referred to, which "highlights the obligation of the management board and supervisory board of listed companies to take into account the interests of the shareholders, the workforce and the other groups related to the company (the stakeholders) to ensure the best interests of the company"[232] and "requires that the company and its governing bodies must be aware of the company's role in the community and its responsibility vis-à-vis society".[233] This statement verifies that "the interests of the company" are not only limited to the interests of shareholders and the workforce; but protecting other corporate stakeholders (such as creditors) and societal interests (such as community) is also in the interests of listed companies.

The historical background of the co-determination system also illustrates that protecting the public interest is an integral part of German corporate governance. The public interest considerations could be discerned from the German co-determination system ever since the provisions of the Employee Co-Determination Act (1976) (the

229 Du Plessis (2017), p. 221.

230 Mager and Meyer-Fackler (2017), p. 33.

231 Subsections 3(3) of the WpÜG.

232 See para 1 of the "Foreword" (at page 2) of the 2020 German CG Code.

233 See para 2 of the "Foreword" (at page 2) of the 2020 German CG Code.

"MitbestG") conferred upon the employee representatives the right of "parity co-determination".[234] At first, a number of the largest and most renowned German companies of that time launched an objection against the constitutionality of the MitbestG before the German Federal Constitutional Court.[235] The opponents contended that such co-determination rights conferred by the MitbestG infringed upon the companies' property rights guaranteed by the Federal Constitution.[236] The Constitutional Court held that the purpose of the parity co-determination provisions under the MitbestG was to promote the common good, thus it was not only in conformity with the Federal Constitution, but also necessary for the promotion of the common good.[237] After that, in another judgment in 1982, the German Supreme Court in Civil Matters held that the provisions of the MitbestG had been passed in the public interest.[238] The Court concluded that "the MitbestG (1976) stretches beyond the interests of the persons immediately affected by it, it indeed serves the common good of the community (…) and aims at the entire national economy…"[239] Thus, according to this historical background, it seems that "the members on the supervisory board are not only obliged to consider the interests of the shareholders and employees when making decisions, but should also take into consideration the general public interest".[240] In a takeover, the co-determination system provides a possibility that employee representatives on the supervisory board may consider the impact of a decision on other corporate stakeholders and societal interests when they participate in the decision-making process of the target.

4.4.3.2 Disclosure of Non-financial Stakeholder Information under the HGB, AktG, WpÜG

The non-financial report obligation of the management board under the HGB and AktG and the disclosure obligation of the acquirer and target with regard to stakeholder issues under the WpÜG aim to reduce the information asymmetries which relevant stakeholders may encounter. Such mechanisms also provide protection to

---

[234] Du Plessis et al. (2017), p. 189. The Employee Co-Determination Act (MitbestG) introduced a kind of "quasi-parity" between the delegates of the shareholders and those of the employees, while the chairperson is elected from among the shareholder delegates and has the casting vote in case of a deadlock between shareholder and employee representatives.

[235] Ibid, see pp. 186–187.

[236] Ibid, see p. 187. Article 14 paras 1 and 2 of the German Federal Constitution provide: "The property and the right of succession into a decedent's estate are guaranteed. Their substance and limits are defined by statute".

[237] Ibid. Collection of Decisions of the German Federal Constitutional Court (BVerfGE) vol. 50, 290 et seq.

[238] Ibid. Collection of Decisions of the German Federal Supreme Court in Civil Matters (BGHZ) vol. 83, 106 et seq. (at 110 et seq.).

[239] Ibid, see pp. 187–188.

[240] Ibid, see p. 154.

the relevant societal interests in a takeover, particularly when combined with the co-determination system.

(1) Obligation of the Management to Make a Non-financial Statement in Corporate Activities

The HGB requires certain large public-interest companies that fall within the categories as listed under Section 289b to include a non-financial statement in their annual management report, which implements Article 19a of the EU Non-financial Reporting Directive (Directive 2014/95/EU).[241] The non-financial statement should include information on at least the following aspects: (i) environmental issues; (ii) employee matters, including information on, for example, measures taken to ensure gender equality, the rights of employees to be informed and consulted, the rights of trade unions; (iii) social matters; (iv) human rights, including information on, for example, the avoidance of human rights violations; (v) the combat against corruption and bribery.[242] Where the company subject to this obligation does not include information on one or more of the above aspects, it must provide a reasonable explanation for the lack of information in this non-financial statement.[243] Thus this non-financial reporting requirement, with regard to the formulation of its content, is implemented on a "comply-or-explain" approach.[244] The AktG stipulates that the supervisory board may instruct an external audit to be performed of the non-financial statement as required by Section 289b of the HGB.[245] The 2020 German CG Code also provides rules requiring that the shareholders and third parties be kept informed by management report which includes reporting on corporate social responsibility ("CSR reporting").[246] The non-financial statement and the CSR reporting usually reflect how a company performs its social responsibilities in its activities. In the event of a takeover, this statement and a report from the management of the acquirer provide the stakeholders of the target and the public with information about how the acquirer may assume its social responsibilities and take into account the interests of the stakeholders in its future activities after the takeover.

---

[241] Subsection 289b(1) of the HGB stipulates three types of capital companies that are subject to this non-financial reporting obligation: (i) those which fulfil the requirements of a large capital company as stipulated in Section 267 (para 3 sentence 1); (ii) those which satisfy the Section 264d of HGB ("capital market-oriented" company); (iii) those that have on average more than 500 employees during the financial year. The translation of subsection 289b(1) in this part referred to Kessedjian and Rivera (2020), p. 410.

[242] Subsection 289c(1) of the HGB.

[243] Subsection 289c(4) of the HGB.

[244] Section 317 of the HGB stipulates that in the audit of the management report, with regard to the requirements under Sections 289b and 289c, it is only necessary to check whether the non-financial declaration or the separate non-financial report has been submitted. Usually without the non-financial statement, the management board's report would be incomplete and would not pass the audit.

[245] Subsections 111(2), 171(1) of the AktG. The supervisory board also has the power to audit a separate non-financial report or a separate consolidated non-financial report if such a report has been prepared.

[246] See Principle 21 of the 2020 German CG Code.

(2) Obligation of the Acquirer and Target to Disclose Information on Stakeholder Issues in a Takeover

The WpÜG provides for specific rules concerning the disclosure of information about the effects of a takeover on non-shareholder stakeholders. When it came into force in 2002, a primary goal of the WpÜG was to "increase access to information for the securities holders concerned and for the target's employees and improve the transparency of the takeover procedure for all parties involved".[247] To achieve this goal, it imposed numerous notification and publication duties on the acquirer, which were not limited to the technical details of the offer, but also extended to, for example, the anticipated consequences of a successful offer for the target, the acquirer's intentions concerning the target given these anticipated consequences.[248] In July 2006, to implement the relevant disclosure requirements on the acquirer company and the board of the target company under the EU Takeover Directive,[249] these notification duties were further amended.[250]

Currently, the WpÜG requires the acquirer to publish a document containing the contents of the bid and the supplementary information of the bid.[251] The supplementary information to be given includes, for example, particulars of: (i) necessary steps which will ensure that the acquirer has at his disposal the funds required for performance of the offer in full, as well as details of the expected consequences of a successful offer for the acquirer's financial position, financial performance, and earnings positions; (ii) the acquirer's intentions with regard to the future business activity of the target and of the acquirer, to the extent the acquirer is affected, particularly the registered office and location of material business units of the company, the use of assets, future obligations, the employees and their representatives, the members of the management bodies, and material changes to the conditions of employment.[252] The information covers the potential impact of the takeover on the target stakeholders the acquirer may anticipate. For example, the financial performance of the acquirer may provide clues to the leverage of the bid, which usually has a deep impact on the financial situation of the target and the interests of its creditors. The acquirer's intention pertinent to the future businesses, the locations of the domicile and main parts of the target may affect stakeholders such as the existing suppliers and the local

247 Stohlmeier (2015), p. 55.

248 Ibid.

249 See Articles 6(3)(i), 9(5) of the EU Takeover Directive.

250 The WpÜG was amended by the Takeover Directive Implementation Act (Übernahmerichtlinie-Umsetzungsgesetz) (Issued on 8 July 2006 (BGBI. I S. 1426). See its official version in German available at: https://www.bgbl.de/xaver/bgbl/start.xav?startbk=Bundesanzeiger_BGBl&start=//*[@attr_id=%27bgbl106s1426.pdf%27]#__bgbl__%2F%2F*%5B%40attr_id%3D%27bgbl106s1426.pdf%27%5D__1621504877742 (accessed 20 May2021). Article 1(7)(13) of this Act amended Sections 11 and 27 of the WpÜG and implemented the disclosure requirements under the EU Takeover Directive. See also Stohlmeier (2015), p. 56: it is observed that "since the German legislator had already foreseen many of these rules when drafting in the original WpÜG, the necessary changes introduced in July 2006 were limited".

251 Section 11 of the WpÜG.

252 Subsection 11(2) of the WpÜG.

community. The potential changes to the position of employees and their representatives also directly bear on the interests of the employee group; and where the planned lay-off reaches a certain scale, the economic development and social stability of the local community may also be affected.

With regard to the disclosure duty of the boards, the WpÜG requires that the management board and the supervisory board of the target should give a substantiated statement on the offer, which contains in particular the anticipated consequences of a successful offer for the target, the employees and their representatives, the employment conditions as well as the locations of the target company.[253] This requirement may further reduce the information asymmetries which the employee representatives encounter when they participate in the decision-making of the supervisory board in a takeover. To this extent, such a statement also provides indirect protection for employees and other stakeholders the employee representatives intend to take into account.

4.4.4 Intermediate Conclusion

In the corporate governance regime, the supervisory board of the target plays an important role in the decision-making process of a takeover. Apart from those actions that are within the competence of the management board, the supervisory board's approval is required for both pre-bid and post-bid anti-takeover actions by the management board. Employee representatives thus have a strong position in takeovers, as can be seen from the Porsche SE/VW AG case, and the interests of employees as well as other societal interests affected by a takeover may be better considered by the boards. Moreover, the obligation of the management to make a non-financial statement in corporate activities in the corporate governance regime, and obligation of the acquirer and target to disclose information on stakeholder issues in a takeover (particularly how the takeover may affect relevant societal interests) in the takeover law regime also provide possibility for more non-shareholder stakeholders to be taken into account in the boards' decisions in takeovers.

4.5 Conclusion

The analysis in this chapter illustrates that under the current regulatory framework of takeovers in Germany, the competition law and FDI screening regulations dedicate focus to protection of the recognized public interest considerations. Meanwhile, the takeover law and corporate governance rules focus on regulating and protecting the interests of target shareholders, employees as well as other societal interests affected by a takeover.

---

[253] Subsection 27(1) of the WpÜG.

Protection of the Legally Recognized Public Interest Considerations

The competition law (the GWB) entitles the Minister of the BMWK to approve anti-competitive takeovers based on certain public interest reasons. This "public interest exemption" mechanism works as a major tool for protecting important societal interests in Germany. In the GWB cases as discussed in this chapter, the Minister has recognized the following considerations as in principle satisfying the "public interest exemption" standard in takeovers: (i) the preservation of important know-how, (ii) the improvement of international competitiveness, (iii) the retention of the employment rate in the region, (iv) the security of the energy supply of the country, (v) the achievement of environmental objectives of the Federal Government, (vi) the preservation of the university hospital and R&D of the university medical faculty, (vii) the defence interest of the country, (viii) the press diversity, (ix) the achievement of healthcare policy objectives and improvement of the healthcare level. The past cases also indicate that the Minister is not always independent from the political factors when making decisions and the recognition of the public interest considerations can be hard to predict in practice.

The AWV and AWG, in the FDI screening regime, also predominantly protect the public interest in foreign takeovers. Since the consecutive reforms of 2017, the scopes of transactions subject to a cross-sector investment review or a sector-specific investment review have been extensively enlarged. The sector-specific review of foreign takeovers remains focused on the defence sector and on protecting the security interest of Germany; the cross-sector review, as required by the EU FDI Screening Regulation, will also take into account the effects of the transaction on other Member State's public order or security. To respond to the COVID-19 crisis, protecting the critical infrastructure in the healthcare area from foreign investors is considered as an indispensable part of the "public order or security". Besides, protecting the "critical technologies" also falls within the "public order or security" interest, and the sectors and activities of companies as listed under such category have also been increased by the reforms in recent years.

Protection of the Interests of Corporate Stakeholders and Other Societal Interests Affected by a Takeover

The protection of the interests of corporate stakeholders (such as shareholders and employees) and other societal interests affected by a takeover (such as the interests of the environment and local community) is mainly observed from the corporate governance mechanisms under corporate law (the AktG) and the decision-making mechanisms under the takeover law (the WpÜG).

The AktG prescribes a co-determination system with employee participation on the supervisory board and requires the management board to act in the interest of the company. According to the WpÜG, where the target company does not "opt-in" for the board-neutrality rule under the EU Takeover Directive, the management board may take anti-takeover actions, either pre-bid or post-bid, with the approval from the supervisory board (except for actions that a diligent and conscientious manager of a company not subject to a takeover offer would have taken and the search for a competing offer). This design gives the supervisory board a prominent role in takeovers and provides the employee representatives on the supervisory board with an opportunity to consider the interests of other stakeholders, inter alia, the employee group. In the private regulation regime, the 2020 German CG Code does not provide specific mechanisms for protecting the relevant stakeholders in the event of a takeover, except for reiterating the co-determination and "CSR reporting" requirements.

In the corporate governance regime, the disclosure requirement on non-financial stakeholder issues under the HGB and the CSR reporting requirement under the 2020 German CG Code provide non-shareholder stakeholders with information about how a company performs its social responsibilities in corporate activities. In a takeover situation, the specific disclosure requirements on the acquirer company and the target boards in the WpÜG concerning the potential consequences of a takeover on relevant stakeholders further reduce the information asymmetries relating to these stakeholders. Such disclosure mechanisms may also work to protect the interests of relevant corporate stakeholders (such as employees, creditors, suppliers) and other societal interests affected by a takeover (such as the local community).

Chapter 5
The Regulatory Framework of China

Abstract This chapter examines the government regulation and private regulation of takeovers in China. It first explores the "public interest exemption" mechanism in China's competition law and the "pre-establishment national treatment plus negative list" mechanism as well as the national security review of foreign investments in China's FDI screening regulations. Following that, this chapter conducts research into the regulations in the corporate-governance-related fields and discusses the protection of shareholders and other stakeholders in the takeover law, corporate law and corporate governance code for listed companies in China. It also pays attention to the unique characteristic of the Chinese economy in which the SOE-related takeovers constitute a considerable portion in the market and examines the relevant societal interests that are regulated in these SOE-related takeovers as well as the regulatory mechanisms.

5.1 Introduction

In China, the "split-share structure reform", which was initiated in 2005 and largely finished at the end of 2006, gradually transferred the previously "non-tradable shares" into tradable shares.[1] It significantly reduced the level of ownership concentration in Chinese listed companies and injected vibrancy to the takeover market.[2] Since 2008, the financial environment for takeovers has also been improved: the restrictions on merchant banks to provide funding for takeover buyers were cancelled, and the private loans between non-financial institutions and online peer-to-peer lending were

[1] He and Kyaw (2018), p. 56: The non-tradable shares were previously owned by the state and legal persons (including enterprises, or public institutions and social organizations with legal personality) and accounted for two-thirds in China's stock market. In 2005, the China Securities Regulatory Commission (CSRC) initiated the share reforms to convert non-negotiable shares into negotiable shares gradually over a period up to 36 months. To learn more about the "split share reform", see Sect. 5.4.4.1 of this chapter.

[2] See Table 1 and Fig. 1 in Huang and Chen (2019), pp. 367–368: Table 1 "Shareholding of the largest shareholders of listed companies", and Fig. 1 "Largest shareholding in Chinese listed companies". Table 1 and Fig. 1 reveal how the ownership concentration in Chinese listed companies reduces after the 2005 reform.

H. Ai, *Protecting Societal Interests in Corporate Takeovers*,
https://doi.org/10.1007/978-981-19-7546-2_5

no longer banned.[3] Against this backdrop, the market environment for takeovers in China has changed a lot in the past fifteen years.

This chapter examines the government regulation and private regulation of takeovers in China and explores the relevant societal interests that are protected under these regulations as well as the relevant protection mechanisms.[4] Section 5.2 analyses the merger control review and "public interest exemption" review mechanism under Chinese competition law—The Anti-Monopoly Law. The focus of discussion will be on how the responsible authority for merger control interprets the considerations relevant to the "public interest exemption" and how it implements the "public interest exemption" review mechanism to approve anti-competition takeovers in practice.

Section 5.3 goes to the FDI screening regime of China and mainly analyses regulations in three fields: (1) the Foreign Investment Law and its implementation regulation which officially establish the "pre-establishment national treatment plus negative list" system for foreign investments and emphasize protecting legitimate interests of foreign investors; (2) the Special Administrative Measures for the Access of Foreign Investment (the "FI Negative List" hereinafter) which stipulates the prohibited and restricted sectors and activities for the market access for foreign investors; and (3) the newly published Measures for the Security Review of Foreign Investment, which rebuilds the national security review system in China.[5] By discussing each of the

---

[3] Huang and Chen (2019), pp. 365–366. In 2008, the China Banking Regulatory Commission prescribed that merchant banks can provide funding for takeover buyers. See Shangye Yinhang Binggou Daikuan Fengxian Zhiyin (商业银行并购贷款风险指引) (Guidelines on the Risk Management of M&A Loans of Commercial Banks) (Promulgated by the China Banking Regulatory Commission on June 12 2008, expired in 2015). In 2015, the Supreme People's Court of the PRC released a judicial interpretation to remove the 10-year ban on private loans between non-financial institutions and uphold the validity of peer-to-peer (P2P) lending. See Guanyu Shenli Minjian Jiedai Anjian Shiyong Falv Ruogan Wenti de Guiding (关于审理民间借贷案件适用法律若干问题的规定) (Provisions of the Supreme People's Court on Several Issues concerning the Application of the Law in Private Lending Cases) (Issued by the Supreme People's Court on 23 June 2015, effective on 1 September 2015, has been modified on 19 August 2020, 29 December 2020). Huang and Chen (2019, p. 365) also argued that the decline of the Chinese stock market in the past five years (2015–2019) also made many Chinese listed companies attractive and vulnerable as takeover targets.

[4] The English translations of the relevant Chinese laws and regulations in this book use the official English versions published on the website of the Chinese Government (if there is any) and the English versions published on the website of PKULAW.CN (if there is any).

[5] It should be noted that there are other important government regulations in the FDI screening regime and applicable to foreign investors at the market access stage, such as the Encouraged Catalogue for Foreign Investment (which stipulates the sectors and industries that foreign investors are encouraged to invest in China) and the Market Access Negative List (which stipulates the prohibited and restricted sectors applicable for both domestic and foreign investors in China). The relevant sectors and activities as stipulated in these regulations may also illustrate what societal interests China aims to protect and regulate in foreign takeovers. However, by contrast, the relevant sectors and activities as stipulated in the FI Negative List give more direct implications in this field, as it is specifically applicable to foreign investors and it specifies the restricted and prohibited sectors instead of encouraged sectors (normally the former indicates the most valued considerations). Therefore, to limit the scope of this book, Sect. 5.3 will only discuss the FI Negative List.

foregoing regulations, Sect. 5.3 aims to disclose how the scope of the regulated societal interests and the regulation approaches under the FDI screening regime have changed over time in China.

Section 5.4 conducts research into the takeover law, corporate law and the corporate governance code for listed companies in China. This section mainly explores how the government regulation and private regulation in these corporate-governance-related fields protect shareholders and other stakeholders of the target company. It analyses which kind of stakeholders and societal interests the current rules in these fields cover and what protection mechanisms are available for them.

One unique characteristic of the Chinese economy lies in the deep involvement of the Government and the Communist Party of China (the "CPC" hereinafter) in the corporate activities of Chinese SOEs. A considerable portion of takeovers and mergers in China was conducted by Chinese SOEs in recent years.[6] The SOEs are subject to specific corporate governance requirements in the corporate law regime and requirements on transfer of shares in other government regulations. Through these specific regulatory requirements, the Government and the CPC may participate in the corporate governance of SOEs and exercise deep influence in SOE-related takeovers to pursue public policies and protect certain public interest considerations. Section 5.4 also examines relevant corporate governance rules applicable to SOEs and specific regulation on SOE-related takeovers to see how the Government and CPC may intervene in SOE-related takeovers and what societal interests they pursue in this process.

Section 5.5 comes to a conclusion of this Chapter.

5.2 Competition Law—The Anti-Monopoly Law

5.2.1 Background to the Public Interest Protection Mechanism

The Anti-Monopoly Law (the "AML" hereinafter) regulates three types of monopolistic conducts in economic activities within the territory of China, of which takeovers fall within the type of "concentration of undertakings".[7] The years 2021 and 2022

---

[6] Zhou et al. (2015), p. 80.

[7] Zhonghua Renmin Gongheguo Fanlongduanfa (中华人民共和国反垄断法) (Anti-monopoly Law of the People's Republic of China) (Promulgated by the National People's Congress of the People's Republic of China on 30 August 2007, amended on 24 June 2022, effective on 1 August 2022). Article 3 lists three monopolistic conducts: (1) monopoly agreements reached between undertakings; (2) abuse of dominant position by undertakings; and (3) concentration of undertakings that lead or may lead to elimination or restriction of competition. Article 25 lists three types of "concentration of undertakings", which include: (1) merger of undertakings; (2) control over other undertakings gained by an undertaking through acquiring their shares or assets; and (3) control over other undertakings or the ability capable of exerting a decisive influence on the same gained by an undertaking through signing contracts or other means.

witnessed milestone reforms in the development of the AML. In October 2021, a Draft Amendment to the AML was released for public comments[8]; on 24 June 2022, China passed an official amendment to the AML ("Amendment 2022" hereinafter) which made an overhaul of this law for the first time after its coming into force in 2008.[9] The Amendment 2022 aims to deal with the key issues that have emerged in China's anti-monopoly enforcement during the past decade, particularly these that have arisen in the development of the digital economy.[10] In November of 2021, China made another big step to enhance its anti-monopoly regulation, by officially announcing the launch of the National Anti-monopoly Bureau (the "National Bureau" hereinafter). Prior to this, in the institutional reform in March 2018,[11] the competence to implement the AML was consolidated and transferred to the Bureau of the State Administration for Market Regulation (the "SAMR Bureau" hereinafter) from three responsible departments: the National Development and Reform Commission (the "NDRC" hereinafter), the State Administration for Industry and Commerce (the "SAIC" hereinafter) and the Ministry of Commerce (the "MOFCOM" hereinafter).[12] The inauguration of the National Bureau reflects China's resolution to accelerate the improvement of the anti-monopoly regulatory system. The National Bureau is still set under the SAMR and subject to the latter's general management.

---

[8] See Ma et al. (24 October 2021). Highlights of the Draft Amendment to the Anti-Monopoly Law. Available at: https://www.hankunlaw.com/newsAndInsights/enLawDetail.html?id=2c91af087a8577e3017cbf89807c0bbf (accessed 19 April 2022); Wei, Y., et al. (15 November 2021), An Interpretation of the Key Points in the Draft Amendment of the PRC Anti-Monopoly Law. Available at: http://www.junhe.com/legal-updates/1582 (accessed 19 April 2022).

[9] See NPC.GOV.CN (24 June 2022). 全国人民代表大会常务委员会关于修改《中华人民共和国反垄断法》的决定 (Decision of the Standing Committee of the National People's Congress on Amending the Anti-monopoly Law of the People's Republic of China). Available at: http://www.npc.gov.cn/npc/c30834/202206/e42c256faf7049449cdfaabf374a3595.shtml (accessed 4 July 2022). The English translation of the amended AML in this book was made by the author giving reference to Antitrust Review (27 June 2022).《中华人民共和国反垄断法》修改前后对照表(双语版) (Contrast Table of Anti-Monopoly Law of the People's Republic of China Before and After Revision (Bilingual Version)). Available at: https://mp.weixin.qq.com/s/8C9nW5t9eZelEPCNTBcH3w (accessed 4 July 2022).

[10] For example, Amendment 2022 introduced a new provision to the AML (Article 9) which provides that "undertakings shall not use data, algorithms, technology, capital advantages and platform rules to engage in monopolistic acts prohibited by this law".

[11] In March 2018, the State Council published the Institutional Reform Proposal: Guowuyuan Jigou Gaige Fangan (国务院机构改革方案) (The State Council Institutional Reform Proposal) (Approved at the First Session of the Thirteenth National People's Congress on March 17 2018).

[12] See Article 2(1) of Guowuyuan Jigou Gaige Fangan (国务院机构改革方案) (The State Council Institutional Reform Proposal). Besides, the SAMR also took over the competence of the Anti-Monopoly Commission of the State Council as listed in Article 9 of the AML. See the competence of the SAMR Bureau available at: http://www.samr.gov.cn/fldj/sjjs/ (accessed 1 June 2022), including (i) drawing up the measures and guidelines of the Anti-monopoly system; (ii) organizing the enforcement work of applying the Anti-monopoly Law; (iii) guiding the enterprises to respond to anti-monopoly suits overseas; organizing and guiding the review work of fair competition; (iv) undertaking the international cooperation and communications of the enforcement of Anti-monopoly Law; (v) undertaking the daily work of the anti-monopoly committee of the State Council.

Nevertheless, as a 'vice-ministerial' level institution, it now has a higher standing than the previous SAMR Bureau. Under the National Bureau, the Anti-monopoly Enforcement Department II (the "Enforcement Department II" hereinafter), which is a general directorate-level department, is now responsible for merger control in China.

Article 1 of the AML stipulates the general objectives of the law, which largely concentrate on the economic interests, including "to prevent and curb monopolistic acts, to protect fair market competition, to encourage innovation, to enhance economic efficiency, to safeguard consumers' interests and the general public interest, and to promote the healthy development of the socialist market economy".[13] Article 34 of the AML[14] allows the enforcement authority (the Enforcement Department II) to permit a concentration of undertakings that leads, or may lead, to elimination or restriction of competition if the parties involved can prove that "the advantages of the concentration to competition obviously outweigh its disadvantages to competition" (the "competition advantage exemption") or that "the concentration is in the public interest" (the "public interest exemption"). Where the enforcement authority decides not to prohibit the concentration, it may impose additional, restrictive conditions to reduce the negative impact exerted by such concentration on competition.[15] The two exemptions reflect both the competition interest and other non-competition public interest considerations the AML aims to regulate; and put together, they form the "public interest exemption review" mechanism in the merger control review procedure. Accordingly, the relevant societal interest considerations as regulated by the AML can be largely divided into two types: (1) the competition interest and relevant economic interest considerations; (2) other non-competition public interest considerations.

Moreover, for a takeover where the acquirer is a foreign investor and which involves national security concerns, Article 38 of the AML[16] stipulates that "a national security review shall be conducted as is required by the relevant State regulations, in addition to the merger control review subject to the AML". The AML does not provide specified provisions with regard to the meaning of the "national security" or the relevant responsibilities or procedures for the security review. Thus, whilst the national security interest is undoubtedly an important public interest the AML aims to protect, the details of the national security review will be discussed in Sect. 5.3 of this chapter, in combination with other FDI screening regulations.

---

[13] Article 1 of the AML. Among others, the objective "to encourage innovation" was added to Article 1 by the Amendment 2022.

[14] The original Article 28 AML before the amendment.

[15] Article 35 of the AML (the original Article 29 AML before the amendment).

[16] The original Article 31 AML before the amendment.

5.2.2 *Protection of the Competition Interest and Non-competition Public Interest Under the AML*

5.2.2.1 Protecting the Competition Interest: The Merger Control Review and the "Competition Advantage Exemption"

The competition interest as regulated under the AML is closely linked with economic considerations such as the "economic efficiency" or the "development of the socialist market economy". This section first analyses the considerations the Enforcement Department II (before October 2021, the SAMR Bureau) is required to take account of when it reviews a takeover or merger's effects on the competition interest; then it explores other economic considerations that are relevant to the competition interest and also explicitly or implicitly protected by the AML.

(1) Considerations Relevant to the Competition Interest under the AML

Article 34 of the AML specifically regulates anti-competitive takeovers by prescribing that "a concentration of undertakings that has or may have the effect of eliminating or restricting competition shall be prohibited". Article 33 AML[17] specifies the considerations the enforcement authority may take into account to review the anti-competitive effects of a takeover, among which, the impact of the takeover on "technology advancement" and on "the development of the national economy" is included.[18] The "development of the national economy" could be interpreted in such a broad way as incorporating all the relevant economic and social factors; the technology advancement is often closely linked with the industrial policies in crucial national industries, such as the defence sector and the high-technology sector.

Pursuant to Article 34, where the advantages of a takeover to competition obviously outweigh its disadvantages to competition, the Enforcement Department II may not prohibit it. To apply for this "competition advantage exemption", the parties to the takeover carry the burden of proving the "obviously outweigh". As the AML is silent on the standard, the Enforcement Department II has a large discretion in assessing "obviously outweigh". In 2020, the SAMR published a document for assessing the impact of concentration of undertakings—Interim Provisions on the Examination of Concentrations between Undertakings, which was amended in 2022.[19] It repeats the considerations under Article 33 of the AML for assessing the overall impact of a

[17] The original Article 27 AML before the Amendment.

[18] Article 33 of the AML. The competition aspects are the most prominent factors, including, for example, the parties' market influence (reflected in the market share and market control), the degree of concentration in the relevant market, and the impact of the concentration on market access, consumers, and other relevant enterprises.

[19] Jingyingzhe Jizhong Shencha Zanxing Guiding (经营者集中审查暂行规定) (Interim Provisions on the Review of Concentrations between Undertakings) (Promulgated by the State Administration for Market Regulation on 23 October 2020, amended on 24 March 2022, effective on 1 May 2022). To support the implementation of the amended AML, the SAMR further revised this Interim Provisions and published Provisions on the Review of Concentration of Undertakings (Draft for Comments) (经营者集中审查规定(征求意见稿)) on 27 June 2022.

concentration of undertaking on competition and does not provide for further specific factors to evaluate the "competition advantages" or to assess the offset between the advantages and harms to competition.[20] It does emphasize that to evaluate the competitive impact of the concentration of undertakings, the authority may also "comprehensively consider the impact of the concentration on the public interest and whether the undertakings participating in the concentration are enterprises on the brink of bankruptcy."[21]

With regard to what considerations can be recognized as "advantages to competition", the Provisions on Mergers and Acquisitions of Domestic Enterprises by Foreign Investors issued in 2006 (the "Provisions on Foreign Mergers and Acquisitions" hereinafter) provided some clues. It stipulated that one of the takeover parties may apply for a review exemption under any of the following circumstances: (i) the takeover may improve the conditions for fair competition in the market; (ii) a loss-making enterprise is taken over and employment is ensured; (iii) the takeover helps the absorption of advanced technologies and the improvement of management personnel and is able to improve the enterprise's international competitiveness; or (iv) the takeover may improve the environment.[22] Nevertheless, in the 2009 version of this regulation (the "Provisions on Foreign Mergers and Acquisitions (2009)" hereinafter), this provision was deleted.[23] This change suggested that the national competition policies of a country vary according to the changing economic, social and political situations and the international environment.[24]

The Interim Provisions on Assessing the Impact of Concentration of Undertakings on Competition (the "Interim Provisions on Assessing the Impact" hereinafter), which was promulgated by the MOFCOM in 2011, provided for more detailed factors for assessing the "competition advantages" a takeover may bring.[25] According to it, the effects of a takeover on the following economic aspects may be

[20] Article 24 of Interim Provisions on the Review of Concentrations between Undertakings.

[21] Article 30 of Interim Provisions on the Review of Concentrations between Undertakings. The newly published Provisions on the Review of Concentration of Undertakings (Draft for Comments) made no change to the content of Article 30 (which simply becomes Article 36 in this new draft regulation).

[22] Guanyu Waiguo Touzizhe Binggou Jingnei Qiye de Guiding (关于外国投资者并购境内企业的规定 (2006)) (Provisions on Mergers and Acquisitions of Domestic Enterprises by Foreign Investors) (2006 Revision). (Promulgated by Ministry of Commerce on 8 August 2006, effective on 8 September 2006, has been modified in 2009). See Article 54.

[23] Guanyu Waiguo Touzizhe Binggou Jingnei Qiye de Guiding (关于外国投资者并购境内企业的规定 (2009修订)) (Provisions on Mergers and Acquisitions of Domestic Enterprises by Foreign Investors) (2009 Revision). (Promulgated by Ministry of Commerce on 22 June 2009, effective on promulgation).

[24] See Ma (2014), p. 46.

[25] Shangwubu Guanyu Pinggu Jingyingzhe Jizhong Yingxiang de Zanxing Guiding (商务部关于评估经营者集中影响的暂行规定) (Interim Provisions on Assessing the Impact of Concentration of Undertakings on Competition) (Interim Provisions on Assessing the Impact) (Promulgated by the MOFCOM on 29 August 2011, effective on 5 September 2011). This document has expired in 2021.

regarded as "competition advantages": (i) positive effects on technology developments (mainly through the integrated resources of the R&D on technology)[26]; (ii) improved economic efficiency, the achievement of "economy of scale" which may reduce the production cost, promote production diversity and therefore benefit the consumers' interests[27]; (iii) increased pressure on other undertakings in the relevant market, which may prompt the other undertakings to improve their product quality, reduce the product price and thus enhance the consumers' welfare[28]; (iv) enhancement of the national economic development resulting from expanded business scales and increased competitiveness and efficiency.[29] In line with Article 33 AML, the Interim Provisions on Assessing the Impact (before it expired) also emphasized that a concentration of undertaking may have negative effects on the above economic interests (the technology development, the consumers' interests, the national economy).[30] The enforcement authority, to decide on a "competition advantage exemption", needs to assess the takeover's advantages as well as its limitations and harms to these economic interests, and estimate whether the advantages offset and "obviously outweigh" the disadvantages. Besides, to make this assessment, it is also required to consider other economic factors, such as whether the undertakings of the concentration are on the brink of bankruptcy.[31]

(2) Considerations of "Economic Efficiency" and "Development of the Socialist Market Economy"

The "economic efficiency" and "development of the socialist market economy (or national economy)" are important benchmarks for evaluating a takeover's effects on competition under the AML, the Interim Provisions on the Review of Concentrations between Undertakings, and the Interim Provisions for Assessing the Impact. The understandings and assessment criteria of "economic efficiency" depend to a large extent on the different types of the market economy (e.g., the capitalist economy and the socialist economy), and vary along with different development stages of the market economy. To this extent, the term "economic efficiency" is better to be explained in combination with the other term "the development of the socialist market economy (or national economy)".

The term "development of socialist market economy" (or national economy) entails advantages for different aspects of economic development, such as a vibrant employment market, high competitiveness of national companies in both domestic and international market, and well-developed R&D capacities of the companies in crucial industries. In the context of China, Shan et al. (2012) argued that "promoting

[26] Article 8 of the Interim Provisions on Assessing the Impact.

[27] Article 9 of the Interim Provisions on Assessing the Impact.

[28] Article 10 of the Interim Provisions on Assessing the Impact.

[29] Article 11 of the Interim Provisions on Assessing the Impact.

[30] Articles 8 ~ 11 of the Interim Provisions on Assessing the Impact.

[31] Article 8 of the Interim Provisions on Assessing the Impact.

the healthy development of the socialist market economy" may imply giving preference to developing the SOEs or specific producers.[32] Weinreich-Zhao (2015) also held that Article 1 of the AML opens the doors to an influx of other policy goals, among which, the industrial policy being the most prominent one.[33] In line with such arguments, Article 8 AML[34] emphasizes the protection of "lawful business operations of undertakings in industries that are under the control of the State-owned economic sector and have a bearing on the lifeline of the national economy or national security".[35] Li (2017) posited that the general expression of Article 8 AML leaves room for exempting anti-monopoly behavior of SOEs.[36] Sun (2015) argued that the enforcement authority has expanded the interpretation on Article 8 and tended to categorize all the SOEs into sectors and industries that "have a bearing on the lifeline of the national economy or national security".[37] Weinreich-Zhao (2015) also posited that this provision may be interpreted to facilitate mergers between SOEs and thus to further an industrial policy aimed at encouraging concentrations and consolidations in the SOE sector.[38]

5.2.2.2 Protecting Other Non-competition Public Interest Considerations: The "Public Interest Exemption"

In the event of a takeover, Article 34 allows the Enforcement Department II to not prohibit a concentration of undertakings that leads or may lead to elimination or restriction of competition if "the concentration is in the public interest".[39] The AML does not provide a detailed interpretation of the "public interest", nor does it give any specific examples of what societal interests could be counted as a "public interest" in the merger control regime.[40] As Article 34 stipulates both the "public interest exemption" and the "competition advantage exemption", the former should be understood in a way as referring to non-competition public interest considerations. Thus, considerations for assessing the "competition advantages" of a takeover as listed under the Interim Provisions on Assessing the Impact and other economic

---

[32] Ma (2014), p. 47. See Shan et al. (2012). China's Anti-Monopoly Law: What is the Welfare Standard?. *Review of Industrial Organization, 41*(1–2), 31–52.

[33] Weinreich-Zhao (2015), p. 63.

[34] The original Article 7 AML before the amendment.

[35] Article 8 of the AML.

[36] Li (2017), p. 122.

[37] Sun (2015), p. 20.

[38] Weinreich-Zhao (2015), pp. 64–67.

[39] Article 34 of the AML.

[40] While the Amendment 2022 proposed eye-catching revisions in relation to many areas of Chinese competition law, it made no change to the original Article 28 AML (which simply becomes Article 34 in the new AML).

considerations that are entailed by the competition interest under the AML shall be excluded from this type of "public interest exemption".[41]

Besides, Article 20 AML[42] also provides that the relevant articles (Articles 17[43] and 18[44]) which prohibit monopoly agreements do not apply to agreements that can be proven to be concluded for several purposes, including "serving public interests in energy conservation, environment protection and disaster relief".[45] As specified in the same law, the term "public interest" in Article 34 and Article 20 should be interpreted in a consistent way. Accordingly, the non-competition public interest considerations that may exempt an anti-competitive takeover must at least incorporate non-exclusive considerations of "energy conservation, environment protection and disaster relief".[46]

The public interest exemption review mechanism (which incorporates both "competition advantage exemption" and other "non-competition public interest exemption" grounds) applies to takeovers and mergers that satisfy the threshold for reviewing a concentration of undertakings as stipulated by the AML. The Enforcement Department II (before October 2021, the SAMR Bureau) is responsible for implementing the public interest exemption review of a takeover. According to Article 30 AML,[47] the Enforcement Department II should first conduct a preliminary review of a concentration within 30 days after it receives the documents or materials required by Article 28[48] from the undertakings concerned. If the Enforcement Department II decides to conduct further review after the preliminary review, Article 31[49] provides for that the second-stage review should be completed within 90 days after such a decision is made. In the second-stage review, the Enforcement Department II should make the decision whether or not to prohibit the concentration and inform the undertakings concerned with its decision. In this process, it must decide whether or not to implement the two exemptions in Article 34. In the second-stage review, one of the undertakings of the concentration concerned could submit to the Bureau its defence

[41] The relevant considerations include, for example, whether the undertaking is on the brink of bankruptcy or may enhance technology advancement (as listed in the Interim Provisions on Assessing the Impact); the industrial policies and other factors that are closely related to the development of the national economy (as stipulated by the AML).

[42] The original Article 15 AML before the amendment.

[43] The original Article 13 AML before the amendment.

[44] The original Article 14 AML before the amendment.

[45] Article 20 of the AML. The purposes listed in Article 20 include: (1) improving technologies, or engaging in research and development of new products; or (2) improving product quality, reducing cost, and enhancing efficiency, unifying specifications and standards of products, or implementing specialized vision of production; (3) increasing the efficiency and competitiveness of small and medium-sized undertakings; (4) serving public interests in energy conservation, environment protection and disaster relief; (5) mitigating sharp decrease in sales volumes or obvious overproduction; (6) safeguarding legitimate interests in foreign trade and in economic cooperation with foreign counterparts; or (7) other purposes as prescribed by law or the State Council.

[46] Li (2019), p. 85.

[47] The original Article 25 AML before the amendment.

[48] The original Article 23 AML before the amendment.

[49] The original Article 26 AML before the amendment.

opinions (competition advantage or other non-competition public interest considerations) and carries the burden of proof after the Enforcement Department II finds anti-competitive effects of the concentration. After assessing such public interest arguments (either competition advantages or other non-competition public interest considerations), the Enforcement Department II, makes the final decision of whether to prohibit or to exempt the concentration within the time limit required by Article 31 of the AML.

5.2.3 *Analysis of Previous Cases Under the AML*

This section discusses three representative cases under the AML: (1) The Coca-Cola/Huiyuan takeover; (2) The CNR/China CSR merger case; (3) The abandoned takeover of Yonghui/Zhongbai. The three cases illustrate how the responsible authorities interpreted the relevant societal interests regulated by the AML in practice. The discussion on the three cases aims to shed some light on the following aspects: (1) Was there a line between the protection of the competition interest and other economic interest considerations (such as the industrial policies and protection of SOEs) in the cases? (2) How did the responsible authorities interpret the national security interest in practice? (3) How was the "public interest exemption" review implemented in practice?

5.2.3.1 The Coca-Cola/Huiyuan Takeover: The Protection of Competition Interest or Industrial Policy?

This case led to much controversy in that MOFCOM, the responsible authority for the merger control review at that time, seemed to incorporate non-competition economic interest considerations, which normally can hardly be deemed as public interest in its decision-making. Thus, the case gave a glimpse of the difficulty in delimiting the relevant societal interests that are regulated under the Chinese merger control regime in practice.

(1) Background of the Case

On 18 March 2009, the MOFCOM prohibited the proposed takeover plan by Coca-Cola of Huiyuan, the largest Chinese fruit juice producer and a company incorporated in the Cayman Islands and registered in Hong Kong.[50] Before this takeover, "Huiyuan" was one of the 25 best known brands in China and a leading brand

[50] See the detailed introduction of this case in Weinreich-Zhao (2015), pp. 93–94. See MOFCOM.GOV.CN (18 March 2009). 商务部关于禁止可口可乐公司收购中国汇源公司审查决定的公告(2009年第22号) (Announcement from the MOFCOM of the Review Decision on Prohibiting the Coca-cola/Huiyuan Takeover) (2009, No.22). Available at: http://fldj.mofcom.gov.cn/aarticle/ztxx/200903/20090306108494.html (accessed 1 March 2021).

in the Chinese juice market.[51] The MOFCOM's decision held that this takeover "would squash the survival space of the domestic medium and small-sized juice producers, restrain domestic enterprises' capacity in competing in the juice market and achieving independent innovation"; and it "would cause negative impacts on the effective competition structure of the Chinese juice market, and hinder a sustainable and healthy development of the Chinese juice industry".[52] The MOFCOM also considered that the takeover parties involved failed to sufficiently prove that the advantages to competition created by this transaction could obviously outweigh its disadvantages or that the transaction would be in the public interest.[53] Based on the above considerations and pursuant to Articles 33, 34 and 35 of the AML,[54] the MOFCOM decided to prohibit this proposed concentration.

(2) Controversy in This Case

It is suspected that instead of conducting a strictly competition-based assessment, the MOFCOM made its decision in this case largely on the grounds of protecting the national brand and the domestic juice industry. As the juice industry can hardly be recognized as a crucial sector of the national economy, it is difficult to regard the protection of this famous brand as an indispensable part of protecting the national economic security or other public interests. Besides, the fact that the MOFCOM's decision and the legal reasoning were so brief further exacerbated the public doubts. Some scholars argued that the decision in this case illustrated the procedural deficiencies in China's merger control review at this stage: the analysis was oversimplified and short; the economic data used for the analysis was not accessible to the public; during the merger control review, no hearing procedure was available and consumers' opinions were not fully heard.[55] Accordingly, it is difficult to exclude other non-competition economic considerations from this prohibition decision.[56] As Weinreich-Zhao (2015) concluded, the last references in the decision to "the competitiveness of small and medium enterprises in China" and "the sustainable and healthy development of the Chinese juice industry" caused suspicion "whether the decision was an illustration of a protectionist application of the AML by the MOFCOM, motivated by industrial policy considerations rather than competition policy goals".[57]

---

[51] Before this takeover, Huiyuan possessed a market share of 46 per cent for pure juice, 39.8% for juice drinks with 26–99% juice content, and 10.3 per cent for juice drinks with less than 25% juice content. See Weinreich-Zhao (2015), p. 93.

[52] MOFCOM.GOV.CN (18 March 2009). 商务部关于禁止可口可乐公司收购中国汇源公司审查决定的公告(2009年第22号) (Announcement from the MOFCOM of the Review Decision on Prohibiting the Coca-cola/Huiyuan Takeover) (2009, No.22).

[53] Ibid.

[54] The original Articles 27, 28, 29 of the AML at that time.

[55] Wei (2013), p. 128; Weinreich-Zhao (2015), p. 303.

[56] Weinreich-Zhao (2015), p. 303.

[57] Ibid, p. 99.

Confronted with the above arguments, the MOFCOM defended its position in a later Press Conference in 2010.[58] It emphasized that the prohibition of the Coca-cola/Huiyuan case was actually an exceptional one compared with the other takeover and merger cases it had approved. According to the then Director of the Anti-monopoly Bureau of the MOFCOM, Ming Shang, until the Press Conference, almost 95% of the cases that were sent for a review received an approval decision, five cases received restrictive conditions, and only one case, Coca-cola/Huiyuan, got a prohibition.[59] When asked whether the Anti-monopoly Bureau was affected by the public cry for protecting the famous national brand when making the final decision in this case, Ming Shang reiterated that "when the Anti-monopoly Bureau reviewed a concentration, it completely based its decision on the competition considerations, which had already been recognized by foreign professionals".[60]

Nevertheless, this case still showed the main problems with the merger control review in China at the early stage after the AML came into force. Without detailed rules on the substantive competition standards for the review, a transparent review procedure and a convincing economic analysis, the merger control review decisions in cases with foreign participants are likely to leave a protectionist impression that the authority largely considers the industrial policy instead of the competition interest.

5.2.3.2 The CNR/China CSR Merger: Advantages to Competition or Other Public Interest Considerations?

The CNR/China CSR case discussed in this section is a merger instead of takeover, but the considerations the Chinese regulators took into account in this case give a good illustration of how they implemented the public interest exemption review mechanism in practice.

In March 2015, MOFCOM unconditionally approved the merger between China's two state-owned train manufactures—the China CNR Corporation Limited (the "CNR" hereinafter) and the China South Locomotive & Rolling Stock Corporation Limited (the "China CSR" hereinafter).[61] After the merger, the China CRRC Corporation Limited (the "CRRC" hereinafter) was established and became a super-giant in both the domestic and international railway transportation equipment market.[62]

---

[58] See MOFCOM.COM.CN (12 August 2010). 商务部召开反垄断工作情况专题新闻发布会 (Ministry of Commerce holds the Special Press Conference on the Implementation of the Anti-monopoly Law). Available at: http://www.mofcom.gov.cn/aarticle/ae/ai/201008/20100807078063.html?%2042452330511%E2%81%8444123207458 (accessed 1 March 2021).

[59] Ibid.

[60] Ibid.

[61] See MOFCOM.GOV.CN (3 April 2015). 2015年第一季度无条件批准经营者集中案件列表 (List of Cases of the Unconditionally Approved Concentrations of Undertakings of the First Quarter of 2015). Available at: http://fldj.mofcom.gov.cn/article/zcfb/201504/20150400932418.shtml (accessed 1 March 2021).

[62] Liu (2016), p. 124. See the news about the merger at Lin, Q. (31 December 2014). 中国南车北车合并变身"中国中车" (The China CSR and CNR Merged into CRRC). Available at: http://www.gov.cn/xinwen/2014-12/31/content_2798737.htm (accessed 22 April 2022).

The CNR and the China CSR together already controlled China's domestic rolling-stock market before the merger.[63] In the international market, in 2010, the China CSR ranked first and CNR ranked third in the world's top 10 largest manufacturers of new rolling stock[64]; between 2011 and 2014, the CNR and the China CSR ranked first and second respectively among the world's rolling stock suppliers for consecutive years before the merger.[65] The two companies claimed that the merger aimed to achieve synergy effects, increase the R&D capability in high-technology, improve the competitive advantages, and promote Chinese high-end equipment manufacturing to go further into the world.[66] Opponents were concerned whether the merger would form a monopoly position in the relevant market in China, which could impede the quick improvement of technologies and the building up of core competitiveness.[67] According to an officer of the State-owned Assets Supervision and Administration Commission of the State Council (the "SASAC" hereinafter), before the proposal of the merger, there were serious competition problems between the China CSR and CNR, particularly by lowering the offer price to win the market overseas.[68] The market regulators worried that the continuation of such situations would incrementally impede the Chinese companies' competitiveness in the international railway manufacturing market.[69] Professionals from the SASAC suggested that the synergy effects gained from the merger would largely strengthen the companies' capacity in R&D of high-technology and improve their international competitiveness.[70] To this

---

63 See the relevant data at Xinhuanet (31 December 2014). Shares of CNR, CSR Surge after Merger Announcement. Available at: https://www.chinadaily.com.cn/business/2014-12/31/content_19208682.htm (accessed 7 July 2022); Macquarie Research (26 June 2014). China CNR Corp: The Other Twin Brother. Available at: http://pg.jrj.com.cn/acc/Res/HK_RES/STOCK/2014/6/26/1efc5efd-629a-420a-a040-4427e3428ebb.pdf (accessed 7 July 2022); Economist Intelligence (6 September 2016). Assessing Mega-mergers through the CSR-CNR Lens. Available at: http://country.eiu.com/article.aspx?articleid=944580878&Country=China&topic=Economy_1 (accessed 7 July 2022).

64 Briginshaw, D. (20 April 2012). CSR tops the rolling stock league, but can it stay there? Available at: https://www.railjournal.com/rolling-stock/csr-tops-the-rolling-stock-league-but-can-it-stay-there/ (accessed 26 April 2022).

65 CRRC (29 March 2016). CRRC Corporation Limited: 2015 Annual Results Announcement. Available at: https://www.crrcgc.cc/Portals/250/pdf/CRRC_AR2015.pdf (accessed 7 July 2022).

66 Lin, Q. (31 December 2014). 中国南车北车合并变身"中国中车" (The China CSR and CNR Merged into CRRC).

67 Ye (28 September 2015). 中车集团正式成立,中国南北车完成合并 (The Establishment of the CRRC Marking the Completion of The Merger Between China CSR and CNR). Available at: https://www.bbc.com/zhongwen/simp/china/2015/09/150928_china_rail (accessed 1 March 2021).

68 Yang & Zhang (26 March 2015). 南北车合并预计6月完成 (Merger Between China CSR and CNR Expected to be Finished in June). Available at: http://dz.jjckb.cn/www/pages/webpage2009/html/2015-03/26/content_3624.htm (accessed 22 April 2022).

69 Zhang (4 November 2014). 院士称南北车早该合并: 搞恶性竞争致海外买家怀疑中国技术 (Academician Said That the Merger between the China CSR and CNR Should Have Taken Place Earlier: Vicious Competition Caused Overseas Buyers to Doubt Chinese Technology). Available at: http://politics.people.com.cn/n/2014/1104/c1001-25968923.html (accessed 7 July 2022).

70 Yang & Zhang (26 March 2015). 南北车合并预计6月完成 (Merger Between China CSR and CNR Expected to be Finished in June).

extent, the merger was even considered as "would provide an important direction for the future Chinese SOE reforms".[71]

Similar to other approval cases, MOFCOM did not publish the reasoning of its decision in this case. The final approval for this merger implied the use of the public interest exemption mechanism for approving anti-competitive concentrations in practice. It illustrated that the "advantages to the international competitiveness" of the Chinese SOEs could overwhelmingly triumph over the potential anti-competition effects in the domestic market; or interpreted from another perspective, the merger provided examples of what is "in the public interest". As argued by the merging parties in this case, promoting the R&D capacity of high technology in China, increasing Chinese SOEs' international competitiveness, and more importantly, providing a good precedent for future Chinese SOE reforms could all be used as "public interest" justifications. The results of the merger did not disappoint the regulator: in 2015, the CRRC undoubtedly ranked first in the 'Top 10 manufacturers of rolling stock ranked by new vehicles' revenue 2015.[72]

5.2.3.3 The Abandoned Takeover of Zhongbai by Yonghui: The National Security Interest in the Retail Sector?

This takeover attracted publicity because this was the first publicly reported case since the NDRC took over the national security review responsibility from MOFCOM in April 2019. It also caused controversy in that it indicated that a national security review may be conducted in the retail sector, where Yonghui and Zhongbai operate their major businesses.

In August 2019, Chinese supermarket chain Yonghui Superstores received the "no prohibition" decision from MOFCOM on its proposed takeover of Zhongbai Holdings, another Chinese retailer.[73] Then in September 2019, Yonghui received a notice from the NDRC stating that this takeover was subject to a national security review,[74] followed by another notification from the NDRC in November 2019

[71] Ibid.

[72] SCIMULTICLIENTSTUDIES (2016). Worldwide Rolling Stock Manufacturers 2016. Available at: https://www.sci.de/fileadmin/user_upload/Flyer_Hersteller_Schienenfahrzeuge.pdf (accessed 22 April 2022).

[73] See Eastmoney (21 August 2019). 永辉超市关于收到国家市场监督管理总局《经营者集中反垄断审查不予禁止决定书》的公告(Announcement from Yonghui Supermarket on Receiving the "No-Prohibition Decision Concerning the Anti-monopoly Review of the Concentration of Undertakings" from the SAMR). Available at: http://data.eastmoney.com/notices/detail/601933/AN201908201344715940,JUU2JUIwJUI4JUU4JUJFJTg5JUU4JUI2JTg1JUU1JUI4JTgy.html (accessed 22 April 2022).

[74] Eastmoney (26 September 2019). 永辉超市关于要约收购中百控股集团股份有限公司的进展公告(Announcement from Yonghui Supermarket on the Progress of the Takeover of Zhongbai). Available at: http://data.eastmoney.com/notices/detail/601933/AN201909251367565887,JUU2JUIwJUI4JUU4JUJFJTg5JUU4JUI2JTg1JUU1JUI4JTgy.html (accessed 22 April 2022).

which initiated a special review of the security concerns in this takeover.[75] According to the NDRC, this takeover was subject to a national security review because the largest shareholder of Yonghui, the Dairy Farm which held almost 20 per cent in the company, was a subsidiary of British conglomerate Jardine Dairy Farm.[76] In December 2019, Yonghui published an announcement on signing a cooperation memorandum and cancelling this takeover offer to Zhongbai.[77] In this announcement, Yonghui mentioned the NDRC's requirement for it to hold a friendly negotiation with the Wuhan State-owned Assets Management Limited Company, the actual controlling shareholder of Zhongbai.[78]

Normally the retail sector is not regarded as a security-sensitive sector. It is neither closely relevant to the defence interest, nor regarded as the frontier of technology development. It is hard to consider the retail sector as bearing crucial importance for the stability of the national economy or the social life order. In this case, the NDRC did not publish the detailed reasoning for its decision online. As a result, the standards for conducting security review in takeovers and mergers with foreign participants remain obscure. From this case, it could be observed that the scope of sectors and industries as relevant to the national security interest, which is a recognized public interest consideration under the AML, is hard to be predicted by participants to takeovers and mergers in China.

5.2.4 Intermediate Conclusion

The foregoing analysis in this section illustrates that the scope of the relevant societal interests as regulated by the AML is much broader than the competition interest. First of all, by incorporating the "economic efficiency" and "development of the socialist market economy" in the general objectives of the AML and stipulating the "advantages to competition" as one exemption to anti-competition takeovers, the

[75] Eastmoney (13 November 2019). 永辉超市关于收到国家发展和改革委员会关于特别审查告知书的公告(Announcement from Yonghui Supermarket on Receiving the Special Review Notification from the NDRC). Available at: http://data.eastmoney.com/notices/detail/601933/AN201911121370671865,JUU2JUIwJUI4JUU4JUJFJTg5JUU4JUI2JTg1JUU1JUI4JTgy.html (accessed 22 April 2022).

[76] Ding (17 December 2019). Yonghui Drops Plans to Increase Stake in Chinese Retailer After National Security Probe. Available at: https://www.caixinglobal.com/2019-12-17/yonghui-drops-plans-to-increase-stake-in-chinese-retailer-after-national-security-probe-101495178.html (accessed 22 April 2022).

[77] STATIC.SSE.COM.CN (17 December 2019). 永辉超市股份有限公司关于签署《合作备忘录》暨取消部分要约收购中百集团的公告 (Announcement from Yonghui Supermarket on Signing the "Memorandum of Cooperation" and Cancelling the Partial Takeover Offer to Acquire Zhongbai Group). Available at: http://static.sse.com.cn//disclosure/listedinfo/announcement/c/2019-12-17/601933_20191217_2.pdf (accessed 22 April 2022).

[78] Ibid.

merger control regime does not only cover the efficiency interest, but also considerations related to the industrial policies of crucial national sectors as well as the protection of SOEs. Then by recognizing the "non-competition public interest" as another exemption for anti-competition takeovers and given the obscure definition of the "public interest" in this law, other non-economic societal interests may also be incorporated under the merger control regime. Among others, the AML specifically regulates the national security interest in foreign takeovers, which refers to not only the defence security, but also entails considerations such as the economic security (the stable operation of national economy), the basic social order (the stability of the society), and the technology and know-how security in foreign takeovers. The cases as discussed in this section reveal that the responsible authorities have large discretion in interpreting and implementing the two public interest exemptions in merger control review.

5.3 Regulations in the FDI Screening Regime

5.3.1 Background and Recent Reforms

The value of the FDI into China has remained at a high level for the past decade. The increase of the FDI value between 2013–2018 is illustrated in Fig. 5.1.[79] In 2019 and 2020, FDI into China kept reaching a record-high value: in 2019, it was 136.7 billion U.S. dollars, up 5.8% from a year earlier[80]; in 2020, it continued to increase by 6.2% year-on-year to 144.3 billion U.S. dollars according to the MOFCOM.[81]

Behind this eye-catching increase were China's changing positions in market access policies for foreign investors and a series of prominent regulation reforms in the FDI screening regime since 2018. In the past, China had been implementing restrictive market access regulation on foreign investments for a long time. The public concerns at that time were that the tremendous economic power and financial forces of certain multinationals would expand too rapidly and gain market powers before domestic firms which lacked advanced technology, efficiency, and capital, could be

[79] ENGLISH.SCIO.GOV.CN (15 March 2019). Quick View of China's Foreign Investment Law. Available at: http://english.scio.gov.cn/infographics/2019-03/15/content_74574531.htm (accessed 1 March 2021).

[80] NEWS.CGTN.COM (21 January 2020). China's FDI up 5.8% in 2019, high-tech industry biggest beneficiary. Available at: https://news.cgtn.com/news/2020-01-21/China-s-FDI-up-5-8-in-2019--NqC5cZVr4k/index.html (accessed 1 March 2021). According to this news report, foreign investment in high-tech industry grew 25.6 per cent in 2019 to 266 billion yuan, accounting for 28.3 per cent of the whole foreign investment.

[81] MOFCOM.GOV.CN (20 January 2021). 2020年我国利用外资增长6.2%，规模创历史新高 (China's utilization of foreign capital increases by 6.2% in 2020, hitting a record high in scale). Available at: http://www.mofcom.gov.cn/article/news/202101/20210103032555.shtml (accessed 1 March 2021).

Fig. 5.1 FDI in China 2013–2018 (US$ billion)[82]

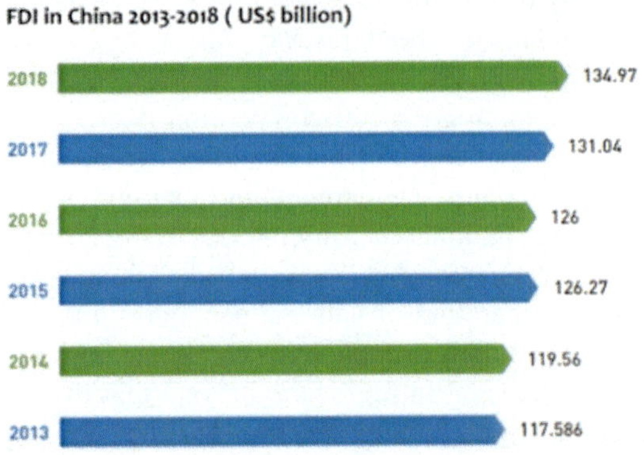

well established.[83] Against that backdrop, foreign investments were subject to strict scrutiny, and more weight was put on protecting domestic industries.[84] This restrictive stand was often criticized for creating an unequal playing field for Chinese companies and their foreign competitors in the global market. Between 2018 and 2021, China has been accelerating its opening up towards foreign investment and promulgated a series of regulations to facilitate the reform. On 28 June 2018, the NDRC and MOFCOM jointly issued the Special Administrative Measures for the Access of Foreign Investment (the "2018 FI Negative List" hereinafter) which applied to regulate the market access for foreign investors in the whole country of China.[85] The 2018 FI Negative List was updated in 2019, 2020, 2021 respectively (the "2019 FI Negative List",[86] the "2020 FI Negative List"[87] and the "2021 FI Negative List"[88]

[82] Figure 5.1 originates from ENGLISH.SCIO.GOV.CN (March 15 2019). Quick View of China's Foreign Investment Law.

[83] Weinreich-Zhao (2015), p. 27.

[84] Ibid.

[85] MOFCOM.GOV.CN (28 June 2018). 发展改革委、商务部令 (2018年第18号): 外商投资准入特别管理措施 (负面清单) (2018年版) (National Development and Reform Commission and the Ministry of Commerce (2018 No. 18): 2018 Special Administrative Measures for the Access of Foreign Investment Access). Available at: http://www.mofcom.gov.cn/article/b/f/201806/20180602760432.shtml (accessed 1 March 2021).

[86] WWW.GOV.CN (30 June 2019).《外商投资准入特别管理措施 (负面清单) (2019年版) 》发布 (The release of the "2019 Special Administrative Measures for the Access of Foreign Investment"). Available at: http://www.gov.cn/xinwen/2019-06/30/content_5404703.htm (accessed 1 March 2021).

[87] WWW.GOV.CN (23 June 2020). 外商投资准入特别管理措施 (负面清单) (2020年版) 说明 (Specification on the 2020 Special Administrative Measures for the Access of Foreign Investment). Available at: http://www.gov.cn/gongbao/content/2020/content_5532623.htm (accessed 1 March 2021).

[88] See WWW.GOV.CN (27 December 2021).《外商投资准入特别管理措施 (负面清单) (2021年版) 》说明(Specification on the "2021 Special Administrative Measures for the Access of Foreign Investment"). Available at: http://www.gov.cn/gongbao/content/2022/content_5679693.htm (accessed 5 June 2022).

hereinafter). In 2019, two crucial regulations in the FDI screening regime were further promulgated. On 15 March 2019, the National People's Congress passed the Foreign Investment Law, which took effect on 1 January 2020.[89] The Foreign Investment Law formally establishes a "pre-establishment national treatment plus negative list" approach to regulate the market access for foreign investments. To ensure the implementation of the Foreign Investment Law, the State Council published the Regulation on Implementing the Foreign Investment Law of the PRC (the "Implementing Regulation" hereinafter) on 31 December 2019, which took effect on the same day as the Foreign Investment Law.[90] The two regulations highlight China's efforts to promote inward foreign investments and standardize the detailed rules on the administration for foreign investments.[91]

Regulation of the national security review of foreign investments is another pillar of the FDI screening regime. Prior to 2020, two regulations dominated the national security review of foreign takeovers: the Notice of the General Office of the State Council on the Establishment of the Security Review System for Mergers and Acquisitions of Domestic Enterprises by Foreign Investors (the "Notice 2011" hereinafter)[92] and the Provisions of the Ministry of Commerce on the Implementation of the Security Review System for Mergers and Acquisitions of Domestic Enterprises by Foreign Investors (the "Provisions 2011" hereinafter).[93] Neither the Foreign Investment Law nor the Implementing Regulation elaborates on the security review system in foreign investment. In December 2020, China promulgated the Measures for the Security Review of Foreign Investment (the "Measures for the Security Review" hereinafter), which became effective on 18 January 2021.[94] This regulation fills in the loopholes in the Foreign Investment Law by providing detailed

[89] Zhonghua Renmin Gongheguo Waishang Touzifa (中华人民共和国外商投资法) (Foreign Investment Law of the People's Republic of China) (Promulgated by the National People's Congress of the People's Republic of China on 15 March 2019, effective on 1 January 2020).

[90] Zhonghua Renmin Gongheguo Waishang Touzifa Shishi Tiaoli (中华人民共和国外商投资法实施条例) (Implementing Regulation for the Foreign Investment Law of the People's Republic of China) (Promulgated by the State Council on 12 December 2019, effective on 1 January 2020).

[91] XINHUANET.COM (31 December 2019). China releases regulation on implementing foreign investment law. Available at: http://www.xinhuanet.com/english/2019-12/31/c_138669461.htm (accessed 1 March 2021).

[92] Guowuyuan Bangongting Guanyu Jianli Waiguo Touzizhe Binggou Jingnei Qiye Anquan Shencha Zhidu de Tongzhi (国务院办公厅关于建立外国投资者并购境内企业安全审查制度的通知) (Notice of the General Office of the State Council on the Establishment of the Security Review System for Mergers and Acquisitions of Domestic Enterprises by Foreign Investors) (Promulgated by the General Office of the State Council on 3 February 2011, effective on 5 March 2011).

[93] Shangwubu Shishi Waiguo Touzizhe Binggou Jingnei Qiye Anquan Shencha Zhidu de Guiding (商务部实施外国投资者并购境内企业安全审查制度的规定) (Provisions of the Ministry of Commerce on the Implementation of the Security Review System for Mergers and Acquisitions of Domestic Enterprises by Foreign Investors) (Promulgated by the Ministry of Commerce on 25 August 2011, effective on 1 September 2011).

[94] Waishang Touzi Anquan Shencha Banfa (外商投资安全审查办法) (Decree No.37 of the National Development and Reform Commission and the Ministry of Commerce: Measures for the Security Review of Foreign Investment) (Promulgated by the National Development and Reform Commission and the Ministry of Commerce on 19 December 2020, effective on 18 January 2021).

provisions on security review of foreign investments and reconstructs the national security review regime.

In addition to the above regulations on the market access and national security review of foreign investments, the Provisions on Foreign Mergers and Acquisitions (2009), which has been briefly discussed in the merger control regime, and the Measures for the Administration of Strategic Investment in Listed Companies by Foreign Investors (the "Measures for Foreign Strategic Investment" hereinafter) also provide for rules regulating relevant societal interests in foreign takeovers.[95]

This section explores the relevant societal interests that are protected under the aforementioned FDI screening regulations in China, with a focus on the regulations on market access and the national security review of foreign investments.

5.3.2 Regulation on Market Access for Foreign Investments

5.3.2.1 The "Pre-establishment National Treatment Plus Negative List" Approach

(1) Market Access Regulation Prior to the Foreign Investment Law

Since 1995, China has adopted a "Catalogue of Industries for Guiding Foreign Investment" (the "Catalogue of Industries" hereinafter), which incorporated the "prohibited, restricted and encouraged industries" to guide foreign investors who intended to conduct investment in China.[96] The Catalogue of Industries was updated several times in the following years until 2017.[97] The regulation on market access for foreign investment into China during this period was established on the basis of the catalogue system, which imposed various approval and recording requirements for foreign investments. For example, the Provisions on Foreign Mergers and Acquisitions (2009) required "that foreign investors shall first obtain approval" from the MOFCOM and its local counterparts before they could take over a domestic enterprise or establish a foreign-invested enterprise in China.[98] According to Administrative Measures for the Confirmation and Recording of Foreign-Funded Projects,

[95] Waiguo Touzizhe dui Shangshi Gongsi Zhanlue Touzi Guanli Banfa (外国投资者对上市公司战略投资管理办法(2012修订)) (Measures for the Administration of Strategic Investment in Listed Companies by Foreign Investors) (2015 Revision) (Promulgated by the Ministry of Commerce, China Securities Regulatory Commission, State Administration of Taxation, State Administration for Industry and Commerce, and State Administration of Foreign Exchange on 28 October 2015, effective on promulgation).

[96] Du, 2020, p. 73. Waishang Touzi Chanye Zhidao Mulu (外商投资产业指导目录 (1995)) (Catalogue of Industries for Guiding Foreign Investment) (1995) (Promulgated by the State Development Planning Commission, State Economic and Trade Commission, and the Ministry of Foreign Trade and Economic Cooperation on 20 June 1995, effective on promulgation, repealed in 2002).

[97] The catalogue was updated at intervals in 1997, 2002, 2004, 2007, 2011, 2015, and 2017, respectively.

[98] Articles 6, 10, 11 of Provisions on Foreign Mergers and Acquisitions (2009).

as to foreign investment projects for which the Catalogue of Industries requires that the Chinese party should hold a controlling shareholding, approval from the NDRC and its local counterparts was necessary; and other foreign investment projects were subject to record-filing requirements.[99] As the record-filing application can be refused by the NDRC and its local counterparts in certain conditions, it was in essence an approval obligation for foreign investors.[100]

Since 2018, a nationwide "negative list" system started to apply to regulate the market access for foreign investment, which largely reduced the approval requirements for foreign investors at the market access stage.[101] The NDRC and MOFCOM jointly issued the 2018 FI Negative List which specifically applied to foreign investors.[102] It incorporated industries in which the foreign investors are prohibited from investing ("prohibited industries") and industries where the foreign investors' access is restricted ("licensed (restricted) industries"). Pursuant to the "negative list" system, only foreign investments in the "licensed industries" are subject to *ex ante* approval (or licence) requirements. For foreign investments in the industries that are out of the negative list, *ex ante* approval from administrative regulators is no longer required, whist they are still subject to *ex post* record-filing requirements.[103]

---

99 Waishang Touzi Xiangmu Hezhun he Beian Guanli Banfa (外商投资项目核准和备案管理办法) (Administrative Measures for the Confirmation and Recording of Foreign-Funded Projects) (Promulgated by the National Development and Reform Commission of China on 17 May 2014, effective on 17 June 2014, amended on 27 December 2014). See Articles 3, 4.

100 Articles 20, 27 ~ 29 of Administrative Measures for the Confirmation and Recording of Foreign-Funded Projects. See Kong, 2019, p. 8.

101 In fact, China started to implement the "negative list" system to regulate the market access for foreign investments in the Shanghai Free Trade Zone in 2013. See SHANGHAI.GOV.CN (30 September 2013). 中国(上海)自由贸易试验区外商投资准入特别管理措施(负面清单)(2013) (The Special Administrative Measures for Access of Foreign Investment to China (Shanghai) Pilot Free Trade Zone (Negative List) (2013). Available at: http://www.shanghai.gov.cn/nw30984/20200820/0001-30984_37036.html (accessed 1 March 2021). After that, in 2015, an updated version of this Negative List (2013) was applied to four free trade zones: Shanghai, Guangdong, Tianjin and Fujian; in 2017, another updated version of it was issued and covered all the pilot free trade zones in China. See discussions on the application of this "negative list" system between 2013 and 2017 in Du (2020), pp. 74–76.

102 See MOFCOM.GOV.CN (28 June 2018). 发展改革委、商务部令(2018年第18号): 外商投资准入特别管理措施(负面清单)(2018年版) (National Development and Reform Commission and the Ministry of Commerce (2018 No. 18): 2018 Special Administrative Measures for the Access of Foreign Investment Access).

103 Du (2020), p. 76. See Waishang TouziQiye Sheli ji Biangeng Beian Guanli Zanxing Banfa (外商投资企业设立及变更备案管理暂行办法) (Interim Measures for the Recording Administration of the Formation and Modification of Foreign-Invested Enterprises) (Promulgated by the Ministry of Commerce on 8 October 2016, effective on Promulgation, amended in 2017 and 2018), Articles 2, 5.

(2) The Deregulated "Pre-establishment National Treatment plus Negative List" Approach

The Foreign Investment Law incorporates general principles such as "to further expand opening-up" and "to vigorously promote foreign investment"[104] and pledges to "build a market environment of stability, transparency, predictability, and fair competition" for foreign investors.[105] To accomplish these goals, it implements an approach of "pre-establishment national treatment plus negative list" to regulate market access for foreign investments.[106] Under this approach, the FI Negative List serves as the first filter screening for foreign investments by stipulating the specific industries, sectors, and businesses that foreign investors are prohibited or restricted from investing in. Foreign investors must not invest in the fields which are prohibited by the negative lists.[107] To invest in a restricted field, foreign investors must obtain approval from the responsible regulators and meet the investment conditions set out by the FI Negative List.[108] In the fields outside of the FI Negative List, the "pre-establishment national treatment" for foreign investments applies, meaning that the treatment accorded to foreign investors and their investments shall be no less favourable than that accorded to domestic investors and their investments at the investment access stage.[109] The new regime turns the previous "*ex ante* approval for each investment" approach into a new "overall record-filing requirements plus approval for items on the negative lists" approach, meaning that only foreign investments in the industries and sectors as listed on the negative lists are subject to *ex ante* approval, others are only subject to record filing requirements.[110] This "pre-establishment national treatment plus negative list" rule formally confirms the deregulated approach for market access which has been gradually established by the "negative list" system since 2013.[111] The Implementing Regulation further reinforces this deregulated stand and reduces the burden on foreign investors by adjusting the relevant regulators' competences for approval and record-filing of foreign investments.[112]

---

[104] Article 1 of the Foreign Investment Law. The Foreign Investment Law applies to four forms of foreign investment in China: (i) a foreign investor forms a foreign-funded enterprise within China alone or jointly with any other investor; (ii) a foreign investor acquires any shares, equities, portion of property, or other similar interest in an enterprise within China; (iii) a foreign investor invests in any new construction project within China alone or jointly with any other investor; (iv) investment in any other manner as specified by a law or administrative regulation of the State Council. See Article 2 of the Foreign Investment Law.

[105] Article 3 of the Foreign Investment Law.

[106] Article 4, para 1 of the Foreign Investment Law.

[107] Article 28, para 1 of the Foreign Investment Law.

[108] Article 28, para 2 of the Foreign Investment Law.

[109] Article 4, para 2 of the Foreign Investment Law.

[110] Kong (2019), p. 7.

[111] Du (2020), p. 76.

[112] See Articles 34 ~ 37 of the Implementing Regulation.

5.3.2.2 The Relevant Societal Interests Regulated by the FI Negative List

The reforms to the market access regulation show the changing scope of the relevant societal interests that are protected in the FDI screening regime in China. The previously strict approval requirements for foreign investments aimed to provide a comprehensive protection for societal considerations that were of importance to the national security, the economic development and the social order. The current approach, by highlighting the most crucial ones in the FI Negative List, largely reduces the scope of the regulated societal interests in FDI activities.

The content of the FI Negative List is subject to adjustment in due time according to the needs for further expansion of the opening up and the economic and social development.[113] The total number of items (the restricted and prohibited industries and sectors) on the 2018 FI Negative List was 48; in the 2019 FI Negative List, the number was reduced to 40, and in 2020, to 33. In 2018, the prohibited areas where foreign investors could not invest covered a wide scope of industries and sectors, including: (1) breeding and fishing; (2) non-ferrous metal and non-metallic mining; (3) nuclear fuels and nuclear radiation processing, Chinese medicinal herb slices processing and patented traditional Chinese medicine manufacturing; (4) tobacco products; (5) air traffic control, the post or domestic express mail delivery services; (6) internet and relevant services; (7) legal services; (8) social survey area; (9) research and experimental development; (10) professional and technical services; (11) protection of wild fauna and flora; (12) compulsory educational institution or a religious educational institution; (13) news and publication areas; (14) radio and television broadcasting, transmission, program making, and operation areas; (15) motion picture production, distribution, and exhibition; (16) cultural relics protection and cultural recreation.[114] In the 2019 FI Negative List, prohibitions for foreign investments were removed from certain manufacturing industries (such as the production of rice paper and ink ingots) and agriculture industries (such as the sectors of development of wild animal and plant resources originating in China and protected by the State); and restrictions on foreign investments were further liberalized in the transportation sector (for example, in the domestic shipping agency industry), the basic infrastructure services sector (for example, in the exploration and development of petroleum and natural gas) and the cultural services sector (for example, in the cinema building area and performance agency profession).[115]

The 2020 FI Negative List further removed prohibition for foreign investments in the sectors of smelting and processing of radioactive minerals, and nuclear fuel production and in air traffic control sectors.[116] Besides, restrictions on foreign investments in industries and sectors of agriculture, basic municipal infrastructure (such as construction and operation of urban water supply and drainage network with

[113] Article 4 of the Implementing Regulation.

[114] See the 2018 FI Negative List.

[115] See the 2019 FI Negative List.

[116] See the 2020 FI Negative List.

urban population of more than 500,000), public transportation (such as in public air transport), and in the financial sectors (such as the securities companies, the securities investment fund management companies, futures companies, and life insurance companies) were further liberalized.[117] In December 2021, China published the most recent 2021 FI Negative List, which takes effects on 1 January 2022. The 2021 FI Negative List further reduces the number of items of the restricted and prohibited industries and sectors from 33 to 31; it fully liberalizes the restrictions on automotive manufacturing and releases the restrictions on television and broadcasting equipment manufacturing.[118] The consecutive adjustments in the 2019, 2020, and 2021 FI Negative List specify China's resolution for a deeper opening-up policy for foreign investment. On the other hand, the societal interests as regulated under the current 2021 FI Negative List are still wide-ranging, including not only the commonly recognized public interest considerations (such as the energy supply safety), but also other economic considerations (such as the development of information technology service and information transmission, protection of some public transportation sectors), and societal and cultural considerations (such as protection of the social survey sector, the media industry, the education industry and legal services). The various aspects of considerations on the negative list make it an "all-embracing" network for protecting the relevant societal interests in foreign takeovers; and it is hard to pinpoint the protection focus of the regulation at the market access stage.

5.3.3 The National Security Review of Foreign Investments

5.3.3.1 National Security Review of Foreign Takeovers Prior to 2020: The Notice 2011 and Provisions 2011

Prior to the promulgation of the Foreign Investment Law in 2019, the national security review of foreign takeovers was mainly regulated by the Notice 2011 and the Provisions 2011. The Foreign Investment Law stipulates that foreign investors "shall not impair" the national security nor the public interest in their investment activities in China.[119] It sets forth that the State will establish a security review system to scrutinize a foreign investment that impacts or may impact the national security; and the decision made upon the security review in accordance with the law will be final.[120] Nevertheless, similar to the AML, it does not specify the meaning of the "national

---

[117] Ibid.

[118] See detailed analysis on the reforms in the 2021 FI Negative List in Xue et al. (5 January 2022). The 2021 Revised Negative List for Foreign Investment. Available at: https://www.hankunlaw.com/downloadfile/newsAndInsights/c65f1d46da88415f1abbf1050c2cae2e.pdf (accessed 5 June 2022).

[119] Article 6 of the Foreign Investment Law. Besides, the Foreign Investment Law also directly interacts with the AML by requiring that foreign investors who acquire a Chinese company through participating in the concentration of undertakings will be subject to the examination rules under the AML. See Article 33 of the Foreign Investment Law.

[120] Article 35 of the Foreign Investment Law.

security". Neither does it give examples of the sectors and industries in which foreign investments may cause security concerns, nor stipulates the specific security review procedure.[121] As a result, after the promulgation of the Foreign Investment Law and the Implementing Regulation (and before the publication of the Measures for the Security Review in December 2020), the Notice 2011 and Provisions 2011 still dominated in the security review regime; and the security review system under the Notice 2011 and Provisions 2011 mainly consisted of the following aspects:

(1) The Scope of the Security Review of Foreign Takeovers

The divergence in the interpretation on the "national security" in the security review in China has existed for a long time: does it only refer to the defence interest of the country, or does it also include the economic security, cultural security and other aspects?

According to the Notice 2011, foreign takeovers that are subject to a security review include two categories: (i) foreign takeovers in the defence sectors and related to defence security, including these in the military industry and entities peripheral to major or sensitive military facilities; (ii) foreign takeovers aiming to obtain actual control of the domestic entities in the sectors of agriculture, energies and resources, infrastructure, transportation, key technology, and the manufacture of major equipment.[122] The Provisions 2011 further stipulate that the decision on whether a foreign takeover falls within the scope of a security review should be made pursuant to the substance and actual impact of such transaction, so that evasion of a national security review in any business structures or business arrangements, including, but not limited to, holding shares on behalf of others, trust, multi-level re-investment, leasing, loans, agreement-based control and overseas transactions, could be avoided.[123]

The Notice 2011 also provides the evaluation criteria for the security review of foreign takeovers. It requires that four aspects shall be scrutinized: (i) the influence of the transaction on the national defence security, including on the capacity of producing domestic products and providing services needed for national defence, and on the relevant infrastructure in the defence sector; (ii) the influence of the transaction on the stable operation of the national economy; (iii) the influence on the basic social life order; and (iv) the influence on the research capacity of the crucial technologies pertaining to national security.[124]

According to the relevant rules under the Provisions 2011 and Notice 2011, it could be observed that the "national security" review in China at this stage not only protected the defence interest. It also aimed to protect societal interests that may have

[121] Article 40 of the Implementing Regulation reiterates that "the State shall establish the foreign investment security review system and conduct a security review of foreign investment that has or may have an impact on national security". However, it does not elaborate on this security review system either.

[122] Article 1 of the Notice 2011. Article 2 of the Notice 2011 provides for the four situations that would constitute a foreign takeover. See also Bian (2018), pp. 81–82.

[123] Article 9 of the Provisions 2011. See also Bian (2018), p. 82.

[124] Article 2 of the Notice 2011. See also Bian (2018), p. 82.

impact on economic security (such as on the crucial technology R&D, and on the stability of the economic development which is often related to the market stability) and considerations that have a deep impact on the social life order.

(2) Responsible Authorities and Relevant Review Procedures

According to the Notice 2011, the Joint Ministerial Conference (the "Joint Conference" hereinafter) is responsible for conducting the national security review of foreign takeovers.[125] The Joint Conference is under the leadership of the State Council, organized and held by the NDRC and MOFCOM (so it is an ad hoc review), and must work in operation with other relevant departments of the specific industries and sectors of the takeover.[126] The Provisions 2011 require that for foreign takeovers that fall under the security review categories under the Notice 2011, the foreign investors involved must first report to the NDRC for a security review.[127] Upon receipt of the review request from the NDRC, the Joint Conference first conducts a general security review, seeking advice from other relevant departments.[128] After the general review, the Joint Conference will formulate a decision of clearance and notify the NDRC in writing provided that the takeover or merger concerned will not threaten national security; where the relevant departments consider that the takeover or merger is a potential threat to national security, a special review will be commenced by the Joint Conference, which should be completed within 60 working days.[129]

The NDRC should notify the applicant and the responsible local Municipal Bureau of commerce and business about the Joint Conference's decision in writing within 5 days after it receives the decision from the Joint Conference: (i) for a transaction which is decided by the Joint Conference as "not having an impact on national security", the foreign applicant may continue the transaction; (ii) for a transaction which is decided by the Joint Conference as "may have an impact on national security" and that has not been conducted yet, the parties involved must terminate the transaction; and (iii) for a transaction which, according to the Joint Conference, has had or may have crucial influence on national security, the NDRC must work in cooperation with other relevant departments and based on the opinions of the Joint Conference to terminate the transaction, or to eliminate the impact through transferring the relevant shares, assets or other effective measures.[130] It should be noted that the Joint

[125] Article 3(1) of the Notice 2011.

[126] Article 3(2) of the Notice 2011. See also Tian (2019), p. 137. According to Article 3(3) of the Notice 2011, the Joint Conference's primary responsibilities include: (i) analysing the influence of a foreign takeover on the national security; (ii) studying and coordinating the major issues in the security review; and (iii) making final decisions in such security review. See also Bian (2018), p. 81.

[127] Article 1 of the Provisions 2011. According to the institutional reform, on 30 April 2019, the NDRC took over the MOFCOM's responsibilities in accepting the applications for security review. See the Notice issued by the NDRC on this change, available at: https://www.ndrc.gov.cn/xxgk/zcfb/gg/201904/t20190430_961220.html (accessed 1 March 2021).

[128] Article 4 (3) of the Notice 2011. See also Bian (2018), p. 83.

[129] Ibid.

[130] Article 4 (6) of the Notice 2011; Article 7 of the Provisions 2011. See also Bian (2018), p. 83; Tian (2019), pp. 138–139.

Conference does not have final power to reject the transaction, and the power for rejection is reserved by the State Council.

5.3.3.2 The New Security Review Regime Under the Measures for the Security Review

In December 2020, the Measures for the Security Review were promulgated and filled the loopholes in the Foreign Investment Law. This regulation was formulated on the basis of the framework as established by the Notice 2011 and Provisions 2011 and the national security review experience in China since 2011. It also responds to the reforms in major jurisdictions such as the U.S., the EU, Germany and the U.K., which all enacted new FDI screening regulations or further expanded the scope of their existing regulation in recent years, particularly in 2020 against the background of the COVID-19 pandemic.[131]

The new security review regime under the Measures for the Security Review was established with several objectives, including for example: (i) to coordinate the relationship between actively promoting foreign investments and safeguarding national security; (ii) to make the security review compatible with the regulation on market access for foreign investments (the "pre-establishment national treatment plus negative list" system); (iii) to prevent and resolve national security risks while avoiding generalization of security reviews.[132] To achieve such objectives, the Measures for the Security Review make some adjustments to the existing rules concerning the responsible authorities, the scope of sectors and activities subject to a security review and relevant procedures, which will be discussed in sequence in this section.

(1) The Responsible Authority

The Measures for the Security Review require that a "Foreign Investment Security Review Working Mechanism shall be established" and the Office of the "Foreign Investment Security Review Working Mechanism" (the "Security Review Office" hereinafter) should take the responsibility for the routine work in relation to the security review.[133] The Security Review Office is located in the NDRC, under the leadership of both the NDRC and MOFCOM.[134] The establishment of the Security

[131] NDRC.GOV.CN (19 December 2020). 健全外商投资安全审查制度，为更高水平对外开放保驾护航 — 外商投资安全审查工作机制办公室负责人就《外商投资安全审查办法》答记者问 (Improve the foreign investment security review system and escort a higher level of opening—Press conference by the head of the Foreign Investment Security Review Working Mechanism Office concerning Measures for the Security Review of Foreign Investment). Available at: https://www.ndrc.gov.cn/xwdt/xwfb/202012/t20201219_1255024.html (accessed 1 March 2021). For example, the U.S. enacted Foreign Investment Risk Review Modernization Act in August 2018; as to the reforms in the U.K. in this field, see Sect. 5.3.3; for reforms in the EU and Germany in this field, see Sect. 5.4.3 of this book.

[132] Ibid.

[133] Article 3 of the Measures for the Security Review.

[134] Ibid.

Review Office changes the ad hoc nature of the Joint Conference in the previous regime and thus reinforces the powers of the authority in the security review. Besides, this design also provides more certainties to foreign investors.

(2) The Scope of Foreign Investments Subject to the Security Review

With regard to the type of transactions, the Measures of Security Review regulate both foreign direct investments and indirect investments in China, including the following circumstances:

- a foreign investor, alone or jointly with other investor(s), invests in a new project or establishes an enterprise in China;
- a foreign investor acquires an equity or asset of an enterprise in China by means of merger or acquisition;
- a foreign investor invests in China by any other means.[135]

In comparison with the previous security review regime under the Notice 2011 and Provisions 2011 which only regulated foreign takeovers of domestic companies with security concerns, the scope of transactions subject to security review under the current regime is enlarged. It covers both takeovers and mergers and applies irrespective of whether the target is a foreign-invested enterprise or domestic enterprise.

With regard to the industries and sectors, under the new regime, foreign investments in the following areas are subject to a security review:

- areas related to the defence security interest, including: (a) the arms industry, an ancillary to the arms industry, or any other fields related to national defence security; and (b) an area surrounding a military installation or an arms industry facility;
- the following areas that are related to national security and where the foreign investor's investment results in the acquisition of the actual control of the enterprise it invests in: (a) important agricultural products; (b) important energy and resources; (c) critical equipment manufacturing; (d) important infrastructure; (e) important transportation services; (f) important cultural products and services; (g) important information technology and internet products and services; (h) important financial services; (i) key technology; or (j) any other important fields that are related to national security.[136]

Pursuant to the Measures for the Security Review, foreign investments falling under the scope of security review are divided into two types: for those taking place in the defence-related fields, there is no threshold of "obtaining the actual control of the enterprise" for a security review; for those in other fields that are related to the national security interest, there is a threshold that the investment will result in the

[135] Article 2 para 2 (1)(2)(3) of the Measures for the Security Review.

[136] Article 4 para 1(1)(2) of the Measures for the Security Review.

foreign investor's acquisition of actual control of the target enterprise.[137] Compared with the previous regime under the Notice 2011 and Provisions 2011, the scope of the second type of investments (those that are considered as related to the national security) is expanded, increasing investments in important cultural products and services, important information and internet products and services, and important financial services. This change reaffirms China's consistent stand in interpreting the "national security" interest, that is, it refers to not only defence security, but also economic security and the social order of the country.

For foreign investments of the two types, the foreign investors or their related parties in China should proactively report the investment to the Security Review Office before making the investment.[138] In addition to this proactive reporting by the relevant parties, the Security Review Office has the power to require the parties to any foreign investment within the scope subject to a security review to make a report.[139] Besides, a relevant agency, enterprise, social group, member of the general public, among others, which deems that any foreign investment affects or may affect national security, may propose a security review to the Security Review Office.[140] Compared with the previous regime where the relevant agencies or enterprises or the public need to first recommend to the NDRC for a review and then the NDRC submits its recommendation to the Joint Conference where it sees the necessity of a review, the current procedure allows the recommendation to be made directly to the Security Review Office and thus streamlines the procedure.

In the event where the foreign investment falls within the reporting scope, but the foreign investor or the related party conducts the investment without reporting, the Security Review Office will order it to report within a specified period; if the relevant parties refuse to do so, the Security Review Office will order it to dispose of its resultant equities or assets within a specified period and take other necessary measures to restore the state as it was before the investment to eliminate the effect on national security.[141]

(3) The Security Review Procedure and Possible Results

The review procedure under the new regime does not change, and still consists of a general review and special review. The general review must be completed within 30 working days of the Security Review Office's decision to conduct a security

---

[137] Article 4 para 1(2), para 2(1)(2) of the Measures for the Security Review. The "acquisition of actual control" includes the following three situations: (1) the foreign investor holds not less than 50% of the equities of the enterprise; (2) the foreign investor holds less than 50% of the equities of the enterprise, but has voting rights that have a material effect on the resolutions of the board of directors or the members' or shareholder meeting; (3) other situations which result in the foreign investor's material effect on, among others, the decision-making of business, personnel, finance, and technology of the enterprise.

[138] Article 4 para 1 of the Measures for the Security Review.

[139] Article 4 para 3 of the Measures for the Security Review.

[140] Article 15 of the Measures for the Security Review.

[141] Article 16 of the Measures for the Security Review.

review.[142] Where the Security Review Office finds that the foreign investment does not affect national security, it will make the decision to pass the security review; where, after the general review, the Security Review Office deems that the national security is affected or may be affected, it will initiate the special review.[143]

The special review must be completed within 60 working days, which is subject to an extension under exceptional circumstances.[144] The Security Review Office will make the following decisions in the special review: (i) where the foreign investment does not affect national security, it will pass the security review; (ii) where the foreign investment affects national security, it will (a) prohibit the investment, or (b) conditionally pass the security review if with conditions the effect on the national security could be eliminated and the relevant parties commit to undertake the conditions in writing.[145] Where the Security Review Office makes a decision to prohibit the foreign investment, if the investment has not been conducted, the relevant parties must not invest; where the investment has already been conducted, the relevant parties will dispose of the equities or assets and take other necessary measures to eliminate the effect on the national security within a specified time.[146] For foreign investments that are conditionally passed, the relevant parties may invest subject to the imposed conditions.[147] The review procedure and potential results of a security review of foreign investments are concluded in Fig. 5.2.

5.3.4 Other Rules for Protecting the Relevant Societal Interests in the FDI Screening Regime

5.3.4.1 More Rules on Protecting the Relevant Societal Interests in China

The Provisions on Foreign Mergers and Acquisitions (2009) and Measures for Foreign Strategic Investment are also applicable to the area of foreign investment review.

The Provisions on Foreign Mergers and Acquisitions (2009) stipulate rules of protecting the public interest and other important societal interests in foreign takeovers. With regard to the competition interest, it requires that foreign investors must not create excessive concentration, eliminate or hinder competition.[148] Pertaining to the non-competition public interest, it stipulates that foreign takeovers and mergers must not disturb the social economic order and the security of the

[142] Article 8 para 1 of the Measures for the Security Review.

[143] Article 8 para 2 of the Measures for the Security Review.

[144] Article 9 para 2 of the Measures for the Security Review.

[145] Article 9 para 1 of the Measures for the Security Review.

[146] Article 12 para 1 of the Measures for the Security Review.

[147] Article 12 para 2 of the Measures for the Security Review.

[148] Article 3 of Provisions on Foreign Mergers and Acquisitions (2009).

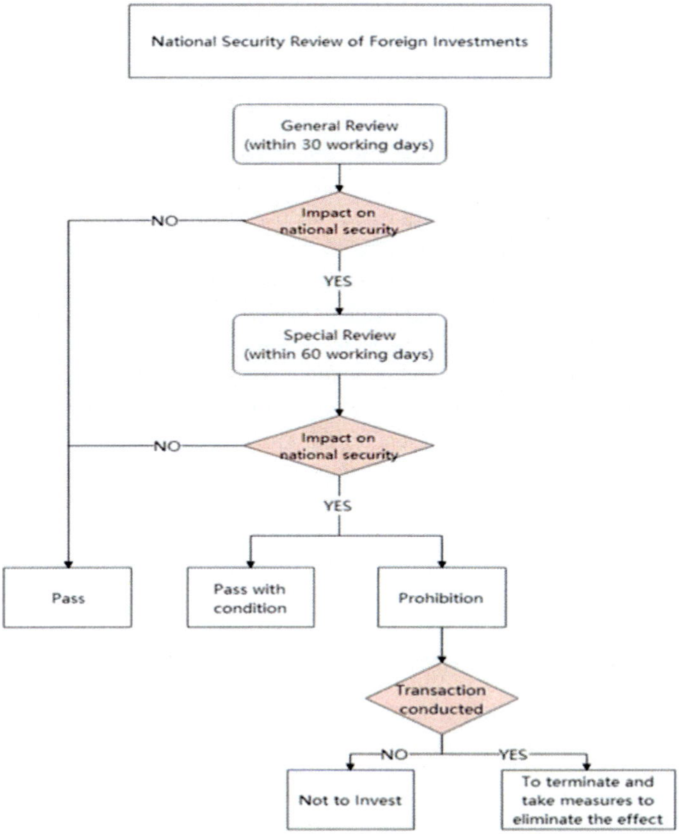

Fig. 5.2 The review procedure and potential results of a national security review of foreign investments[149]

national economy.[150] As to other societal interests, it sets forth requirements for foreign investors that their mergers and acquisitions of domestic enterprises must not lead to the loss of state-owned assets,[151] and they must comply with the industrial, land and environmental protection policies as stipulated in laws and administrative regulations.[152] In addition, it also emphasizes the protection of the domestic enterprises which possess a well-known trademark or China's time-honored brand.[153]

The Measures for Foreign Strategic Investment apply to a certain scale of medium and long-term investments by foreign investors ("foreign strategic investments")

[149] Figure 5.2 was formulated by the author based on the relevant rules in the Measures for the Security Review.

[150] Articles 3, 12 of Provisions on Foreign Mergers and Acquisitions (2009).

[151] Article 3 of Provisions on Foreign Mergers and Acquisitions (2009).

[152] Article 4 of Provisions on Foreign Mergers and Acquisitions (2009).

[153] Article 12 of Provisions on Foreign Mergers and Acquisitions (2009).

where the foreign investors obtain A-share stocks (i) of listed companies that have completed the split-share structure reform; and (ii) of newly listed companies after the split-share structure reform.[154] It incorporates requirements that foreign strategic investments must not impair national economic security and public interests.[155] In June 2020, the MOFCOM published draft amendment to this regulation ("The 2020 Amendment (Draft) of Measures for the Administration of Foreign Strategic Investment").[156] The new amendment will be applicable to foreign investors obtaining and holding A-share stocks of listed companies for a certain period of time (referred to as "foreign strategic investment") through (i) transfers by agreement, (ii) targeted issuance of new shares by listed companies, (iii) takeover bid, and (iv) other methods prescribed by national laws and regulations.[157] It also changes the "national economic security" consideration to "national security", which enlarges the scope of societal interests that may be regulated under the new version (such as the national defence security).[158] The new amendment also refers to the "negative list" system and stipulates that foreign strategic investment must not be conducted in listed companies of the "prohibited sectors" on the FI Negative List; as to "restricted sectors", the

[154] Article 2 of Provisions on Foreign Mergers and Acquisitions (2009). For the definition of "A-share stocks", see Huang (2014), pp. 254–255: "Depending on the nationality of eligible traders and the currencies in which the shares are traded, 'A-shares' refer to those that are limited to domestic investors, including individuals, legal persons, and the state, with both the principal and dividends denominated in the local currency, the Chinese Yuan (CNY). Before the "split-share structure reform", "A-shares" were further subdivided into three subsets in China: "State shares", "legal person shares", and "public individual shares", and only "public individual shares were "tradable shares" which might be freely traded on the stock exchange; the other two types were called "non-tradable shares". For more information on the "split-share structure reform", see Sect. 5.4.4.1 of this book.

[155] Article 4 para 1 of Provisions on Foreign Mergers and Acquisitions (2009).

[156] On 30 July 2018, the five departments published a new draft of amendment and sought for public opinions. See MOFCOM.GOV.CN (30 July 2018). 商务部关于《关于修改(外国投资者对上市公司战略投资管理办法)的决定 (征求意见稿) 》公开征求意见的通知 (Notice of the Ministry of Commerce on Public Consultation on the Decision on Amending the Measures for the Administration of Strategic Investment in Listed Companies by Foreign Investors (Draft)). Available at: http://www.mofcom.gov.cn/article/b/g/201809/20180902788872.shtml (accessed 1 March 2021). On 18 June 2020, in order to ensure the good connection between this regulation and the Foreign Investment Law, the MOFCOM adjusted the revised plan again and published a new draft of the amendment on this regulation. See the 2020 Amendment (Draft) of Measures for the Administration of Foreign Strategic Investment at WZS.MOFCOM.GOV.CN (18 June 2020). 商务部关于《外国投资者对上市公司战略投资管理办法 (修订草案公开征求意见稿) 》公开征求意见的通知 (Notice of the Ministry of Commerce on Public Consultation on the Decision on Amending the Measures for the Administration of Strategic Investment in Listed Companies by Foreign Investors (Draft)), available at: http://wzs.mofcom.gov.cn/article/n/202006/20200602975158.shtml (accessed 3 March 2021).

[157] Article 2 of the 2020 Amendment (Draft) of Measures for the Administration of Foreign Strategic Investment.

[158] Article 3(1) of the 2020 Amendment (Draft) of Measures for the Administration of Foreign Strategic Investment.

strategic investment must satisfy the requirements on shareholding, senior management, etc.[159] Moreover, the new amendment adds a rule of security review to foreign strategic investments, specifying that "where strategic investment involves national security review, the relevant provisions of the foreign investment security review system shall be followed".[160]

5.3.4.2 Rules Protecting the Legitimate Interests of Foreign Investors

The Foreign Investment Law and the Implementing Regulation also provide for rules to protect the legitimate interests of foreign investors and to facilitate their foreign investments in China.

At the post-investment operating stage, the Foreign Investment Law requires that "all national support policies for the development of enterprises shall be equally applied to foreign-invested enterprises".[161] It further provides that "unless otherwise stipulated by laws and administrative regulations, governmental authorities at all levels shall not impair the legitimate rights and interests of or impose any additional obligations on foreign-invested enterprises; they shall not set any market access and withdrawal conditions, and shall not intervene in the normal production and distribution activities of foreign-invested enterprises".[162] The stipulation of protecting the intellectual property rights of foreign investors and foreign-funded enterprises is further progress in the Foreign Investment Law.[163]

The Implementing Regulation reinforces the stand of equal treatment at the post-investment operating stage by specifying in a more detailed way that "the government should treat domestic and foreign-invested enterprises lawfully and equally in, among others, government funding, land supply, tax and fee cuts, licence awarding, standard setting, project application, and human resources policies".[164] The Implementing Regulation clearly stipulates that "foreign investment will not be expropriated by the State; in special cases where expropriation is necessary for public interest, legal procedures should be followed in a non-discriminatory manner, and timely compensation should be made based on market value".[165] This provision mentions the "public interest", but leaves space for the government to further interpret this term.

---

159 Article 3 (5) of the 2020 Amendment (Draft) of Measures for the Administration of Foreign Strategic Investment.

160 Article 21 of the 2020 Amendment (Draft) of Measures for the Administration of Foreign Strategic Investment.

161 Article 9 of the Foreign Investment Law.

162 Article 24 of the Foreign Investment Law.

163 Article 22 of the Foreign Investment Law.

164 Article 6 of the Implementing Regulation.

165 Article 21 of the Implementing Regulation.

5.3.5 *Intermediate Conclusion*

The regulations in the FDI screening regime as discussed in this section illustrate that the national security interest is only one of the many considerations which the Chinese regulators deem as crucial societal interests in foreign investments. At the market access stage, the FI Negative List shows that foreign investments in the areas of, for example, agriculture, resource and energy, public transportation, culture, media, education, legal services are still subject to some restrictions. Accordingly, the relevant societal interests that are related to these areas are under protection. In the past years, the sectors and industries on the FI Negative List have been reduced consecutively. This liberalization indicates a deregulated approach for market access regulation for foreign investments. The newly promulgated Foreign Investment Law and its Implementing Regulation also reaffirm China's policy to further open up the market for foreign investments. Meanwhile, the newly adopted Measures for the Security Review indicate that whilst China is striving to promote the openness of its market, its firm stand to protect the national security interest never changes. It is also observed that in China, the term "national security" does not only refer to defence security, but also covers considerations that may have an impact on the stable development of the national economy and the order of social life. Altogether, the current FDI screening regulation in China allows the regulators to protect a broad spectrum of societal interests in foreign takeovers, including not only the commonly recognized public interest (such as defence interest), but also other economic and societal considerations.

5.4 Takeover Law, Corporate Law and Corporate Governance Code

5.4.1 *Background*

In addition to the foregoing public laws, private laws such as the takeover law, the corporate law and private regulation in the field of corporate governance in China also incorporate mechanisms for protecting shareholders and other stakeholders of the target company in takeovers.

Measures for the Administration of the Takeover of Listed Companies (the "2006 Takeover Measures" hereinafter) are the applicable takeover law for listed companies in China,[166] and the China Securities Regulatory Commission (the "CSRC" hereinafter) is the responsible regulator in this field.[167] The 2006 Takeover Measures

[166] Shangshi Gongsi Shougou Guanli Banfa (上市公司收购管理办法) (2020年修订) (Measures for the Administration of the Takeover of Listed Companies) (2020 Revision) (Promulgated by China Securities Regulatory Commission on 17 May 2006, amended in 2008, 2012, 2014, 2020).

[167] Article 10 of the 2006 Takeover Measures.

focus on protecting the shareholders of the target by giving the shareholder meeting the power of approving post-offer anti-takeover actions taken by the board of directors. The rules pertinent to taking anti-takeover measures and the fiduciary duties of controlling shareholders, directors and management under the 2006 Takeover Measures reflect the basic corporate governance rules under the 2005 PRC Company Law (the "Company Law" hereinafter).[168] Apart from the shareholders, in the corporate governance field, the Company Law and some private regulations also provide protection for other stakeholders of the companies. For example, the Company Law and the self-regulatory Corporate Governance Code for Listed Companies (the "2018 Chinese CG Code" hereinafter)[169] both incorporate rules requiring a company to perform corporate social responsibilities (the "CSR" hereinafter); and the 2018 Chinese CG Code has specific reporting requirements for listed companies with regard to their performance in environmental protection and other CSR matters. Moreover, takeovers involving Chinese SOEs are usually subject to specific regulations promulgated by the State Council, the Central Committee of the CPC and their affiliated organs. Such regulations specifically stipulate the objectives and corporate governance structure of Chinese SOEs and often impose requirements on the SOEs to protect certain societal interests in their corporate activities.[170]

This section analyses these corporate-governance-related mechanisms in China. It first explores the protection mechanisms for target shareholders under the 2006 Takeover Measures, the Company Law and the 2018 Chinese CG Code. Following that, it examines what other stakeholders next to shareholders are taken into account as well under the Chinese takeover law, corporate law and corporate governance code and what the protection mechanisms are. In the end, it discusses the rules under the Company Law and other government regulations that specifically regulate the corporate governance of Chinese SOEs or applicable to SOE-related takeovers to see what societal interests the SOEs often pursue in their activities.

[168] Zhonghua Renmin Gongheguo Gongsifa (中华人民共和国公司法)(2018修订)(Company Law of the People's Republic of China) (2018 Revision) (Promulgated by Standing Committee of the National People's Congress on 29 December 1993, amended in 2005, 1999, 2004, 2013 and 2018). The law underwent major amendments in 2005, and relatively minor changes in 1999, 2004, 2013 and 2018. Hence it is customarily abbreviated as the 2005 PRC Company Law.

[169] Shangshi Gongsi Zhili Zhunze (上市公司治理准则)(Code of Corporate Governance for Listed Companies) (Promulgated by China Securities Regulatory Commission on 30 September 2018, effective on promulgation).

[170] In China, State-owned enterprises (SOEs) include the "wholly state-owned enterprises", "wholly state-owned companies", and "state-owned capital holding companies" that the State Council and local governments perform the responsibilities of investors on behalf of the State. These SOEs are supervised by the SASAC at the central government level or by their local agencies. See SASAC.GOV.CN (4 July 2019). 什么样的企业是国有企业? (What is State-owned enterprise?). Available at: http://www.sasac.gov.cn/n2588040/n2590387/n9854212/c11647665/content.html (accessed 1 April 2021).

5.4.2 *Protection of the Shareholders*

Relevant rules on the decision-making power of shareholders in major corporate issues under the Company Law and rules on shareholder power to approve post-bid anti-takeover measures under the 2006 Takeover Measures reflect that protecting the shareholders is the main objective of the corporate law and takeover law regime. The protection focus on shareholders is also reflected in the requirements on the fiduciary duties of directors and management under the 2006 Takeover Measures, the Company Law, the 2018 Chinese CG Code and other self-regulatory instruments by the stock exchanges—Shanghai Stock Exchange (the "SSE" hereinafter) and the Shenzhen Stock Exchange (the "SZSE" hereinafter).[171] Within the shareholder group, the 2006 Takeover Measures, through the "mandatory bid rule", give the minority shareholders an opportunity to leave the company after the controlling shareholder of the company changes.[172] Moreover, the requirements on the fiduciary duties of controlling shareholders or actual controllers of the target under the 2006 Takeover Measures also provide an extra protection to minority shareholders.[173]

---

[171] The SSE and SZSE are both under the direct guidance of the CSRC, and their principal management is appointed by the CSRC. The two stock exchanges are committed to developing China's multi-tiered capital market comprising the Main Board (in SSE), the Sci-Tech Innovation board (in SSE), the SME Board (in SZSE), and the ChiNext Board (in SZSE). See the history and development of the SSE at: http://english.sse.com.cn/aboutsse/overview/ (accessed 2 March 2021); see the history and development of the SZSE at: http://www.szse.cn/English/about/overview/index.html (accessed 2 March 2021).

[172] Article 47 of the 2006 Takeover Measures. This mandatory bid rule is also stipulated in Articles 65, 73 of the 2005 PRC Securities Law (Zhonghua Renmin Gongheguo Zhenquanfa (中华人民共和国证券法)(2019 修订)(Securities Law of the People's Republic of China (2019 Revision)) (Promulgated by the Standing Committee of the National People's Congress on 29 December 1998, amended in 2004, 2005, 2013, 2014, 2019, effective on 1 March 2020). This law underwent major amendments in 2005, and relatively minor changes in 2004, 2013 and 2014. Hence it is customarily abbreviated as the 2005 PRC Securities Law.

[173] Articles 7, 53 of the 2006 Takeover Measures. Article 7 requires that "the controlling shareholders or actual controllers of the target company shall not misuse their rights to impair the legitimate interests of the target company and other shareholders", and "where the controlling shareholders or actual controller and their related parties have impaired the legitimate interests of the company and other shareholders, they shall actively eliminate the damage before transferring the controlling rights of the target company". Article 53 requires that in the event of a takeover by agreement, "if the controlling shareholder(s) of the listed company is to transfer its control by agreement, it shall investigate on the eligibility, credit status, and the takeover intention of the acquirer, and disclose the relevant investigations in its report on equity changes". In the private regulation field, the SSE and SZSE have issued conduct guidelines for controlling shareholders and actual controllers of the listed companies, which also stipulate the fiduciary duties of the controlling shareholders and actual controllers when they transfer their control rights. See for example, SSE.COM.CN (26 July 2010). 关于发布《上海证券交易所上市公司控股股东、实际控制人行为指引》的通知(Notification on issuing The Conduct Guidelines for Controlling Shareholders and Actual Controllers of the Shanghai Stock Exchange). Available at: http://www.sse.com.cn/lawandrules/sserules/main/listing/stock/c/c_20190228_4727827.shtml (accessed 2 March 2021). Article 4.8 of this Conduct Guidelines required that "the controlling shareholders or actual controllers of the listed companies shall not use the transfer of control rights to impair the legitimate interests of

5.4.2.1 Shareholders' Decision-Making Power in a Takeover

(1) Shareholders' Decision-making Power in Major Corporate Issues in the Company Law

In the corporate governance regime, companies in China have a two-tier board structure—board of directors and board of supervisors,[174] and the corporate governance system under the Company Law is basically shareholder-centred in that the shareholder meeting is the final decision maker in major corporate issues.[175]

The decision-making power of the shareholders is reflected in, among others, the following aspects: (i) electing and changing directors and supervisors who are not employee representatives; (ii) making resolutions on an increase or decrease of the company's registered capital; (iii) making resolutions on the merger, division, change of company form, disbanding, liquidation of the company; and (iv) revising the articles of association of the company.[176] In contrast, the board of directors is accountable to the shareholder meeting and implements the resolutions made by the shareholder meeting.[177] The board of directors decides on the company's business and investment plans (e.g., the annual financial budget plans, the profit distribution plans, plans on the increase and decrease of registered capital and issuance of corporate bonds, and plans on merger, division, change of company form), and on the internal management systems of the company (e.g., the establishment of the company's internal management departments, the hiring or dismissing of the manager and his salary and compensation).[178] Based on this design, in a takeover, the shareholder meeting of the target has the power to decide on issues such as modifying the articles of association, increasing or decreasing the company capital, and disposing of company assets, which are sometimes used as defensive measures in practice.[179] Meanwhile, the board of directors of the target still has the power to decide on the company's operational businesses in this process, and to elaborate on the relevant plans of the defensive measures for submission to the shareholder meeting.

With regard to the role of the supervisory board in a takeover, the Company Law requires that "the board of supervisors of a joint-stock limited company in China

---

the listed company and other shareholders (duty of loyalty)" and that "the controlling shareholders or actual controllers shall, in due diligence, conduct reasonable investigation and disclose the relevant information on matters such as the acquirer's qualifications, credit status, transfer intention, intention on reorganization, and capability to perform the contract (duty of diligence)".

[174] Articles 51, 117 of the Company Law.

[175] Huang and Chen (2019), p. 274. See Articles 36, 98 of the Company Law.

[176] Articles 37, 99 of the Company Law. See also Huang and Chen (2019), p. 274.

[177] Articles 46, 108 of the Company Law. See also Huang and Chen (2019), p. 274.

[178] Ibid.

[179] Article 103 of the Company Law requires resolutions on the modifying of the articles of association, the increase and decrease of registered capital, and on the merger, division, dissolution or change of company form shall be adopted by shareholders representing two thirds or more of the voting rights of the shareholders in presence at the shareholder meeting. For resolutions on other corporate matters, the adoption threshold is half of the voting rights of the shareholders in attendance.

should consist of both shareholder representatives and employee representatives, and the ratio of the latter should be no less than one third of the total number of the supervisors".[180] The employee representatives on the supervisory board should be elected by the employees of the company (either through the assembly of the representatives of the employees, the assembly of employees, or through other democratic means).[181] The Company Law does not confer the supervisory board with a decision-making power in major corporate issues such as in a takeover. The primary responsibilities of the supervisors include, for example, checking the financial affairs of the company and supervising the duty-related acts of the directors and senior managers.[182] Where any director or senior manager's act impairs the interests of the company, the board of supervisors may require him (her) to make corrections; where their duty-related act infringes any law or administrative regulation, the board of supervisors may put forward proposes on the removal of them, and initiate a lawsuit in the court against them if the act causes loss to the company.[183] Based on these designs, in theory, the supervisory board may supervise the directors and senior managers' fulfilment of their fiduciary duties in a takeover. Nevertheless, in practice, the members on the supervisory board are often chosen from shareholders and employees through an election process which is dominated by the majority shareholder(s) and the board of directors.[184] Thus whether they can conduct this supervisory role independently is often doubted. In fact, the board of supervisors in China is often seen as a figurehead.[185]

(2) Restriction on the Anti-takeover Actions of the Board of Directors Under the 2006 Takeover Measures

Article 33 of the 2006 Takeover Measures explicitly restricts the power of the board of directors in taking actions after the acquirer makes an informative announcement of a bid and until the bid is completed.[186] It requires that during this period, the board of directors, without approval from the shareholder meeting, must not take actions that might produce significant effects on the assets, liabilities, entitlements or business performances of the target.[187] Article 33 also gives examples of such actions, including but not limited to disposing of the assets or conducting external investments of the company, adjusting the main businesses, guarantees or loans of the company.[188] During the period after the announcement of the bid and until the bid is completed, the target company can still continuously engage in normal business operations or implement the resolutions made by the shareholder meeting, and the

[180] Article 117 para 2 of the Company Law.

[181] Articles 37 (2), 117 of the Company Law.

[182] Articles 53, 118, 149, 151 of the Company Law.

[183] Ibid.

[184] Huang and Chen (2019), p. 388.

[185] Ibid.

[186] Article 33 of the 2006 Takeover Measures.

[187] Ibid.

[188] Ibid.

restriction on the board of directors' actions does not apply to these matters.[189] Pursuant to Article 33, the shareholder meeting has the final power to take anti-takeover measures. It should be noted that: (i) the restriction on the board of directors applies only to actions that may significantly change the assets or liabilities of the company; (ii) the restriction only applies to actions taken after the announcement of a takeover bid. Thus, this provision still leaves room for the board of directors to take post-bid defensive measures that have no significant influence on the assets or liabilities of the company or take defensive measures prior to the announcement of a bid.[190]

In practice, the legitimacy of some of the board of directors' measures is questionable under the current laws. For example, when confronted with a takeover bid, listed companies in China often modify their articles of association and introduce articles such as the "golden parachute rule" or the "staggered board rule" to add obstacles for the acquirer to obtain the control of the company.[191] The two stock exchanges sometimes issue an "enquiry letter" ("letter of concerns") to these target companies, asking them to reply and explain the legitimacy of the anti-takeover measures taken by the board of directors. For instance, in December 2015, a Shenzhen-listed company called Longping Gaoke proposed to revise its articles of association to introduce a restriction on the shareholder right to nominate directors.[192] In January 2016, SSE sent an enquiry letter to the company, asking if there was any legal basis for introducing these proposed provisions; and two days later, Longping Gaoke dropped the proposal.[193] The self-regulatory mechanism of enquiry letter, although with no enforcement power on the target company, provides external pressure on the target company. It makes the board of directors of the target to be more cautious when setting up anti-takeover defences that may harm the interests of the new acquirer shareholder. To that extent, it also protects the shareholder interests and safeguards the decision-making power of them.

---

[189] Ibid.

[190] Huang and Chen (2019), p. 376.

[191] For a detailed analysis of the anti-takeover measures in practice in China, see Huang (2014), pp.296–306; Zeng and Lin (2020), pp. 209–211.

[192] Huang and Chen (2019), p. 390.

[193] Ibid. Some other companies, such as China BaoAn and Bai Lilian, refused to give up their anti-takeover provisions after receiving letters of enquiry from stock exchanges, arguing that these provisions were necessary to fend off bad-faith takeovers.

5.4.2.2 Fiduciary Duties of the Board of Directors and Management to Shareholders

Article 8 of the 2006 Takeover Measures prescribes the duty of loyalty and duty of diligence of the directors and management of the target, requiring that "the directors and management treat all the acquirers equally, make decisions and take measures in the interests of the company and the shareholders, and do not misuse their powers to set up improper obstacles for the takeover, or use the target's resources to provide the acquirer with financial aid or impair the legitimate interests of the company and its shareholders".[194] These requirements aim to prevent the directors and management from seeking self-interest in takeovers at the expense of the target company and its shareholders. This provision corresponds with Article 147 of the Company Law which stipulates the directors, supervisors and senior managers' duties of loyalty and diligence to the company. It should also be noted that the management and the directors' fiduciary duties apply to the whole process of a takeover, meaning that, even in the prior-bid stage, the management and the board must take the interests of the company and the shareholders rather than their self-interests into consideration when trying to set any defensive measures.

Moreover, the fiduciary duties of the directors in a takeover are also reflected in the rules on their investigation and reporting obligations. In the event of a takeover bid, Article 32 of the 2006 Takeover Measures requires that "the board of directors of the target shall investigate on the eligibility, credit situation and takeover intention of the acquirer, analyse the conditions of the bid, and give advice on whether the shareholders should take the offer, and hire independent financial consultants to provide professional opinions"; and "within 20 days after the acquirer announces the bid, the board of directors of the target shall publish a report ('target board report') as well as the professional opinions from the independent financial consultant".[195] According to a document published by the CSRC, the "target board report" serves to disclose major information about the target and provide opinions and recommendations on the bid to the target shareholders.[196] On the one hand, the requirements on the board of directors under Article 32 may help reduce the information asymmetry between the target shareholders and the acquirer; and with the opinions from the board of directors and other professional financial consultant, the target shareholders may make more informed decisions on a bid. On the other hand, it should be noted

[194] Article 8 of the 2006 Takeover Measures.

[195] Article 32 of the Company Law.

[196] See Gongkai Faxing Zhengquan de Gongsi Xinxi Pilu Neirong he Geshi Zhunze di Shibahao—Beishougou Gongsi Dongshihui Baogaoshu (公开发行证券的公司信息披露内容和格式准则第18号—被收购公司董事会报告书 (2020年修正))(Guidelines for the Content and Format of Information Disclosure of Publicly Offering Company(No.18)—Report of the Board of Directors of the Acquired Company) (2020 Revision) (Promulgated by the CSRC on 4 August 2006, revised on 30 March 2020). See Sects. 5.2–5.5.

that the fiduciary duties in this article still focus on protecting target shareholders, with the other stakeholders largely ignored.[197]

5.4.3 Protection of Other Stakeholders

Apart from target shareholders, the takeover law, corporate law and corporate governance code of China also stipulate mechanisms to protect the interests of other corporate stakeholders and other common societal interests. The relevant mechanisms mainly consist of two parts: (i) general principles of protecting the public interest and requirements that the acquirer should disclose information about future plans for some stakeholders in the 2006 Takeover Measures; (ii) rules on CSR in the Company Law and the 2018 Chinese CG Code.

5.4.3.1 Rules on Protecting Other Stakeholders in the 2006 Takeover Measures

The 2006 Takeover Measures mention the protection of the "public interest" in takeovers by requiring in the general principle that "corporate takeovers shall not impair national security and public interests"; and "where a takeover involves industrial policies of the State, access requirements for an industry and transfer of state-owned shares, and are subject to approval from the relevant authorities, it may only be conducted after such approval is obtained".[198] The 2006 Takeover Measures do not specify the concept of "public interest". As a result, the CSRC has the discretion to interpret these terms by giving reference to other government regulations and intervene in individual cases based on such principles. With regard to other stakeholders, the 2006 Takeover Measures stipulate the circumstances where a listed company must not be taken over, which focus on situations of the bidder's incompetence, including "where the bidder is in a large amount of debt, gets involved in any major illegal act or seriously untrustworthy conduct within the last three years, and is in one of the circumstances as listed in Article 146 of the Company Law".[199] To some extent, this restriction secures the solvency capability of the target and shields

---

197 Article 15 of Guidelines for the Content and Format of Information Disclosure of Publicly Offering Company (No.18)—Report of the Board of Directors of the Acquired Company. Article 15 (2) particularly specifies that "The title page of the report of the board of directors shall state…all directors of the company have fulfilled their fiduciary duties, and the recommendations to shareholders are made objectively and prudently based on the overall interests of the company and all shareholders".

198 Article 4 of the 2006 Takeover Measures. Article 1 of the Securities Law also enunciates its purposes of "protecting the legitimate rights and interests of investors, safeguarding the economic order and public interests of society in regulating the issuing and trading of securities". Similarly, there is no explicit explanation under it on the "economic order" and "public interests".

199 Article 6 of the 2006 Takeover Measures.

the target from highly-leveraged hostile takeovers. In this sense, it may indirectly protect corporate stakeholders such as employees and creditors. Moreover, the 2006 Takeover Measures specify that in a takeover bid, the acquirer should disclose its future plans (for the next 12 months) "for adjusting the assets, businesses, personnel, organizational structure…" in its offer report.[200] Such disclosure provides the board of directors and the relevant stakeholders in the target with information about the takeover's potential consequences on the relevant stakeholders.

5.4.3.2 Rules on CSR in the Company Law and 2018 Chinese CG Code

The Company Law and the 2018 Chinese CG Code incorporate rules on CSR. This section mainly explores what kinds of societal interests are covered by these CSR rules, and whether such CSR requirements form a fiduciary duty of directors and management to the non-shareholder stakeholders in a takeover.

(1) CSR Rules in the Company Law

Article 147 of the Company Law explicitly stipulates that "the directors, supervisors and senior managers have a duty of loyalty and duty of diligence to the company".[201] The expression of "duty to the company" of the directors, supervisors and senior managers denotes the possibility of protecting other non-shareholder stakeholders in corporate activities. However, this provision does not specify the stakeholders to which such fiduciary duty applies. In the same provision, it only requires that "the directors, supervisors or senior managers shall not accept any bribe or other illegal gains by taking the advantage of his (her) powers or encroach on the property of the company".[202] Article 5 of the Company Law stipulates the corporate social responsibilities of a company in China. It provides for that "when conducting business operations, a company shall…act in good faith, accept the supervision of the government and general public, and assume social responsibilities".[203] This CSR rule seems to impose a duty to the companies to protect non-shareholder stakeholders in their activities, including takeovers.

Nevertheless, this CSR requirement has been the subject of much controversy since the Company Law came into force. Scholars have disputes whether companies should pursue the interests of other stakeholders in their activities and whether this requirement constitutes an enforceable duty of the directors. From the perspective of many Chinese scholars, Article 5 of the Company Law only serves as a general principle to encourage companies to take into account non-shareholder stakeholders; and they argue that it does not directly impose a fiduciary duty on the directors and managements to non-shareholder stakeholders in China.

[200] Articles 17(4), 29 (11) of the 2006 Takeover Measures.

[201] Article 147 of the Company Law.

[202] Ibid.

[203] Article 5 of the Company Law.

For example, Liu (2006) argued that "the foothold of companies to assume CSR should be profit-making, that is, assuming social responsibilities is only a necessary cost (or a tool) for the companies to maximize their profits; otherwise, it will be detrimental to social development".[204] Similarly, Zhou and Zhang (2009) held that "emphasizing the CSR should first be established on the basis of respecting the company's profit-making purpose; and it is against the original objective of this provision to equate the social responsibilities of the company with its profit-making nature or to use the CSR requirement to deny its profitability nature".[205] Chinese scholars usually agree that the corporate social responsibilities of a company consist of both "legal obligations" and "other responsibilities": the "legal obligations" refer to that companies should abide by laws and regulations to conduct their activities; and the "other responsibilities" mainly include "moral responsibilities", meaning that in addition to what the laws and regulations require them to comply in their activities, the companies should also abide by social and business ethics and accept the supervision of the government and the public.[206] Shi et al. (2008) once argued that "at this stage, in China, the emphasis on and adherence to the companies' legal obligations should be the foundation for promoting the CSR requirement".[207] They also held that Article 5 of the Company Law in essence "only gives a moral call to companies without adding any specific legal obligations".[208] Other scholars were concerned that too much emphasis on the CSR requirement would make it an instrument utilized by the Government for achieving public interests, which would impose extra burdens on companies.[209] They held that a distinction should be drawn between the "public interest" the achievement of which should be the task of the Government and the companies' social responsibilities[210]; they also worried that the CSR requirement would provide the Government with an excuse to intervene in the activities of companies.[211]

There is also dispute over the subject of such responsibilities as well as towards which stakeholders the company owes such responsibilities. For example, Shi et al. (2008) posited that the "subject", "object" and the content of this CSR requirement under Article 5 were all unclear.[212] Li (2010) argued that "a company's social responsibilities are generally borne by the board of directors of the company".[213] He held that the company's social responsibilities are almost equivalent to the responsibilities of the board of directors to the society in many cases; and the directors, instead of

204 Liu (2006), p. 539.

205 Zhou and Zhang (2009), p. 61.

206 See for example, Lou (2008), p. 38; Li (2010), pp. 123–124.

207 Shi et al. (2008), p. 48.

208 Ibid.

209 Li (2010), p. 122.

210 Ibid.

211 Shi et al. (2008), p. 48.

212 Ibid.

213 Li (2010), p. 122.

being the agents of the shareholders, are actually implementing an original authorization which is independent of the shareholders.[214] Li (2010) posited that "undertaking social responsibilities often means that a trade-off and compromise must be made between the interests of shareholders and the interests of society"; thus, "it is against natural justice to make the shareholders undertake such responsibilities".[215] Li (2010) further divided the social responsibilities of a company into three tiers and analysed the board of directors' fiduciary duty to shareholders and duty to other stakeholders based on this division. From his perspective, the first tier of the company's social responsibilities is the "legal obligations" of the company, and at this level, the board of directors' fiduciary duty to the shareholders and to other stakeholders is consistent in that they both require the board to make business decisions in compliance with laws and regulations.[216] The second tier of a company's social responsibilities, according to Li (2010), consists of the responsibilities to other stakeholders based on the requirements of business ethics, while the third tier consists of the higher level of responsibilities which is to use the corporate resources to give back to society for charity purposes.[217] As to these two tiers, Li (2010) held that the board should try to consider the other stakeholders' interests on the premise of protecting the shareholders and fulfilling their fiduciary duties to shareholders; and in this sense, "the process of realizing the CSR is actually the process of making compromises between the interests of shareholders and other stakeholders".[218]

Regarding the stakeholders towards whom the board of directors may owe a fiduciary duty, Shi (2019) gave a detailed analysis.[219] According to Shi (2019), whether the CSR requirement under Article 5 imposes a fiduciary duty to the board of directors and management to non-shareholder stakeholders should be discussed depending on different types of stakeholders and on different operational situations of a company.[220] As to the employee protection, Article 17 of the Company Law stipulates that "companies shall protect the legitimate interests of the employees"; and Article 18 further provides for protection mechanisms a company should have in place for the employees, including for example "establishing labour unions in the company and conducting activities through the labour union to protect the employees' legitimate interests", "soliciting the opinions from the labour union as well as employees when deciding on restructuring or any major issues relating to business operations, or formulating any important bylaws", etc.[221] Shi (2019) argued that, whilst Article 5 does not explicitly specify that employees fall within the scope of stakeholders covered by the CSR, the content concerning employee protection in Articles 17 and

[214] Ibid, see pp. 122–123.

[215] Ibid.

[216] Ibid, see p. 125.

[217] Ibid, see p. 124.

[218] Ibid, see p. 125.

[219] Shi (2019), pp. 59–79.

[220] Ibid, see p. 71.

[221] Article 18 of the Company Law.

18 should be regarded as an important part of CSR.[222] Nevertheless, he also held that acknowledging employee protection as part of the CSR does not mean that directors and management have a fiduciary duty to the employees; from his perspective, employee protection should first be achieved through the labour law and social welfare law instead of the company law.[223] According to Shi (2019), in corporate activities, employees should be regarded as part of the CSR stakeholders and should be protected by the explicit stipulation such as Articles 17 and 18 of the Company Law; except for that, employee protection should be achieved by mechanisms under the labour law or other social welfare laws, rather than by imposing a fiduciary duty on directors and management under the Company Law.

With regard to other non-shareholder stakeholders, Shi (2019) held a similar opinion. For example, as to creditors of a company, Shi (2019) argued that the Company Law already provides for specific rules to protect creditors.[224] According to Shi (2019), it is not realistic to impose on the directors and management a fiduciary duty to creditors when the company is in a normal operational state; because in that situation, the company and its creditors are two parties to one transaction, the directors and management should represent the company's interests to negotiate with the creditors, rather than to protect or prioritize the creditors' interest in this process.[225] Only when the company is in bankruptcy or on the brink of bankruptcy, is there a possibility that the directors and management owe this fiduciary duty to creditors and protect their interests against the opportunistic behaviour of shareholders.[226] Moreover, as to the relationship between the company and the local community, Shi (2019) held that when a company moves out from the local community, there might be some expected losses to the community (for example, the reduction in taxation); nevertheless, these losses, which are usually called as "positive losses" are hard to be remedied through the fiduciary duties as it is difficult to delimit the scope of such losses.[227]

In a nutshell, according to Shi (2019), the CSR requirement under Article 5 does not directly lead to directors and management's fiduciary duties to non-shareholder stakeholders. In normal operational decisions, these stakeholders are either protected by the rules under the Company Law which directly and explicitly stipulate their interests (such as Articles 17 and 18) or laws in other regimes (such as the environment law, labour law); only under some exceptional circumstances of structural decisions of

---

[222] Shi (2019), p. 63.

[223] Ibid, p. 72. Shi also argued that where these laws were deficient to protect the stakeholders, they should be amended first.

[224] Ibid, see pp. 72–73: The protection mechanisms for creditors include for example, rules on capital contribution of shareholders and profit distribution of the company, rules concerning mergers and divisions, dissolution and liquidation of the company; except for these rules, the core pillar for protecting creditors lies in the mechanisms in the contract law, and the relevant rules under the Company Law cannot lead to fiduciary duties of the directors and management and impose on them requirements for protecting creditors.

[225] Ibid, see p. 73.

[226] Ibid.

[227] Ibid, see p. 74.

the company, may the directors and management owe a fiduciary duty to some of the other stakeholders (such as a fiduciary duty to creditors in a bankruptcy situation).[228] Similarly, Zhu (2008) also agreed that the achievement of social responsibilities of companies did not only result from the rules provided by the Company Law; instead, it required a cooperation of a variety of laws and regulations, including for example, the specific laws for consumer protection, the laws regulating product safety, the tort law, and the compulsory disclosure systems in these law regimes.[229]

Besides, the Company Law does not incorporate specific mechanisms for implementing this CSR requirement. The 2018 Chinese CG Code provides for mechanisms such as CSR reporting to encourage listed companies to protect non-shareholder stakeholders.

(2) CSR Rules in the 2018 Chinese CG Code

The 2018 Chinese CG Code is the major private regulatory instrument in the field of corporate governance in China. In principle, it requires the listed companies to fulfil their corporate social responsibilities and respect the basic rights and interests of relevant stakeholders.[230] It has a separate chapter (Chap. 8) on "stakeholders, environmental protection, and corporate social responsibilities".[231]

Regarding the scope of stakeholders, Article 83 of the 2018 Chinese CG Code requires that "listed companies should take account of the legitimate interests of creditors, employees, customers, suppliers, the community and to conduct efficient communication and cooperation with them to promote sustainable and healthy development of the company".[232] This provision lists the major non-shareholder stakeholders that are often discussed under the CSR notion; the examples it gives do not seem to be exhaustive as it uses the word "等" (meaning "and so on") after the specification of "community". In Article 86, it also requires listed companies "to actively implement the concept of green development, integrate the requirements for ecological environmental protection into the development strategy and corporate governance process, to actively participate in the construction of ecological civilization, and play a demonstrative and leading role in pollution prevention and treatment, resources conservation, ecological protection, and other respects."[233] Moreover, it

[228] Ibid, see p. 79. Shi (2019) made reference to Bainbridge (1992), who divided corporate decisions into "operational decisions" and "structural decisions", the latter include takeovers. See Bainbridge, S. M. (1992). Interpreting non-shareholder constituency statutes. *Pepp. L. Rev.*, *19*(3), 971–1026, pp. 976–979. Shi (2019) also acknowledged that in a takeover case, directors may take anti-takeover measures for non-shareholder stakeholders as some case law permits (such as the Unocal Corp. v. Mesa Petroleum Co. case (493 A 2d 946 (Del. 1985)), which was discussed in Bainbridge, 1992, pp. 980–981); but in these situations, the main concern is to prevent directors and management from utilizing this fiduciary duty to pursue self-interest by taking anti-takeover measures in the name of protecting non-shareholder stakeholders. See Ibid, pp. 75–76.

[229] Zhu (2008), p. 32.

[230] Article 3 para 2 of the 2018 Chinese CG Code.

[231] Chapter 8 of the 2018 Chinese CG Code.

[232] Article 83 of the 2018 Chinese CG Code.

[233] Article 86 of the 2018 Chinese CG Code.

enlarges the scope of stakeholders and puts forward the broad CSR requirement in Article 87, requiring that listed companies "should actively perform social responsibilities in terms of community welfare, disaster relief, public welfare, etc., while maintaining the company's sustainable development, improving business performance, and protecting the interests of shareholders"; and "should be encouraged to provide pair assistance for poverty-stricken counties or poverty-stricken villages, and actively connect and support the poverty-stricken areas to develop industries, cultivate talents, and promote employment".[234] It can be seen that the 2018 Chinese CG Code recognizes the protection of a large scope of non-shareholder stakeholders in the corporate activities of listed companies.

Pertinent to the specific protection mechanisms for the abovementioned stakeholders, the 2018 Chinese CG Code stipulates that "listed companies should provide necessary conditions for safeguarding the rights and interests of stakeholders"; and "when their legitimate rights and interests are infringed, stakeholders should have the opportunity and channels to obtain relief according to law".[235] Thus, it leaves room for listed companies to design their own protection mechanisms. In the field of employee protection, the 2018 Chinese CG Code requires that "the board of directors, the board of supervisors and the management should establish diversified communication channels with employees, and listen to their opinions on the company's operations, financial status, and major issues involving employees' interests".[236] Moreover, it incorporates a voluntary reporting mechanism on stakeholder issues which encourages listed companies "to voluntarily disclose information that may affect shareholders and other stakeholders' decisions".[237] Among all the stakeholders it mentions in the foregoing provisions, the 2018 Chinese CG Code explicitly stipulates that "the listed companies should disclose environmental information and its fulfilment of social responsibilities related to matters such as poverty alleviation in accordance with laws, regulations and the requirements of competent authorities".[238]

According to Zeng and Lin (2020), the provisions concerning disclosure on stakeholder issues and other CSR-related matters in the 2018 Chinese CG Code formulate the basic framework on disclosure of information about Environmental, Social and Governance (the "ESG" hereinafter) in China.[239] They also observed that, while the number of voluntary CSR disclosure reports provided by listed companies on the two stock exchanges—the SSE and the SZSE has been increasing year by year, the total number of disclosure on environmental information and other CSR matters

---

234 Article 87 of the 2018 Chinese CG Code.

235 Article 84 of the 2018 Chinese CG Code.

236 Article 85 of the 2018 Chinese CG Code.

237 Article 91 of the 2018 Chinese CG Code. The mandatory information disclosure requirement subject to laws and regulations for listed companies is stipulated in Articles 88 of the 2018 Chinese CG Code.

238 Article 95 of the 2018 Chinese CG Code.

239 Zeng and Lin (2020), p. 150. "ESG" matters are among the main concerns of the OECD corporate governance principles.

remains low.[240] In 2020, to further encourage listed companies to pay attention to CSR matters, particularly environmental protection in their activities, the SZSE modified its evaluation standards on information disclosure of listed companies.[241] Currently, ESG criteria of "whether to actively disclose the performance on environmental, social responsibility and corporate governance (ESG) and whether the content of the disclosure report is substantial and complete" are included in the assessment on information disclosure of listed companies on the SZSE.[242] The disclosure report on CSR matters as required by the 2018 Chinese CG Code or ESG matters as required by the SZSE may help reduce the information asymmetries between the public, non-shareholder stakeholders and the companies in a takeover.

The implementation of the 2018 Chinese CG Code differs from the traditional "comply or explain" approach. The code itself explicitly requires that listed companies in China "should act in the spirit of it to enhance corporate governance"[243]; and the market regulator—the CSRC and its affiliated agencies (the local Securities Regulatory Bureaus) are responsible for supervising the conduct of the listed companies and to urge the companies to adopt effective measures to make corrections in the case of major problems in their corporate governance.[244] For example, the local Securities Regulatory Bureaus may conduct on-site inspection of the listed companies to see if their organizational designs and activities comply with the rules in the corporate governance code; in the cases where the companies deviate from the rules, they may conduct interviews with the management team and order them to make corrections.[245] Based on these designs, listed companies are under pressure to disclose how they perform on the ESG matters to the CSRC and SZSE, and are thus motivated to take into account the interests of relevant stakeholders in their activities such as takeovers.

---

240 Ibid, pp. 129–130.

241 SZSE (4 September 2020). 关于发布《深圳证券交易所上市公司信息披露工作考核办法(2020年修订)》的通知(Notice on Issuing Measures for the Evaluation of Information Disclosure of Listed Companies on the Shenzhen Stock Exchange (Revised in 2020)). Available at: http://www.szse.cn/disclosure/notice/general/t20200904_581281.html (accessed 2 March 2021).

242 See Articles 6(5), 16 of Measures for the Evaluation of Information Disclosure of Listed Companies on the Shenzhen Stock Exchange (Revised in 2020).

243 Article 2 of the 2018 Chinese CG Code.

244 Article 6 para 1 of the 2018 Chinese CG Code.

245 Chen (2020), pp. 238–243.

5.4.4 *Regulation on Relevant Societal Interests in SOE-Related Takeovers*

5.4.4.1 Background: The Split-Share Structure Reform and the Predominant Position of SOEs in China

SOEs are considered to be the backbone of the socialist economy of China.[246] During China's reform of transitioning the planned economy to a market economy, one uncompromised principle was "maintaining the leading status of SOEs in key industries and important enterprises".[247] Nevertheless, before 2005, the shares owned by the State in companies were not tradable on the market.[248] Despite holding non-tradable shares, the State (by virtue of the SASAC) enjoyed the same voting, cash flow, and other legal rights as their public counterparts, and it could avoid the stock market risk borne by public shares.[249] The basic principles of "one share, one vote" and "equal share, equal rights" in the Securities Law thus turned into "law on the books" for a "sliced and diced" market.[250] In 2005, the CSRC initiated the split-share structure reform to convert non-negotiable shares into negotiable shares gradually over a period up to 36 months.[251] As of November 2020, there were 1,151 listed SOEs

---

246 WWW.GOV.CN (13 November 2020). 做强做优做大国有资本和国有企业—来自首届国有经济研究峰会的观察 (Strengthening and Optimizing State-owned Capital and State-owned Enterprises—Observations from the First State-owned Economy Research Summit). Available at: http://www.gov.cn/xinwen/2020-11/13/content_5561170.htm (accessed 27 February 2021). In 2019, the total assets of enterprises under the supervision of the state-owned assets system across China reached 201.3 trillion yuan, an increase of 1.5 times compared with 2012; from 2012 to 2019, the accumulated taxes and fees paid by enterprises under the supervision of state-owned assets in the country accounted for about a quarter of the national tax revenue during the same period; in 2019, R&D investment by enterprises under the supervision of state-owned assets exceeded 1 trillion yuan, accounting for about half of the country. In another speech in 2015, President Xi Jinping also emphasized that "the State-owned enterprises, especially centrally managed enterprises, are in a predominant position in major industries and key areas that are related to national security and the lifeline of the national economy and are an important pillar of the national economy" (see FINANCE.PEOPLE.COM.CN (27 July 2015). 发展混合所有制经济的新视角 (A new perspective on developing a mixed ownership economy), available at: http://finance.people.com.cn/stock/n/2015/0727/c67815-27363334.html (accessed 2 March 2021).

247 See Zhonggong Zhongyang Guanyu Guoyouqiye Gaige he Fazhan Ruogan Zhongda Wenti de Jueding (中共中央关于国有企业改革和发展若干重大问题的决定) (The Decision of the Central Committee of the Communist Party of China on Major Issues Concerning the Reform and Development of State-Owned Enterprises) (Promulgated by the Central Committee of The Communist Party of China on 22 September, 1999, effective on promulgation).

248 He and Kyaw (2018), p. 49; Sheng (2015), p. 50: At that time, the Chinese listed companies had dual classes of A-shares: two thirds of total Chinese stock shares were non-tradable shares owned by the State and legal persons; and the other one third was tradable shares owned by individual shareholders.

249 He and Kyaw (2018), p. 49.

250 Sheng (2015), p. 50.

251 See Zhongguo Zhengquan Jiandu Guanli Weiyuanhui Guanyu Shangshi Gongsi Guquan Fenzhi Gaige Shidian Youguan Wenti de Tongzhi (中国证券监督管理委员会关于上市公司股权分置改

in China, accounting for 28% of the total number of listed companies, and the market capitalization of them accounted for 44% of the total market capitalization.[252] Among the Fortune 500 Chinese companies in 2020, there were 265 SOEs, accounting for 53%.[253] Chinese SOEs are also the key force in mergers and takeovers in the market: in 2020, 167 of China's Fortune 500 companies have completed 1072 mergers and acquisitions; among them, there were 104 Chinese SOEs, which have implemented 567 mergers and takeovers.[254] On the one hand, these takeovers and mergers consolidated resources and production capacities of central and local SOEs and enhanced market efficiency.[255] On the other hand, SOE-related takeovers are subject to specific regulation by the Government and the CPC, which often aim to pursue certain public policies and protect special public interest considerations through SOE activities. Section 5.4.4.2 continues to analyse the approaches the Government and CPC have adopted to intervene in SOE-related takeovers; Sect. 5.4.4.3 concludes the societal interests the Government and the CPC aimed to protect through the regulation and intervention.

5.4.4.2 Regulatory Approaches by the Government and CPC in SOE-Related Takeovers

The Government and the CPC usually exert deep influence in the corporate activities of the Chinese SOEs. According to Zhang (2014), Chinese SOEs often maintain strong networks of bureaucrats and officials and are burdened with political objectives in their economic activities.[256] The study by Chan et al. (2012) showed that Chinese listed companies with a politically connected CEO or Chairman seem to be free from financing constraints in the market.[257] They probably have easier access to

革试点有关问题的通知) (Notice of the China Securities Regulatory Commission on Piloting the Share-trading Reform of Listed Companies) (Issued by the China Securities Regulatory Commission on 29 April 2005, effective on promulgation) (Expired). This regulation initiated the reform of the split-share structure and stipulated the period of lockups for the previously "non-tradable" shares. See He and Kyaw, 2018, p. 56; Sheng, 2015, pp. 45-46, 281–285.

[252] WWW.GOV.CN (13 November 2020). 做强做优做大国有资本和国有企业—来自首届国有经济研究峰会的观察 (Strengthening and Optimizing State-owned Capital and State-owned Enterprises—Observations from the First State-owned Economy Research Summit). Of the 1,151 listed SOEs, 394 were central state-owned listed companies, and 757 were local state-owned listed companies.

[253] SASAC.GOV.CN (28 September 2020). 2020 年中国 500 强企业分析报告: 发展迈上新高度, 国民共进开新局 (Analysis Report on China's Fortune 500 Companies in 2020: New Height of Development and New Game Launched by the Citizens). Available at: http://www.sasac.gov.cn/n2588020/n2877938/n2879597/n2879599/c15556421/content.html (accessed 27 February 2021).

[254] Ibid.

[255] CSRC.GOV.CN (13 December 2017). Speech by CSRC Vice Chairman Jiang Yang on 2017 CCTV Financial Forum and Chinese Listed Companies Summit. Available at: http://www.csrc.gov.cn/csrc_en/c102031/c1372369/content.shtml (accessed 2 March 2021).

[256] Zhang (2014), p. 445.

[257] Chan et al. (2012), p.166.

external credit via either the personal connection of the company's top management, explicit preferential policy treatment, or they are perceived by lenders to have implicit government guarantee.[258] Another study by Cull et al. (2015) corresponded to this observation by finding that "firms with non-government-appointed CEOs tend to face tighter financial constraints due to their inferior political status in the Chinese market".[259] With regard to takeovers, Zhou et al. (2015) posited that SOE acquirers may enjoy favourable financial support, such as privileged bank loans, government subsidies, and so forth.[260] Since the outcomes of takeovers often primarily rely on the acquirers' financial resources, SOE acquirers tend to be more competitive than their privately owned counterparts. Against this background, Chen et al. (2011) further posited that except for the SOEs, private companies in China are also incentivized to establish political connections with the Government and the CPC.[261]

The Government and CPC may exert influence on SOE related takeovers from three aspects: (i) through the State ownership (by virtue of the SASAC or holding companies), the Government can participate in the decision-makings in the SOE-related takeover as the controlling shareholder; (ii) by the compulsory requirement of establishing Party organizations in the SOEs and the power to appoint senior executives of the SOEs, the CPC can actively participate in the SOEs' corporate activities, including takeovers; (iii) with the power to allocate important societal and economic resources (e.g., approving the bank loans, appropriating the land), the Government can affect the SOEs and other listed companies' funding for a takeover.[262]

(1) Regulation by SASAC and Its Local Agencies

In Chinese SOEs, owing to the agency costs and an omnipresent bureaucracy, the State used to play a virtually non-existent role with respect to the monitoring of management in companies with the State as the controlling shareholder.[263] This is considered as the reason for the "insider control" problem, meaning that the insiders such as directors and management have an effective or actual control of the company.[264]

To deal with this problem, in 2003, the Chinese government created the SASAC which acts as a fiduciary of the State to manage its ownership interests in Chinese

258 Ibid.

259 Cull et al. (2015), p. 288.

260 Zhou et al. (2015), p. 81.

261 Chen et al. (2011), p. 240.

262 Ma et al. (2013), p. 100; Chang and Wong, 2004, p. 621.

263 Huang and Chen (2019), p. 387. This unique phenomenon was called Guoyougu Suoyouzhe Quewei ("no functional proprietor of the state-owned shares").

264 Ibid.

SOEs.[265] Pursuant to the Enterprise State-Owned Assets Law,[266] the SASAC is entitled with the shareholder rights on behalf of the Government in Chinese SOEs. One of the SASAC's objectives is to "separate the government's social and public management functions from its role as the investor of the state-owned assets".[267] Except for the exercise of the shareholder rights, the SASAC is not allowed to intervene directly in the management or day-to-day operations of the SOEs.[268] Under this mechanism, the State was expected to only serve as the owner, and the SASAC controlled the shares of the listed companies directly or indirectly through SOEs.[269] In many listed SOEs, there is often a third layer of agents (except for the first layer of the State Council and local governments, and the second layer of the SASAC and its local branches) to represent the State to exercise the shareholder rights, namely the holding company of listed SOEs.[270] The holding companies are SOEs which are completely owned by the SASAC or the local governments, and they are also the registered holder of the State shares in listed SOEs.[271]

In the event of a takeover, according to Measures for the Supervision and Administration of the Transactions of State-owned Assets of Enterprises, "the transfer of the State shareholding in the SOEs needs to be reviewed by the SASAC and its agencies, and in the situation where the transfer of the shareholding leads to a change in the State's control, approval from the local government is also required".[272]

(2) Regulation by the CPC and Its Party Organizations

With regard to the role of the CPC in the corporate governance of SOEs, the Company Law requires Chinese companies to establish organizations of the CPC and to carry

---

[265] Zhang (2014), p. 438. See also Weinreich-Zhao (2015), p.16: In addition to the SASAC, other regulatory bodies were established for SOEs in specific strategic sectors. For example, the China Banking and Insurance Regulatory Commission oversees the respective industries and controls all state-owned assets in relevant SOEs. For other nonessential industries (such as machinery, electronics, chemicals, and textiles), in which private investments were allowed to enter, the government dissolved the government ministries overseeing these industries and replaced them with chambers of commerce or trade associations representing and coordinating various interests.

[266] Zhonghua Renmin Gongheguo Qiye Guoyou Zichanfa (中华人民共和国企业国有资产法) (Law of the People's Republic of China on the State-Owned Assets of Enterprises) (Promulgated by the Standing Committee of the National People's Congress on 28 October 2008, effective on 1 May 2009). See Articles 12, 16, 18, 21, 30 ~ 38.

[267] Zhang (2014), p. 439. See also Weinreich-Zhao (2015), p. 16: the large national SOEs are controlled by central SASAC, the remaining SOEs are controlled by regional SASACs at provincial and local levels.

[268] Articles 6, 14 of Law of the People's Republic of China on the State-Owned Assets of Enterprises.

[269] Wang and Xiao (2009), p. 106.

[270] Chen (2014), p. 12.

[271] Ibid.

[272] Qiye Guoyou Zichan Jiaoyi Jiandu Guanli Banfa (企业国有资产交易监督管理办法) (Measures for the Supervision and Administration of the Transactions of State-owned Assets of Enterprises) (Promulgated by SASAC and Ministry of Finance of The People's Republic of China on 24 June 2016, effective on promulgation). See Articles 6~7. See also Zeng and Lin, 2020, pp. 155–156.

out activities of the Party.[273] The CPC's leadership is also emphasized during the reforms of corporate governance structure of SOEs.

On 30 December 2019, the Central Committee of the CPC issued a trial regulation on the primary-level Party organizations' work in SOEs, which became effective on publication and stipulates that: "(i) SOEs shall incorporate the requirements for the Party-building work into their articles of association; (ii) shall stipulate that the research and discussion among the Party organizations in the SOEs are the prerequisite procedure for the board of directors and the management team to decide on major corporate issues; and (iii) that the Party organizations have a legitimate position in the corporate governance structure of the SOEs".[274] The major corporate issues that need to be discussed before the board of directors and the management team can make a decision, include but are not limited to: "(i) the principal issues in the reorganization of the corporate asset and the transfer of the property rights of the SOE; (ii) the establishment and adjustment of the corporate organizational structure; (iii) the formulation and modification of important charter rules; and (iv) the major issues related to securing the production, company stability, employee interests, and corporate social responsibilities".[275] Besides, the trial regulation also empowers the Party organization to strengthen its leadership in and control of the selection of the personnel in SOEs.[276] According to this, the CPC has the actual power in appointing and supervising senior executives of the SOEs.[277] In fact, many of the Government-appointed executives of listed SOEs were previously CPC officials.[278] Based on

[273] Article 19 of the Company Law. Article 5 of 2018 Chinese CG Code also requires that state-controlled listed companies should "incorporate requirements related to the Party building work into their articles of association in accordance with the Company Law and relevant regulations, and by giving due considerations to the companies' actual situations such as ownership structure and business management". See also WWW.GOV.CN (24 August 2015). 中共中央、国务院关于深化国有企业改革的指导意见 (Guiding Opinions of the Central Committee of the Communist Party of China and the State Council on Deepening the Reform of State-owned Enterprises). Available at: http://www.gov.cn/zhengce/2015-09/13/content_2930440.htm (accessed 28 February 2021). It also requires that the improvement of corporate governance should be unified with the reinforcement of the CPC's leadership in SOEs, and the charter of the SOEs should incorporate the party-building requirements.

[274] See WWW.GOV.CN (5 January 2020). 中国中央印发《中国共产党国有企业基层组织工作条例 (试行) 》(The Central Committee of the CPC issues Trial Regulation on the Work at Primary-level Party Organizations of SOEs). Available at: http://www.gov.cn/zhengce/2020-01/05/content_5466687.htm (accessed 2 March 2021). Article 13.

[275] Article 15 of Trial Regulation on the Work at Primary-level Party Organizations of SOEs.

[276] Article 11 (4) of Trial Regulation on the Work at Primary-level Party Organizations of SOEs.

[277] See also Bernier et al. (2020), p. 204: in regard to the Government's and CPC's influence on the senior personnel of the SOEs, "SASAC has the power to assess the economic performance of central SOEs and assign their leaders an annual grade ranging from A to E, which determines whether the leaders of central SOEs will receive compensation higher or lower than a fixed baseline; SASAC also appoints the top leadership positions—Party secretary, general manager, and board chairman—for non-core central SOEs"; as to core central SOEs, the CPC exercises the appointment authority over the leadership of companies.

[278] Ding et al. (2014), p. 155.

these designs, the CPC, by virtue of the Party organizations in the SOEs, could play a crucial role in the decision-making process of a SOE-related takeover.

5.4.4.3 The Dual Goals of Chinese SOEs and the Relevant Societal Interests that are Regulated in SOE-Related Takeovers

(1) The Dual Goals of Chinese SOEs in Their Corporate Activities

As an extension of government functions, Chinese SOEs usually carry dual goals of achieving economic benefits and protecting the public interest.[279] The Chinese Government and the CPC promulgated regulations concerning the SOE reforms and the comprehensive economic reforms of the country, which stipulate the public welfare objectives SOEs should undertake in their activities. Such objectives could often be discerned in SOE-related takeovers and illustrate the most crucial societal interests the Government and the CPC aim to protect.

For example, the Law on the State-Owned Assets of Enterprises requires that "the State should promote the state-owned capital to concentrate on crucial industries and sectors that are linked to the economic lifeline and national security of the country".[280] The Decision of the Central Committee of the CPC on Some Major Issues Concerning Comprehensively Deepening the Reform further stresses that "State-owned capital management should make greater contributions in providing public services, developing important forward-looking strategic industries, protecting the ecological environment, supporting scientific and technological progress, and safeguarding national security".[281] The 2020 Government Work Report further proposed to "improve the effectiveness of SOE reform and implement the three-year action for the SOE reform" and that "SOEs should focus on main responsibilities and main businesses, improve market-oriented operating mechanisms and core competitiveness".[282]

---

[279] Liu and Xu (2017), p. 32.

[280] Article 7 of Law of the People's Republic of China on the State-Owned Assets of Enterprises. In consistence with this stance, the State-owned capital in the future reforms would be further concentrated on important industries, areas, and infrastructures that are related to national security and people's livelihood, as well as the forward-looking strategic industries. See XINHUANET.COM (7 June 2017). 不断完善国企改革的三个体系 (To Continuously improve the three systems of state-owned enterprise reform). Available at: http://www.xinhuanet.com/politics/2017-06/07/c_1121099080.htm (accessed 2 March 2021).

[281] CHINA.ORG.CN (17 January 2014). 中共中央关于全面深化改革若干重大问题的决定 (Decision of the CCCPC on Some Major Issues Concerning Comprehensively Deepening the Reform). Available at: http://www.china.org.cn/chinese/2014-01/17/content_31226494.htm (accessed 2 March 2021).

[282] XINHUANET.COM (29 May 2020). 政府工作报告—2020年5月22日在第十三届全国人民代表大会第三次会议上(The Government Work Report—Delivered at the Third Session of the 13th National People's Congress of the People's Republic of China on 22 May 2020). Available at: http://www.xinhuanet.com/politics/2020-05/29/c_1126051808.htm (accessed 28 February 2021).

Moreover, according to the guiding opinions on the SOE reforms issued by the Central Committee of CPC and the Central Government, Chinese SOEs are categorized into two types—"profit-making SOEs" and "public welfare SOEs" given the different emphases of their social and economic functions.[283] The "profit-making SOEs" refer to "SOEs that are primarily burdened with economy-boosting functions. They are expected to "run in accordance with the marketization requirements to enhance the vitality of the state-owned economy, amplify the function of state-owned capital, and realize the preservation and appreciation of the state-owned assets".[284] For these SOEs, the Government would "strengthen the assessment of their roles in serving the national strategies, ensuring national security and national economic development, and in developing forward-looking strategic industries and completing 'special tasks'".[285] In contrast, the main goals of "public welfare SOEs" are "to protect people's livelihood, serve the society and provide public products and services" and "to introduce market mechanisms to improve the efficiency and capacity of public services".[286] The Government's regulatory strategies towards the two types of SOEs are also differentiated, aiming at promoting a better integration of the economic efficiency and social welfare.[287] Liu and Xu (2017) observed that in the process of SOE reforms, their two major functions—to boost the national economy and to enhance the public welfare, were not well balanced: on the one hand, many SOEs made a large number of short-term investments and repeated constructions to excessively pursue economic benefits; on the other hand, the Government's intervention in many public welfare SOEs were diluted, leading to the poor achievement in public welfare goals.[288] Against this background, how to enhance the public welfare goals of the SOEs and protect the relevant societal interests in their activities has become one hot topic of SOE's corporate governance reform.

(2) The Relevant Societal Interests Chinese SOEs Pursue in Takeovers

Among all the societal interests the "profit-making SOEs" and "public welfare SOEs" are expected to serve, considerations such as protecting national security, ensuring the supply of public products and services and enhancing the international competitiveness (as shown by the CNR/China CSR case in Sect. 5.2.3) are usually observed in SOE-related takeovers. In addition, the Government may pursue other societal interests through the regulation on SOE-related takeovers. For example, Wei (2014) observed that the Government sometimes also intervenes in SOE-related takeovers to achieve the following objectives: "(i) to help the local SOEs out of financial deficit; (ii) to promote the adjustment of industrial structure; (iii) to cure potential negative

[283] WWW.GOV.CN (13 September2015). 中共中央、国务院关于深化国有企业改革的指导意见 (Guiding Opinions of the Central Committee of the Communist Party of China and the State Council on Deepening the Reform of State-owned Enterprises).

[284] Ibid.

[285] Ibid.

[286] Ibid.

[287] Ibid.

[288] Liu and Xu (2017), p. 32.

externalities caused by takeovers (such as unemployment and loss of state-owned assets, and the social instability caused by such problems)".[289] Chen (2014) found that many of the SOE-related takeovers are initiated by the Government to cultivate the growth of local enterprises.[290] Zhou et al. (2015) found that SOE acquirers may have governmental support to help them acquire target companies in industries under tight government control, and may dominate the takeover competition against privately owned enterprises through the government intervention.[291] Moreover, potential problems are also observed in the Government's intervention. Pan et al. (2008) found that except for achieving the public interest objectives, the governments sometimes strived to intervene in takeovers and mergers involving the local SOEs to pursue personal career promotions.[292] Pan et al. (2008) concluded that local governments' interventions have a negative impact on the takeover and merger performance for profitable listed SOEs and a positive impact on the takeover and merger performance for in-loss listed SOEs.[293] Wei (2014) found that the Government may pursue rent-seeking in the approval procedure of a takeover.[294]

Pertaining to the CPC's role in takeovers, on the one hand, Ding et al. (2014) showed that when the Party organization participates in the SOE governance, the level of the merger and acquisition premiums that the SOE seller requires when selling the state-owned assets or equity is higher.[295] Chen and Lu (2014) argued that the participation of Party organizations in the corporate governance of the SOEs helps to curb the low-price transfer of state-owned assets or equity, which effectively avoids the potential loss of state-owned assets.[296] On the other hand, however, the much too high takeover price (which is much higher than the real price in the market) may not be conducive to the success of the takeover as well as the effective allocation of assets in the market.[297]

---

[289] Wei (2014), pp. 61–67, 81. For example, the Government may set "soft constraints" to the takeover parties, such as making it a prerequisite for the parties to solve the unemployment problem and the compensation fees for laid-off workers. Moreover, the local Government may also be incentivized to intervene in takeovers to achieve personal career promotion.

[290] Chen (2014), p. 13.

[291] Zhou et al. (2015), p. 81.

[292] Pan et al. (2008), pp. 42–43.

[293] Ibid. See p. 51.

[294] Wei (2014), p. 81.

[295] Ding et al. (2014), p. 118.

[296] Chen and Lu (2014), p. 119.

[297] Ibid.

5.4.5 *Intermediate Conclusion*

The takeover law in China (the 2006 Takeover Measures) protects the interests of target shareholders mainly by giving them the power to decide on the board's post-bid anti-takeover actions and requiring the directors to investigate and provide opinions on the acquirer's offer. The interests of other stakeholders are covered by the Company Law and the 2018 Chinese CG Code, which incorporate CSR requirements and advanced CSR standards to encourage companies to consider the relevant societal interests in their activities. Nevertheless, to what extent these CSR rules may play a role in takeovers is open for further discussion. The Government and CPC conduct specific regulation on SOE's activities such as takeovers. Thus, in SOE-related takeovers, the legally recognized public interest considerations in other laws as well as the public policies of the Government are often pursued by the Chinese SOEs.

5.5 Conclusion

This chapter analyses the regulatory framework of China in protecting the relevant societal interests in takeovers. Within this framework, government regulation in China covers various societal interests in takeovers with the focus on protecting public interests in the merger control regime and FDI screening regime and on protecting target shareholders in the takeover law regime and corporate law regime. In the private regulation field, the 2018 Chinese CG Code provides some protection to non-shareholder stakeholders mainly by stipulating the CSR requirements.

Protection of the Recognized Public Interest Considerations

In the merger control regime, the AML provides for a public interest exemption review mechanism to allow the merger control authority (the Enforcement Department II within the National Bureau) to use "advantages to the competition" (the "competition advantage exemption") and the "public interests" (the "public interest exemption") to release takeovers that (may) have anti-competition effects. The "competition advantage exemption" directly reflects the protection of the competition interest, which is closely related to the economic considerations as denoted by the "development of the socialist market economy (or national economy)" in the AML. Concerning other non-competition public interest, the AML does not provide an explicit interpretation, but it requires a national security review in foreign takeovers with a national security concern. Past cases illustrated that the industries and sectors as related to this security interest consideration go beyond the defence sector and cover many fundamental areas of the national economy. Besides, public interest considerations as listed in Article 20 AML for exempting monopoly agreements ("energy conservation, environment protection and disaster relief") also fall under this non-competition public interest group. The enforcement authority did not provide reasoning for its approval decisions in a merger control review; thus, it remains unclear how the enforcement authority makes its assessment in this public interest exemption review and whether this mechanism has ever been implemented in practice.

In the FDI screening regime, China adopts a "pre-establishment national treatment plus negative list" system to regulate foreign investments at the market access stage and a security review system of foreign investments after market access. The total number of items on the FI Negative List (the restricted and prohibited sectors and activities) has been consecutively reduced since 2018, which shows that China is incrementally liberalizing its market for foreign investors. On the other hand, the societal interests as regulated under the current 2021 FI Negative List are still wide-ranging, including not only the commonly recognized public interest considerations (such as the energy supply safety), but also other economic considerations (such as protection of some public transportation sectors) and societal and cultural considerations (such as protection of the social survey sector). Moreover, according to the Measures for the Security Review, which were issued in December 2020, foreign investments subject to a security review are not only limited to the defence sectors; foreign takeovers in other sectors (such as important agricultural products, important energy and resources, important transportation services, important cultural products, important information technology and internet products and services, important financial services, key technology, etc.) may also be recognized by the responsible authority (the Security Review Office) as relevant to national security and lead to a security review. Thus, the regulation in the FDI screening regime provides an "all-embracing" network for protecting various societal interests in foreign takeovers.

Moreover, takeovers involving Chinese SOEs are subject to specific regulation and intervention by the Government and CPC. In the event of a takeover, Chinese SOEs are often tasked to achieve public policies and public interest considerations such as protecting the national security, safeguarding the supply of public products and services, and enhancing the international competitiveness of SOEs.

Protection of the Interests of Corporate Stakeholders and Other Common Societal Interests

Protection of the target shareholders is the main subject of the takeover law regime and corporate law regime. The Company Law allocates the decision-making power in major corporate issues to the shareholder meeting; meanwhile, the directors and management are imposed with a fiduciary duty to the shareholders. In line with this, the 2006 Takeover Measures restrict the board of directors' power to take post-bid anti-takeover measures and require the directors and management to fulfil their fiduciary duties to shareholders in a takeover by conducting investigations and reporting to help shareholders reduce information asymmetries. Meanwhile, the Company Law requires companies to perform social responsibilities in their activities. It does not explain what kind of stakeholders and societal interests fall within the scope of this CSR requirement. Only in other provisions, the Company Law stipulates mechanisms for protecting the employees and creditors in corporate activities. The 2018 Chinese CG Code provides examples of the CSR performance of listed companies, including protecting stakeholders such as creditors, employees, customers, suppliers, the community, the environment, etc., and stipulates a CSR reporting requirement on listed companies. Moreover, in the private regulation field, to further encourage listed companies to pay attention to CSR matters, particularly environmental protection in their activities, the stock exchange (SZSE) also modified its evaluation standards on information disclosure of listed companies to incorporate ESG criterion. Such CSR rules and ESG standards may encourage listed companies to consider the relevant stakeholders' interests in corporate governance and takeover activities.

Chapter 6
Comparison and Evaluation of the Regulatory Frameworks of the U.K., Germany and China

Abstract This chapter compares and evaluates the protection of the public interest, the interests of corporate stakeholders and other societal interests in the three jurisdictions based on the discussions in Chaps. 2–5. It first analyses the similarities and differences in the scope of relevant societal interests that are protected as well as the specific protection mechanisms under the government regulation (including the competition law, FDI screening law, takeover law, and corporate law) and private regulation (the national corporate governance code) of takeovers in the three jurisdictions. Following that, it conducts a normative evaluation of the roles of the protection mechanisms in protecting the relevant societal interests by reviewing their advantages and problems in dealing with the market failure problems that may be caused as a result of takeovers.

6.1 Introduction

Based on the analysis in Chaps. 3–5, this chapter conducts a comparison and evaluation of the regulatory frameworks of takeovers in the U.K., Germany and China.

Section 6.2 first conducts a comparison of the protection mechanisms for the public interest, the interests of corporate stakeholders, and other societal interests in the three jurisdictions. The comparison explores the similarities and differences in the protection mechanisms and relevant societal interests under the government regulation (including competition law, FDI screening law, takeover law, and corporate law) and private regulation (which here refers mainly to the national corporate governance code) of the three jurisdictions. As the analysis of the competition law and FDI screening law in previous chapters covered both substantive (i.e. the relevant societal interests that are regulated) and procedural aspects (i.e. the procedures and responsible authorities for implementing the protection mechanisms), the comparison in Sect. 6.2 concerning these public laws also consists of these two aspects. Furthermore, because the procedural aspects were not relevant for the discussion of the takeover law, corporate law and the national corporate governance codes in

H. Ai, *Protecting Societal Interests in Corporate Takeovers*,
https://doi.org/10.1007/978-981-19-7546-2_6

previous chapters, this chapter also focuses only on the substantive content of the protection mechanisms in these regimes.

Section 6.3 follows the comparative legal analysis by giving a normative evaluation of the protection mechanisms based on the law and economics framework presented in Chap. 2. The evaluation aims to examine the strengths and weaknesses of the protection mechanisms for different societal interests and to explore what lessons can be drawn from the current regimes. Section 6.3 begins by giving an overview of the market failures relating to different societal interests in takeovers, which were discussed in Chap. 2 and will serve as the benchmark for the evaluation. Then it gives a review to specify what market failure(s) the protection mechanisms, as discussed in Sect. 6.2, may address. Following that, Sect. 6.3 analyses the strengths and weaknesses of the protection mechanisms in the three jurisdictions. It first discusses the theoretical advantages and disadvantages of government regulation and private regulation in curing market failures; then it analyses the strengths as well as the weaknesses (problems) of the protection mechanisms in the three jurisdictions in curing the market failure(s) and protecting different societal interests.

Following the comparison and evaluation in this chapter, Chap. 7 will answer the research questions by concluding the observations from Chaps. 2 to 6 and provide recommendations for (potential) future reforms to the regulatory frameworks of takeovers in the three jurisdictions.

6.2 Comparison of the Protection Mechanisms

6.2.1 Introduction

Under the regulatory framework of takeovers in the U.K., Germany and China, the protection of public interest considerations is mainly achieved by means of the national competition laws and FDI screening laws. This section first compares these laws in the three jurisdictions. In China, in addition to competition law and FDI screening regulations, the corporate law and some other government regulations incorporate specific rules concerning the corporate governance of SOEs and SOE-related takeovers. Based on such rules, the Government and the CPC in China may intervene in SOE-related takeovers to pursue public policies in the name of protecting "the public interest". The relevant mechanisms in this field contrast with the U.K. and Germany and will also be discussed in this section.

Apart from the recognized public interest considerations, the interests of corporate stakeholders of the target and other societal interests are also covered by the regulatory frameworks of the three jurisdictions. For the purpose of this book, "corporate stakeholders" have been defined earlier as "those who have direct contractual relationships with the company and often bear the direct consequences of a takeover"; and the examples of this group as discussed in previous chapters mainly include the shareholders, board of directors, and the employees of the target.[1] Moreover, other societal aspects such as the environment and the local community may also bear the consequences of a takeover, whilst usually no contractual relationship exists between them and the target. The U.K., Germany and China employ their national takeover law, corporate law and corporate governance code to balance and protect the interests of the corporate stakeholders and other societal interests. The protection mechanisms largely consist of rules of: (i) the decision-making power of the target company in a takeover; (ii) the board of directors' duty to consider other stakeholders and the companies' social responsibilities ("CSR" rules); (iii) the disclosure of stakeholder issues in corporate activities, inter alia takeovers; and (iv) the engagement mechanisms for non-shareholder stakeholders in corporate decisions. This section also compares these mechanisms in the three jurisdictions. The comparison focuses on the substantive aspects of the mechanisms, such as the objectives of the mechanisms and the relevant societal interests they cover. As procedural issues (inter alia the relevant enforcement procedures) are not of relevance to these corporate-governance-related laws and documents as discussed in Chaps. 3–5, they are not incorporated in the comparison of this section.

6.2.2 *Protection Mechanisms for the Legally Recognized Public Interest Considerations*

6.2.2.1 National Competition Laws

In the merger control regime, the national competition laws of the three jurisdictions (the EA 2002 in the U.K., the GWB in Germany and the AML in China) all stipulate provisions to protect the competition interest by prohibiting or restricting takeovers and mergers with anti-competitive effects. Meanwhile, the GWB and the AML incorporate a "public interest exemption" mechanism to allow the responsible authorities to "exempt" takeovers with anti-competitive effects for other public interest reasons; and the EA 2002 adopts a "public interest intervention" mechanism to empower the responsible authority to intervene in takeovers based on specific public interest considerations.

(1) Substantive Comparison: Protection Mechanisms and Recognized Public Interest Considerations

Regarding the "public interest exemption", the GWB and the AML use a similar terminology for exempting takeovers with anti-competitive effects. The GWB presents the "public interest" reasons as "advantages to the economy as a whole (that) outweigh the restraint to competition" and "overriding public interest".[2] The

[1] See the definition of "corporate stakeholders" in this book in Sect. 1.2.2.

[2] Section 42 of the GWB.

"public interest exemption" provision under the AML was inspired by the GWB[3]: public interest reasons become relevant when "the advantages of the concentration to competition obviously outweigh its disadvantages to competition" or when "the concentration is in the public interest".[4] Both "the advantages to the economy as a whole" and "the advantages of the concentration to competition" indicate that the responsible authorities, when deciding on the exemption, would consider the advantages the takeover may bring to competition and measure the advantages with the harms for competition. The terms "economy as a whole" and "obviously outweigh" suggest that the criteria for granting this exemption can be very high. As to the meaning of the "public interest", both the GWB and the AML remain silent. This silence, which seems intentional, leaves the responsible authority—the Minister of the BMWK ("the Minister") in Germany and the National Bureau in China with wide discretion in interpreting the public interest arguments in individual cases.

The recognized public interest reasons in German and Chinese case law and competition practice teach us that there are several differences between the two jurisdictions. The GWB cases as discussed in Chap. 4 show that the takeover parties in Germany may apply for a public interest exemption through a Ministerial Authorization using various arguments. Among the arguments submitted by the takeover parties, the Minister has recognized the following ones as in principle falling within the "advantages to the economy as a whole" or the "overriding public interest": (i) preservation of important know-how, (ii) improvement of international competitiveness, (iii) retention of the employment rate in the region, (iv) security of the energy supply of the country, (v) achievement of the environmental objectives of the Federal Government, (vi) preservation of a university hospital and the R&D of the university's medical faculty, (vii) the defence interest of the country, (viii) press diversity, (ix) achievement of the healthcare policy objectives and improvement of the healthcare level. In contrast with Germany, the approval decisions made by the merger control authority in China—the Enforcement Department II within the National Bureau (the SAMR Bureau before October 2021, and the MOFCOM before 2018) provides limited information about how it assessed and recognized the "public interest" considerations in past takeover and merger cases. It is unclear whether this public interest exemption mechanism has ever been implemented in practice in China. According to the cases as discussed in Chap. 5, protecting the State-owned economy and increasing the international competitiveness of Chinese SOEs were the major factors the Chinese regulator would consider in its approval of takeovers and mergers with potential anti-competition harms. It should be noted that the AML specifically lists the national security interest in Article 38 and the public interest considerations for exempting monopoly agreements (energy conservation, environment protection and disaster relief) in Article 20. In theory, the takeover parties may use these arguments to apply for an exemption. The newly published Amendment 2022 made no change to the content of the relevant public interest provisions in the AML (which simply become Articles 34, 38 and 20 of the law after the amendment). Regarding the

[3] Wang (2008a), p. 6. See also Wang (2008b), p. 81.

[4] Article 34 of the AML.

restriction for implementing the exemption mechanism, the GWB clearly provides that a Ministerial Authorization may be granted "only if the scope of the restraint of competition does not jeopardize the market economy system".[5] The AML does not provide for such restriction.[6] Consistent with this, in the proposed CNR/China CSR merger, it seems that the potential effects of the merger on the Chinese market were not fully taken into account in the final approval decision.[7]

The function of the "public interest intervention" mechanism in the EA 2002 of the U.K. differs from that of the "public interest exemption" mechanisms in the GWB and the AML. The "public interest intervention" mechanism allows the Secretary of State in the U.K. to intervene in several merger situations (a relevant merger situation, a special merger situation, and before 31 December 2020 a European relevant merger situation) based on specific public interest considerations. The Secretary of State may either make an adverse public interest finding where the takeover or merger infringes the public interest or make no finding at all if he(she) decides that no public interest consideration is relevant to the transaction concerned. Thus, this public interest intervention mechanism would not only lead to an exemption as the public interest exemption mechanism does. In some contrary situations, the Secretary of State may confirm that the takeover or merger causes harmful effects on the public interest and take actions to remedy, mitigate or prevent such effects. Therefore, it differs from the public interest exemption mechanism which only aims to approve takeovers and mergers with anti-competition harms, given their public interest benefits.

The recognized public interest considerations under the EA 2002 that allow for the Secretary of State to intervene in a takeover underwent major changes in recent years. Before 2020, the recognized public interest considerations in a relevant merger situation included (i) national security, (ii) relevant considerations in newspaper and media mergers (such as accurate presentation of news, free expression of opinion, and plurality of media ownership), and (iii) maintaining the financial stability (such as the continuity of banking services and the protection of depositors).[8] At this stage, in a European relevant merger situation and a special merger situation, it was the national security and considerations related to newspaper and media mergers that allowed for this public interest intervention.[9] To this extent, the scope of the recognized public interest considerations in the U.K. was more clear but much narrower than that in the German regime.

Against the background of the COVID-19 pandemic, the U.K. Government added a new public interest consideration in Sect. 58 of the EA 2002 in June 2020: the need to

---

[5] Subsection 42 (1) of the GWB.

[6] In contrast, Article 20 of the AML provides for restrictions for exempting a monopoly agreement on a public interest basis, that is the undertakings concerned need to prove that the agreement reached will not substantially restrict competition in the relevant market and that the consumers can share the benefits derived therefrom.

[7] See the discussion on the CNR/China CSR merger in Sect. 5.2.3.2.

[8] Section 58 of the EA 2002.

[9] Sections 59, 67, 68 of the EA 2002.

maintain in the U.K. the capability to combat and mitigate the effects of public health emergencies. This new consideration would allow the Secretary of State to intervene in future takeovers where the target operates in public health sectors. Moreover, based on this consideration, the Secretary of State may intervene in takeovers in other sectors as well, for example, where the target company designs and makes parts for cars (considering its potential capability to produce ventilators during a public health emergency), provides internet service, operates in the food supply chain or in the delivery sector (given that goods and services in these sectors may be increasingly demanded in a lockdown time during a public health emergency). Therefore, after this reform, the scope of industries and sectors that may be recognized as relevant to the "public interest" in takeovers seems to have been extensively enlarged; consequently, uncertainty in the interpretation of the public interest considerations under the EA 2002 has increased.

Since 4 January 2022, the national security interest under the EA 2002 has been replaced by virtue of the U.K. Security Act 2021, which establishes a separate national security review regime in takeovers and mergers. Under the new regime of the U.K. Security Act 2021, the Government's intervention power in takeovers and mergers with national security concerns is expanded as there is no minimum turnover or share of supply threshold for the Secretary of State to intervene. The U.K. Security Act 2021 also removed the type of mergers in the defence industry from the special merger situation category. Currently, the recognized public interest considerations in a special merger situation only include those that are related to newspaper and media mergers. Moreover, because of the Brexit, since 31 December 2020, the Secretary of State's public interest intervention in European relevant merger situation no longer applies.

(2) Procedural Comparison: Responsible Authorities and Relevant Procedures

More obvious differences are observed when comparing the responsible authorities and relevant procedures for implementing the "public interest exemption" mechanism and "public interest intervention" mechanism.

The GWB clearly separates the authority responsible for implementing the public interest exemption (the Minister) from that responsible for a regular merger control (the BKartA). It confines the BKartA to consider just the competition effects of the takeover or merger concerned, and only after the BKartA makes the decision to prohibit the takeover, can the parties concerned apply to the BMWi for a Ministerial Authorization. The Minister, based on the opinions given by the Monopolies Commission, independently makes decisions on the application for public interest exemption. In contrast, the AML does not distinguish between authorities responsible for merger control and authorities responsible for implementing the public interest exemption. The Enforcement Department II within the National Bureau (the SAMR Bureau before October 2021, and the MOFCOM before 2018) is responsible for reviewing whether a takeover or merger gives rise to any anti-competition effects and for authorizing a public interest exemption. Another difference between China and Germany lies in the fact that there is no other advisory authority in China for the public interest exemption decision. The AML also requires the State Council to establish an Anti-monopoly Commission. However, this Anti-monopoly Commission mainly acts its duties at the macro-control level, such as formulating and drafting policies and guidelines, organizing investigation and assessment of competition as a whole and publishing assessment reports.[10] To this extent, the role of the Chinese Anti-monopoly Commission largely differs from that of the Monopolies Commission in Germany.

The design of the responsible authorities for the "public interest intervention" mechanism in the U.K. differs from both the two-tier authorities (the BKartA and the Minister) in Germany and the one-tier authority (the Enforcement Department II) in China. In the U.K., both the CMA and the Secretary of State play an important role in a public interest intervention procedure whilst the latter dominates the initiation of the intervention and the final decisions on the adverse public interest findings. According to the EA 2002, the CMA is responsible for reviewing the anti-competitive outcome of a merger situation ("a substantial lessening of competition" within the market in the U.K.) and for deciding on the actions that need to be taken to cure the anti-competitive outcome.[11] When the Secretary of State believes that the public interest consideration(s) as listed under Section 58 is/are relevant to that merger concerned, it may give a public interest intervention notice in a relevant merger situation ("PIIN"), a European Intervention Notice (before 31 December 2020) in a European merger situation ("EIN"), or a Special Intervention Notice in a special merger situation ("SIN") to the CMA. Then, based on the report from the CMA, the Secretary of State decides whether the takeover or merger situation concerned operates against the public interest and makes a reference to the CMA. The CMA, pursuant to the grounds brought forward in the reference (only adverse public interest effect, or both substantial lessening of the competition and adverse public interest effect), provides its findings to the Secretary of State, and the latter finally decides whether the takeover or merger operates or may be expected to operate against the public interest. The Secretary of State must take into consideration the CMA's view concerning the competition issues. Nevertheless, given the public interest findings it finally makes, the Secretary of State may decide on a different outcome to address the competition issues, including for example, to clear the merger, make a reference, or to accept undertakings made by the merger parties, which might be different from those proposed by the CMA to resolve any competition concerns.[12] In addition to the CMA, other regulators may also participate in this public interest intervention procedure. For example, in a case of newspaper or media merger, the Ofcom is also required to provide an investigation report to the Secretary of State.

Therefore, it could be observed that the authorities responsible for the public interest intervention review in the U.K. differ from those in Germany, which strictly

[10] Article 12 of the AML (the original Article 9 AML before the amendment).

[11] Subsections 22(1), 33(1), 35(1)(2), 36(1)(2) of the EA 2002.

[12] Competition & Market Authority (CMA) (13 December 2018). Merger Remedies. Available at: https://assets.publishing.service.gov.uk/government/uploads/system/uploads/attachment_data/file/764372/Merger_remedies_guidance.pdf (accessed 8 May 2021).

separates the merger control authority (the BKartA) from the public interest exemption authority (the Minister). The CMA in the U.K. acts both as the responsible authority for the merger control and the advisory institution of the Secretary of State in the public interest intervention review. By conducting investigations and providing reports to the Secretary of State, the CMA's role in the public interest intervention review resembles that of the Monopolies Commission in Germany. This U.K. model also differs from the one-tier decision-making model in China considering the fact that, except for the Enforcement Department II, there is no other authority participating in the public interest exemption review process.

Concerning other procedural issues, the GWB cases as discussed in Chap. 4 illustrated that the German model attaches importance to the transparency of the public interest exemption procedure and a strong basis of reasoning for making a decision. Prior to the Minister's decision on the public interest exemption, the Monopolies Commission first gives its opinions to the Minister, which often provide the public with an overview of the weight of the relevant societal interests in the takeover or merger concerned. Where the Minister's decision deviates from the opinions of the Monopolies Commission, it will state the reasons for the deviation in its final decision.[13] In the decision-making process of the Minister, the parties to the takeover or merger and the Monopolies Commission have a right to a public hearing.[14] In addition to this, undertakings concerned and third parties who claim that the decision may infringe upon their rights have a right to appeal against the Minister's decision.[15] With these mechanisms, the transparency and the persuasiveness of the final decision are increased. Similar with Germany, in the U.K., the reports from the CMA to the Secretary of State normally provide a detailed analysis of the public interest issues in the merger situation concerned. The participation of other regulators in specific areas (such as Ofcom in media mergers) and their opinions to the CMA or the Secretary of State also enhance the persuasiveness of the final decisions from the Secretary of State. Moreover, the EA 2002 provides remedies for the related parties to the public interest intervention by allowing that any person aggrieved by a decision of the CMA, Ofcom or the Secretary of State in relation to a relevant merger situation or a special merger situation may apply to the Competition Appeal Tribunal (CAT) for a review of that decision.[16]

In comparison, the AML only mandates the enforcement authority to publish its decisions where it prohibits or conditionally approves a takeover or merger.[17] The publication of other unconditional approval decisions is left to the discretion of the enforcement authority.[18] In practice, the unconditionally approved cases as published by the Enforcement Department II (the SAMR Bureau before October 2021, and the MOFCOM before 2018) contained no factual findings or legal analysis.

[13] Subsection 42(1) of the GWB.

[14] Subsection 56 (7) of the GWB.

[15] Subsections 73 (2)(4) of the GWB.

[16] Subsection 120(1) of the EA 2002.

[17] Article 36 of the AML (the original Article 30 AML before the amendment).

[18] Article 52 of the AML (the original Article 44 AML before the amendment).

As a result, it is usually unclear to the public whether a case was unconditionally approved because no anti-competition effect was found or because the undertakings successfully proved that the individual case satisfied the conditions for a public interest exemption. The CNR/China CSR merger as discussed in Chap. 5 showed that the public seemed suspicious about the potential public interest justifications behind the approval decision in this case. Moreover, the AML allows those who are not satisfied with the decision made by the enforcement authority in accordance with Article 34 (the original Article 28) to bring an administrative action before the court; however, prior to bringing the administrative action to the court, one has to first apply for an administrative reconsideration.[19] The AML does not specify who has the right to apply for the administrative reconsideration or administrative action. Thus, in contrast with the U.K. and Germany, this design increases the difficulty of the relevant parties in seeking remedies.

6.2.2.2 FDI Screening Laws

Before 2020, the FDI screening regulation in the U.K. and Germany contrasted with that in China mainly in that the former focused on protecting the national security interests whilst the latter adopted an "all-embracing" approach to protect a wide range of societal interests in foreign takeovers. After 2020, against the background of the COVID-19 pandemic and the changing international environment, all of the three jurisdictions have made modifications to their FDI screening regulation to strengthen the responsible authorities' power of reviewing foreign takeovers. In the U.K. and Germany, the scope of the regulated public interest considerations under the FDI screening regime was largely extended; meanwhile, China, although continuing its all-embracing approach, further highlighted the protection of the national security interest in its FDI screening regime. This section compares the substantive and procedural aspects of the FDI screening regulation in the three jurisdictions. The focus of the comparison is on the substantive content of the FDI screening regulation, by exploring "what are the public interest considerations which the three jurisdictions aim to protect in foreign takeovers" and "what are the protection mechanisms".

(1) Substantive Comparison: Protection Mechanisms and Recognized Public Interest Considerations

a. *The "All-embracing" Protection Approach for Various Public Interest Considerations in China*

The FDI screening regulation in China mainly consists of three tiers: (i) market access regulation on inward foreign investments; (ii) regulation on national security review of foreign takeovers; (iii) other administrative regulation on foreign takeovers.

The Foreign Investment Law of China formally established a "pre-establishment national treatment plus negative list" ("the FI Negative List") approach to restrict the

[19] Article 65 of the AML (the original Article 53 AML before the amendment).

market access for foreign investments.[20] The FI Negative List stipulates the "prohibited" and "restricted" industries and sectors for foreign investments: foreign investors cannot invest in the "prohibited" fields; to invest in a restricted field, foreign investors must obtain approval from the responsible regulators and meet the investment conditions as set out by the FI Negative List.[21] In the fields that are not on the FI Negative List, the "pre-establishment national treatment" applies, meaning that the treatment accorded to foreign investors and their investments will be no less favourable than that accorded to domestic investors and their investments at the market access stage.[22] The items on the FI Negative List do not only aim to protect the national security interest; in fact, they also involve protecting various considerations relevant to the economic development (such as the development of information technology services and the protection of some public transport sectors) and the social order of China (such as protection of the media industry, the education sector and legal services). Thus, this FI Negative List serves as an "all-embracing" protection mechanism for the relevant societal interests at the market access stage. Since 2018, according to the policy of "further deepening the opening up", the items on the FI Negative List have been largely reduced year by year, which indicated a deregulation trend in the FDI screening regime of China. However, in essence, the basic principle of the "all-embracing" protection approach has remained unchanged.

Another supporting pillar of the FDI screening regime in China is the regulation of national security review in foreign takeovers. Before 2020, the national security review of foreign takeovers was mainly regulated by Notice 2011 and Provisions 2011. According to the two documents, a security review should be conducted not only in foreign takeovers in the defence-related sectors; foreign takeovers aiming to obtain actual control of the domestic entities in other economic sectors such as agriculture, energies and resources, infrastructure, transportation, key technology, and the manufacture of major equipment are also subject to a security review. The various sectors illustrated that the national security review in China at this stage also featured the "all-embracing" protection approach, regulating not only the national defence security, but also other societal interests that are closely related to the economic security and social life order. In December 2020, China adopted the Measures for the Security Review, which rebuilt the national security review regime by further enlarging the scope of foreign takeovers subject to a security review and establishing a new review authority (the Security Review Office). The new regime continues to recognize the "national security" as including not only defence security, but also economic security and the social order of the country. Under the new regime, foreign investments in important cultural products and services, important information and internet products and services and important financial services are also regarded as related to the national security interest.

---

[20] There are two "negative lists" in the FDI screening regime in China: the MA Negative List regulates market access for both domestic and foreign investments, and the FI Negative List specifically regulates foreign investments. Chapter 5 only discusses the regulation under the FI Negative List.

[21] Article 28 of The Foreign Investment Law.

[22] Article 4 para 2 of The Foreign Investment Law.

In addition to the "negative list" system and the national security review, the "all-embracing" protection approach in China is also reflected in two specific regulations on foreign takeovers: The Provisions on Foreign Mergers and Acquisitions (2009) and Measures for Foreign Strategic Investment. The two documents stipulate the protection of societal interests such as the security of the national economy, the state-owned assets, industry, land and environmental policies, etc.

b. *The Security-review-centred Protection Approach in the U.K. and Germany*

In comparison with China's three-tier regulation, the FDI screening regulation in the U.K. and Germany seems much more simplified and mainly consists of the rules of security review in foreign takeovers. The security review in the two jurisdictions used to largely focus on protecting the national defence security. In recent years, both the U.K. and Germany have been expanding the scope of foreign takeovers subject to a security review and enlarging the relevant public interest considerations this security review undertakes to protect.

Differing slightly from Germany and China, before November 2020, the U.K. did not have a separate FDI screening regulation which specifically applied to foreign takeovers. At that stage, the EA 2002 in the competition law regime applied irrespective of the nationality of investors and allowed the Secretary of State to intervene on national security grounds in foreign takeovers which satisfied the turnover or share of supply threshold and had triggered a merger control review. Before 2017, the U.K. had been taking a relatively lenient stance in the FDI screening area and the Government only conducted ad hoc reviews based on national security concerns in some foreign takeovers. Since 2017, the rising national security risks from foreign hostile takeovers of U.K. companies made the Government reconsider its lenient stance and imposed pressure on reforms in this area. In 2018, the U.K. Government tried to expand its intervention power in foreign takeovers taking place in areas that were considered as closely related to the national security by lowering the thresholds for a relevant merger situation in such areas.[23] The Government also published a White Paper (the 2018 White Paper) which explained in detail the trigger events that may give rise to national security risks and permit Government intervention.

In Germany, before 2020, the AWV and the AWG already established a separate FDI screening regime, which differed from the situation in the U.K. and seemed more similar to China. Nevertheless, in terms of the protection mechanisms, Germany shares more similarities with the U.K. in that it also mainly relied on a security review of foreign takeovers. In comparison with the U.K., before 2020, the security review mechanisms in Germany were much more complex and the Government of Germany also took a stronger intervention stance than the U.K. in this area at that time.

The AWV and AWG provide for rules concerning a sector-specific investment review and a cross-sector investment review of foreign takeovers in Germany. The

[23] See more about this reform in Sect. 3.3.1.

sector-specific investment review applies solely to foreign takeovers in security-sensitive areas and particularly protects the defence interests of Germany. By comparison, the cross-sector investment review concerns not only the defence interest. It applies to any foreign takeovers satisfying the threshold of the acquisition of shareholdings, regardless of the sectors where the takeover takes place, and examines whether the "public order or security" of Germany is endangered in a foreign takeover. In 2017 and 2018, Germany already conducted two reforms to enlarge the scope of sectors subject to a security review. According to the two amendments in 2017 and 2018, takeovers were subject to a cross-sector investment review where a non-EU resident acquired ownership of at least 25 per cent of the voting rights of a domestic company and 10 per cent of the voting rights of a domestic companyin particularly sensitive sectors.[24] During this period, takeovers in "sensitive sectors" to which the 10 per cent threshold applied included acquisitions of a company that operated in sectors such as critical infrastructure, developed or modified software for critical infrastructure operation, or was active in telecommunications surveillance, rendered cloud computing services, had a licence for telematics infrastructure, or was in the media industry and was characterized by particular topicality and breadth of impact.[25] The public interest considerations as relevant to the "public order or security" of Germany included for example, "the peaceful coexistence of nations", "foreign relations of Germany", and "the health and life of human beings". Thus, before 2020, the relevant public interest considerations that were protected under the FDI screening regulation in Germany had already gone beyond the defence interest.

The reforms towards a strengthened national security review in the U.K. and Germany in recent years were mainly triggered by the increasing foreign takeovers of domestic companies in the security-related sectors and high-technology sectors in the two jurisdictions. Such reforms during this period contrasted with the deregulation reforms in China which were mainly reflected in the decreasing number of items on its "negative list" for market access. In 2020, both the U.K. and Germany lengthened their strides in taking reforms to enhance the Government's intervention power in foreign takeovers; and pursuant to these reforms, the scope of societal interests that are regulated through the security review in the two jurisdictions was further extended.

In November 2020, the U.K. Security Bill 2020 was published, which became the U.K. Security Act 2021 and came into force on 4 January 2022. The U.K. Security Act 2021 establishes a new, separate FDI screening regime. Compared with the FDI screening regime under the EA 2002, the new regime does not include a minimum turnover or share of supply threshold for the Government's review of foreign takeovers with national security concerns. The U.K. Security Act 2021 introduces a mandatory notification requirement for takeovers in seventeen key sectors of the economy which are of high national security risks. In addition to the traditional defence-related sectors, the seventeen sectors also include these that were previously

---

[24] See more about this reform in Sect. 4.3.1.

[25] Subsection 55(1) of the AWV.

not regarded as closely linked to the security interest (such as communications, transport).[26] For takeovers that are not in the specified high-risk sectors, investors are also encouraged to submit a notification if the transaction constitutes a "trigger event" and could raise national security risks and the Secretary of State has a "call-in" power to intervene and conduct an in-depth national security assessment in these takeovers. As a result, it is hard to pinpoint the scope of sectors that may be subject to a security review and the relevant societal interests that would be regulated under this security review. Therefore, to some extent, the new U.K. regime shows some features of the "all-embracing" approach in China.

To respond to the COVID-19 crisis and the new EU FDI screening framework, Germany made a series of reforms to the AWV and AWG to further strengthen its security review in foreign takeovers since 2020. The main changes under the new regime are reflected in two aspects: (i) the cross-sector investment review would not only aim at protecting the public order and security of Germany, but would also consider a takeover's potential effects on the public order and security of other Member States or programs of a Union interest, which makes the interpretation of the "public order and security" much more complex; (ii) the sectors of companies subject to a cross-sector investment review and activities of companies subject to a sector-specific investment review were both largely extended, indicating an expansion of the societal interests that will be regulated in the name of "public order or security".[27] Among other reforms, through the Fifteenth Amendment to the AWV, Germany added takeovers in the healthcare sector to the scope of a cross-sector investment review to protect critical healthcare infrastructures.

The FDI screening reforms in the U.K., Germany and China since 2020 had in common that the three jurisdictions all strengthened the Government's powers in security reviews of foreign takeovers through extending the sectors of takeovers subject to a security review and expanding the interpretation of the "security interest". Compared with the U.K. and China, the reforms in Germany in 2020 particularly added the societal interests related to the country's capability to combat the COVID-19 crisis as new public interest considerations in the FDI screening regime and adapted to the new FDI screening regime of the EU. In contrast to Germany and China, the U.K. Security Act 2021 for the first time established a separate FDI screening regulation in the U.K. When compared with the two other jurisdictions, China, on the one hand, still continued its all-embracing protection approach; on the other hand, the newly adopted Measures for the Security Review in 2020 in China highlighted the importance of protecting the "national security interest" and reinforced the security review in foreign investments, which responded to and converged with the reforms in the U.K. and Germany.

---

[26] For more about these proposed sectors, see Sect. 3.3.2.

[27] See the detailed discussion of the reforms in this field in Sect. 4.3.2.

(2) Procedural Comparison: Responsible Authorities and Relevant Procedures

Consistent with its three-tier "all-embracing" regulation, the design of the responsible authorities and relevant procedures in China also seems more complex than that in the U.K. and Germany.

In the U.K., before the promulgation of the U.K. Security Act 2021, the Secretary of State was responsible for a security review in foreign takeovers based on the public interest considerations under the EA 2002, particularly the national security interest. The relevant procedures and the cooperative role of the CMA in this process were subject to the rules concerning the public interest intervention mechanism under the EA 2002. The U.K. Security Act 2021 separated the security review from the merger control review. Under the current regime, the CMA will no longer be involved in the national security assessment; the Secretary of State for Business, Energy and Industrial Strategy, along with the newly established Investment Security Unit, will undertake the national security assessment and decide on the outcome of the review. In Germany, the BMWK is responsible for both the cross-sector and sector-specific investment review in foreign takeovers. As the Minister of the BMWK is also responsible for the "public interest exemption" mechanism in the merger control regime, the procedure of the FDI screening thus largely overlaps with the public interest exemption procedure.

In China, at the market access stage, the NDRC, MOFCOM and their local counterparts and the sector regulators are responsible for implementing the FI Negative List. Before the publication of the Measures for the Security Review in 2020, the Joint Conference, an ad hoc institution which was under the leadership of the State Council and organized and held by the NDRC and MOFCOM was responsible for conducting a security review at the convention of the NDRC. According to the Measures for the Security Review, the Security Review Office was established and replaced the ad hoc Joint Conference. The Security Review Office is still under the leadership of both the NDRC and MOFCOM and takes the responsibility for the routine work of the security review. Thus, as a result of the recent reforms after 2020, the U.K., Germany and China are converging in that they now all have in place a permanent institution responsible for the security review in foreign takeovers, which again reflects the strengthened FDI screening regulation approach in the three jurisdictions.

6.2.2.3 State Intervention in SOE-Related Takeovers: Protection Mechanisms and Recognized "Public Interest" Considerations

In China, SOEs usually carry dual objectives of achieving economic benefits and protecting the public interest. The Chinese Government can exert deep and multi-faceted influence in SOE-related takeovers by exercising the shareholder rights and its power in allocating important societal and economic resources in the market. The Chinese Communist Party (CPC) can also actively participate in SOE-related takeovers to achieve public policy objectives through its Party organizations in the SOEs and its power to appoint senior executives of the SOEs. The relevant rules in the corporate law and other government regulations concerning the corporate governance of the Chinese SOEs and regulating SOE-related takeovers thus serve as a unique regime for protecting the public interest in takeovers, which contrasts with the U.K. and Germany in this field.

In China, SOEs retain absolute control of the key industries and areas that are closely related to the national security interest (both defence security and economic security). Both the "profit-making SOEs" and the "public-welfare SOEs" can function as a vehicle for protecting the public interest. The "public-welfare SOEs" are naturally burdened with the task to assure the supply of public services and achieve the public interest in their corporate activities. The "profit-making SOEs" are primarily burdened with economy-boosting functions, particularly in enhancing the vitality of the state-owned economy, preserving the state-owned assets, and developing strategic industries. As their main businesses often take place in the sectors that bear crucial influence on the national economy or that are closely related to the national security, they are also expected to protect the public interest in these areas. The Chinese Government and the CPC employ several mechanisms to assure the achievement of the public interest objectives in SOE-related takeovers. The SASAC represents the State to exercise the shareholder rights in the SOEs; meanwhile, it exercises a supervision role in the SOE-related takeovers. The transfer of State shareholding in SOEs needs to be reviewed by the SASAC and its agencies, and where the transfer of the shareholding leads to a change of control, approval from the local government is also required. In terms of the role of the CPC, discussions among the Party organizations in the SOEs are the prerequisite procedures before the board of directors and the management team decide on major corporate issues, and the Party organization has a leadership in the selection of the senior personnel in the SOEs. The Government and the CPC can therefore exert deep influence in the decision-making process of the SOEs in a takeover. Consequently, the public policy objectives of the Government and CPC are often incorporated in the decisions of SOE-related takeovers. Among others, protecting the national security (including both defence security, economic security and social life order) and increasing the international competitiveness of an SOE are often in a priority position of the decisions. In addition, the Government sometimes may intervene in SOE-related takeovers to help local SOEs out of financial deficit, to adjust the industrial structure or to solve a large-scale unemployment problem.[28]

In comparison with China, in the U.K. and Germany, the Government mainly exerts its influence on some privatized companies and intervenes in some hostile takeovers of such companies through the use of "golden shares", the legitimacy of which has been challenged by the CJEU in case law. The two jurisdictions lack similar government regulation mechanisms as in China which specifically target the corporate governance of SOEs and pursue public interest objectives through SOE-related activities. In the U.K., the Government introduced the first large-scale and comprehensive dismantling of SOEs in Europe.[29] After 1945, the nationalized industries

[28] See the relevant discussion in this regard in Sect. 5.4.4.

[29] Bernier et al. (2020), p. 128.

in the U.K. were established as "public corporations" and were managed by boards appointed by ministers. The boards of such "public corporations" were expected to be the "high custodian of the public interest" and run the industries efficiently and effectively in the public interest.[30] Following the privatization efforts in the 1980s and 1990s, the number of SOEs in which the State-owned shares largely dropped. However, the privatization wave did not change the public interest expectations on these companies. For example, the privatized companies in the energy sectors are still required to pursue public objectives such as security of supply and environmental sustainability. The regulators are involved in planning investments in the privatized utilities sectors; and major privatized utilities in the energy, telecommunications and transport sectors are still subject to an on-going degree of State regulation and political intervention.[31] However, in takeovers involving these companies, the Government in the U.K. mainly relies on the government regulations in the merger control regime and FDI screening regime to intervene to pursue public policy objectives. In the field of corporate governance, before the Brexit, the U.K. Government used "golden shares" as an anti-takeover measure to prevent hostile takeovers and to restrict foreign influence in the strategic sectors. In Germany, similarly, the Federal Government in previous cases also used "golden shares" as a defence in takeovers of some major privatized companies. The German Federal Government can intervene in the shareholding transaction in these companies and the responsible Federal ministry is required to use its influence to ensure that the supervisory bodies of the companies in which the State has a majority shareholding take the special interests of the Federation into consideration in their activities.[32] The Federal Budget Code ("BHO") sets rules for State participation in private-law enterprise, and a review of ownership takes place every 2 years.[33] The Federal Government can hold interests in privatized companies if there is an important interest on the part of the Federation and the purpose intended by the Federation cannot be achieved better or more efficiently in any other way.[34]

In the previous "golden shares" case law, the CJEU found that the "golden shares" provisions usually infringed the fundamental freedoms under the TFEU.[35] It accepted certain public interest reasons as justifications for the maintenance of golden shares, such as[36] "(i) safeguarding of availability of the telecommunications network in the

[30] Ibid, p. 139.

[31] Ibid, p. 137.

[32] See Subsection 65 (6) of the BHO.

[33] OECD (2018). Privatisation and the broadening of ownership of State-owned enterprises. Available at: https://www.oecd.org/daf/ca/Privatisation-and-the-Broadening-of-Ownership-of-SOEs-Stocktaking-of-National-Practices.pdf (accessed 5 May 2021), pp. 14, 22, 38.

[34] See Subsection 65 (1) of the BHO.

[35] Consolidated versions of the Treaty on European Union and the Treaty on the Functioning of the European Union (TFEU) [2016] OJ C202/1. See Article 63 (free movement of capital) and Article 49 (freedom of establishment).

[36] See conclusions of the public interest justifications in Szabados (2015), p. 1124; Papadopoulos (2021), p. 62.

event of crisis, war, or terrorism[37]; (ii) safeguarding of energy supply linked to the public security[38]; (iii) protecting the interests of workers and minority shareholders and the general interest that a big sized company would affect.[39] Concerning the public security reason, the CJEU requires that "public security may only be relied on in the event of a genuine and sufficiently serious threat to a fundamental interest of society".[40] Meanwhile, the Court rejected the idea that purely economic reasons (such as ensuring the conditions of competition or the prevention of a possible disruption of the capital market) could constitute valid justifications for a restriction of the free movement of capital.[41] Moreover, the restriction measures as imposed by the Government apply equally to nationals of the Member State concerned and of other EU Member States and should comply with the principle of proportionality.[42] In most of the golden share cases, the Member States successfully convinced the CJEU with the public interest considerations for justifying the restrictions on the fundamental freedoms; nevertheless, they usually failed to prove that the principle of proportionality had been complied with.[43] For example, in *Commission v. Italy,*[44] the CJEU accepted that "the minimum supply of energy resources and goods essential to the public, the continuity of public service, national defence, the protection of public policy and public security, and health emergencies may justify a restriction on the free movement of capital".[45] Nevertheless, the Court held that "the Italian rules did not satisfy the proportionality test".[46] Only in one golden shares case—the *Commission v. Belgium,*[47] did the CJEU accept the justification from the Belgian Government considering that "the Member State's special powers were based on an *ex post* authorization system and subject to strict time limits, a formal statement of reasons for the decision, and effective judicial review".[48]

In the two cases—*Commission v. United Kingdom* in 2003 and *Commission v. Germany* in 2007 as discussed in Chaps. 3 and 4 respectively, the CJEU decided

---

37 Case C-171/08 *Commission v. Portugal*, Judgment of the Court of 8 July 2010, see para 72.

38 Ibid, see para 84; see also Case C-212/09 *Commission v. Portugal*, Judgment of the Court of 10 November 2011, see para 82.

39 Case C-112/05 *Commission v. Germany*, Judgment of the Court of 23 October 2007.

40 Ibid, p. 1125.

41 Ibid. See Case C-171/08 *Commission v. Portugal*, Judgment of the Court of 8 July 2010, paras 70–71.

42 Papadopoulos (2021), p. 59: "according to the *Gebhard* test introduced by the CJEU, national measures which hinder or make less attractive the exercise of free movement of capital or freedom of establishment can be justified if they satisfy four specific conditions (i) they must be applied in a non-discriminatory manner; (ii) they must be justified by imperative requirements in the general interest; (iii) they must be suitable for securing the attainment of the objective that they pursue; and (iv) they must not go beyond what is necessary in order to attain it".

43 Ibid, p. 61.

44 Case C-326/07 *Commission v. Italy*, Judgment of the Court of 26 March 2009.

45 Szabados (2015), p. 1126.

46 Ibid.

47 Case C-503/99 *Commission v. Belgium*, Judgment of the Court of 4 June 2002.

48 Szabados (2015), pp. 1126–1127; see also Papadopoulos (2021), pp. 58, 61.

that the golden shares held by the Government constituted a restriction on the free movement of capital; and the U.K. and Germany failed to prove that general public interest reasons in the two cases justified such restrictions.[49] The CJEU's strict stance in explaining and recognizing the public interest justifications for "golden shares" restricts its use in the U.K. and the EU. Thus, compared with the Government and CPC's influence on SOE-related takeovers in China, the Government's intervention in the U.K. and Germany in takeovers of major privatized companies to protect public interests seems much less strong.

6.2.3 Protection Mechanisms for the Interests of Corporate Stakeholders and Other Societal Interests

6.2.3.1 Protection of the Interests of Target Shareholders

Among all the corporate stakeholders, protecting the shareholders of the target company is the primary objective of the takeover laws, corporate laws and the corporate governance codes of the three jurisdictions. The major protection mechanism for shareholders are the rules allocating the decision-making power of the target in a takeover. An evident difference exists between Germany and the other two jurisdictions in that the supervisory board and employees in Germany play an important role in the decision-making process of a takeover, whilst in the U.K. and China the shareholder meeting dominates this process and has exclusive power. Within the shareholder group, the takeover laws in the three jurisdictions all incorporate a "mandatory bid" rule to provide for extra protection for minority shareholders.

(1) Shareholders' Exclusive Decision-making Power in the U.K. and China

In the takeover law regime of the U.K., the City Code restricts the actions taken by the target board that may have the effect of frustrating the bid or preventing the shareholders from deciding on the merits of the bid during the course of an offer or where the board believes that a bona fide offer might be imminent.[50] This "non-frustration rule" exclusively allocates the power of taking anti-takeover measures to the general meeting of shareholders when a bid is on the horizon. Under this model, the shareholder meeting of the target has the final power to decide on the merits of a takeover offer, and correspondingly, the shareholders' interests are protected from the potential misuse of power by the board of directors.[51] The takeover law in China adopts a similar decision-making model. The 2006 Takeover Measures in China restrict the board of directors from taking actions that might produce significant

[49] See analysis about the two golden share cases in Sects. 3.4.2.2 and 4.4.2.3.

[50] Rule 21.1(a) of the City Code.

[51] Under this "non-frustration rule", the board may still take actions such as searching for an alternative friendly acquirer to compete with the existing one (the "white knight") or taking pre-offer "embedded defences". See the discussion in Sect. 3.4.2.2.

effects on the assets, liabilities, entitlements or business performances of the target company after the acquirer makes an informative announcement of a bid and until the bid is completed.[52] During this period, such anti-takeover actions should be approved by the shareholder meeting of the target. To this extent, the decision-making models in China and the U.K. have in common that they both give the target shareholders an exclusive power to decide on the merit of a takeover.

Nevertheless, within this "shareholder decides" model, there is still a difference between the U.K. and China. The "non-frustration rule" in the U.K. applies when a takeover bid is "on the horizon", including when an announcement has been made by the acquirer or even when the acquirer has not yet made the takeover announcement but the target board believes that a bona fide offer might be imminent. In China, the restriction on the board of directors only explicitly applies after an "informative announcement" is made by the acquirer; and the 2006 Takeover Measures are silent on whether this restriction also applies to pre-bid anti-takeover measures by the board of directors. In practice, the board of directors of many companies in China often takes advantage of this gap and tries to incorporate anti-takeover clauses in the company's articles of association to generate a deterrent effect to potential acquirers. These clauses often protect the board of directors and allow them to take certain anti-takeover measures when confronted with a hostile takeover (e.g., the "staggered board clause", the "golden parachute clause", clauses that restrict the acquirer's rights to dominate directors or extend the matters subject to a special voting rule, or clauses to increase the acquirer's obligations to report and disclose). The board of directors in China, through these clauses, may gain a stronger role in takeovers than their counterpart in the U.K.

(2) The Supervisory Board's Decision-making Power in Germany

The German model in this area differs from the U.K. and China in that the supervisory board of the target plays a decisive role concerning the management board's anti-takeover measures. Germany opts out of the "board neutrality" rule under the EU Takeover Directive. The takeover law in Germany (WpÜG) provides the target company with the freedom to either "opt-in" and follow the strict "board neutrality rule" in the EU Takeover Directive, or to choose, in the articles of association, to follow the less restrictive default provisions in the WpÜG concerning the anti-takeover measures. In the first situation where the target opts in, its management board and supervisory board in principle are prohibited from taking anti-takeover actions during the time the acquirer's decision to make a bid is published and until the result of the bid is made public; nevertheless this prohibition is subject to four exceptions, one of which is that the general meeting of shareholders authorizes the management board and the supervisory board to take such actions.[53] In the second

52 This restriction on the board of directors in the 2006 Takeover Measures applies only to actions that may significantly change the assets or liabilities of the company and taken after the announcement of a takeover bid. See the discussion in Sect. 5.4.2.1.

53 See discussion about these exceptions in Sect. 4.4.2.2. The other three exceptions include: (i) actions taken by the management board in the normal course of business; (ii) actions taken outside

situation where the target follows the less restrictive rules under the WpÜG, in principle the management board is prohibited from taking anti-takeover actions during the pending takeover offer. Such prohibition is also subject to several exceptions, of which one is that the post-offer actions taken by the management board have been specifically approved by the supervisory board.[54] Regarding the anti-takeover measures taken by the management board prior to the publication of an offer, the WpÜG requires an authorization from the general meeting of shareholders as well as the consent of the supervisory board.[55] Thus, apart from those actions that can be solely decided by the board of directors, for other anti-takeover actions, either pre-bid or post-bid, the supervisory board's approval is required. Consequently, the role of the shareholder meeting's anticipatory authorization for the pre-bid anti-takeover actions seems marginal, given that the board of directors can take post-bid actions with only the approval of the supervisory board. To this extent, the shareholder meeting's decision-making role in a takeover in Germany is comparatively weak; meanwhile, the supervisory board in Germany gets the actual and final decision-making power.

In summary, concerning the protection of shareholders from the board of directors' misuse of anti-takeover measures, the German model (where the companies do not "opt-in" for the "board neutrality rule") contrasts with the U.K. and China mainly in that the German supervisory board's consent is decisive for the board of directors' anti-takeover measures. With regard to the post-offer anti-takeover measures, Germany differs from the other two jurisdictions in that after the board of directors makes the initiatives of the measures, the supervisory board in German companies rather than the shareholder meeting should give consent to these measures (as in the U.K. and China). As to the pre-bid anti-takeover actions, Germany contrasts with the U.K. in that in addition to the consent from the shareholder meeting, the former also requires the consent from the supervisory board. Germany also contrasts with China concerning the pre-bid anti-takeover actions in that the Chinese takeover law (the 2006 Takeover Measures) is silent as to which corporate organ (either the shareholder meeting or the board of directors) should approve such pre-bid anti-takeover measures. Although China also adopts a "two-tier" board system, the supervisory board and the co-determination by employees in China only have a token role in practice, which obviously differs from the German model. In a takeover, the supervisory board in Chinese companies therefore differs from its counterpart in Germany as the former's approval is not required. Moreover, as a result of the prominent role of the supervisory board, the employee representatives on the supervisory board in Germany may also have a more important role in the decision-making process of a takeover than the employees in the U.K. and China.

---

the normal course of business, to the extent that they serve the realization of decisions that were made and partially realized prior to the decision to make an offer; and (iii) the search for competition offers ("the white knight"). See Subsection 33a(2) of the WpÜG.

[54] The other two exceptions are: (i) actions that a diligent and conscious manager of a company not subject to a takeover offer would have taken as well; (ii) the search for competing offers ("the white knight"). See Section 33 (1) of the WpÜG.

[55] Ibid. See subsection 33 (2) of the WpÜG.

6.2.3.2 Protection of the Interests of Non-shareholder Corporate Stakeholders and Societal Stakeholders

The interests of other non-shareholder stakeholders in takeovers are usually stipulated by the general principles and rules concerning the fiduciary duties of the board and management in the corporate law, takeover law and the corporate governance code. In the U.K., Germany and China, the relevant protection mechanisms include provisions that require the board and management to consider the "interest of the company" and the companies to fulfil their corporate social responsibilities ("CSR"), rules pertinent to the disclosure of information on non-shareholder stakeholder matters, and rules that allow non-shareholder stakeholders to participate in corporate decisions.

(1) Principles of Protecting Other Stakeholders

In addition to protecting the shareholder interests, the corporate laws and corporate governance codes for listed companies of the three jurisdictions have similar principles requiring the companies to take into account the interests of other stakeholders in their activities.

In the U.K., the CA 2006 defines the directors' duties to "promote the success of the company" and to "have regard to" a number of non-shareholder stakeholders in their decisions and to value the build-up of a long-term relationship with them.[56] The CA 2006 gives a non-exhaustive list of examples of the stakeholders that the directors should "have regard to", including employees, suppliers, customers, and creditors of the company, and the community and the environment the company may have an impact on.[57] This provision, as a reflection of the "enlightened shareholder value" in the U.K., is often compared with its previous "shareholder primacy" tradition which focused exclusively on protecting the shareholders in corporate activities.[58] In the self-regulatory regime, the 2018 U.K. Corporate Governance Code (the "2018 U.K. CG Code") emphasizes building positive relationships between the company and its stakeholders and strengthening stakeholders' voice at the board level, and the 2018 Guidance on Board Effectiveness (the "2018 U.K. Guidance") gives examples of the key stakeholders of a listed company, including the workforce, customers, suppliers, regulators, government, bondholders, banks and other creditors, trade unions and community groups.[59]

Similarly, in Germany, the 2020 German Corporate Governance Code (the "2020 German CG Code") highlights the obligation of the management board and supervisory board of listed companies to take into account "the workforce and the other groups related to the company to ensure the best interests of the company"[60] and requires the company to be aware of its responsibilities to the community

[56] Section 172 of the CA 2006.

[57] Subsections 172(1)(3) of the CA 2006.

[58] See discussions in Sect. 3.4.2.1.

[59] See discussions in Sect. 3.4.3.3.

[60] See para 1 of the "Foreword" (at page 2) of the 2020 German CG Code.

and the society.[61] The Company Law in China has a similar CSR provision as Germany, requiring companies to assume social responsibilities in their activities.[62] In contrast with the U.K., the CSR provisions in Germany and China do not provide detailed examples of the relevant stakeholders. In Germany, among all the other stakeholders, the 2020 German CG Code only emphasizes the interests of "workforce" and "community". In China, the Company Law specifies the protection of employees.[63] As a complement, the corporate governance code for listed companies (the "2018 Chinese CG Code") recognizes the protection of a large scope of other stakeholders. The corporate stakeholders it lists include creditors, employees, customers and suppliers.[64] Regarding other societal stakeholders, it requires the listed companies to actively perform social responsibilities in terms of community welfare, environmental protection, disaster relief and poverty alleviation.[65]

The above principles of protecting other stakeholders apply to general corporate activities rather than specifically targeting at takeovers. In the event of takeovers, the City Code in the U.K. provides for mechanisms of the "post-offer undertakings" and "post-offer intention statements" to encourage the takeover parties to consider the interests of non-shareholder stakeholders of the target. Through the two mechanisms, the takeover parties could make post-offer arrangements concerning the target's employees, locations, its R&D investment, the sustainable development of the environment, and the prosperity of the local community.[66] Where the takeover parties specify that their arrangements belong to "post-offer undertakings", these arrangements are legally binding for the period specified in the undertaking.In case of breach, the Takeover Panel in the U.K. is able to obtain an order from the court to seek compliance from the takeover party that makes such promises,or to use its disciplinary power such as issuing a statement of censure to the takeover party.[67] In contrast, the takeover laws in China and Germany do not provide for such protection mechanisms concerning the arrangement of other stakeholders. In China, the 2006 Takeover Measures stipulate that "corporate takeovers shall not impair national security and public interests" in the general principles; in Germany, the WpÜG only sets forth that "the management and supervisory board of the target company must act in the interests of the target company".[68]

(2) Disclosure of Information on Stakeholder Matters

Another corporate governance mechanism for protecting other stakeholders in the three jurisdictions is the disclosure of information about stakeholder matters given

[61] See para 2 of the "Foreword" (at page 2) of the 2020 German CG Code.

[62] Article 5 of The Company Law.

[63] Article 18 of The Company Law.

[64] Article 83 of the 2018 Chinese CG Code.

[65] Articles 86, 87 of the 2018 Chinese CG Code.

[66] Rules 19.5 (post-offer undertakings), 19.6 (post-offer intention statements) of the City Code.

[67] Rules 19.5 (h)(i), 10(d), 11 of the City Code.

[68] Subsections 3 (3) of the WpÜG.

by the board of directors, which aims to reduce information asymmetries between the company and their non-shareholder stakeholders.

The relevant provisions concerning non-financial reporting on stakeholder matters are stipulated by the corporate law or commercial law in the U.K. and Germany and the corporate governance code in China. The non-financial reporting requirement in the national laws of the U.K. and Germany implemented the relevant provisions of the EU Non-financial Reporting Directive (Directive 2014/95/EU). In the U.K., the CA 2006 imposes a reporting obligation on listed companies and large companies with more than 500 employees to include the following non-financial information in its strategic report, including, for example, the environmental matters, matters concerning the company's employees, and social, community and human rights issues, etc.[69] In addition to this non-financial information statement, in January 2022, a "sustainability information statement" was further inserted into the CA 2006 as part of the strategic report, which came into force on 6 April 2022.[70] Currently, the CA 2006 requires that both the non-financial and sustainability information statement should contain the climate-related financial disclosures of the company.[71] This non-financial reporting requirement is implemented on a "comply or explain" basis, meaning that where the strategic report does not contain the above stakeholder information, it must state which kind of information it does not contain.[72]

Similar to the U.K., the German Commercial Code (HGB) also incorporates rules to implement the non-financial reporting requirement under the Directive 2014/95/EU. It requires certain large public-interest companies to include a non-financial statement in their annual management report, which should contain aspects such as environmental issues, employee matters, social matters and human rights.[73] The implementation of this stakeholder report in Germany also follows a "comply or explain" approach, which is comparable with the U.K. again.[74] In addition, as an implementation of the relevant rules under the EU Takeover Directive,[75] the City Code and WpÜG stipulate the duties of the acquirer to publish its intentions concerning the future business of the target (such as information about potential changes to the employment, the locations of the company), and the duties of the target board(s) to give its opinions (as well as the reasons) on the takeover offer (such as the board's views on anticipated consequences of the takeover on employment).[76]

In China, the corporate governance regime incorporates more specific disclosure requirements than the takeover law regime. The 2018 Chinese CG Code provides

---

69 Sections 414(C)(7), 414CA, 414 CB of the CA 2006.

70 The "sustainability information statement" was inserted into section 414(C)(2) of the CA 2006 by virtue of The Companies (Strategic Report) (Climate-related Financial Disclosure) Regulations 2022 (S.I. 2022/31).

71 Section 414CB(A1) of the CA 2006.

72 Subsection 414(C)(7), 414CB(4) of the CA 2006.

73 Subsection 289c(1) of the HGB.

74 See subsection 414(C)(7) of the CA 2006, subsection 289c(4) of the HGB.

75 See Articles 6(3)(i), 9(5) of the EU Takeover Directive.

76 See Rule 24 (1)(2) of the City Code, subsection 27 (1) of the WpÜG.

for rules which encourage the listed companies to disclose information that may affect other stakeholders' decisions.[77] It particularly requires listed companies to disclose environmental information and their performance of social responsibilities such as poverty alleviation efforts.[78] These CSR disclosure requirements in the 2018 Chinese CG Code do not follow the "comply or explain" approach as its counterparts in the U.K. and Germany, as the 2018 Chinese CG Code explicitly requires that listed companies should "act in the spirit of it and make and amend the articles of association and other relevant governance strategies in compliance with it".[79] Moreover, to further encourage listed companies to fulfil to the CSR matters, one of the stock exchanges in China—SZSE modified its evaluation standards in 2020 on information disclosure of listed companies. It incorporated the considerations "whether to actively disclose the performance on environmental, social responsibility and corporate governance" and "whether the content of the disclosure report is substantial and complete" in the assessment of information disclosure of companies listed on the SZSE.[80] Unlike in the U.K. and Germany, the 2006 Takeover Measures in China only require that the acquirer should incorporate in the offer document its plans for "adjusting the assets, businesses, personnel, organizational structure" for the future 12 months[81]; and there is no such disclosure requirement on the target board concerning the potential consequences of the takeover on other stakeholders.

The disclosure mechanisms in the three jurisdictions may also provide protection to the relevant stakeholders by providing them with essential information about how a takeover may impact their interests. Nevertheless, in the event of a takeover, the role of such disclosure mechanisms in protecting other stakeholders still largely depends on whether these stakeholders can engage and participate in the decision-making process of the target and make their voices heard or interests represented.

(3) Mechanisms for Other Stakeholders to Engage in a Takeover Decision

In the three jurisdictions, only Germany provides other stakeholders (particularly the employees) with a mechanism to participate in approving the anti-takeover measures (through the supervisory board and the co-determination system).

In the U.K. and China, although the corporate law and corporate governance code require the companies to have regard to non-shareholder stakeholders and assume social responsibilities in their activities, the relevant stakeholders lack direct access to participate in the decision-making in takeovers. For example, in the U.K., the corporate law CA 2006 only requires directors to "have regard to" other stakeholders without providing engagement mechanisms for the other stakeholders in major corporate decisions. Employees at larger companies (those with more than fifty employees)

[77] Article 91 of the 2018 Chinese CG Code.

[78] Article 95 of the 2018 Chinese CG Code.

[79] Article 2 of the 2018 Chinese CG Code.

[80] See Articles 6(5), 16 of Measures for the Evaluation of Information Disclosure of Listed Companies on the Shenzhen Stock Exchange (Revised in 2020).

[81] Article 29(11) of the 2006 Takeover Measures.

in the U.K. have the right to information about the development of corporate activities and the economic situation of the company and the right to consultation about major corporate changes, particularly redundancies.[82] In the self-regulatory regime, the 2018 U.K. CG Code sets out mechanisms for workforce engagement on the board by requiring the board of directors to employ one or a combination of the following methods: (i) a director appointed from the workforce; (ii) a formal workforce advisory panel; and (iii) a designated non-executive director.[83] The implementation of these mechanisms follows the "comply or explain" approach. In the event where the board has not chosen one or more of them, it should explain what alternative arrangements are in place and why it considers that they are effective.[84] Thus, in a takeover situation, the engagement of employees on the board is still up to the target company; even when the target has in place such mechanisms, given the fact that the board of directors has limited decision-making power in a takeover, it is even harder for the employees to participate in the takeover. Regarding other non-shareholder stakeholders, there is no existing engagement mechanism for them to participate in a takeover process to "supervise" the board of directors to "have regard to" their interests.

The Company Law in China provides that companies should have in place mechanisms for employee engagement in corporate activities, including for example "establishing trade-unions in the company and conducting activities through the union to protect the employees' legitimate interests", "soliciting the opinions from the union as well as employees when deciding on restructuring or any major issues relating to business operations, or formulating any important bylaws".[85] In the self-regulatory regime, the 2018 Chinese CG Code requires that "the board of directors, the board of

[82] See Section 20 of Information and Consultation of Employees Regulations 2004 (Statutory Instrument 2004 No. 3426) of the U.K. This document followed and implemented the General Framework for Informing and Consulting Employees (Directive 2002/14/EC) at the EU level and provides employees in large companies with rights to be informed and consulted on a wide range of business issues. According to Directive 2002/14/EC, the information and consultation ("I&C" hereinafter) right of employees covers data on a company's "recent and probable development of activities and economic situation, employment structure and probable development, especially if there is a threat to jobs, and decisions that could lead to substantial changes in the way work is organized or in contractual relations". See EUR-LEX.EUROPA.EU. EU General Rules on Employee Information and Consultation. Available at: https://eur-lex.europa.eu/legal-content/EN/TXT/?uri=LEGISSUM%3Ac10817 (accessed 9 July 2021). See also EUROFOUND (20 January 2011). Information and consultation practice across Europe five years after the EU Directive. Available at: https://www.eurofound.europa.eu/publications/report/2011/industrial-relations/information-and-consultation-practice-across-europe-five-years-after-the-eu-directive (accessed 9 May 2021), pp. 1–5: The I&C bodies which are the vehicle for the I&C rights guaranteed by Directive 2002/14/EC include works council, employee councils, cooperation committees, representative trade union structures and elected employee representatives.

[83] Provision 5 of the 2018 U.K. CG Code.

[84] Ibid.

[85] Article 18 of The Company Law.

L error
rror: IllegalOperatorSequence
perator: 0xc1
osition: 1065020

supervisors and the management should establish diversified communication channels with employees, and listen to their opinions on the company's operations, financial status, and major issues involving employees' interests".[86] Nevertheless, similar to the U.K., whilst these mechanisms may engage target employees in a takeover process, they only provide them with rights of information and consultation, which still differ from the right of determination as enjoyed by the employee representatives on the supervisory board in Germany.

In Germany, similar to the U.K., employees enjoy information and consultation rights as stipulated by the relevant rules at the EU level.[87] In addition to such information and consultation rights, different from the U.K. and China, employees in Germany also have a participation right. The AktG and the 2020 German CG Code incorporate requirements for co-determination and employee participation on the supervisory board. The mandatory requirement for employee representatives on the supervisory board of large corporations in theory provides a potential for the "interest of the employees" to be considered in corporate decisions. The decision-making power of the supervisory board in takeovers provides the employee representatives with an opportunity to directly participate in a takeover process and increases the possibility of achieving the "interest of the company" as a whole instead of merely the shareholder interests.

6.3 Evaluation of the Protection Mechanisms

This section evaluates the strengths and weaknesses (problems) of the current regulatory frameworks of the three jurisdictions in protecting different societal interests. It first provides an overview of the market failure(s) that may arise as a result of takeovers and shows how they may affect the relevant societal interests (see Table 6.1). Then it summarizes the protection mechanisms in the three jurisdictions (see Table 6.2) and illustrates which market failure(s) the protection mechanisms may address (see Table 6.3). Following that, it discusses the theoretical strengths and weaknesses of "government regulation"[88] and "private regulation"[89] in solving

---

[86] Article 85 of the 2018 Chinese CG Code.

[87] See also EUROFOUND (20 January 2011). Information and consultation practice across Europe five years after the EU Directive: in Germany, the employees or trade unions have the right to initiate works councils, which are the I&C bodies. According to Kraakman et al. (2017, p. 91), "even if works councils cannot influence major corporate decisions, the information flow they provide may create trust between companies and their employees as mandatory employee representation on the board".

[88] For the purpose of discussion in this section, the term "regulation" used in the following parts actually equates to the "government regulation" as used in other parts of this book, which refers to "rules formulated by the government (laws and other legal instruments). See the definition of "government regulation" in this book in Sect. 1.2.3.

[89] Among the different forms of private regulation (like private standards and certification systems), this book primarily discusses self-regulation. See the definitions of the concepts "private regulation" and "self-regulation" in Sect. 1.2.3.

market failures, which provides basic ideas about the potential advantages and disadvantages of the protection mechanisms in takeovers. After the theoretical analysis, this section examines the strengths and weaknesses of the protection mechanisms in the three jurisdictions from three aspects: (i) their aims, (ii) their content, and (iii) their enforcement and compliance. The "aims" of a rule or a mechanism usually explain what societal interests "should" be protected and why, and imply the ideal situation after the implementation of the mechanism. The "content" specifies the detailed aspects of the mechanism and indicates the major factors which public authorities and private agencies take into account when formulating the mechanism. The "compliance" level reveals how the societal interests are actually protected in practice. Altogether, analysis of the three aspects aims to explain "what societal interests should be protected", "how they are protected', and "what are the factors that influence the effectiveness of the protection mechanisms".

6.3.1 *Review of the Protection Mechanisms: What Market Failures Do They Solve?*

For the purpose of this research, the benchmark for evaluating the effectiveness of the regulatory frameworks in the three jurisdictions is their role in addressing the relevant market failure(s) that may arise as a result of takeovers, as discussed in Chap. 2. Therefore, before directly diving into the analysis of strengths and weaknesses, this section first examines what market failure(s) the protection mechanisms may potentially cure.

6.3.1.1 Overview of the Market Failures in Takeovers

As discussed in Chap. 2, apart from the potential efficiency gains generated, a takeover sometimes causes efficiency losses in the form of market failures. That is, increases in market power (monopoly), negative externalities, severe information asymmetries, and undersupply of public goods may occur in takeovers and thereby affect different societal interests. Table 6.1 illustrates the market failure(s) a takeover may cause and their potential influence on the legally recognized public interest considerations, the interests of corporate stakeholders and other societal interests affected by a takeover.[90]

From Table 6.1, it is clear that the legally recognized public interest considerations, the interests of corporate stakeholders and other societal interests affected by a takeover all carry a risk of being susceptible to the market inefficiencies a takeover may cause, either before, during or after the takeover. Among the four types of market failure, the problems of negative externalities and severe information asymmetries

[90] It should be noted that not all takeovers would cause such market failures problems and not all of these problems would always coexist in a single takeover.

Table 6.1 Market failures relating to different societal interests in takeovers

Relevant societal interests	Market failures			
	Market power	Negative externalities	Information asymmetries	Public goods
Legally recognized public interest considerations	Yes (Monopoly and harms on the competition interest)	Yes (e.g., Negative externalities on the national security)	Yes (e.g., Information asymmetries between the public, the regulator, and the takeover parties)[91]	Yes (e.g., Undersupply of "public goods" after a takeover of the SOE or privatized public company in the armaments industry)
Interests of corporate stakeholders	N/A[92]	Yes (e.g., (1) Squeezing out of long-term shareholders who disagree with a hostile bid; (2) redundancies after a takeover; (3) higher risk of insolvency of the target faced by the creditors in a highly-leveraged takeover)	Yes (e.g., Information asymmetries (1) between the shareholders of the target; (2) between the shareholders and the board of the target; (3) between the acquirer and the corporate stakeholders of the target)	N/A
Other societal interests affected by a takeover	N/A	Yes (e.g., Negative externalities on environment and the local community where the takeover party changes corporate strategies concerning these stakeholders)	Yes (e.g., Information asymmetries between the takeover party who makes post-offer promises and the stakeholders who bear an interest in such promises)	N/A

[91] See the examples of such information asymmetries in Sect. 2.2.2.2.

[92] It should be noted that to the extent that corporate stakeholders are also consumers or suppliers in the same market, their interests may also be hurt by the presence of market power (monopoly); but such effect would be indirect.

Table 6.2 Overview of protection mechanisms for legally recognized public interest considerations

Government regulation	Jurisdictions			
	Protection mechanisms	The U.K	Germany	China
Competition law	Applicable regulation(s)	Enterprise Act 2002 (EA 2002)	Act against Restraints of Competition (GWB)	Anti-Monopoly Law (AML)
	Recognized public interest considerations	**Competition interest and other public interest** (national security (before 4 January 2022); public interest considerations in newspaper and media mergers; financial stability; capability to combat/mitigate public health emergencies)	**Competition interest and other public interest** ("advantages to the economy as a whole"; "an overriding public interest")	**Competition interest and other public interest** ("advantages to competition"; "public interest")
	Protection mechanism(s)	**Merger control and the "public interest intervention"** (To deal with the problems of **"monopoly", "negative externalities",** and **"information asymmetries"**)	**Merger control and the "public interest exemption" authorization** (To deal with the problems of **"monopoly", "negative externalities",** and **"information asymmetries"**)	**Merger control and the "public interest exemption" authorization** (To deal with the problems of **"monopoly", "negative externalities"**)
	Responsible authorities	Secretary of State, CMA	BkartA (for merger control), Minister of the BMWK (for public interest exemption authorization)	Enforcement Department II of the National Bureau (the SAMR Bureau before October 2021)

(continued)

Table 6.2 (continued)

Government regulation	Jurisdictions			
	Protection mechanisms	The U.K	Germany	China
FDI screening regulation	Applicable regulation(s)	(1) EA 2002 (before 4 January 2022) (2) National Security and Investment Act (The U.K. Security Act 2021)	(1) AWV (2) AWG[93]	(1) For market access regulation: FI Negative List, The Foreign Investment Law (2) For security review of foreign takeovers: Notice 2011, Provisions 2011, Measures for the Security Review of Foreign Investment (Measures for the Security Review) (3) Others: Provisions on Foreign Mergers and Acquisitions (2009), Measures for the Administration of Foreign Strategic Investment (Measures for Foreign Strategic Investment)
	Recognized public interest considerations	**National security interest**	**National security interest (public order or security, the defence interest), capability to respond to public health crisis, etc.**	**National security (the defence interest, the economic security, social life order), protection of state-owned assets, etc.**

(continued)

[93] Amendments to the AMV and AWG in recent years mainly include the Fifteenth, Sixteenth and Seventeenth Amendment to the AWV, and the First Amendment to the AWG. For more information about these amendments, see Sect. 4.3.2.2.

Table 6.2 (continued)

Government regulation	Jurisdictions			
	Protection mechanisms	The U.K	Germany	China
	Protection mechanism(s)	**National security review of foreign takeovers** (To deal with the problems of **"negative externalities"**, **"information asymmetries"**, and **undersupply of "public goods"**)	**National security review of foreign takeovers** (To deal with the problems of **"negative externalities"**, **"information asymmetries"**, and **undersupply of "public goods"**)	**"Pre-establishment national treatment plus negative list" at market access stage, National security review of foreign takeovers, Other administrative regulation of foreign takeovers** (To deal with the problems of **"negative externalities"**, **"information asymmetries"**, and **undersupply of "public goods"**)
	Responsible authorities	Secretary of State, Investment Security Unit	BMWK	(1) NDRC, MOFCOM and their local agencies, and the sector regulators (for implementing the "negative list" at the market access stage and for administrative regulation) (2) The Security Review Office (for the security review)

(continued)

Table 6.2 (continued)

Government regulation	Jurisdictions			
	Protection mechanisms	The U.K	Germany	China
Corporate law and other government regulation	Applicable regulation(s)	–	–	(1) Company Law, (2) A Trial Regulation on the Work at Primary-level Party Organizations of SOEs (3) Other regulatory documents on state-owned assets and development of SOEs
	Recognized public interest considerations	–	–	**Protection of state-owned assets, international competitiveness of SOEs, national security interest, etc.**

(continued)

Table 6.2 (continued)

Government regulation	Jurisdictions			
	Protection mechanisms	The U.K	Germany	China
	Protection mechanism(s)	**Use of "golden shares"** (To deal with the problems of **"negative externalities"** and **undersupply of "public goods"**)	**Use of "golden shares"** (To deal with the problems of **"negative externalities"** and **undersupply of "public goods"**)	**(1) The SASAC and its local agencies' regulation of share transfer of SOEs** **(2) The CPC organization's participation in major corporate issues and leadership in appointing senior personnel of SOEs** **(3) Division of "public interest SOEs" and "profit-making SOEs"** (To deal with the problems of **"negative externalities"** and **undersupply of "public goods"**)

Table 6.3 Overview of protection mechanisms for the interests of corporate stakeholders and other societal interests affected by a takeover

Government regulation and private regulation	Jurisdictions			
	Protection mechanisms	The U.K	Germany	China
Takeover law	Applicable regulation(s)	City Code on Takeovers and Mergers (The City Code)	Securities Acquisition and Takeover Act (WpÜG)	Measures for the Administration of the Takeover of Listed Companies (2006 Takeover Measures)
	Recognized societal interests	**Interests of shareholders (protection focus) and of other stakeholders**	**Interests of shareholders (protection focus) and of other stakeholders (inter alia, employees)**	**Interests of shareholders (protection focus) and of other stakeholders (inter alia, employees)**
	Protection mechanism(s)	**(1) "Non-frustration rule" on the board of directors' anti-takeover actions** **(2) "Mandatory bid" rule** (To deal with the "**negative externalities**" to **shareholders**)	**(1) Supervisory board's power of deciding the anti-takeover actions** **(2) "Mandatory bid" rule** (To deal with the "**negative externalities**" to **shareholders**)	**(1) Restriction on the board of directors' post-offer anti-takeover actions** **(2) "Mandatory bid" rule** (To deal with the "**negative externalities**" to **shareholders**)

(continued)

Table 6.3 (continued)

Government regulation and private regulation	Jurisdictions				
	Protection mechanisms		The U.K	Germany	China
			Obligation of the acquirer and target board to disclose information on stakeholder issues	**Obligation of the acquirer and target board to disclose information on stakeholder issues** (To deal with the **"negative externalities"**, and **"information asymmetries" to other stakeholders**)	**Obligation of the acquirer to disclose its plans for "adjusting the assets, businesses, personnel, organizational structure" for the future 12 months** (To deal with the **"negative externalities"**, and **"information asymmetries" to other stakeholders**)
			"Post-offer undertakings", "Post-offer intention statements" (To deal with the **"negative externalities"**, and **"information asymmetries" to other stakeholders**)		
Corporate law and private regulation of corporate governance	Corporate law	Applicable regulation(s)	Companies Act 2006 (CA 2006)	German Commercial Code (HGB); Stock Corporation Act (AktG)	Company Law
		Recognized societal interests	**Interests of the company (Interests of shareholders and other stakeholders)**	**Interests of the company (Interests of shareholders, employees, and other stakeholders)**	**Interests of the company (Interests of shareholders, mention of the corporate social responsibilities)**

(continued)

Table 6.3 (continued)

Government regulation and private regulation	Jurisdictions				
	Protection mechanisms		The U.K	Germany	China
		Protection mechanism(s)	**Requirement on directors to "have regard to" other stakeholders** (To deal with the "**negative externalities**" **to other stakeholders**)	**Co-determination system and employee participation on the supervisory board** (To deal with the "**negative externalities**", and **"information asymmetries" to other stakeholders**)	**(1) Requirement on companies to assume social responsibilities ("CSR" rules)** **(2) Requirement on companies to solicit the employees' opinions in certain major corporate issues** (To deal with the **"negative externalities"**, and **"information asymmetries" to other stakeholders**)
			The board of directors' strategic report on non-financial stakeholder issues (To deal with the **"information asymmetries" to other stakeholders**)	**The board of directors' strategic report on non-financial stakeholder issues** (To deal with the **"information asymmetries" to other stakeholders**)	
	Self-regulation of corporate governance	Applicable regulation(s)	2018 U.K. Corporate Governance Code (2018 U.K. CG Code)	German Corporate Governance Code (2020 German CG Code)	Code of Corporate Governance for Listed Companies (2018 Chinese CG Code)
		Recognized societal interests	**Interests of shareholders and other stakeholders (employees, customers, suppliers, creditors, etc.)**	**Interests of shareholders and other stakeholders (employees, etc.)**	**Interests of shareholders and other stakeholders (creditors, employees, customers, suppliers, community, environment, etc.)**

(continued)

Table 6.3 (continued)

Government regulation and private regulation	Jurisdictions				
	Protection mechanisms		The U.K	Germany	China
		Protection mechanism(s)	**Engagement mechanisms for other stakeholders on the board (inter alia, workforce**[94] **engagement mechanisms)** (To deal with the "**negative externalities**", and "**information asymmetries" to other stakeholders**)	**(1) Requirement on the board of directors' CSR reporting** **(2) Requirement on the board of directors to consider other stakeholders** (To deal with the "**negative externalities**", and "**information asymmetries" to other stakeholders**)	**(1) Required disclosure on environment information and CSR performance such as poverty alleviation efforts;** **(2) Voluntary disclosure on other information that may affect other stakeholders** (To deal with the "**negative externalities**", and "**information asymmetries" to other stakeholders**)

[94] It should be noted that the term "workforce" is broader than "employees" as used in Section 172 of the CA 2006 (i.e., those with a direct contract of employment with the company). The "workforce" might include agency workers, contractors and people with "zero hours" contracts. See Financial Reporting Council. 2018 UK Corporate Governance Code – FAQs. Available at: https://www.frc.org.uk/directors/corporate-governance-and-stewardship/uk-corporate-governance-code/2018-uk-corporate-governance-code-faqs (accessed 30 April 2021).

are relevant to all the three types of societal interests, although the forms and extent of the negative externalities and information asymmetries may differ. The monopoly problem and undersupply of public goods are mainly affecting the crucial public interest considerations (e.g., the competition interest, the national security). Correspondingly, the protection mechanisms for different societal interests differ in the government regulation and private regulation.

6.3.1.2 Overview of Mechanisms for the Protection of Different Societal Interests

Tables 6.2 and 6.3 show how the legally recognized public interest considerations, the interests of corporate stakeholders and other societal interests affected by a takeover are protected in the three jurisdictions, respectively. The relevant societal interests, protection mechanisms, and the specific types of market failure that may be addressed by the protection mechanisms are highlighted in the two tables.

(1) Overview of Protection Mechanisms for Legally Recognized Public Interest Considerations

From Table 6.2, it is obvious that public laws in the competition law regime and the FDI screening regime of the three jurisdictions play a dominant role in dealing with market failures relating to the public interest.

The merger control rules in the national competition laws primarily deal with the potential creation of a dominant undertaking as the result of a takeover, that is, a situation in which the increase in market power acquired by an undertaking because of the takeover would otherwise result in higher prices, lower output and social deadweight losses. Meanwhile, the public interest intervention mechanism in the U.K. and the public interest exemption mechanisms in Germany and China may cure the negative externalities to other crucial public interest considerations (for example, the national security interest) following a takeover. Concerning the possible information asymmetries that may occur between the takeover parties, the regulators and the general public, the public interest intervention statement given by the Secretary of State in the U.K. and the opinions and decisions given by the Monopolies Commission and the Minister of the BMWK in Germany may alleviate such problems. In China, the reasoning for the approval decisions from the Enforcement Department II is (often) not published and there is no other department or agency involved in implementing this public interest exemption mechanism. Accordingly, the information asymmetries in this field are not really addressed.

In the FDI screening regime, the national security review in the three jurisdictions deals with the information asymmetries between the regulator and the foreign investors and may reduce the potential threat (negative externality) to the national security interest. In China, the all-inclusive "negative list" at the market access stage also protects other societal interests from the negative externalities of foreign takeovers. Moreover, from another perspective, the FDI screening mechanisms restrict foreign investors from entering into crucial sectors such as national defence and thus guard against potential under-provision and under-consumption of public goods in these areas.

As one special regime for protecting the public interest, the corporate law and other government regulation in China which regulate SOEs' activities may also deal with the market failures in an SOE-related takeover. For example, in a takeover where the target is an SOE, the negative externalities may include the loss of the State-owned assets in the process of change of control, large-scale unemployment and the detriment to high-technology development in some strategic areas. The specific regulation concerning SOE-related takeovers may reduce such negative externalities as well as preventing the undersupply of some public goods, given the dominant position of Chinese SOEs in producing and supplying goods such as sanitation infrastructure, defence equipment, etc. As discussed earlier in this book, in the U.K. and Germany, the Government may use "golden shares" in privatized SOEs to pursue a "public interest" in hostile takeovers; nevertheless, such "golden shares" are restricted by the CJEU. In its previous case law, to protect the basic freedoms as stipulated by the TFEU, the CJEU only recognized certain public interest considerations (such as safeguarding energy supply that is linked to public security, safeguarding the telecommunications network in the event of crisis, war, or terrorism) and imposed strict procedural conditions to justify the use of golden shares. Compared with the robust mechanisms for regulating SOE-related takeovers in China, the role of golden shares in the U.K. and Germany in reducing negative externalities to public interest considerations and protecting the public goods in takeovers, seems marginal.

(2) Overview of Protection Mechanisms for Interests of Corporate Stakeholders and Other Societal Interests Affected by a Takeover

Table 6.3 shows that the takeover law, corporate law and the corporate governance code in the three jurisdictions play a primary role in dealing with the negative externalities and information asymmetries relating to the interests of corporate stakeholders and other societal interests that are affected by a takeover but are not legally recognized as public interest considerations.

The decision-making rules on the anti-takeover measures in the takeover laws of the three jurisdictions mainly deal with the agency problems between the board and the shareholders and aim to protect the shareholder group from negative externalities. Moreover, the three jurisdictions give the minority shareholders of the target company another protection through the "mandatory bid rule", which deals with the agency problem between the majority and minority shareholders and helps address the negative effects to the latter.

The takeover laws in the U.K. and Germany also potentially address the problems of severe information asymmetries and negative externalities relating to other stakeholders. The "post-offer undertakings" and "post-offer intention statements"[95] in the U.K. encourage the takeover parties to consider the potential negative externalities a takeover may cause to corporate stakeholders (e.g., the employees, creditors) as well

[95] See the analysis of the "post-offer undertakings" and "post-offer intention statements" in Sect. 3.4.3.1.

as other societal stakeholders (e.g., the environment and local community). Such mechanisms mainly intend to reduce negative externalities on the stakeholders and information asymmetries between the company and its stakeholders in the post-offer stage. The disclosure requirements on the acquirer and target board(s) in the City Code and WpÜG concerning the takeovers' anticipated consequences to relevant stakeholders, and the disclosure requirement concerning the acquirer's offer document in the 2006 Takeover Measures intend to relieve the information asymmetries between the company and its stakeholders during the takeover process. Compared with the U.K. and Germany, the Chinese rules in this field are formulated in a more general way[96] and do not require the target board(s) to provide opinions about the anticipated consequences of the takeover on other stakeholders.[97] To this extent, the disclosure mechanism in the Chinese takeover law seems to play a less effective role in alleviating the potential information asymmetries other stakeholders encounter than the City Code and WpÜG.

In the corporate governance regime, the term "interests of the company" under the corporate laws in the three jurisdictions seems different from the "interests of shareholders" and may be employed by the board(s) to address negative externalities to other stakeholders in takeovers. In the U.K., in line with this, the CA 2006 provides for a list of relevant stakeholders and considerations the board is encouraged to "have regard to" in their decisions. In Germany, the co-determination and employee participation mechanisms under the AktG enable the supervisory board to particularly consider the interests of the employee group. In China, the Company Law incorporates a CSR rule; nevertheless, it remains disputable in China whether this CSR requirement constitutes a fiduciary duty on the board of directors towards other stakeholders.

The similar rules relating to stakeholder protection under the corporate governance codes for listed companies in the three jurisdictions play a complementary role to the corporate laws in addressing negative externalities to other stakeholders in corporate activities. For example, the 2018 U.K. CG Code emphasizes that companies should build positive relationships with their stakeholders and provide mechanisms to strengthen stakeholders' voice (particularly the workforce engagement) on the board. The 2020 German CG Code highlights that the company and its governing bodies must be aware of the company's role in the community and its responsibility vis-à-vis society. The 2018 Chinese CG Code also incorporates a separate chapter on "stakeholders, environmental protection, and corporate social responsibilities" and requires listed companies to actively perform their social responsibilities. In principle, these mechanisms also incentivize a target company to consider the negative consequences on non-shareholder stakeholders. Nevertheless, it could be observed that currently, the engagement mechanisms for other stakeholders to participate in

[96] Article 29(11) of the 2006 Takeover Measures only requires the acquirer to incorporate in the offer document its plans for "adjusting the assets, businesses, personnel, organizational structure" for the future 12 months.

[97] Article 32 of the 2006 Takeover Measures only requires that the target board should publish a report ("target board report") to give advice on whether the shareholders should take the offer.

corporate decisions in the U.K. and Germany are mainly tailored for the employees. Thus, it is likely that the interests of the employee group may be better considered in takeovers compared to other stakeholders in the two jurisdictions. Although the Chinese Company Law adopts a two-tier board system and requires that joint-stock limited companies should have employee representatives on the supervisory board, the supervisory board in China does not have actual decision-making powers as in Germany, and the role of employee representatives in China differs a lot from that in Germany.[98] The Company Law and the 2018 Chinese CG Code require the boards to seek opinions from the employees when deciding on major corporate issues which may affect employees' interests.[99] In theory, these requirements may play a role in addressing negative externalities and information asymmetries relating to employees. Nevertheless, considering the fact that there are no specific supporting engagement measures for the employees or other stakeholders to actually participate in the board of directors' decisions, and it is totally up to the target company to decide whether to consult these stakeholders' opinions and how to assume the CSR duties, such provisions may easily turn into an empty slogan in practice.

6.3.2 *Strengths and Weaknesses of the Protection Mechanisms*

To further analyse the strengths and weaknesses of the current protection mechanisms under the regulatory frameworks of takeovers in the three jurisdictions, this section first discusses the theoretical advantages and disadvantages of government regulation and private regulation in curing market failures.

6.3.2.1 Theoretical Advantages and Disadvantages of Government Regulation and Private Regulation

(1) Government Regulation

According to the public interest approach, "regulation" is a possible remedy for market failure and a measure to protect the interests of the public at large.[100] The assumption is that democratically elected government (and its administrative agencies), which is responsible for the formulation of regulation, takes into account the public interest from the outset. The strict procedural requirements make it difficult for the regulatory agencies to formulate or modify the rules randomly, and thus increase the certainty among the public. Furthermore, the potential legal sanctions

[98] See Sect. 5.4.2.1.

[99] Article 18 of The Company Law, Article 85 of the 2018 Chinese CG Code.

[100] For discussion about the public interest approach and private interest approach of regulation, see Sect. 2.3.1.

for breach of obligation and the supervision by the enforcement authorities guarantee compliance with the rules.[101]

In some situations, the above strengths of regulation may become its weaknesses and decrease its effectiveness for curing market failure problems. Firstly, the strict procedural requirements for regulation mean that the costs for formulating, implementing and enforcing regulation can be unavoidably high. Potential delays in adjusting the current regulation to solve new problems in the market seem common and might be further intensified by the bureaucratic systems and thoughts of the public authorities.[102] Apart from the administrative costs of formulating, implementing and enforcing regulation, the costs of regulation also include "costs in the form of distortions caused by regulatory intervention in other markets", given that each intervention (through regulation) is likely to create distortions in other markets.[103] Secondly, as the private interest approach suggests, regulation may just reflect the specific demand of special interest groups. Politicians who are in charge of formulating regulation, from the perspective of this approach, are also "utility maximisers" and "may be interested in maximizing power, the size of their bureaucracy, the number of votes, financial gains from lobbying groups etc."[104] Interest groups may thus lobby for protective regulation or more lenient regulation, depending on their own demand.[105] The distribution of control among the interest groups (for example, certain powerful industries and their company members) may change overtime, thus the regulation may only present the most competitive group interest at the time of formulation.[106] The third concern lies in that, as powerful outsiders (that is, representatives of the interest groups) may dominate the rule-making process of regulation, their lack of expertise in the areas to which the regulation applies would reduce the quality and credit of regulation and affects its effectiveness in the market.

(2) Private Regulation

Private regulation has advantages that may be able to address some of the above weaknesses of regulation.

Firstly, private regulation agencies are often less bureaucratic when compared with the public authorities, and the procedural requirements for making and modifying private regulation are less rigid than that of regulation.[107] To that extent, private regulation seems to have the advantage of flexibility over regulation in adapting to

[101] See the discussion of these advantages of regulation in Van den Bergh (2008), pp. 4–5. Van den Bergh argues that from an economic perspective, regulation may be preferred to liability rules inter alia because it can be enforced by criminal sanctions, which is likely to have a greater deterrent effect than a duty to compensate.

[102] Stigler (1971), pp. 7, 11. The costs of the election, operation and maintaining of the organization of the public authorities would all increase the possibilities of delays.

[103] Philipsen (2018), pp. 542–543.

[104] Ibid, p. 543.

[105] Ibid.

[106] Stigler (1971), pp. 6–7.

[107] Philipsen (2018), p. 545.

the market environment.[108] Secondly, private regulatory agencies often consist of people and experts who come from the specific industries and professions that are being regulated and are better trained than their counterparts in the public authorities.[109] Private agencies are usually considered as having better information on the activities that need to be regulated and more expertise in dealing with the market problems in the specific areas of the regulated activities.[110] The lower information costs also reduce the total costs for formulating and modifying private regulation compared to government regulation. Thirdly, as self-regulatory rules and mechanisms are often formulated by the experts and representatives from the industry or profession, the members being regulated are often more willing and committed to follow them.[111] The costs of compliance therefore would be minimized. Besides, it is also expected that, self-regulation (as one form of private regulation) may achieve greater inspectorial depth of the market problems than regulation.[112]

On the other hand, these advantages of private regulation also indicate its underlying weaknesses in other situations. Firstly, with regard to the incentives, the self-regulatory nature of the agencies means that its members may lack the incentives to make and implement private regulation.[113] Even though they may be more capable than the public authorities in regulating business activities, they are not necessarily more willing to write rules to address the market problems or regulate them effectively.[114] Secondly, the content of private regulation may also be susceptible to the intervention by interest groups (through lobbying). There is a risk that private regulation may be deliberately tailored by some interest groups to help them deviate from the existing rules in regulation and thus serve private interests at the expense of the public interest.[115] Moreover, without strict procedural requirements, the content of private regulation may be modified randomly, which creates uncertainty for market players or even gaps and inconsistencies with the existing regulation rules. Thirdly, another obvious disadvantage of private regulation presented by theoretical literature

---

[108] However, it should be noted that this "flexibility" advantage of private regulation may not always hold true. In some cases, private regulation forms may not be more flexible than regulation, for example, when comparing the private certification system with the (public) licensing. See ibid, p. 545.

[109] Ayres and Braithwaite (1992), p. 104.

[110] Philipsen (2018), p. 544. This is the least disputable argument in favour of private regulation. See Philipsen (2003), p. 160.

[111] Ayres and Braithwaite (1992), p. 113. See also Philipsen (2018), p. 545: the fact that private regulation rules are formulated and enforced by one's peers may increase one's willingness to comply with them, compared to the rules formulated and enforced by government agencies far away.

[112] Ibid, p. 104.

[113] Ibid, pp. 105–106. Some scholars also pointed out that "some forms of private regulation lack democratic legitimacy" (see Philipsen (2018), p. 546); and "the capacity of a self-regulation agency to make rules governing the activities of an association or profession may itself constitute an abuse if it lacks democratic legitimacy in relation to members of the association or profession" (see Ogus (1995), p. 98; Page (1986), p. 163).

[114] Ibid.

[115] Philipsen (2018), p. 546.

lies in that it may lack appropriate enforcement and sanctioning mechanisms.[116] For example, scholars found that self-regulatory agencies have a poor record of enforcing their standards against recalcitrant members.[117] Even if they have the necessary powers, the private agencies may be hesitant to take actions considering that there is often inadequate sanction, limited personnel and resources as well as the fear of the adverse public reaction after the sanction.[118] As a result, the implementation of private regulation mainly depends on non-legal sanctions such as reputational harms and peer pressure.[119]

6.3.2.2 Strengths and Weaknesses of the Protection Mechanisms in the Three Jurisdictions

The theoretical analysis of the advantages and disadvantages of government regulation and private regulation provides the foothold for examining the strengths and weaknesses (problems) of the protection mechanisms under the current regulatory frameworks of takeovers in the three jurisdictions. To achieve this aim, this section examines three aspects of the protection mechanisms for protecting the societal interests: (i) their aims; (ii) their content; (iii) their enforcement or implementation.

(1) Aims

The current protection mechanisms in the three jurisdictions only focus on regulating part of the societal interests in takeovers.

Consistent with the presumption of the public interest approach of regulation, the protection mechanisms as provided by the public laws in the three jurisdictions play a prominent role in protecting the crucial public interests in takeovers. The public interest considerations they regulate usually have a great influence on the safety and well-being of the country. The scope of the public interest considerations is defined on a national basis and is not exactly the same in the three jurisdictions. Nevertheless, in all of the three jurisdictions, the competition laws recognize the competition interest and the national security interest as the most crucial public interest considerations in takeovers and mergers: the merger control rules primarily prevent the creation of monopoly position as a result of takeovers or mergers; the public interest intervention mechanism in the U.K. (before January 2022) and public interest exemption mechanisms in Germany and China address potential negative externalities to national security and secure supply of public goods in the defence area. The national security review mechanism in the FDI screening regulations in the three jurisdictions mainly addresses negative externalities foreign takeovers may cause to the security interest; meanwhile, it also deals with potential risks to undersupply of public goods (inter alia, national defence). In China, apart from the security interest,

[116] Ibid.

[117] Ogus (1995), p. 99.

[118] Hopt (2011), p. 63.

[119] Ibid, p. 64.

market access regulation of foreign takeovers addresses negative externalities to other societal interests as well.

In contrast, the competition laws and FDI screening regulations are not structured to touch upon the internal corporate governance of the takeover parties and do not provide for protection mechanisms for corporate stakeholders. Concerning other societal stakeholders (such as the local community and the environment), it seems that government regulation in the above regimes has an incentive to expand to cover more aspects of them in takeovers. In the U.K., the new public interest consideration that was added to the EA 2002 in 2020 allows the Government to intervene in takeovers of companies that are active in the public health areas (such as in researching a vaccine or in manufacturing PPE); and the new national security review regime established by the U.K. Security Act 2021 further expands the Government's power to intervene in takeovers and mergers with security concerns. the In Germany, the previous cases of the "public interest exemption" system show that the Government sometimes has recognized environmental interests and employment of the local community as "public interest" considerations in takeovers. The amendments to the German FDI screening laws since 2020 also enlarge the scope of considerations that fall within the "national security" category and add new considerations in the public health area. In China, the all-embracing "negative lists" regulating the market access stage for foreign investors still protect a large scope of societal interests in foreign takeovers, although the number of considerations of this "negative list" has been reduced over the years.

The takeover laws, corporate laws and private regulation of corporate governance in the three jurisdictions, to some extent, fill the gap in protecting corporate stakeholders. Protection mechanisms in these areas mainly deal with the information asymmetries and negative externalities faced by the shareholders in corporate activities. Through an indirect way and as a secondary aim, they also provide protection for the interests of other stakeholders, including corporate stakeholders (mainly the employees) and other external societal stakeholders (such as the environment and local community). For example, the emphasis of the "interests of the company" in the corporate laws encourages the target board, when giving opinions to the shareholders about the takeover offer, to consider the negative externalities the takeover may have on other stakeholders; and the corporate governance codes which absorb advanced international CSR standards provide good examples for listed companies to protect the interests of other stakeholders in their activities. In contrast, these corporate-governance-related laws and documents are limited in scope and fail to reach out to protect the crucial public interest in takeovers.

(2) Contents

The different aims of public laws, private laws and private regulation deeply affect the content (inter alia, the level of detail) of the protection mechanisms in the three jurisdictions.

Protection mechanisms under the competition laws and FDI screening regulations which stipulate the protection of the public interest in takeovers are usually formulated in a general way, with no clear definition and scope of the "public interest" specified. As to the private laws, the takeover laws of the three jurisdictions provide rather detailed content about protecting target shareholders; with regard to other societal interests affected by a takeover, the relevant provisions under the takeover laws and corporate laws are also formulated in a comparatively general way, with more principles than detailed instructions. The corporate governance codes, in contrast, combine general principles and detailed advanced corporate governance standards. Moreover, within the three jurisdictions, the FDI screening regulations in China constitute an exception to the generality feature of the public laws. The three-tier FDI screening regulations in China are formulated in a rather complex and detailed way. After reforms in recent years, the content of the current FDI screening laws in the U.K. and Germany became more specific and detailed than in the past regime. The advantages and disadvantages of different levels of details of the relevant protection mechanisms are as follows.

First of all, the relevant public interest provisions in the competition laws of the three jurisdictions and the FDI screening rules of the U.K. and Germany prior to the reforms in 2020 show a generality in the content and provide no specific definition for the "public interest". This generality seems intentional, which mainly takes into account the complex procedural requirements for reformulating government regulation to adapt to new changes, the bureaucratic nature of public authorities and the resulting potential delays in this process. On the one hand, such generality does enable the protection mechanisms under the government regulation to deal better with new challenges in the future as they are not particular to specific issues and may act as a buffer when new problems emerge. For example, the relevant provisions of public interest protection in the competition law of the U.K. (EA 2002) are formulated in a very general way and intend to leave room for adding new considerations in the future. This design enables the Government to introduce new consideration of "combatting public health emergencies" to respond to the COVID-19 crisis in 2020. On the other hand, generality often means vagueness and can lead to conflicts in the interpretation and enforcement of the rules. In practice, it gives the public authorities much discretion in interpreting and implementing the relevant rules, which can be observed from the public interest exemption mechanisms in Germany and China. Moreover, when faced with new challenges, the general content of the government regulation may be deficient and more detailed explanatory documents or supplementary laws may still be needed. The recent reforms in the FDI screening regime of the U.K. illustrate this situation. When the Government's stand towards foreign takeovers in the U.K. gradually tightened in recent years, the previously general security review rules under its competition law were no longer satisfactory. The Government proposed regulatory reforms in this field at first, which were then followed by an new law (the U.K. Security Act 2021, the initial form of it was the U.K. Security Bill 2020).[120] In this process, to adapt to the new regulatory demands, a series of public procedures were unavoidable.

Secondly, contrary to being too general, some of the public laws are formulated in a too detailed way, which may raise problems of lack of flexibility and increase

[120] See discussion about the reforms in the FDI screening regime in the U.K. in Sect. 3.3.2.

the transaction costs for potential acquirers. The most obvious example of this type is China's "negative lists" for foreign investors at the market access stage. They are all formulated in a quite detailed way which specify every sector and industry that foreign investors are not allowed or restricted to invest in. On the one hand, this design seems helpful to foreign investors by providing them with explicit guidance and certainty. On the other hand, given that the lists are revised on an annual basis, the legal certainty and guidance may turn into higher costs for foreign investors to learn and adapt to the changing system.

Thirdly, in the private law regime, the corporate laws in the three jurisdictions require the companies to consider other stakeholders in their activities through general principles (for example, the CSR rule in the Chinese Company Law). The relevant provisions give companies more autonomy to adopt different, innovative mechanisms to protect other stakeholders in takeovers. Nevertheless, without supplementary rules in other regulations or representative cases in practice that further specify the aim of the company and duties of the directors, these general principles may easily become empty slogans. For example, in the U.K., the "enlightened shareholder value" that features in the CA 2006 does not differ much from the previous "shareholder value" tradition in that there is a lack of detailed rules specifying how directors may protect other stakeholders in corporate activities. In China, the CSR rules give little hint to the board of directors whether they also have a duty to consider the environment, the local community and other stakeholders in their decisions. Thus, in takeovers, such corporate governance provisions seem only to provide an indirect and marginal role in protecting these stakeholders.

In the end, in comparison with the government regulation, corporate governance codes for listed companies in the three jurisdictions combine the use of general principles and detailed specifications of protection mechanisms. For example, the 2018 U.K. CG Code provides for stakeholder engagement mechanisms, particularly employee engagement in corporate decisions. More importantly, the self-regulatory nature of the code makes it much simpler and easier to be modified than the public laws and private laws. Thus, such corporate governance mechanisms may fill in the gaps in the general content as well as the delays in the procedures for reformulating the government regulation mechanisms.

(3) Enforcement and Compliance

The effectiveness of the protection mechanisms also largely depends on the level of enforcement and compliance with the government regulation and private regulation.

a. *Enforcement of the Protection Mechanisms in Government Regulation*

The implementation of the competition law and FDI screening regulations in the three jurisdictions mainly relies on the enforcement by the responsible public authorities. In the three jurisdictions, the responsible authorities for merger control (the CMA in the U.K., the BKartA in Germany, and the Enforcement Department II in China) may impose restrictive measures or legal sanctions on the parties concerned where a takeover or merger causes anti-competitive harms. With regard to the public interest intervention and public interest exemption mechanisms, the competition laws in the U.K. and Germany, when compared with China, provide for more specific and detailed enforcement rules (such as rules of the divisions of powers of the responsible authorities, the transparency of the procedure and the final decisions). In the FDI screening regime, public authorities for the national security review in the three jurisdictions scrutinize and decide whether a foreign takeover causes (or may cause) harms to the security interest. China's "all-embracing" regulatory approach and detailed market access rules provide foreign investors with a clearer view of the future than the comparatively general provisions in this field in the U.K. and Germany before the two jurisdictions conducted reforms in recent years. Such foresight in China creates more deterrent effects to foreign investors and improves the enforceability of the FDI screening mechanisms. After the U.K. and Germany's continuous reforms, the current FDI screening rules in the two jurisdictions provide for a clearer scope of activities, sectors and industries that are subject to the security review, which promotes the enforcement of this protection mechanism. Nevertheless, currently, the Government in the U.K. and Germany still has wide discretion in interpreting the newly added activities, sectors and industries in the relevant rules, which may lead to uncertainty for the foreign investors and increase their costs of compliance with the new laws in the near future.

In addition, other designs of the responsible authorities in the three jurisdictions also have an impact on the enforcement of the protection mechanisms under the competition laws and FDI screening regulations. These include, for example, the level of expertise of the personnel, the level of bureaucracy of the authorities, and the division of powers and cooperation between different authorities. Given the facts that (i) the merger control history in China is short compared to that of the U.K. and Germany, (ii) the Enforcement Department II in China has an exclusive power of implementing the merger control rules and public interest exemption mechanism, and (iii) the use of economic analysis in reviewing takeovers and mergers in China is less established, the enforcement of the public interest exemption mechanism in the AML seems to fall behind its counterparts in the U.K. and Germany, as reflected in the lack of relevant cases in China in this area. With regard to the FDI screening regulations, on the contrary, the enforcement of the relevant protection mechanisms in China has been in the leading position for a long time among the three jurisdictions.

The enforcement of the protection mechanisms under the corporate law and takeover law differs from that of the public law mechanisms in that (i) the public authorities' supervisory role is comparatively weakened (particularly regarding the protection mechanisms for non-shareholder stakeholders), and (ii) the parties to the takeovers have more autonomy to decide on the implementation of the relevant mechanisms. Market regulators of takeovers usually play an active role in supervising the acquirer and target's compliance with protection mechanisms that address negative externalities (such as the "non-frustration rule" and "mandatory bid rule") and information asymmetries (such as the mandatory disclosure requirements on the acquirer and target board) relating to the shareholders. By comparison, as to the rules of protecting other stakeholders, the board(s) of the target usually enjoy the autonomy to decide whether and how to implement them in takeovers. Such stakeholder-protection rules are often formulated in a general way with no explicit implementation guidance for the board(s) (such as the rules on the directors' duty to "have regard to" other stakeholders under the CA 2006 in the U.K. and the CSR provision under the Chinese Company Law). In takeovers, it seems difficult for the regulators to monitor and evaluate the implementation of these mechanisms; as a result, the target board(s) often lack(s) incentives to comply with these general requirements and really take into account the stakeholders' interests in their decisions.

b. *Compliance with the Protection Mechanisms in Private Regulation*

As discussed earlier in this section, private agencies which formulate private regulation may have more expertise in regulating the specific area, but they may lack both incentives and resources to monitor the compliance with these instruments.

In the U.K., self-regulation of takeovers has a long tradition, especially as reflected in the self-regulatory nature of the City Code and the Takeover Panel at the outset, and the peer pressure on which self-regulation largely relies is also much more developed in the U.K.[121] In the corporate governance regime, the 2018 U.K. CG Code is implemented on a "comply or explain" approach, meaning that the implementation is still up to the listed companies.[122] The Financial Reporting Council (the "FRC" hereinafter) sets the standards under the corporate governance code, monitors and takes actions to promote the quality of corporate reporting.[123] The FRC also emphasizes that the corporate governance code "is monitored by investors and based on the underlying principles of good governance".[124] The FRC publishes its findings in the year concerning corporate reporting in the U.K. in an "Annual Review of Corporate Governance and Reporting" based on "the evidence gathered through its monitoring of annual reports and accounts, broad outreach with stakeholders and the evidence gathered by external parties".[125] The annual review published by the FRC in January 2020 found that the declared compliance with the 2016 Corporate Governance Code remained high: of the 288 non-investment companies reviewed, 73 per cent claimed full compliance, and 95 per cent reported that they were either complying with all, or all but one or two, of its 54 provisions.[126] The annual review also noticed that many listed companies noted in their annual reports published in 2019 the actions

---

[121] Hopt (2011), p. 64. See the self-regulatory nature of the City Code and the Takeover Panel in Sect. 3.4.2.2.

[122] In the U.K., the principles of the 2018 U.K. CG Code are implemented on a "comply or explain" basis, see Sect. 3.4.3.3.

[123] See the foreword part of the 2018 U.K. CG Code.

[124] Financial Reporting Council (26 October 2016). FRC Response to the BEIS Select Committee Corporate Governance Inquiry. Available at: https://www.frc.org.uk/getattachment/e1e0b17a-b0b9-444f-9ef4-e5b91dd37b45/FRC-Response-to-the-BEIS-Select-Committee-Corporate-Governance-Inquiry.pdf (accessed 1 May 2021). See "FRC responsibilities" at pp. 4–5.

[125] Financial Reporting Council. Annual Review of Corporate Reporting. Available at: https://www.frc.org.uk/accountants/corporate-reporting-review/annual-review-of-corporate-reporting (accessed 1 May 2021).

[126] Financial Reporting Council (January 2020). Annual Review of the UK Corporate Governance Code. Available at: https://www.frc.org.uk/getattachment/53799a2d-824e-4e15-9325-33eb6a30f063/Annual-Review-of-the-UK-Corporate-Governance-Code,-Jan-2020_Final-Corrected.pdf

they were planning to take in preparation for full reporting, and in some cases, they stated early adoption of some elements of the 2018 U.K. CG Code.[127]

The content of the German corporate governance code is recognized and supported by its corporate law; thus the code is referred to as "self-regulation in the shadow of the law".[128] The 2020 German CG Code also follows the "comply or explain" approach.[129] The "Government Commission on the German Corporate Governance Code" (the "GCGC Commission" hereinafter) formulates the standards in the code and reviews the code on an annual basis.[130] The GCGC consists of representatives of the management board and supervisory board of German listed companies and their stakeholders (for example, the institutional and retail investors, academics, auditors and trade unions).[131] Past study found that the compliance rate with the code was stable at a generally high level: for example, the average acceptance level of the "shall" provisions (the recommendations which are subject to the "comply or explain" approach) was 97.7 per cent for DAX-companies, and 95.9 per cent for MDAX-companies in 2017.[132]

Nevertheless, it is worth noting that the "comply or explain" approach implies that even failure to comply with the code is still regarded as "compliance" as long as explanation(s) is given by the companies for the deviation. Thus, beneath the high compliance rate as observed in the U.K. and Germany, the quality of the compliance may still be problematic and needs to be further improved. For example, the FRC review in the U.K. also found that although around half of the sampled FTSE 100

(accessed 1 May 2021). In this annual review, the FRC assessed the corporate governance in the U.K. by considering the quality of reporting against the 2016 U.K. Corporate Governance Code and commented on the "early adoption" by FTSE 100 companies of the 2018 Corporate Governance Code. It reviewed a selection of third-party research and the data used here was from the annual survey by Grant Thornton. See Grant Thornton (2019). Corporate Governance Review 2019. Available at: https://www.grantthornton.co.uk/globalassets/1.-member-firms/united-kingdom/pdf/publication/2019/corporate-governance-review-2019.pdf (accessed 8 May 2021).

[127] Ibid. The 2018 U.K. CG Code was published in July 2018 and applies to premium listed companies for accounting years beginning on or after 1 January 2019; therefore, reporting would be part of the annual reports published in 2020.

[128] Hopt (2011), pp. 14–15.

[129] The "recommendations" in the 2020 German CG Code are implemented on a "comply or explain" approach; with regard to the "suggestions" (the "should provisions"), the listed companies are "encouraged", not "required" to give a specific explanation if they do not implement such rules. For more discussion of the 2020 German CG Code, see Sect. 4.4.3.

[130] The full name of GCGC Commission is "Regierungskommission Deutscher Corporate Governance Kodex". See its homepage available at: https://www.dcgk.de/en/commission.html (accessed 1 May 2021).

[131] Ibid. The members of the GCGC Commission are appointed by the German Federal Minister of Justice and Consumer Protection.

[132] CORPGOV.LAW.HARVARD.EDU (18 September 2018). Study of the German Corporate Governance Code Compliance. Available at: https://corpgov.law.harvard.edu/2018/09/18/study-of-the-german-corporate-governance-code-compliance/ (accessed 8 May 2021). The study evaluated the declarations of conformity published by 76 companies listed in the key German stock market indices DAX (30) and MDAX (50) to analyse the compliance of these companies with the German Corporate Governance Code in 2017. See also Zeng and Lin (2020), pp. 291–295.

companies provided purpose statements, the quality of the statement varied greatly, which indicated that many of these companies may have not sufficiently considered the views of stakeholders in their purpose.[133] The German corporate governance code also contains the "should" provisions, which refer to "suggestions" that can be deviated from without explanation. The study on the compliance with it found that only 7 per cent of the companies reviewed follow that suggestion[134]; besides, the proportion of "precautionary" and "highly precautionary" deviations from the "recommendations" still remained unsatisfactorily high.[135] In line with this, in takeovers, the protection mechanisms for stakeholders in the corporate governance code may not be implemented by the takeover parties but still be counted as "complied" if an explanation is given. To that extent, the actual effectiveness of the self-regulatory corporate governance mechanisms in the U.K. and Germany seems hard to assess.

The implementation of the 2018 Chinese CG Code differs from the traditional "comply or explain" approach. The 2018 Chinese CG Code itself explicitly requires that listed companies in China "shall act in the spirit" of it; and the market regulator (the CSRC and the local Securities Regulatory Bureaus) can monitor the listed companies' compliance with it and urge them to adopt effective measures to make corrections in the case of major problems in their corporate governance.[136] For example, the local Securities Regulatory Bureaus may conduct on-site inspection of the listed companies to see if their organizational designs and activities comply with the rules in the corporate governance code; in the cases where the companies deviate from the rules, they may conduct interviews with the management team and order them to make corrections. The strong supervisory role of the public authorities in the implementation of the code increases the Chinese listed companies' incentives to comply with the relevant disclosure and transparency requirements in takeovers; and it also distinguishes the Chinese corporate governance code from its counterparts in the U.K. and Germany.

6.4 Conclusion

The comparison of the protection mechanisms in this chapter illustrated the similarities and differences regarding the relevant societal interests under the regulatory frameworks of takeovers in the U.K., Germany and China. What the three jurisdictions have in common is that (1) their public laws (competition laws and FDI screening laws) stipulate some recognized public interest considerations in takeovers (such as the competition interest and the national security interest); (2) their private

[133] Financial Reporting Council (January 2020). Annual Review of the UK Corporate Governance Code. See p. 9.

[134] CORPGOV.LAW.HARVARD.EDU (18 September 2018). Study of the German Corporate Governance Code Compliance.

[135] Ibid.

[136] See Sect. 5.4.3.2.

laws (takeover laws, corporate laws) and national corporate governance codes mainly regulate the interests of corporate stakeholders (inter alia, target shareholders), and only provide general principles for protecting other societal interests affected by a takeover (such as environmental interests and interests of the local community). Meanwhile, differences exist in the recognized public interest considerations, intervention mechanisms, relevant procedures and responsible authorities as far as the public law mechanisms are concerned; and in the degree of protection for certain stakeholders (such as shareholders and employees) and decision-making roles of the corporate organs (such as the shareholder meeting and the board(s)) as far as the private law mechanisms and national corporate governance codes are concerned.

The evaluation part of this chapter explored what market failures the protection mechanisms may address in takeovers, and their strengths and weaknesses in addressing the market failures relating to different societal interests. The public laws, private laws and national corporate governance codes only aim at protecting a certain part of societal interests and addressing the relevant market failures in takeovers, respectively. The different levels of details of the content affect the level of compliance of the protection mechanisms. Based on the above-mentioned observations from the comparison and evaluation, Chap. 7 will summarize answers to the research questions put forward in Chap. 1 and provide recommendations for future changes in the U.K., Germany and China.

Chapter 7
Conclusion and Recommendations

Abstract This chapter draws final conclusions of the whole research and provides recommendations for future reforms in the three jurisdictions in the field of takeover regulation. It first summarizes the answers to the three sub-questions that have been explored in Chaps. 2, 3, 4, 5, 6. Following that, this chapter answers sub-question 4 of this book, that is, "*Based on the strengths and weaknesses of the current regulatory frameworks and protection mechanisms, what recommendations can be made for future reforms in the three jurisdictions?*" In the end, it illustrates the limitations of this research.

7.1 Introduction

This book examined the regulatory frameworks of the U.K., Germany and China for protecting societal interests in corporate takeovers. The central research question as proposed in Chap. 1 is: *What are the societal interests that may be affected by a takeover, are these protected under the current regulatory frameworks of the U.K., Germany and China; (and if so) how are they protected and what recommendations can be made for future reforms in the three jurisdictions?* To answer this research question, Chaps. 2, 3, 4, 5, 6 explored and answered three sub-questions:

Sub-question 1: What market failure(s) can be caused by a takeover and what kinds of societal interests are affected?

Chapter 1 provided preliminary definitions of the concepts "relevant stakeholders" and "relevant societal interests" and made the presumption that "a takeover may affect a wide range of societal interests". Chapter 2 proceeded to answer this sub-question by conducting an economic analysis of the market failure(s) that may arise as a result of takeovers and explored the relevant societal interests relating to the market failure(s). It found that market failure(s) may affect three types of societal interests: (i) the interests of corporate stakeholders with whom target companies have a contractual relationship, (ii) the legally recognized public interest considerations, and (iii) other societal interests affected by a takeover. This finding responded to the presumption in Chap. 1 that "a takeover may affect a wide range of societal

H. Ai, *Protecting Societal Interests in Corporate Takeovers*,
https://doi.org/10.1007/978-981-19-7546-2_7

interests" and illustrated the importance of protecting the relevant societal interests in takeovers.

Sub-question 2: What are the relevant societal interests that are currently regulated in the three jurisdictions and which protection mechanisms are used?

Chapters 3, 4, 5 examined the government regulation (competition law, FDI screening regulations, takeover law, and corporate law) and private regulation (mainly the national corporate governance code) in the U.K., Germany and China respectively. Each of the three chapters explored the three types of societal interests that are protected by the government regulation and private regulation and the specific protection mechanisms.

Sub-question 3: What are the similarities and differences between the regulatory frameworks of the three jurisdictions, and what are the strengths and weaknesses of these frameworks in addressing the relevant market failure(s) and protecting societal interests in takeovers?

Chapter 6 conducted a comparison of the protection mechanisms in the three jurisdictions and discussed the strengths and weaknesses of these regulatory frameworks in solving the market failure(s) relating to different societal interests.

In this chapter, Sect. 7.2 summarizes the answers to the above Sub-questions 1 to 3. Following that, Sect. 7.3 answers Sub-question 4 of this book, that is, "*Based on the strengths and weaknesses of the current regulatory frameworks and protection mechanisms, what recommendations can be made for future reforms in the three jurisdictions?*" In the end, Sect. 7.4 illustrates the limitations of this research.

7.2 Answers to the Research Questions

Based on the analysis in Chaps. 2, 3, 4, 5 and 6, answers to Sub-questions 1 to 3 can be summarized as follows:

Market Failures May Arise as a Result of Takeovers and Affect the "Relevant Societal Interests", Which Include (i) the Interests of Corporate Stakeholders, (ii) the Legally Recognized Public Interest Considerations, and (iii) Other Societal Interests Affected by a Takeover

Depending on how many stakeholders are affected (which usually directly determines the different degrees of influence on society) and whether the stakeholders are directly related to the target company through a contractual relationship, the societal interests that may be affected by the consequences of a takeover ("the relevant societal interests") can be categorized into three types:

Type 1: ***The interests of corporate stakeholders*** *who have a direct contractual relationship with the target company and usually directly bear the consequences of the takeover, such as shareholders and employees of the target company.*

Apart from the corporate stakeholders of the target, the interests of other societal stakeholders which may be affected by a takeover can be further divided into two types:

Type 2: ***The legally recognized public interest considerations*** *which are explicitly stipulated by laws and usually have a far-reaching impact on the whole country; the most quoted example of this type is the national security interest in a foreign takeover.*

Type 3: ***Other societal interests affected by a takeover*** *which also have wide social impact but are not legally recognized as "public interest"; the environmental interests and the interests of the local community where the target company resides are the representative examples of this type.*

Four Types of Market Failures Are Observed in Takeovers and Respond to the Presumption that "Takeovers May Have Varied Effects on the Relevant Stakeholders and Societal Interests"[1]

The four types of market failures that are observed in takeovers include the following:

Type 1: Concentration of the acquirer and target company after a takeover may result in ***an increase of market power (potential monopoly)****, which in some situations harms the competition interest.*

Type 2: ***Severe information asymmetries*** *may exist between the acquirer, the corporate stakeholders of the target (such as the shareholders, directors, supervisors, employees,* etc.*) and the market regulators before, during a takeover or in the post-takeover stage.*

Compared with the acquirer, corporate stakeholders of the target and the public regulators are in a disadvantaged information position concerning the acquirer's future plans about the target and the potential impact of the takeover on the stakeholders. Severe information asymmetries may affect the decisions of the relevant stakeholders, such as the shareholders' decisions to accept the offer, the board's decision to take defensive measures and the regulators' decisions to prevent or restrict certain foreign takeovers in security-sensitive areas.

Type 3: ***Negative externalities*** *may occur in takeovers.*

In some situations, the acquirers conduct a restructuring of the target after the takeover, which often leads to lay-offs and causes negative externalities on the employees' interests. In other situations, after the takeover, the target moves the key factories out of the country or changes its strategies in corporate social responsibilities (such as abandoning its environmental-friendly production process or materials), which harms the interests of the local community or the environment. In these circumstances, the interests of corporate stakeholders and other societal interests bear the negative consequences of the takeovers.

Type 4: Takeovers may threaten the supply of ***public goods****.*

Takeovers may threaten the supply of some public goods. For example, in the situation where the acquirer comes from a foreign country and the target operates in the national defence area or areas relating to public healthcare, the success of the takeover may cause shortages in the supply of public goods in these areas and create risks for the national security.

The U.K., Germany and China establish regulatory frameworks consisting of government regulation (including public laws and private laws) and private regulation

---

[1] See the presumption in Sect. 1.2.2.

(mainly referring to the corporate governance codes) to address market failures and protect the relevant societal interests in takeovers.

Public Laws (Competition Law and FDI Screening Laws) in the Three Jurisdictions Recognize and Protect Certain Public Interest Considerations in Takeovers

The competition laws and FDI screening laws in the three jurisdictions recognize certain public interest considerations in takeovers and mergers and provide for mechanisms to address market failures relating to these public interest considerations. The scope of the recognized public interest considerations differs in the three jurisdictions. Recent reforms suggested that the competition laws and FDI screening laws have been expanding by regulating an increasing number of societal interests in the name of "protecting the public interest".

(1) *The Competition Laws in the Three Jurisdictions Address the Market Failure of Market Power and Protect the Competition Interest Through Merger Control Rules; Meanwhile, They Incorporate a "Public Interest Intervention" or "Public Interest Exemption" Mechanism to Deal With Negative Externalities, Severe Information Asymmetries and Shortage in the Supply of Public Goods and Protect Other Public Interest Considerations*

The "public interest intervention" mechanism in the EA 2002 of the U.K. used to protect the national security interest (before 4 January 2022), the public interest considerations relevant to newspaper and media mergers (for example, media plurality, free expression, standards objectives, etc.), and stability of the financial market. In 2020, to respond to the COVID-19 pandemic, the U.K. added a new public interest consideration in the EA 2002, that is, "protecting the capability of the country in combatting and mitigating public health emergencies".

The "public interest exemption" mechanisms in Germany (in the GWB) and in China (in the AML) are formulated in general provisions and do not provide for explicit public interest considerations. The responsible authorities for implementing this mechanism in Germany (the Minister of the BMWK and the Monopolies Commission) have recognized various societal interests as of "public interest" in previous cases, including for example, the defence interest, environmental objectives of the Federation, press diversity, achievement of the healthcare policy objectives and improvement of the healthcare level. Previous cases in this area also suggested that German authorities, when explaining the "public interest" in individual cases, were faced with the challenge of making the explanation in a consistent way whilst amending the scope of the "public interest" to adapt to the ever-changing environment.

The AML in China explicitly stipulates "protecting national security interest" in foreign takeovers, which includes not only the defence interest, but also the economic security and social life order of the country. The AML also lists public interest considerations for exempting monopoly agreements (including energy conservation, environmental protection and disaster relief). There were no past cases in China which explicitly implemented the "public interest exemption" rule and could provide clues for other recognized public interest considerations, and the newly published Amendment 2022 made no change to the public interest provisions of the law. The merger control cases that were discussed in Chap. 5 showed that protecting the State-owned economy and increasing the international competitiveness of Chinese SOEs were major factors for Chinese regulators' approval decisions in takeovers or mergers with potential anti-competitive effects.

(2) *National Security Review of Foreign Takeovers is the Major Pillar of the FDI Screening Regulation. After a Series of Major Reforms in Recent Years, Currently, the Security Review in the Three Jurisdictions Addresses Not Only Negative Externalities on the Commonly Recognized Defence Interest and Shortage in the Supply of Public Goods (National Defence), But Also Regulates an Increasing Number of Other Societal Interests in the Name of Protecting the Security Interest of the Country*

The FDI screening regulations in the three jurisdictions all provide for a national security review mechanism for foreign takeovers. In China, in addition to the security review, there is more complex market access regulation and administrative regulation of foreign takeovers compared with the U.K. and Germany.

For a long time, the focus of this security review in the U.K. and Germany has been on protecting the defence interest. In recent years, consecutive reforms in this field took place in the two jurisdictions (inter alia since 2020), which significantly enlarged the scope of sectors and activities that are deemed as relating to the "security interest" in foreign takeovers and subject to a security review. The Government's powers in the U.K. and Germany to review foreign takeovers are currently largely strengthened.

The FDI screening regulations in China consist of three parts: (i) the market access regulation for foreign investments through the "negative list" system; (ii) the national security review of foreign investments; (iii) other administrative regulation of foreign takeovers. Based on this design, the Chinese model aims to regulate a wide variety of societal interests and addresses potential negative externalities relating to them in foreign takeovers (such as the development of information technology service, protection of some public transportation sectors, protection of the media industry, the education investment and legal services, etc.). Whilst the number of sectors and activities as regulated by the FI Negative List at the market access stage has been reduced on a yearly basis, the underlying "all-embracing" approach has never changed. In 2020, China also strengthened its national security review and enlarged the scope of activities subject to a security review, which shared similarities with the reforms in the U.K. and Germany.

(3) *A Noticeable Difference Between China and the Other Two Jurisdictions Lies in That China Has in Place Specific Corporate Governance Rules and Administrative Regulations for SOEs, According to Which Chinese SOEs Should Pursue Public Policies of the Government and the CPC in Takeovers in the Name of Protecting "Public Interest"*

The Chinese Government and CPC intervene regularly in the corporate governance and activities of Chinese SOEs. The "public interest" which Chinese SOEs aim to protect, often reflects the public objectives of the Government and the CPC and includes considerations such as improving SOEs' international competitiveness and promoting technological advancement of the country.

The U.K. and Germany lack such regulations which specifically target SOEs' corporate governance and activities. In some cases, the Government in the two jurisdictions relied on "golden shares" to prevent hostile takeovers of major privatized companies in the name of protecting the "public interest". The CJEU in its case law held that "golden shares" could constitute restrictions to the basic freedoms under the TFEU. It adopted a strict stance in interpreting and accepting the public interest considerations (such as securing the energy supply and national security) and applying procedures (inter alia the proportionality test) for justifying the use of golden shares. The golden share cases in the U.K. (before Brexit) and Germany that were discussed in Chaps. 4 and 5 did not pass the CJEU's test.

Private Laws (Takeover Law and Corporate Law) and National Corporate Governance Codes in the Three Jurisdictions Protect the Interests of Corporate Stakeholders (Primarily the Shareholders) and Other Societal Interests Affected by a Takeover by Stipulating the Decision-making of Anti-takeover Measures, the Disclosure Requirements for the Acquirer and Target Board, and the Social Responsibilities of the Company (the "CSR" Rules)

(1) *Takeover Laws of the Three Jurisdictions, Through the Rules That Restrict the Board of Directors' Anti-takeover Measures and Rules That Require the Acquirer and Target Board to Disclose Information About the Takeover Offer, Directly Regulate the Negative Externalities and Severe Information Asymmetries Relating to Target Shareholders*

In the takeover laws of the three jurisdictions, the rules on the board of directors' anti-takeover measures deal with the agency problems between the shareholders and the board of directors of the target. In the U.K. and China, the shareholder meeting decides on the board of directors' anti-takeover measures (in the U.K., this power applies to both the pre-bid and post-bid anti-takeover measures, whilst in China, it only explicitly applies to the post-bid stage).[2] This design aims to ensure that shareholders of the target have the opportunity to decide on the merits of an offer. The German model differs from the U.K. and China in that, apart from the actions that are within the competence of the management board,[3] other anti-takeover measures of the management board are subject to the approval of the supervisory board. This

[2] It should be noted that in the U.K. and China, the decision-making power of the shareholder meeting is subject to certain exceptions, meaning that the board of directors may still take some actions in a takeover process without the approval from the shareholder meeting, for example, the board may search for an alternative friendly acquirer to compete with the existing one (the "white knight").

[3] For example, where the target company does not "opt-in" to abide by the stricter rules on the board(s)' anti-takeover measures under the EU Takeover Directive, the management board can take the following actions pending a takeover offer without consent from the supervisory board: (i) actions that a diligent and conscientious manager of a company not subject to a takeover offer would have taken; (ii) the search for a competing offer (the "white knight").

design thus gives the supervisory board and the employee representatives a prominent role in takeovers. Besides, the rules that require the acquirer to disclose information about the offer in the three jurisdictions and rules that require the target board to give opinions to shareholders about the offer in the U.K. and Germany address severe information asymmetries between the acquirer and target shareholders.

(2) *Apart from Shareholder Protection, Takeover Laws in the U.K. and Germany Also Address Severe Information Asymmetries Relating to Other Stakeholders by Requiring the Acquirer Company and Target Board(s) to Disclose the Takeover's Anticipated Consequences to Other Stakeholders. The Chinese Takeover Law Lacks Such Disclosure Requirement Relating to Other Stakeholders. Moreover, Compared with the Takeover Laws in Germany and China, Takeover Law in the U.K. Provides More Direct Protection to Other Stakeholders by the "Post-offer Undertaking" and "Post-offer Intention Statement" Mechanism*

The City Code in the U.K. and the WpÜG in Germany implemented the disclosure requirements under the EU Takeover Directive. The EU Takeover Directive imposes on the acquirer company and the target board(s) duties to disclose information about the anticipated consequences which a takeover may have on non-shareholder stakeholders (such as potential changes to the employment situation and location of the target). Such requirements may reduce the information asymmetries encountered by relevant stakeholders. Nevertheless, given the fact that other stakeholders in the U.K. and Germany have no direct mechanisms to engage in the board(s)'s decision (except for the co-determination by employees in Germany), the role of such a disclosure requirement in protecting their interests seems rather limited.

Compared with these disclosure requirements, the "post-offer undertakings" and "post-offer intention statements" in the City Code show that takeover law has a potential to provide other stakeholders with direct and concrete protection as well. The "post-offer undertakings" (with binding effect) and "post-offer intention statements" (with no binding effect) allow and encourage the acquirer and the target company (through the board of directors) to make arrangements for other stakeholders during the takeover process, which help to reduce the negative externalities a takeover may cause. The monitoring role of the takeover regulator (in the U.K., the Takeover Panel) is important in ensuring the takeover parties' compliance with their promises. In contrast with the City Code and WpÜG, the 2006 Takeover Measures in China do not require the acquirer or target board to disclose information about a takeover's impact on other stakeholders; nor does it incorporate direct protection mechanisms such as the "post-offer undertakings" or "post-offer intention statements".

(3) *Corporate Governance Mechanisms in the Three Jurisdictions Do Not Regulate Specific Public Interest Considerations. They Only Play a Marginal Role in Addressing the Negative Externalities and Severe Information Asymmetries Relating to the Interests of Corporate Stakeholders and Other Societal Interests Affected by a Takeover*

The basic corporate governance designs in the corporate laws and the national corporate governance codes in the three jurisdictions, particularly the rules on the corporate organs' powers and directors' fiduciary duties in corporate activities, lay a basis for the shareholder protection mechanisms in the takeover laws. Apart from this, the corporate laws and national corporate governance codes stipulate general principles about stakeholder protection and CSR requirements in corporate activities. The relevant societal interests that are usually specified in these corporate governance rules include the interests of the employees, creditors, consumers of the company, the interests of the local community where the company resides and the interests in protecting the environment. For example, corporate laws in the three jurisdictions require that the board of directors should act in the interests of the company (rather than in the interests of shareholders). More specifically, in the U.K., Sect. 172 of the CA 2006 requires the directors to "have regard to" the stakeholders' interests in their decisions, and in China, Article 5 of the Company Law requires the company to take up its social responsibilities. The national corporate governance codes provide for similar principles and recommendations for listed companies.

In principle, the board of directors of the target in the three jurisdictions can rely on these rules to formulate anti-takeover actions when it considers that the acceptance of the takeover offer would be against the interests of these non-shareholder corporate stakeholders (such as the employees, creditors, suppliers) or violate the company's social responsibilities (such as environmental protection). Nevertheless, in the meantime, target shareholders may be willing to accept the offer and sell their shares, and the role of these corporate governance rules differs in the jurisdictions depending on whether the board(s) has the decision-making power in takeovers. In the U.K. and China, where the shareholder meeting has the power to decide on the anti-takeover measures, it is likely that the board's anti-takeover actions would not be approved. To this extent, the role of these corporate governance rules which require the board to consider other stakeholders' interests in their decisions is limited in a takeover. In such a situation, a better protection mechanism for these societal interests may be to incentivize the shareholders to consider other stakeholders' interests and the corporate social responsibilities in their takeover decision. Moreover, the generality of the content (such as Sect. 172 of the CA 2006 in the U.K.) of these corporate governance rules, the lack of guidance for the implementation of the CSR requirements (such as Article 5 of the Company Law in China) and lack of liability rules for the breach of these rules also reduce the effectiveness of the corporate governance mechanisms in a takeover situation. In Germany, as the management board can take anti-takeover measures with the consent of the supervisory board, there is more possibility that the two boards could rely on these corporate governance rules to consider other stakeholders' interests and the CSR of the company.

The disclosure rules on non-financial stakeholder issues in the corporate laws and corporate governance codes in the three jurisdictions at first sight seem to reduce information asymmetries between the takeover parties and non-shareholder stakeholders. In a similar way, however, given that the corporate laws in the three jurisdictions do not provide engagement mechanisms for other stakeholders in the board's decisions (except for the employee co-determination in Germany), such disclosure rules play a rather indirect role in protecting the stakeholders. In the U.K., the corporate governance code (the 2018 U.K. CG Code) does set out mechanisms for stakeholder engagement (inter alia the workforce engagement). Nevertheless, as the code follows the "comply or explain" approach, the implementation of these mechanisms is thus still at the discretion of the board of directors of the company.

7.3 Recommendations for Future Reforms

Based on the strengths and weaknesses of the current regulatory frameworks of the three jurisdictions as analysed in Chap. 6, some recommendations can be made for future reforms.

Recommendation 1: Expansion of the Recognized Public Interest Considerations in the Competition Law and FDI Screening Laws Should Be Conducted Cautiously and Should Follow the Principles of "Necessity" and "Proportionality"

The national competition law and FDI screening laws of the U.K., Germany and China stipulate and regulate some public interest considerations in takeovers. In all of the three jurisdictions, the competition interest and national security interest are recognized as the most crucial public interest considerations by these public laws. In contrast, protecting the interests of corporate stakeholders is not the regulatory task of these laws. Traditionally, the U.K. and Germany interpreted the national security interest in a way that was closely related to the defence interest. China, from the beginning, accepted that the national security interest included not only the defence interest, but also other societal interests which might affect the economic security and social life order.

Apart from the legally recognized public interest considerations, other societal interests which in the past were not recognized by these public laws as belonging to the "public interest" may become of crucial importance in emerging takeovers and have a wide impact on the public at large. A case in point is the public healthcare interest, which before 2020, was not an explicitly recognized public interest consideration in the public laws in the U.K. Analysis in Chaps. 3 and 4 showed that in 2020, the U.K. and Germany modified their competition law or FDI screening laws to incorporate more considerations relating to the country's capacities to combat public health emergencies against the pandemic background. Questions then arise: (i) in what circumstances, should the competition law or FDI screening laws be modified to add new societal interests as legally recognized public interest considerations? and (ii) what principles should be followed for the expansion of the public laws for this purpose?

A country's choice of whether to expand the public law mechanisms to address the negative externalities on new societal interests often differs between jurisdictions and may change over time. For instance, in the U.K., the job cuts after the Kraft/Cadbury takeover gave rise to a public appeal for modifying the EA 2002 to allow the Secretary of State to intervene in foreign takeovers and protect more societal interests (such as the employment in the local community) on the grounds of the "public interest".[4] Nevertheless, after many changes in recent years, the EA 2002 still does not recognize "securing employment" or "protecting the interests of local community" as public interest reasons which allow for public interest intervention in takeovers. Compared with the U.K., in Germany, through the "public interest exemption" procedure in the GWB, the Minister of the BMWK recognized in the past cases the "retention of the employment rate in the region" and "environmental objectives of the Federal government" as "public interest" reasons which may exempt a takeover with anti-competitive harms.[5] In China, the FDI screening regulations, in particular the Negative List at the market access stage, stipulate many societal interests which are usually not recognized as public interest considerations in the other two jurisdictions (such as "the protection of the domestic enterprises which possess a well-known trademark or China's time-honoured brand").[6] In general, different jurisdictions have different standards for assessing whether to accept new societal interests as legally recognized "public interest" in their public laws. Also, the standard within one jurisdiction may vary at different times, which often leads to inconsistency in the public authorities' interpretation of the relevant public interest rule, as can be observed from the German case law in Chap. 4.[7] For future reforms, the three jurisdictions should take into account two main factors when deciding whether to modify their public laws to recognize new societal interests as public interest considerations in takeovers: (i) the impact of the relevant societal interests on society; (ii) whether the private laws already contain mechanisms or have the potential to be modified to protect these societal interests.

As far as the first factor (the impact of the societal interests) is concerned, in essence, a takeover is a control transaction between the acquirer and the target shareholders and belongs to the corporate governance realm of the acquirer and the target company.[8] Only when a takeover's impact goes far beyond the takeover parties and reaches out to other societal interests outside the companies, should the public laws be employed. The responsible authorities for implementing the public laws should assess whether the affected societal interests of the takeover are of crucial importance to the country at the time the takeover takes place on a case-by-case basis; and only when the answer is yes, should the public interest protection mechanisms in the public laws be resorted to. To make such an assessment, the geographical impact of the societal interests should be considered.

For example, in Germany, when assessing whether to accept "the employment interest" as "public interest" consideration, the Minister of the BMWK in past cases held that "only when a takeover generated negative externalities on the employment

[4] See the discussions of this case in Sect. 2.2.2.3.

[5] See the discussions of the "retention and creation of jobs" in Sect. 4.2.2.1.1.

[6] See Article 12 of Provisions on Foreign Mergers and Acquisitions (2009). See the discussion in Sect. 5.3.4.1.

[7] See the discussions of the relevant GWB cases in Sect. 4.2.2.

[8] See the discussion of the nature of takeovers in Sect. 1.2.1 and Sect. 2.1.

of the region instead of just the companies, it might be deemed as a public interest issue".[9] To decide the social importance of the unemployment problem, the Minister assessed the unemployment rate of the region affected by the transaction, the average unemployment rate of a wider region (usually the average national rate), and in some cases, the prevalence of unemployment among certain occupational groups. The Minister's assessment aimed at distinguishing the employment issue at the "general public" level from the employee protection at the corporate governance level. As shown in the German cases, the difference between the two levels lies in that stakeholder protection at the corporate governance level was considered by the public authorities as an internal corporate governance issue and should, if possible, be left to private law mechanisms which provide the companies with a certain degree of autonomy (such as the anti-takeover measures in the takeover law and the CSR rules in the corporate law). In contrast, stakeholder protection at the "general public level" usually involved the legally recognized public interests in the public laws and should be addressed by the relevant public law mechanisms. Thus, in takeovers, protection of the target employees first belongs to the internal corporate governance issue and employees should first rely on the takeover law, corporate governance rules and the labour law to seek protection. Only in exceptional cases where the unemployment issue after the takeover becomes a regional or even national problem, it may become a public interest issue (when it is recognized by the public authorities as of "public interest") and be regulated by the public interest mechanisms in the competition law or FDI screening laws. Similarly, protection of the environment and the local community in principle belongs to the corporate governance realm of the target company (which is often stipulated as part of the corporate social responsibilities) and should be addressed by the private law mechanisms. Only in cases where a takeover directly threatens the national environment objectives or when the interests of the general public of the local regions are harmed, may the public interest mechanisms in the public laws be considered after a rigorous assessment.

The second factor for the jurisdictions to assess whether to expand their public laws to recognize and protect new societal interests should be whether there are protection mechanisms in the existing private laws, and if not, whether the private laws can be modified to protect these societal interests. The premise for the discussion is that in the emerging takeovers, some societal interests which were previously not recognized as "public interest" considerations in the public laws suddenly become of crucial importance, and the existing takeover law or corporate governance rules do not incorporate protection mechanisms for them or the existing mechanisms are not enough. When confronted with new circumstances, to avoid too much intervention by the public authorities in the corporate governance regime, before directly expanding their competition law or FDI screening laws to recognize new public interest considerations, the jurisdictions should first assess whether the takeover law or corporate governance rules could be modified to regulate these societal interests. For example, when confronted with the COVID-19 pandemic, protecting the country's capabilities to combat public health emergency becomes a new societal

[9] See the discussions of the "retention and creation of jobs" in Sect. 4.2.2.1.

interest of crucial importance for the whole country. The takeover law mechanisms (such as rules on anti-takeover measures or the takeover parties' arrangements for different stakeholders) and corporate governance rules (such as the general principles for corporate social responsibilities) seem rather powerless in securing this societal interest in (foreign) takeovers. In such a situation, expanding the competition law or FDI screening laws to recognize the new societal interest as public interest becomes the first choice for the jurisdictions and would allow the public authorities to act promptly and powerfully to respond to the emergency.

The expansion of public law mechanisms to regulate new societal interests in the name of protecting public interest should follow the principle of proportionality. For example, also in the context of the COVID-19 pandemic, the U.K. added an additional public interest consideration to the EA 2002 in June 2020 as "the need to maintain in the U.K. the capability to combat, and to mitigate the effects, of public health emergencies".[10] This expansion enables the U.K. Government to scrutinize and take actions in takeovers and mergers in the relevant sectors (e.g., public health sector, such as vaccine researchers, drug manufacturers, and medical supply companies). From the perspective of the Government itself, the adding of this new public interest consideration is "a necessary and proportionate measure to address the risk which takeovers and mergers may pose to the U.K.'s ability to respond to the COVID-19 pandemic or future public health emergencies".[11] It emphasized that companies relating to the country's capability to combat COVID-19 (or any future public health emergency) should not be subject to takeovers or mergers that are against the public interest; and that if they are taken over, the Government must be able to intervene to ensure that the transaction does not undermine this capability.[12] The U.K. Government also pointed out the economic uncertainty and short-term impact to the share price or profitability of the businesses as a result of the pandemic, to justify that the intervention measure is proportionate.[13] Nevertheless, this new public interest consideration, after the amendment, would also allow the U.K. Government to intervene in takeovers in a broad scope of sectors, including for example, a takeover of a company that provides internet services or in the food supply chain, "given the potential for increased demand for internet services in a lockdown situation or disruption to food supply".[14] As these areas seem to differ from the traditional public health considerations, the expansion of public intervention in such areas therefore causes doubts about the proportionality of the measures in the public consultation. Public authorities may first conduct public consultations with the affected groups about the proportionality of the expansion of the public law mechanisms.[15] For example, in

[10] Department for Business, Energy and Industrial Strategy (June 2020). Enterprise Act 2002: Changes to the public interest grounds for intervention in merger cases (Guidance 2020).

[11] Ibid.

[12] Ibid.

[13] Ibid.

[14] Ibid.

[15] For the OECD definition of "public consultation" and the tools that are usually used for public consultation in different jurisdictions, see OECD.ORG. Background Document on Public

the FDI screening regime, the U.K. Government first proposed seventeen sectors in the U.K. Security Bill 2020 (the initial form of the U.K. Security Act 2021) which it perceived as bearing the highest national security risks.[16] In the public consultation about this reform, relevant businesses and investors expressed their concerns that many of the proposed sector definitions were very broad in scope and needed to be further specified.[17] The U.K. Government, in its response to the consultation, significantly narrowed the definitions of the seventeen sectors to ensure that the new FDI screening regime was targeted and proportionate.[18] In future reforms, the U.K. Government may also issue White Papers or Green Papers for public opinions before legislative changes are finalized,[19] the regulatory agency in Germany that circulates a proposal for comment may arrange a public hearing for public opinions,[20] and public authorities in China may also seek public opinions on the amendment of laws by issuing public announcements and collecting public feedback.[21]

Recommendation 2: In the Takeover Law Regime, Germany and China Should Learn from the U.K. by Introducing Mechanisms to Incentivize the Acquirers to Make Arrangements for Stakeholders, and the U.K. Should Reinforce the Implementation of the Current "Post-offer Undertaking" and "Post-offer Intention Statement" Mechanisms

In the private law regime, the three jurisdictions may modify their takeover law to either introduce new mechanisms (in Germany and China) or strengthen the existing mechanisms (in the U.K.) to incentivize the acquirer to consider other stakeholders of the target in a takeover.

Compared with Germany and China, the City Code in the U.K. plays a more direct role in addressing negative externalities on non-shareholder stakeholders as

Consultation. Available at: https://www.oecd.org/mena/governance/36785341.pdf (accessed 13 July 2021).

[16] See Sect. 3.3.2.

[17] Ibid.

[18] Ibid.

[19] For introduction to the "White Papers", see UK Parliament. White Papers. Available at: https://www.parliament.uk/site-information/glossary/white-paper/ (accessed 13 July 2021). For introduction to the "Green Papers", see UK Parliament. Green Papers. Available at: https://www.parliament.uk/site-information/glossary/green-papers/ (accessed 13 July 2021).

[20] See OECD.ORG. Background Document on Public Consultation.

[21] For example, the SAMR issued an announcement to seek for public opinions about the modification of the AML in January 2020 and then published its explanation of the acceptance of the public opinions in February 2020. See SAMR.GOV.CN (2 January 2020). Announcement for Public Opinions on "Revision of The Anti-Monopoly Law (Draft for Public Opinions) from the SAMR (市场监管总局就《<反垄断法 > 修订草案 (公开征求意见稿) 》公开征求意见的公告). Available at: http://www.samr.gov.cn/hd/zjdc/202001/t20200102_310120.html (accessed 1 March 2021). SAMR.GOV.CN (28 February 2020). Explanation of the Acceptance of Public Opinions on "Revision of The Anti-Monopoly Law (Draft for Public Opinions) (《< 反垄断法 > 修订草案 (公开征求意见稿) 》社会公众意见采纳情况的说明). Available at: http://www.samr.gov.cn/hd/zjjg/202004/t20200414_314212.html (accessed 13 July 2021).

it employs mechanisms of "post-offer undertakings" and "post-offer intention statement" to incentivize the acquirer to make arrangements for other stakeholders. Acquirers are often incentivized to make such promises to relieve public concerns, get support from the regulators for the takeover (inter alia when the acquirer is a foreign investor) and to gain a good reputation of performing social responsibilities. Compared with "one-size-fits-all" binding promises which may increase the costs for the acquirers and deter them from making takeover offers at the outset, one of the advantages of the U.K. mechanisms is that the City Code provides the acquirers with freedom to choose between binding promises (post-offer undertakings) and non-binding ones (post-offer intention statements). This design gives the acquirer more autonomy and can increase their incentives to keep promises in later stages.

In the future, Germany and China should introduce such mechanisms in their takeover laws. Similarly, instead of setting rigid requirements which impose duties on the acquirers, the takeover laws in the two jurisdictions can leave the choice to the acquirers and allow them to decide whether to make such arrangements and (if yes) to make their promises binding on them. As the U.K. practice suggested, although the acquirers were not obliged to make binding promises towards corporate stakeholders (such as employees) and other societal stakeholders (such as the environment and local community), in many cases they still chose to do so in order to address public or political concerns (inter alia in foreign hostile takeovers).[22] To improve the effectiveness of these mechanisms, the takeover laws in the three jurisdictions should encourage the acquirers to consult the relevant stakeholders' opinions when tailoring the arrangements. For the acquirers that choose to make the arrangements as binding ones, the takeover laws should introduce a specific regulator to regularly review their fulfilment of promises in the post-offer stage (for example, in the U.K., the Takeover Panel conducts this task, the monitoring role of which needs to be improved). The takeover laws should further stipulate remedies for the relevant stakeholders whose interests are affected by the acquirers' break of promises.

In addition, China should learn from the U.K. and Germany about their disclosure rules in the takeover laws which require the acquirer and target board to provide information about the takeover's anticipated consequences for the stakeholders. Currently, the 2006 Takeover Measures in China ask the acquirer to disclose its "follow-up plans for adjusting the assets, businesses, personnel, organizational structure or articles of association of the listed company for the future 12 months" in its offer document.[23] For future reforms, the 2006 Takeover Measures should provide for more explicit examples of the relevant stakeholders and societal interests this rule aims to protect (such as the target's employees, the local community, the environmental protection policies, etc.). Moreover, the 2006 Takeover Measures should learn from the other two jurisdictions by requiring the target board(s) to give its opinions about how the offer may impact relevant stakeholders and its advice or plans about stakeholder protection. Such opinions and advice may at least give some guidance to the relevant

---

[22] See discussion of past cases where the acquirers made such post-offer undertakings in Sect. 3.4.3.1.

[23] Article 29(11) of the 2006 Takeover Measures.

stakeholders and reduce the information asymmetries between them and the acquirer. Besides, the target board(s)'s advice or plans can provide the acquirer with inspiration to make later arrangements for the stakeholders. In the U.K. and Germany, to improve the effectiveness of the existing disclosure mechanisms in their takeover laws, future reforms should require the directors, when giving opinions about how the offer could affect different stakeholders and societal interests, to conduct detailed research of the acquirer's follow-up actions towards the target's businesses and employees in its previous takeovers (if there were any).

Recommendation 3: In the Three Jurisdictions, Future Reforms in the Corporate Governance Regime Should Work Towards Incentivizing the Board to Introduce More Engagement Mechanisms for Non-shareholder Stakeholders, and Towards Incentivizing the Shareholders to Better Take into Account Other Stakeholders' Interests in Their Decisions and to Disclose Their Engagement Policy in the Company with Regard to the Stakeholder Matters

As the analysis of the corporate governance rules in the three jurisdictions illustrated, corporate governance mechanisms only play an indirect role in protecting the relevant societal interests in takeovers. Corporate laws in the three jurisdictions mainly deal with the agency problems relating to the shareholders, and the relevant rules of stakeholder protection and CSR requirement are often formulated as general principles. Although there are disclosure requirements for the board about non-financial stakeholder issues in the U.K. and Germany, given the lack of engagement mechanisms for non-shareholder stakeholders in their corporate laws (only in Germany, the corporate law specifies co-determination by employees on the supervisory board), such disclosure plays a limited role in protecting the relevant societal interests in takeovers.

In the future, the three jurisdictions should introduce new corporate governance mechanisms to incentivize the target company to more seriously consider the interests of non-shareholder corporate stakeholders and other societal interests affected by a takeover. The choice of new corporate governance mechanisms is directly affected by the different decision-making models in takeovers in the jurisdictions. In contrast with the current "shareholder meeting decides" model of the anti-takeover measures in the U.K. and China (in China this applies mainly to the post-bid anti-takeover measures), the German model, where the boards decide, gives non-shareholder stakeholders (inter alia the employee group) more possibilities to engage and to be considered in a takeover decision. This book is not going to judge which model is better in takeovers, because the decision-making model in one jurisdiction is normally rooted in its corporate governance tradition and may not fit in well with the corporate governance regime of the other jurisdiction. Nevertheless, it should be noted that recommendations for future reforms in the corporate governance regime differ depending on whether the shareholder meeting decides or the board(s) decides on the anti-takeover measures in the jurisdiction.

(1) *To Incentivize the Board of Directors to Introduce More Engagement Mechanisms for Non-shareholder Stakeholders*

In the three jurisdictions, the corporate laws should require the board of directors to introduce an "advisory stakeholder panel" and a designated "non-executive director" representing different groups of stakeholders.[24] The presumptions are that (i) the stakeholder panel represents not only the views of employees, but also other groups of stakeholders, including for example, the representatives of the suppliers, local community, environmental protection organizations; and (ii) the members of the panel could meet without the board and report the views of different stakeholder groups to the board through the non-executive directors.[25] In this way, the board of directors in the three jurisdictions could learn about the stakeholders' main concerns in a takeover. In Germany, with the opinions from the advisory stakeholder panel, the board of directors could better consider the stakeholders' interests when tailoring anti-takeover actions. In the U.K. and China, with the feedback from the advisory stakeholder panel, the board of directors could give opinions to the shareholders which take into account the takeover's comprehensive consequences on different stakeholders. Moreover, the participation of the stakeholder panel and opinions from the stakeholder representatives could help the board of directors to make better arrangements together with the acquirer for the stakeholders in situations such as the post-offer undertakings in the U.K.

However, it does not seem feasible for the corporate law to specify every stakeholder such a panel should represent. Moreover, some stakeholder groups (e.g. climate or human rights NGOs) are already playing an increasingly active role in lobbying public authorities to introduce CSR aims (such as preventing climate change) into regulatory policies on corporate activities.[26] There is a possibility that once the corporate law introduces concrete stakeholder engagement mechanisms in major corporate decisions, stakeholders such as the climate or human rights NGOs will put further pressure on the board or (and) public authorities by, for example, organizing boycotts against the takeover offer. To this extent, in future reforms, the corporate law should leave the board with the autonomy to decide which stakeholders such as an "advisory stakeholder panel" represents and what societal interests the board considers should prevail in a takeover when there is conflict between the

[24] See discussions about such mechanisms in Esser, I.-M. and MacNeil, I. (2019) Disclosure and engagement: stakeholder participation mechanisms. *European Business Law Review*, 30(2), pp. 201–221. Available at: http://eprints.gla.ac.uk/166091/7/166091.pdf (accessed 25 June 2021).

[25] Ibid.

[26] Recent studies found that some NGOs which are financed by the EU or Member State funding were openly arguing against the core values of the European Union. For example, the NGOs have organized campaigns to object to the EU's trade policies, suggesting that the EU trade policies "contributed to growing inequality, social dislocation and environmental disasters"; some of the NGOs rejected scientific knowledge and launched an anti-vaccination movement. See Bauer, Matthias & Carvalho, João (January 2020). NGO Lobbying—How to Ensure Accountability and Transparency at the EU Level. Available at: https://ecipe.org/blog/ngo-lobbying/ (accessed 16 July 2021).

shareholder interests and other societal interests.[27] In Germany, where the board of directors decides to take anti-takeover action, it needs to explain whether its actions are for the reasons of protecting non-shareholder stakeholders or for CSR reasons. The supervisory board, in its decision to approve these anti-takeover actions, also needs to specify why it considers that other stakeholders' interests should prevail and on which corporate governance rules it bases its decision. In the U.K. and China, where the board of directors' opinions to the shareholders about the offer do not take into account the takeover's potential impact on other stakeholders, it should also specify its considerations.

(2) *To Incentivize the Shareholders to Better Take into Account Other Stakeholders' Interests and to Disclose Their Engagement Policy with Regard to the Stakeholder Matters*

In addition to the engagement mechanisms for diverse stakeholder groups on the board, future reforms in the three jurisdictions should also incentivize shareholders to consider other stakeholders' interests in their corporate decisions.

In practice, institutional investors (such as insurance companies, investment banks, mutual funds, pension funds, investment trusts, etc.)[28] are playing an increasingly active role in influencing the conduct and corporate governance of listed companies in the U.K.,[29] Germany,[30] and China.[31] With regard to the societal interests shareholders may take into account, the "Principles for Responsible Investment"

---

[27] For example, in a takeover, shareholders would like to sell their shares whilst other stakeholder groups (such as the employees, representatives of the local community or some environmental protection organizations) prefer to pressure the board to take anti-takeover action.

[28] An institutional investor is an investment entity having a huge disposal of assets for investment. For introduction of these types of institutional investors, see INVESTORSUK. Institutional investors. Available at: https://www.investorsuk.co.uk/institutional-investors/ (accessed 19 July 2021).

[29] Institutional investors in the U.K. have increased sharply from the 1960s; by the 1990s, pension funds and insurance companies were the most prominent holders of equity; currently, institutional investors still hold a significant portion of shares in the market, and the U.K. is recognized as having the strongest tradition of active ownership in all European countries. See Ivanova, M. (2017). Institutional Investors as Stewards of the Corporation: Exploring the challenges to the monitoring hypothesis. *Business Ethics: A European Review, 26* (2), 175–188. Available at: https://onlinelibrary.wiley.com/doi/10.1111/beer.12142 (accessed 6 June 2022). See pp. 176–178.

[30] Germany, according to the source from ECB on 31 December 2020, is the largest fund market in the EU. See BVI.DE. Germany is the largest EU fund market. Available at: https://www.bvi.de/en/about-the-industry/germany-eus-largest-market/ (accessed 19 July 2021).

[31] In China, compared with mature overseas markets, institutional investors still account for a relatively low overall share of the stock market, but in recent years, the proportion of institutional investors' shareholding has gradually increased and the capital market is undergoing structural changes in China. See XINHUANET.COM (29 December 2020). The proportion of institutional investors has increased and the capital market is undergoing structural changes (机构投资者占比提升, 资本市场正在发生结构性变化). Available at: http://www.xinhuanet.com/money/2020-12/29/c_1126919534.htm (accessed 19 July 2021). See also XINHUANET.COM (23 March 2021). The proportion of shareholding by institutional investors in the A-Stock market continuously increases (A股机构投资者持股占比持续提升). Available at: http://www.xinhuanet.com/fortune/2021-03/23/c_1127243821.htm (accessed 19 July 2021).

launched by the United Nations (the "UN PRI" hereinafter) integrate the Environmental, Social and Governance (the "ESG" hereinafter) standards with investments and encourage investors to engage with the companies based on such factors when making investment decisions.[32] The ESG investing, broadly speaking, refers to an investment approach "that seeks to incorporate environmental, social and governance factors into asset allocation and risk decisions, so as to generate sustainable, long-term financial returns".[33] As to the ESG criteria, the environmental factors usually include "natural resource use, carbon emissions, energy efficiency, pollution and sustainability initiatives"; social factors include "workforce related issues and broader societal issues such as human rights, community, product responsibility"; and governance factors include considerations such as "board independence and diversity, shareholder rights, corporate ethics, etc."[34]

In the U.K. and Germany, the national provisions which implemented the EU Shareholder Rights Directives already incorporate the ESG standards.[35] According to Directive (EU) 2017/828, "institutional investors and asset managers shall develop and publicly disclose an engagement policy that describes how they integrate shareholder engagement in their investment strategy", and that "the policy shall describe how they monitor investee companies on relevant matters, including strategy, financial and non-financial performance and risk, capital structure, social and environmental impact and corporate governance…"[36] National provisions in the U.K. and Germany stipulate the disclosure and transparency requirements with regard to the institutional shareholders and asset managers' engagement policy, which should describe, among others, how they monitor the investee companies on the ESG matters.[37] These disclosure requirements are implemented on a "comply or explain"

---

[32] UNPRI.ORG. About the PRI. Available at: https://www.unpri.org/pri/about-the-pri (accessed 24 June 2021).

[33] Boffo, R., & Patalano, R. (2020). ESG Investing: Practices, Progress and Challenges (OECD Paris), available at: https://www.oecd.org/finance/ESG-Investing-Practices-Progress-Challenges.pdf (accessed 15 July 2021). See p. 6. Research has shown that the engagement by investors with companies on the ESG issues can create value for both the companies and investors. See UNPRI.ORG (26 April 2018). How ESG Engagement Creates Value For Investors and Companies. Available at: https://www.unpri.org/download?ac=4637 (accessed 19 July 2021).

[34] Ibid.

[35] See Directive 2007/36/EC (Directive 2007/36/EC of the European Parliament and of the Council of 11 July 2007 on the exercise of certain rights of shareholders in listed companies [2007] OJ L 184/17) and Directive (EU) 2017/828 (Directive (EU) 2017/828 of the European Parliament and of the Council of 17 May 2017 amending Directive 2007/36/EC as regards the encouragement of long-term shareholder engagement [2017] OJ L 132/1). The two directives "encourage long-term shareholder engagement to ensure that decisions are made for the long-term stability of a company and take into account environmental and social issues". See summary of the aims of the two Directives available at: https://eur-lex.europa.eu/summary/EN/uriserv:l33285 (accessed 15 July 2021).

[36] Article 3 g of Directive (EU) 2017/828.

[37] In the U.K., the transparency requirements of institutional investors and asset managers under Directive (EU) 2017/828 were implemented by the FCA in COBS 2.2B of the FCA Handbook. See Financial Conduct Authority (FCA). COBS 2.2B SRD requirements. Available at: https://www.handbook.fca.org.uk/handbook/COBS/2/2B.html (accessed 22 August 2021). In Germany,

basis, meaning that institutional investors and asset managers should either comply with them or give a clear and reasoned explanation why they have chosen not to comply with one or more of these requirements.[38] In the future, the U.K. and Germany should enhance the engagement practice and disclosure of the engagement policy of the institutional shareholders concerning the ESG matters by for example, encouraging market regulators to monitor more actively the compliance with these requirements and improving the relevant standards for a "clear and reasoned explanation" where the institutional shareholders choose not to follow the requirements. In China, the 2018 Chinese CG Code, the implementation of which differs from the traditional "comply or explain" approach, formulated the basic framework on disclosure of information about the ESG matters. In 2020, stock exchange such as the SZSE included the report on the ESG matters (for example, whether the company actively discloses its ESG performance and whether the content of the disclosure report is substantial and complete) as part of the assessment on information disclosure of companies listed on it. In future reforms, China should promote and expand the use of the ESG standards in its corporate governance regime by for example, introducing more detailed rules about the ESG performance and disclosure requirements into the company law and corporate governance code for listed companies and strengthening the market regulators' supervision of listed companies' disclosure of their ESG performance.

These reforms about the shareholders' ESG performance and disclosure could help shareholders to alleviate information asymmetries in a takeover situation. For example, shareholders can refer to the ESG ratings of the acquirer's previous investment experience.[39] Such ESG ratings can help the shareholders (also the board(s) and other stakeholders) to better distinguish whether the acquirer only intends to make short-term exploitation of the target and to estimate how the acquirer will conduct its future ESG performance after the takeover.[40] The target shareholders, inter alia institutional investors which have become signatories of the PRI and have committed to pursue ESG integration, when making their decisions whether to transfer the shares, should consider more about the impact of this takeover on the ESG issues (such as environmental protection, development of local community, working situation of employees, protection of human rights, etc.). Moreover, in the three jurisdictions,

---

the transparency requirements are stipulated in Sect. 134b of the AktG in Germany. See Federal Financial Supervisory Authority (BaFin). What ARUG II means for companies and BaFin. Available at: https://www.bafin.de/SharedDocs/Veroeffentlichungen/EN/Fachartikel/2020/fa_bj_2003_Aktionaersrechterichtlinie_en.html (accessed 22 August 2021).

[38] See Article 3 g of Directive (EU) 2017/828.

[39] See Boffo, R., & Patalano, R. (2020). ESG Investing: Practices, Progress and Challenges (OECD Paris), p. 40: the ESG ratings usually provide two main types of ESG scores of a company—an "ESG disclosure score" and an "ESG risk management score". The "ESG disclosure score" focuses on how the company reports its information regarding sustainability, and the "ESG risk management score" tries to assess the main risks the company faces in the terms of ESG.

[40] Ibid, see pp. 7–8, 40: it should be noted that ESG ratings can vary greatly from one rating agency to another given that they may employ different frameworks, scoring methodologies, key indicators, data use, qualitative judgment, etc.; moreover, the size of the company, location in which the company operates, industry and materiality issues can also affect the ultimate ESG scores.

the board of the target can search for another company with better ESG rating scores as its "white knight" during the takeover.

7.4 Limitations of the Research

This research contributes to the existing literature about takeover regulation mainly through the integrated approach it applied: (i) instead of analysing only one or two of the takeover law regimes, corporate governance regimes, competition law regimes, or FDI screening regimes of the U.K., Germany and China, it examined the relevant rules and protection mechanisms in all of these regulatory regimes in order to provide an overall picture of stakeholder protection in the three jurisdictions; (ii) instead of only focusing on the protection of the shareholders and other corporate stakeholders in takeovers, it also shed light on how the legally recognized public interest considerations and other common societal interests are regulated in these laws or corporate governance rules. Nevertheless, the current research is still subject to certain limitations which future research could address.

First of all, in view of the choice of jurisdictions, the current research, although implementing a comparative approach, limits itself to three jurisdictions—the U.K., Germany and China. The relevant rules and protection mechanisms at the EU level are only touched upon to the extent that they have been implemented by the national laws of the U.K. (before Brexit) and Germany. Future integrative research could explore the regulatory framework for different societal interests in takeovers at the EU level as well as other geographical contexts where the takeover market is either developed or developing at a high pace (such as the U.S. and the Netherlands).

Secondly, the current research largely relies on a traditional legal analysis. Although it also conducts a law and economics analysis to explore the necessities and justifications for regulating takeovers and protecting different societal interests, it only applies basic market failure theory rather than employing other in-depth economic analysis or tools. Future research could adopt more tools of the law and economics approach, especially those for evaluating the effectiveness of the relevant protection mechanisms (for example, by assessing the costs and benefits of different regulatory mechanisms).

Moreover, this research has important implications for policymakers and market players in that it fills the knowledge gap of interpreting the term "public interest" in takeovers by examining the recognized public interest considerations in the competition law and FDI screening laws of the three jurisdictions. However, it must be admitted that in practice, the public interest considerations in these public laws are usually deeply affected by the political environment and international relations. This research, owing to its limited length, does not pay much attention to areas like public choice, political science and international relations. Future integrative research on takeovers could analyse the major considerations for defining the "public interest" in the public laws by exploring these relevant disciplines and conducting inter-disciplinary methods.

Summary

Corporate takeovers may have positive as well as negative effects on the different stakeholders involved. This book addressed the question "*What are the societal interests that may be affected by a takeover, are these protected under the current regulatory frameworks of the U.K., Germany and China; (and if so) how are they protected and what recommendations can be made for future reforms in the three jurisdictions?*" To answer this research question, the book discussed four sub-questions: (1) What market failure(s) can be caused by a takeover and what kinds of societal interests are affected? (2) What are the relevant societal interests that are currently regulated in the three jurisdictions and which protection mechanisms are used? (3) What are the similarities and differences between the regulatory frameworks of the three jurisdictions, and what are the strengths and weaknesses of these frameworks in addressing the relevant market failure(s) and protecting societal interests in takeovers? (4) Based on the strengths and weaknesses of the current regulatory frameworks and protection mechanisms, what recommendations can be made for future reforms in the three jurisdictions? The main research findings of the book are as follows:

1. **Market failures may arise as a result of takeovers and affect the "relevant societal interests", which include (i) the interests of corporate stakeholders, (ii) the legally recognized public interest considerations, and (iii) other societal interests affected by a takeover.**

Chapter 1 provided preliminary definitions of the concepts "relevant stakeholders" and "relevant societal interests" and made the presumption that "a takeover may affect a wide range of societal interests". Chapter 2 conducted an economic analysis and found that four types of market failures may arise as a result of takeovers: increase of market power (potential monopoly), severe information asymmetries, negative externalities, and undersupply of public goods. It also observed that the market failure problems may affect three types of societal interests: (i) the interests of corporate stakeholders with whom target companies have a contractual relationship, (ii) the legally recognized public interest considerations, and (iii) other societal interests affected by a takeover. This finding responded to the presumption in Chapter 1 and

H. Ai, *Protecting Societal Interests in Corporate Takeovers*,
https://doi.org/10.1007/978-981-19-7546-2

illustrated the importance of protecting the relevant societal interests in takeovers by government regulation and private regulation.

2. **Public laws (competition law and FDI screening laws) in the three jurisdictions recognize and protect certain public interest considerations in takeovers; private laws (takeover law and corporate law) and national corporate governance codes in the three jurisdictions mainly protect the interests of corporate stakeholders (primarily the shareholders) and other societal interests affected by a takeover.**

Chapters 3–5 examined the government regulation (including public laws such as the competition law and FDI screening regulations, and private laws such as the takeover law and corporate law) and private regulation (mainly the national corporate governance code) in the U.K., Germany and China respectively. Each of the three chapters explored the three types of societal interests that are protected by the public laws, private laws and the national corporate governance codes and the specific protection mechanisms. Chapter 6 conducted a comparison of the protection mechanisms in the three jurisdictions and discussed the strengths and weaknesses of these regulatory frameworks in solving the market failure(s) relating to different societal interests.

The book found that public laws (competition law and FDI screening laws) in the three jurisdictions all recognize and protect certain public interest considerations in takeovers. The competition laws in the three jurisdictions address the market failure of market power and protect the competition interest through merger control rules. Meanwhile, they incorporate a "public interest intervention" (as in the EA 2002 of the U.K.) or "public interest exemption" mechanism (as in the GWB of Germany and in the AML of China) to deal with negative externalities, severe information asymmetries and undersupply of public goods and protect other public interest considerations. The EA 2002 of the U.K. recognizes four types of public interest considerations in takeovers: the national security interest (deleted from the EA 2002 by virtue of the U.K. Security Act 2021), the public interest considerations relevant to newspaper and media mergers, the stability of the financial market, and the capability of the country in combatting and mitigating public health emergencies (added in 2020 to respond to the COVID-19 pandemic). By comparison, the "public interest exemption" mechanisms in the GWB of Germany and in the AML of China are formulated in general provisions and do not provide for explicit public interest considerations.

In the FDI screening regime, the three jurisdictions all provide for a national security review mechanism for foreign takeovers. In China, in addition to the security review, there is more complex market access regulation and administrative regulation of foreign takeovers compared to the U.K. and Germany. After a series of major reforms in recent years, currently, the national security review in the three jurisdictions addresses not only negative externalities on the commonly recognized defence interest and shortage in the supply of public goods (national defence), but also regulates an increasing number of other societal interests in the name of protecting the security interest of the country. In 2020, to respond to the COVID-19 pandemic, the three jurisdictions significantly enlarged the scope of sectors and activities that are deemed as relating to the "security interest" in foreign takeovers and subject to a security review.

The book also observed that takeover laws of the three jurisdictions, through the rules that restrict the board of directors' anti-takeover measures and rules that require the acquirer and target board to disclose information about the takeover offer, directly regulate the negative externalities and severe information asymmetries relating to target shareholders. Apart from shareholder protection, takeover laws in the U.K. and Germany also address severe information asymmetries relating to other stakeholders by requiring the acquirer company and target board(s) to disclose the anticipated consequences of the takeover to other stakeholders. The Chinese takeover law lacks such disclosure requirement relating to other stakeholders. Moreover, compared with the takeover laws in Germany and China, takeover law in the U.K. provides more direct protection to other stakeholders by the "post-offer undertaking" and "post-offer intention statement" mechanism. Corporate governance mechanisms in the three jurisdictions do not regulate specific public interest considerations. They only play a marginal role in addressing the negative externalities and severe information asymmetries relating to the interests of corporate stakeholders and other societal interests affected by a takeover.

3. **Based on the strengths and weaknesses of the current regulatory frameworks of the three jurisdictions, the book provides three recommendations for future reforms in the U.K., Germany and China.**

Chapter 7 summarized the answers to Sub-questions 1 to 3 and gave recommendations for future reforms in the three jurisdictions. The book provided the argument that apart from the legally recognized public interest considerations in the current competition laws and FDI screening laws of the three jurisdictions, other societal interests which in the past were not recognized by these public laws as belonging to the "public interest" may become of crucial importance in emerging takeovers and have a wide impact on the public at large. Chapter 7 brought forward two main factors the three jurisdictions should take into account when deciding whether to modify their public laws to recognize new societal interests as public interest considerations in takeovers in the future: (i) the impact of the relevant societal interests on society; (ii) whether the private laws already contain mechanisms or have the potential to be modified to protect these societal interests. Chapter 7 proposed that the three jurisdictions should modify their takeover law to either introduce new mechanisms (in Germany and China) or strengthen the existing mechanisms (in the U.K.) to incentivize the acquirer to consider other stakeholders of the target in a takeover. As to the corporate governance regime, the book holds that the three jurisdictions should introduce new corporate governance mechanisms to incentivize the target company to more seriously consider the interests of non-shareholder corporate stakeholders and other societal interests affected by a takeover. The main recommendations the book provides are as follows:

Recommendation 1: Expansion of the recognized public interest considerations in the competition law and FDI screening laws should be conducted cautiously and should follow the principles of "necessity" and "proportionality".

Recommendation 2: With regard to the takeover law regime of Germany and China, these jurisdictions can learn from the U.K. by introducing mechanisms to incentivize the acquirers to make arrangements for stakeholders, and the U.K. should reinforce the implementation of the current "post-offer undertaking" and "post-offer intention statement" mechanisms.

Recommendation 3: In the three jurisdictions, future reforms in the corporate governance regime should work towards incentivizing the board to introduce more engagement mechanisms for non-shareholder stakeholders, and towards incentivizing the shareholders to better take into account other stakeholders' interests in their decisions and to disclose their engagement policy in the company with regard to the stakeholder matters.

Bibliography

Regulations and self-regulatory rules:

Regulations and Directives of the EU:

1. Communication from the Commission Guidance to the Member States concerning foreign direct investment and free movement of capital from third countries, and the protection of Europe's strategic assets, ahead of the application of Regulation (EU) 2019/452 (FDI Screening Regulation) (C (2020) 1981 final) [2020] OJ C 99 I/01.
2. Directive 2006/46/EC of the European Parliament and of the Council of 14 June 2006 amending Council Directive 78/660/EEC on the annual accounts of certain types of companies, 83/349/EEC on consolidated accounts, 86/635/EEC on the annual accounts and consolidated accounts of banks and other financial institutions and 91/674/EEC on the annual accounts and consolidated accounts of insurance undertakings [2006] OJ L 224/1.
3. Directive 2017/1132 of the European Parliament and of the Council of 14 June 2017 relating to certain aspects of company law [2017] OJ L 169/46.
4. TFEU
   Consolidated version of the Treaty on the Functioning of the European Union (TFEU) [2016] OJ C 202/1.
5. The EC Merger Regulation
   Council Regulation (EC) No 139/2004 of 20 January 2004 on the control of concentrations between undertakings [2004] OJ L 24/1.
6. The EU FDI Screening Regulation
   Regulation (EU) 2019/452 of the European Parliament and of the Council of 19 March 2019 establishing a framework for the screening of foreign direct investments into the Union [2019] OJ L 79 I/1.
7. The EU Non-financial Reporting Directive
   Directive 2014/95/EU of the European Parliament and of the Council of 22 October 2014 amending Directive 2013/34/EU as regards disclosure of non-financial and diversity information by certain large undertakings and groups Text with EEA relevance [2014] OJ L 330/1.
8. The EU Takeover Directive
   Directive 2004/25/EC of the European Parliament and of the Council of 21 April 2004 on takeover bids [2004] OJ L 142/12.

H. Ai, *Protecting Societal Interests in Corporate Takeovers*,
https://doi.org/10.1007/978-981-19-7546-2

Regulations and self-regulatory rules of the U.K.:

9. CA 2006
   Companies Act 2006.
10. EA 2002
    Enterprise Act 2002.
11. The City Code
    The City Code on Takeovers and Mergers.
12. The Enterprise Act 2002 (Share of Supply Test) (Amendment) Order 2018.
13. The Enterprise Act 2002 (Share of Supply Test) (Amendment) Order 2020.
14. The Enterprise Act 2002 (Turnover Test) (Amendment) Order 2018.
15. The Enterprise Act 2002 (Turnover Test) (Amendment) Order 2020.
16. The U.K. Security Act 2021
    National Security and Investment Act 2021.
17. The U.K. Security Bill 2020
    National Security and Investment Bill 2020.
18. The 2017 Green Paper
    National Security and Infrastructure Investment Review – The Government's review of the national security implications of foreign ownership or control.
19. The 2018 U.K. CG Code
    The 2018 U.K. Corporate Governance Code.
20. The 2018 White Paper
    National Security and Investment: A consultation on proposed legislative reforms.

Regulations and self-regulatory rules of Germany:

21. AktG
    Stock Corporation Act.
22. AWG
    The Foreign Trade and Payments Act.
23. AWV
    The Foreign Trade and Payments Ordinance.
24. BHO
    The Federal Budget Code.
25. GWB
    Act against Restraints of Competition.
26. HGB
    The German Commercial Code.
27. The Fifteenth Amendment to the AWV.
28. The First Amendment to the AWG
    The First Law to amend the Foreign Trade Act and other Laws.
29. The Seventeenth Amendment to the AWV.
30. The Sixteenth Amendment to the AWV.
31. The 2020 German CG Code
    The 2020 German Corporate Governance Code.
32. WpÜG
    The Securities Acquisition and Takeover Act.

Regulations, policy documents and self-regulatory rules of China:

Major regulations and self-regulatory rules:

33. AML
Zhonghua Renmin Gongheguo Fanlongduanfa (中华人民共和国反垄断法) (Anti-monopoly Law of the People's Republic of China) (Promulgated by the National People's Congress of the People's Republic of China on 30 August 2007, amended on 24 June 2022, effective on 1 August 2022).
34. Company Law
Zhonghua Renmin Gongheguo Gongsifa (中华人民共和国公司法) (2018修订) (Company Law of the People's Republic of China) (2018 Revision) (Promulgated by Standing Committee of the National People's Congress on 29 December 1993, amended 2005, 1999, 2004, 2013 and 2018).
35. Foreign Investment Law
Zhonghua Renmin Gongheguo Waishang Touzifa (中华人民共和国外商投资法) (Foreign Investment Law of the People's Republic of China) (Promulgated by the National People's Congress of the People's Republic of China on 15 March 2019, effective on 1 January 2020).
36. Implementing Regulation
Zhonghua Renmin Gongheguo Waishang Touzifa Shishi Tiaoli (中华人民共和国外商投资法实施条例) (Implementing Regulation for the Foreign Investment Law of the People's Republic of China) (Promulgated by the State Council on 12 December 2019, effective on 1 January 2020).
37. Measures for Foreign Strategic Investment
Waiguo Touzizhe dui Shangshi Gongsi Zhanlue Touzi Guanli Banfa (外国投资者对上市公司战略投资管理办法(2015修订) (Measures for the Administration of Strategic Investment in Listed Companies by Foreign Investors) (2015 Revision) (Promulgated by the Ministry of Commerce, China Securities Regulatory Commission, State Administration of Taxation, State Administration for Industry and Commerce, and State Administration of Foreign Exchange on 28 October 2015, effective on promulgation).
38. Notice 2011
Guowuyuan Bangongting Guanyu Jianli Waiguo Touzizhe Binggou Jingnei Qiye Anquan Shencha Zhidu de Tongzhi (国务院办公厅关于建立外国投资者并购境内企业安全审查制度的通知) (Notice of the General Office of the State Council on the Establishment of the Security Review System for Mergers and Acquisitions of Domestic Enterprises by Foreign Investors) (Promulgated by the General Office of the State Council on 3 February 2011, effective on 5 March 2011).
39. Provisions on Foreign Mergers and Acquisitions (2009)
Guanyu Waiguo Touzizhe Binggou Jingnei Qiye de Guiding (关于外国投资者并购境内企业的规定 (2009修订)) (Provisions on Mergers and Acquisitions of Domestic Enterprises by Foreign Investors) (2009 Revision) (Promulgated by Ministry of Commerce on 22 June 2009, effective on promulgation).
40. Provisions 2011
Shangwubu Shishi Waiguo Touzizhe Binggou Jingnei Qiye Anquan Shencha Zhidu de Guiding (商务部实施外国投资者并购境内企业安全审查制度的规定) (Provisions of the Ministry of Commerce on the Implementation of the Security Review System for Mergers and Acquisitions of Domestic Enterprises by Foreign Investors) (Promulgated by the Ministry of Commerce on 25 August 2011, effective on 1 September 2011).
41. Securities Law
Zhonghua Renmin Gongheguo Zhenquanfa (中华人民共和国证券法) (2019年修订) (Securities Law of the People's Republic of China (2019 Revision)) (Promulgated by the Standing Committee of the National People's Congress on 29 December 1998, amended in 2004, 2005, 2013, 2014, 2019, effective on 1 March 2020).

42. The 2006 Takeover Measures
Shangshi Gongsi Shougou Guanli Banfa (上市公司收购管理办法) (2020年修订) (Measures for the Administration of the Takeover of Listed Companies) (2020 Revision) (Promulgated by China Securities Regulatory Commission on 17 May 2006, amended in 2008, 2012, 2014, 2020).
43. The 2018 Chinese CG Code
Shangshi Gongsi Zhili Zhunze (上市公司治理准则) (Code of Corporate Governance for Listed Companies) (Promulgated by China Securities Regulatory Commission on 30 September 2018, effective on promulgation).
44. The 2018 FI Negative List
Special Administrative Measures for the Access of Foreign Investment (2018).
45. The 2019 FI Negative List
Special Administrative Measures for the Access of Foreign Investment (2019).
46. The 2020 FI Negative List
Special Administrative Measures for the Access of Foreign Investment (2020).
47. The 2021 FI Negative List
Special Administrative Measures for the Access of Foreign Investment (2020).
48. Measures for the Security Review
Waishang Touzi Anquan Shencha Banfa (外商投资安全审查办法) (Measures for the Security Review of Foreign Investment) (Promulgated by the National Development and Reform Commission and the Ministry of Commerce on 19 December 2020, effective on 18 January 2021).

Other regulations, policy documents and self-regulatory rules:

49. Gongkai Faxing Zhengquan de Gongsi Xinxi Pilu Neirong he Geshi Zhunze di Shibahao – Beishougou Gongsi Dongshihui Baogaoshu (公开发行证券的公司信息披露内容和格式准则第18号 – 被收购公司董事会报告书 (2020年修正)) (Guidelines for the Content and Format of Information Disclosure of Publicly Offering Company(No.18) – Report of the Board of Directors of the Acquired Company) (2020 Revision) (Promulgated by the CSRC on 4 August 2006, revised on 30 March 2020).
50. Guanyu Shenli Minjian Jiedai Anjian Shiyong Falv Ruogan Wenti de Guiding (关于审理民间借贷案件适用法律若干问题的规定) (Provisions of the Supreme People's Court on Several Issues concerning the Application of the Law in Private Lending Cases) (Issued by the Supreme People's Court on 23 June 2015, effective on 1 September 2015, modified on 19 August 2020, 29 December 2020).
51. Guanyu Waiguo Touzizhe Binggou Jingnei Qiye de Guiding (关于外国投资者并购境内企业的规定 (2006)) (Provisions on Mergers and Acquisitions of Domestic Enterprises by Foreign Investors) (2006 Revision) (Promulgated by Ministry of Commerce on 8 August 2006, effective on 8 September 2006, modified in 2009).
52. Guowuyuan Jigou Gaige Fangan (国务院机构改革方案) (The State Council Institutional Reform Proposal) (Approved at the First Session of the Thirteenth National People's Congress on 17 March 2018).
53. Jingyingzhe Jizhong Shencha Zanxing Guiding (经营者集中审查暂行规定) (Interim Provisions on the Review of Concentrations between Undertakings) (Promulgated by the State Administration for Market Regulation on 23 October 2020, amended on 24 March 2022, effective on 1 May 2022).
54. Qiye Guoyou Zichan Jiaoyi Jiandu Guanli Banfa (企业国有资产交易监督管理办法) (Measures for the Supervision and Administration of the Transactions of State-owned Assets of Enterprises) (Promulgated by SASAC and Ministry of Finance of The People's Republic of China on 24 June 2016, effective on promulgation).
55. Shangwubu Guanyu Pinggu Jingyingzhe Jizhong Yingxiang de Zanxing Guiding (商务部关于评估经营者集中影响的暂行规定) (Interim Provisions on Assessing the Impact of Concentration of Undertakings on Competition) (Promulgated by the MOFCOM on 29 August 2011, effective on 5 September 2011) (Expired).

56. Waishang Touzi Qiye Sheli ji Biangeng Beian Guanli Zanxing Banfa (外商投资企业设立及变更备案管理暂行办法) (Interim Measures for the Recording Administration of the Formation and Modification of Foreign-Invested Enterprises) (Promulgated by the Ministry of Commerce on 8 October 2016, effective on Promulgation, amended in 2017 and 2018).
57. Waishang Touzi Xiangmu Hezhun he Beian Guanli Banfa (外商投资项目核准和备案管理办法) (Administrative Measures for the Confirmation and Recording of Foreign-Funded Projects) (Promulgated by the National Development and Reform Commission of China on 17 May 2014, effective on 17 June 2014, amended on 27 December 2014).
58. Zhonggong Zhongyang Guanyu Guoyouqiye Gaige he Fazhan Ruogan Zhongda Wenti de Jueding (中共中央关于国有企业改革和发展若干重大问题的决定) (The Decision of the Central Committee of the Communist Party of China on Major Issues Concerning the Reform and Development of State-Owned Enterprises) (Promulgated by the Central Committee of The Communist Party of China on 22 September 1999, effective on promulgation).
59. Zhonghua Renmin Gongheguo Qiye Guoyou Zichanfa (中华人民共和国企业国有资产法) (Law of the People's Republic of China on the State-Owned Assets of Enterprises) (Promulgated by the Standing Committee of the National People's Congress on 28 October 2008, effective on 1 May 2009).

Books and book chapters:

60. Ayres, I., & Braithwaite, J. (1992). *Responsive Regulation: Transcending the Deregulation Debate*. Oxford University Press.
61. Bechtold, R., & Bosch, W. (2018). *Gesetz gegen Wettbewerbsbeschränkungen: (§1–96, 185, 186): Kommentar* (9. Auflage. ed.). C.H. Beck.
62. Bernier, L., Florio, M., & Bance, P. (Eds.). (2020). *The Routledge Handbook of State-Owned Enterprises*. Routledge.
63. Bian, C. (2018). *National security review regimes of foreign investment: A comparative study in China, the US and the EU*. Doctoral dissertation, Erasmus University Rotterdam.
64. Bozeman, B. (2007). *Public values and public interest: Counterbalancing economic individualism*. Georgetown University Press.
65. Busche, J., & Röhling, A. (2014). *Kölner Kommentar zum Kartellrecht*. Carl Heymanns.
66. Button, M. (2018). *A Practitioner's Guide to The City Code on Takeovers and Mergers 2018/2019* (30th ed.). Sweet & Maxwell.
67. Cahn, & Donald, D. C. (2018). *Comparative Company Law: Text and Cases on the Laws Governing Corporations in Germany, the UK and the USA* (2nd ed.). Cambridge University Press.
68. Chen, J. (2014). *Regulating the Takeover of Chinese Listed Companies*. Springer.
69. Cooter, R., & Ulen, T. (2016). *Law and Economics*. Berkeley Law Books.
70. Davies, P. L., & Worthington, S. (2016). *Gower's Principles of Modern Company Law*. Sweet & Maxwell.
71. Du, D. (2020). *A comparative study of the legislative designs concerning foreign takeover bids of listed companies: China and the Netherlands*. Doctoral dissertation, Erasmus University Rotterdam.
72. Du Plessis, J. J., et al. (2017). *German Corporate Governance in International and European Context* (3rd ed.). Springer.
73. Du Plessis, J. J., et al. (2018). *Principles of Contemporary Corporate Governance* (4th ed.). Cambridge University Press.
74. Faure, M. G. (2001). *Environmental Law and Economics* (N.J. Philipsen (ed.), 2006).
75. Freeman, R. E. (1984). *Strategic Management: A Stakeholder Approach*. Boston Pitman.
76. Gerner-Beuerle, C., & Schilling, M. A. (2019). *Comparative Company Law*. Oxford University Press.
77. Griffin, S. (2006). *Company Law: Fundamental Principles* (4th ed.). Pearson Education.
78. Hopt, K., et al. (2009). Obstacles to corporate restructuring: Observations from a European and German perspective. In Tison (Ed.), *Company Law and Financial Regulation* (pp. 373–395). Cambridge University Press.

79. Huang, R. H. (2014). *Securities and Capital Markets Law in China*. Oxford University Press.
80. Kessedjian, C., & Rivera, H. F. C. (Eds.). (2020). *Private International Law Aspects of Corporate Social Responsibility*. Springer Nature.
81. Kraakman, R. H., et al. (2017). *The Anatomy of Corporate Law: A Comparative and Functional Approach*. Oxford University Press.
82. Liu, A. (2019). *Regulating genetically modified crops in view of environmental risks: China's implementation of international obligations*. Doctoral dissertation, Maastricht University.
83. Majone, G. (1996). *Regulating Europe*. Routledge.
84. Ma, J. (2014). *Comparative Analysis of Merger Control Policy: Lessons for China*. Intersentia.
85. Mattei, U. (1997). *Comparative Law and Economics*. University of Michigan Press.
86. McConville, M. (Ed.). (2017). *Research Methods for Law*. Edinburgh University Press.
87. Ogus, A. (2004). *Regulation: Legal Form and Economic Theory*. Bloomsbury Publishing.
88. Parker, J., & Majumdar, A. (2016). *UK Merger Control* (2nd ed.). Hart Publishing.
89. Payne, J. (2002). *Takeovers in English and German Law*. Hart Publishing.
90. Philipsen, N. (2003). *Regulation of and By Pharmacists in the Netherlands and Belgium: An Economic Approach* (Vol. 45). Intersentia.
91. Rühmkorf, A. (2015). *Corporate Social Responsibility, Private Law and Global Supply Chains*. Edward Elgar Publishing.
92. Peyer, S. (2012). Germany: E.on & Ruhrgas: Merging competition and industrial policy. In B. Rodger (Ed.), *Landmark Cases in Competition Law: Around the World in Fourteen Stories* (Vol. 53, pp. 121–144). Kluwer Law International BV.
93. Sheng, J. (2015). *China's Listed Companies: Conflicts, Governance and Regulation*. Wolters Kluwer Law & Business.
94. Smits, J. M. (2012). *The Mind and Method of The Legal Academic*. Edward Elgar Publishing.
95. Sondergutachten der Monopolkommission (Band 2): Wettbewerbliche und strukturelle Aspekte einer Zusammenfassung von Unternehmen im Energiebereich (VEBA/Gelsenberg). Nomos Verlagsgesellschaft, Baden-Baden (1975). ISBN 3-7890-0154-6.
96. Sondergutachten der Monopolkommission (Band 3): Zusammenschlußvorhaben der Kaiser Aluminium & Chemical Corporation, der Preussag AG und der Vereinigte Industrie-Unternehmungen AG. Nomos Verlagsgesellschaft, Baden-Baden (1975). ISBN 3-7890-0159-7.
97. Sondergutachten der Monopolkommission (Band 4-6): Zusammenschlußvorhaben der Deutsche Babcock AG mit der Artos-Gruppe. Nomos Verlagsgesellschaft, Baden-Baden (1977). ISBN 3-7890-0311-5.
98. Sondergutachten der Monopolkommission (Band 4-6): Zusammenschlußvorhaben der Thyssen Industrie AG mit der Hüler Hille GmbH. Nomos Verlagsgesellschaft, Baden-Baden (1977). ISBN 3-7890-0311-5.
99. Sondergutachten der Monopolkommission (Band 8): Zusammenschlußvorhaben der Deutschen BP AG und der VEBA AG. Nomos Verlagsgesellschaft, Baden-Baden (1979). ISBN 3-7890-0489-8.
100. Sondergutachten der Monopolkommission (Band 10 und 12): Zusammenschlußvorhaben der IBH Holding AG mit der WIBAU AG. Nomos Verlagsgesellschaft, Baden-Baden (1982) (ISBN 3-7890-0768-4.
101. Sondergutachten der Monopolkommission (Band 18): Zusammenschlußvorhaben der DAIMLER-BENZ AG mit der MESSERSCHMITT-BÖLKOW-BLOHM GmbH. Nomos Verlagsgesellschaft, Baden-Baden (1989). ISBN 3-7890-1847-3.
102. Sondergutachten der Monopolkommission (Band 19): Zusammenschlußvorhaben der MAN Aktiengesellschaft und der Gebrüder Sulzer Aktiengesellschaft. Nomos Verlagsgesellschaft, Baden-Baden (1982). ISBN 3-7890-2170-9.
103. Stearns, M. L. (2017). A Public Choice Perspective. In T. S. Ulen (Ed.), *Methodologies of Law and Economics* (pp. 44–71). Edward Elgar Publishing.
104. Stohlmeier, T. (2015). *German Public Takeover Law* (3rd ed.). Kluwer Law International.

105. Tian, X. (2019) (田昕清). *Comparative study on the security review system of foreign investment and its significance to China* (外资安全审查制度比较研究及对我国的借鉴意义). Doctoral dissertation of the Graduate School of China Foreign Affairs University (外交学院2019届博士研究生学位论文).
106. Tsagas, G. (2017). Section 172 of the companies act 2006: Desperate times call for soft law measures. In N. Boeger, & C. Villiers (ed.), *Shaping the Corporate Landscape: Towards Corporate Reform and Enterprise Diversity* (pp. 131–150). https://ssrn.com/abstract=2996090,https://doi.org/10.2139/ssrn.2996090.
107. Varottil, U., & Wan, W. Y. (2017). *Comparative Takeover Regulation: Global and Asian Perspectives*. Cambridge University Press.
108. Vieweg, K., & Fischer, M. (2019). *Wirtschaftsrecht*. Nomos.
109. Weinreich-Zhao, T. (2015). *Chinese Merger Control Law: An Assessment of Its Competition-policy Orientation After the First Years of Application*. Springer.
110. Wei, X. (2014) (魏星). *Research on the effect and function positioning of Government intervention in Chinese M&As* (中国公司并购中政府干预效应及其职能定位研究). Doctoral dissertation of the Graduate School of Chinese Academy of Social Sciences (中国社会科学院研究生院博士论文).
111. Zeng, B., & Lin, W. (2020) (曾斌 & 林蔚然). *The Logic of Capital Governance* (资本治理的逻辑). China Legal Publishing House (中国法制出版社).

Journals and online articles:

112. Aguilera, R. V., & Jackson, G. (2010). Comparative and international corporate governance. *The Academy of Management Annals, 4*(1), 485–556.
113. Akerlof, G. A. (1970). The market for "lemons": Quality uncertainty and the market mechanism. *The Quarterly Journal of Economics, 84*(3), 488–500.
114. Armour, J., Black, B., Cheffins, B., & Nolan, R. (2009). Private enforcement of corporate law: An empirical comparison of the United Kingdom and the United States. *Journal of Empirical Legal Studies, 6*(4), 687–722.
115. Armour, J., Jacobs, J. B., & Milhaupt, C. J. (2011). The evolution of hostile takeover regimes in developed and emerging markets: An analytical framework. *Harvard International Law Journal, 52*, 219–285.
116. Armour, J., & Skeel, D. A., Jr. (2007). Who writes the rules for hostile takeovers, and why?—The peculiar divergence of US and UK takeover regulation. *Georgetown Law Journal, 95*, 1727–1794.
117. Block, W. E. (1983). Public goods and externalities: The case of roads. *The Journal of Libertarian Studies, 7*(1), 1–34.
118. Borochin, P., Ghosh, C., & Huang, D. (2019). Target information asymmetry and takeover strategy: Insights from a new perspective. *European Financial Management, 25*(1), 38–79.
119. Budzinski, O., & Stöhr, A. (2018). Die Ministererlaubnis Als Element Der Deutschen Wettbewerbsordnung: Eine Theoretische Und Empirische Analyse (The Public Interest Exception (Ministererlaubnis) in German Merger Control: A Theoretical and Empirical Analysis of the Instrument). https://papers.ssrn.com/sol3/papers.cfm?abstract_id=3226967.
120. Chalaczkiewicz-Ladna, K., & MacNeil, I. (2020). Engaging stakeholders in corporate decision-making through strategic reporting: An empirical study of FTSE 100 companies (Part 2). *European Business Law Review, 31*(2), 209–242. http://eprints.gla.ac.uk/177301/.
121. Chang, E. C., & Wong, S. M. (2004). Political control and performance in China's listed firms. *Journal of Comparative Economics, 32*(4), 617–636.
122. Chan, K. S., Dang, V. Q., & Yan, I. K. (2012). Chinese firms' political connection, ownership, and financing constraints. *Economics Letters, 115*(2), 164–167.
123. Chen, C. J., et al. (2011). Rent-seeking incentives, corporate political connections, and the control structure of private firms: Chinese evidence. *Journal of Corporate Finance, 17*(2), 229–243.

124. Chen, M. (2020) (陈铭宇). Analysis on the application of Corporate Governance Code for Listed Companies in administrative supervision measures: Analysis of the role of local securities regulatory bureaus in corporate governance supervision. (行政监管措施中《上市公司治理准则》适用情况分析 – 浅析地方证监局的公司治理监管角色. *Multi-Level Capital Market Analysis (多层次资本市场研究)*, 2, 236–248.
125. Chen, S., & Lu, C. (2014) (陈仕华 & 卢昌崇). Can the governance participation by the Party organizations in State-owned enterprise effectively suppress the "loss of state-owned assets" in mergers and acquisitions? (国有企业党组织的治理参与能够有效抑制并购中的"国有资产流失"吗? *Management World (管理世界)*, *5*, 106–120.
126. Cull, R., et al. (2015). Government connections and financial constraints: Evidence from a large representative sample of Chinese firms. *Journal of Corporate Finance, 32*, 271–294.
127. Davies, P., & Hopt, K. J. (2018). Non-shareholder voice in bank governance: Board composition, performance and liability. In *European Corporate Governance Institute (ECGI)-Law Working Paper* (413).
128. Ding, S., et al. (2014). Executive political connections and firm performance: Comparative evidence from privately-controlled and state-owned enterprises. *International Review of Financial Analysis, 36*, 153–167.
129. Draper, P., & Paudyal, K. (2008). Information asymmetry and bidders' gains. *Journal of Business Finance & Accounting, 35*(3–4), 376–405.
130. Esser, I.-M., MacNeil, I., & Chalaczkiewicz-Ladna, K. (2018). Engaging stakeholders in corporate decision-making through strategic reporting: an empirical study of FTSE 100 companies. *European Business Law Review, 29*(5), 729–772. http://eprints.gla.ac.uk/151965/7/151965.pdf.
131. Esser, I.-M., & MacNeil, I. (2019) Disclosure and engagement: stakeholder participation mechanisms. *European Business Law Review, 30*(2), 201–221. http://eprints.gla.ac.uk/166091/7/166091.pdf.
132. Fisher, D. (2009). The enlightened shareholder—Leaving stakeholders in the dark: Will section 172 (1) of the Companies Act 2006 make directors consider the impact of their decisions on third parties? *International Company and Commercial Law Review, 20*(1), 10–16.
133. Freeman, R. E., Wicks, A. C., & Parmar, B. (2004). Stakeholder theory and "the corporate objective revisited." *Organization Science, 15*(3), 364–369.
134. Gugler, K., Mueller, D. C., Yurtoglu, B. B., & Zulehner, C. (2003). The effects of mergers: An international comparison. *International Journal of Industrial Organization, 21*(5), 625–653.
135. Hankir, Y., Rauch, C., & Umber, M. P. (2011). Bank M&A: A market power story? *Journal of Banking & Finance, 35*(9), 2341–2354.
136. Hantke-Domas, M. (2003). The public interest theory of regulation: Non-existence or misinterpretation? *European Journal of Law and Economics, 15*(2), 165–194.
137. He, W., & Kyaw, N. A. (2018). Ownership structure and investment decisions of Chinese SOEs. *Research in International Business and Finance, 43*, 48–57.
138. Hillman, A. J., & Keim, G. D. (2001). Shareholder value, stakeholder management, and social issues: What's the bottom line? *Strategic Management Journal, 22*(2), 125–139.
139. Hirschleifer, D. (1995). Mergers and acquisitions: Strategic and informational issues. *Handbooks in Operations Research and Management Science, 9*, 839–885.
140. Hopt, K. J. (2011). Comparative corporate governance: The state of the art and international regulation. *The American Journal of Comparative Law, 59*(1), 1–73.
141. Höpner, M., & Jackson, G. (2006). Revisiting the Mannesmann takeover: How markets for corporate control emerge. *European Management Review, 3*(3), 142–155.
142. Huang, R. H., & Chen, J. (2019). The rise of hostile takeovers and defensive measures in China: Comparative and empirical perspectives. *European Business Organization Law Review, 20*, 363–398.
143. Kacperczyk, A. (2009). With greater power comes greater responsibility? Takeover protection and corporate attention to stakeholders. *Strategic Management Journal, 30*(3), 261–285.

144. Kang, J.-K., & Kim, J.-M. (2010). Do foreign investors exhibit a corporate governance disadvantage? An information asymmetry perspective. *Journal of International Business Studies, 41*(8), 1415–1438.
145. Kong, Q. (2019) (孔庆江). The relationship and connection between the foreign investment law of the People's Republic of China and other laws and regulations (《中华人民共和国外商投资法》与相关法律的衔接与协调). *Journal of SUIBE* (上海对外经贸大学学报), *26*(3), 5–13.
146. Li, G. (2017) (李国海). On the exemption of state-owned enterprises by the anti-monopoly law (论反垄断法对国有企业的豁免. *Law Review (法学评论), 4*, 115–123.
147. Li, H. (2019) (李华武). The substantive rule system of the anti-monopoly exemption of takeovers and mergers in China: Theoretical explanation and empirical research (我国并购反垄断豁免的实体规则体系: 理论阐述与实证研究. *Hubei Social Sciences (湖北社会科学), 3*, 80–87.
148. Li, J. (2010) (李建伟). The definition of the connotation and the construction of realization mechanism of corporate social responsibility—From the perspective of directors' fiduciary duties (论公司社会责任的内涵界定与实现机制建构 以董事的信义义务为视角). *Tsinghua Law Review* (清华法学), *4*(2), 120–129.
149. Lim, E (2017). Judicial intervention in directors' decision-making process: Section 172 of the companies act 2006. *Journal of Business Law 169*, 2018. https://ssrn.com/abstract=3103345.
150. Liu, C. (2006) (刘诚). Positioning of corporate social responsibility (公司社会责任的定位). *Peking University Law Journal* (中外法学), *18*(5),530–540.
151. Liu, D., & Xu, D. (2017) (刘大洪, & 许丹琳). Research on the path and legal guarantee of the party organization's participation in the governance of state-owned enterprises—From the perspective of the reform of state-owned enterprises (党组织参与国企公司治理的路径与法律保障研究 – 以国企分类改革为视角). *Journal of Central South University (Social Science)* (中南大学学报 (社会科学版)), *23*(5), 31–38.
152. Liu, G. (2016) (刘桂清). The defence of public interest in anti-competitive concentration of undertakings: The path choice and system construction (反竞争经营者集中的公共利益辩护: 路径选择与制度建构). *Tribune of Political Science and Law* (政法论坛), *34*(5), 124–135.
153. Lou, J. (2008) (楼建波). The literary interpretation on and implementation path of the first paragraph of Article 5 of the PRC Company Law: Also on the significance of corporate social responsibility at the ethical level (中国公司法第五条第一款的文义解释及实施路径: 兼论道德层面的企业社会责任的意义). *Peking University Law Journal* (中外法学), *20*(1),36–42.
154. Ma, L., Wang, Y., & Shen, X. (2013). 马连福, 王元芳 & 沈小秀). Party organization governance, redundant employees and executive compensation contract of State-owned enterprise (国有企业党组织治理, 冗余雇员与高管薪酬契约. *Management World (管理世界), 5*, 100–115.
155. Mager, F., & Meyer-Fackler, M. (2017). Mergers and acquisitions in Germany: 1981–2010. *Global Finance Journal, 34*, 32–42.
156. Manne, H. G. (1965). Mergers and the market for corporate control. *Journal of Political Economy, 73*(2), 110–120.
157. Marcoux, A. M. (1998). Who are the stakeholders?: The failure of the stakeholder-as-contractor view. *Business and Professional Ethics Journal, 17*(3), 79–108.
158. Marcus, G. (2000). Issues for consideration in mergers and takeovers from a regulatory perspective. *BIS Review, 60*, 1–12.
159. Martynova, M., & Renneboog, L. (2008). A century of corporate takeovers: What have we learned and where do we stand? *Journal of Banking & Finance, 32*(10), 2148–2177.
160. Miles, S. (2012). Stakeholder: Essentially contested or just confused? *Journal of Business Ethics, 108*(3), 285–298.
161. Nyombi, C. (2015). A critique of shareholder primacy under UK takeover law and the continued imposition of the Board Neutrality Rule. *International Journal of Law and Management, 57*(4), 235–264.

162. Nyombi, C., Mortimer, T., & Lewis, R. (2015). Shareholder primacy and stakeholders' interests in the aftermath of a takeover: a review of empirical evidence. *International Business Law Journal*, 161–186.
163. Officer, M., Poulsen, A. B., & Stegemoller, M. (2006). Information asymmetry and acquirer returns. In *University of Southern California Working Paper.*
164. Ogus, A. (1995). Rethinking self-regulation. *Oxford Journal of Legal Studies, 15*, 97–108.
165. Ogus, A. (2000). Self-regulation. *Encyclopedia of Law and Economics, 5*, 587–602.
166. Page, A. C. (1986). Self-regulation: The constitutional dimension. *The Modern Law Review, 49*(2), 141–167.
167. Pan, H., et al. (2008). Government intervention, political correlation, and local SOE's M&A activities (政府干预, 政治关联与地方国有企业并购). *Economic Research Journal (经济研究), 4*(1), 41–52.
168. Papadopoulos, T. (2021). COVID-19 crisis and screening of foreign direct investments in EU privatized companies. *International Trade Law & Regulation (sweet & Maxwell), 27*(1), 54–75.
169. Patrone, M. R. (2011). Sour chocolate: The U.K. Takeover Panel's improper reaction to Kraft's acquisition of Cadbury. *Int'l L. & Mgmt. Rev., 8*, 63–86.
170. Philipsen, N. J. (2007). The law and economics of professional regulation: What does the theory teach China? *Economic Analysis of Law in China* (pp. 112–150). Edward Elgar.
171. Philipsen, N. J. (2018). The role of private actors in preventing work-related risks: A law and economics perspective. *European Public Law, 24*(3), 539–554.
172. Pucheta-Martínez, M. C., & López-Zamora, B. (2018). Engagement of directors representing institutional investors on environmental disclosure. *Corporate Social Responsibility and Environmental Management, 25*(6), 1108–1120.
173. Ringe, W. G. (2015). Changing law and ownership patterns in Germany: Corporate governance and the erosion of Deutschland AG. *The American Journal of Comparative Law, 63*(2), 493–538.
174. Schneper, W. D., & Guillén, M. F. (2004). Stakeholder rights and corporate governance: A cross-national study of hostile takeovers. *Administrative Science Quarterly, 49*(2), 263–295.
175. Schwarcz, S. L. (2016). Misalignment: Corporate risk-taking and public duty. *Notre Dame L. Rev., 92*, 1–50.
176. Shi, J., Xiao, Z., & Feng, H. (2008) (史际春, 肖竹 & 冯辉). Study on corporate social responsibility: Legal duty, moral responsibility and the others (论公司社会责任:法律义务、道德责任及其他). *Journal of Capital Normal University (Social Sciences Edition)* (首都师范大学学报(社会科学版)), (02), 39–51.
177. Shi, T. (2019) (施天涛). The ideal and reality of Article 5 of the Company Law: How can the company's social responsibility be implemented? (《公司法》第5条的理想与现实: 公司社会责任何以实施?). *Tsinghua University Law Journal* (清华法学), *13*(05), 57–79.
178. Stigler, G. J. (1971). The theory of economic regulation. *The Bell Journal of Economics and Management Science, 2*(1), 3–21.
179. Szabados, T. (2015). Recent golden share cases in the jurisprudence of the Court of Justice of the European Union. *German Law Journal, 16*(5), 1099–1130.
180. Sun, J. (2015) (孙晋), On the application of the review system for concentration of undertakings in the mergers and acquisitions of state-owned enterprises (论经营者集中审查制度在国有企业并购中的适用. *Journal of East China University of Political Science and Law (华东政法大学学报), 4*, 17–26.
181. Tate, R. C. (2012). Section 172 CA 2006: The ticket to stakeholder value of simply tokenism. *Aberdeen Student L. Rev., 3*, 112–119.
182. Van den Bergh, R. (2008). Towards better regulation of the legal professions in the European Union. In *Rotterdam Institute of Law and Economics Working Paper Series, No. 2008/07.*
183. Wang, K., & Xiao, X. (2009). Ultimate government control structures and firm value: Evidence from Chinese listed companies. *China Journal of Accounting Research, 2*(1), 101–122.

184. Wang, X. (2008a) (王晓晔). Analysis of the anti-monopoly law of the People's Republic of China (《中华人民共和国反垄断法》析评. *Chinese Journal of Law (法学研究), 4*, 68–82.
185. Wang, X. (2008b) (王晓晔). Comment on the concentration of undertakings in the anti-monopoly law (《中华人民共和国反垄断法》中经营者集中评析. *Law Science Magazine (法学杂志), 1*, 2–7.
186. Wei, D. (2013). Antitrust in China: An overview of recent implementation of anti-monopoly law. *European Business Organization Law Review, 14*(1), 119–139.
187. Werner, B. (2017). National responses to the European Court of Justice case law on Golden Shares: The role of protective equivalents. *Journal of European Public Policy, 24*(7), 989–1005.
188. Wu, H., & Wei, W. (2005) (吴宏伟, & 魏炜). The value of anti-monopoly law (论反垄断法的价值目标. *The Jurist (法学家), 3*, 92–98.
189. Zhang, A. H. (2014). Foreign direct investment from China: Sense and sensibility. *Northwestern Journal of International Law & Business, 34*, 395–453.
190. Zhou, B., et al. (2015). Does state ownership drive M&A performance? *Evidence from China. European Financial Management, 21*(1), 79–105.
191. Zhou, Y., & Zhang, H. (2009) (周友苏&张虹). Reflection and transcendence: An interpretation on corporate social responsibility (反思与超越: 公司社会责任诠释). *Tribune of Political Science and Law* (政法论坛), *27*(1), 57–63.
192. Zhu, C. (2008) (朱慈蕴). Corporate Social Responsibility: Wandering between legal obligation and ethical standards (公司的社会责任: 游走于法律责任与道德准则之间). *Peking University Law Journal* (中外法学), *20*(1), 29–35.